Death
at the Ballpark

Death at the Ballpark

*A Comprehensive Study
of Game-Related Fatalities of Players,
Other Personnel and Spectators
in Amateur and Professional Baseball,
1862–2007*

ROBERT M. GORMAN
and DAVID WEEKS

McFarland & Company, Inc., Publishers
Jefferson, North Carolina, and London

Library of Congress Cataloguing-in-Publication Data

Gorman, Robert M.
Death at the ballpark : a comprehensive study
of game-related fatalities of players, other personnel and
spectators in amateur and professional baseball, 1862–2007 /
Robert M. Gorman and David Weeks.
p.   cm.
Includes bibliographical references and index.

ISBN 978-0-7864-3435-0
illustrated case binding : 50# alkaline paper ∞

1. Baseball — Miscellanea.
2. Baseball injuries — United States.
3. Baseball — United States.
4. Deaths.
I. Weeks, David.
II. Title.
GV873.G68   2009   796.357 — dc22   2008036625

British Library cataloguing data are available

On the cover: Illustration depicting the death of Edward Likely
from a self-inflicted foul tip in Lincoln, Nebraska,
on June 13, 1887 (*St. Louis Globe-Democrat*);
Calla lily illustration by Mark Durr

Manufactured in the United States of America

*McFarland & Company, Inc., Publishers
Box 611, Jefferson, North Carolina 28640
www.mcfarlandpub.com*

To Bill Kirwin, mentor and friend—
your encouragement and support will never be forgotten.
—Robert M. Gorman

To my good friend Dr. T. R. Machen,
who taught me long ago that you can accomplish
almost anything with a little ingenuity and perseverance.
Also, to my two children, Sarah and Alden, who ensure
that I never have a boring day.
—David Weeks

And to all the victims and their survivors.
We hope that we have dealt with your tragedy in a respectful manner.

Acknowledgments

While in the great game of baseball the pitcher is officially given the win (or the loss), the success of his team is clearly not due to his efforts alone. He has eight other teammates on the field with him, and their skill on defense and ability at bat has as much, if not more, impact on the outcome than what the man on the mound does. The same can be said about researching and writing a book. Authors, like pitchers, are ultimately responsible for the results, but they do not do it alone.

We would like to begin by thanking all those librarians out there who generously supplied us the microfilm and other resources we needed to complete our project. They are the silent partners of the research process and we are truly fortunate to have them. Most especially we thank Carrie Volk, head of the interlibrary loan department at Dacus Library, Winthrop University, who, assisted by Ann Thomas, went to extraordinary lengths — including cajoling, begging, and beseeching libraries around the country — to secure the materials we needed. In addition, Ms. Volk was invaluable in taking our rather poor PDFs and microfilmed and photocopied illustrations and turning them into something usable for this book.

We are deeply indebted to Dr. R. Norman Taylor, M.D., of Rock Hill, South Carolina, who served as an expert advisor concerning matters medical, particularly those cases covered in chapter 9. He helped clarify many of the fine points of medicine and provided additional insight and understanding as to the nature of illness and disease.

We are beholden to Dr. Jason Silverman, teacher, scholar and racquetball player extraordinaire, who spent countless hours proofreading the final product of our labors. His suggestions have made this a much better work. Our thanks, too, to Peter Morris, author of the award-winning *A Game of Inches*, and Trey Strecker, editor of *Nine: A Journal of Baseball History and Culture*, for their invaluable critical comments on the draft manuscript.

Of course, none of this would have been possible without the loving support of our wives, Jane Gorman and Laura Weeks. They were there for us day in and day out as we dwelled in the land of death.

Any errors or omissions in this study are those of the authors alone. We encourage readers to contact us via email (gormanr@winthrop.edu or weeksd@winthrop.edu) or at the Dacus Library, Winthrop University, Rock Hill, SC 29733, concerning corrections or additional information.

Table of Contents

Preface

When one thinks of baseball, rarely do thoughts of tragedy come to mind. It is a game associated with warm, sunny days and leisurely outings to the local ballpark. Yet injury and death have been associated with the game from its beginnings.

Even the most casual fan has heard about baseball's most renowned fatality, the beaning death of Cleveland Indians player Ray Chapman. On the afternoon of August 20, 1920, the Yankees notorious headhunter, Carl Mays, threw a pitch that struck Chapman on the left temple. A surgical attempt to save Chapman's life proved futile and Cleveland's 29-year-old shortstop died early the next morning. It is the only undisputed case of a play-related fatality among players in the major leagues.

Little known are the literally hundreds of fatalities among players, field personnel, and fans that have occurred in other baseball settings, including minor league, semipro, college and high school, and sandlot games. At one time, in fact, baseball was considered the most dangerous of all sports in terms of the number of injuries and fatalities.

What follows is a comprehensive study of game-related baseball fatalities among players, field personnel, and fans at all levels of play in the United States. Rather than merely recounting the deaths, we will place them in context, addressing the factors that led to them and the changes in the game that resulted from them, including style of play, the development of protective equipment, crowd control, stadium structure, and so forth. Earlier versions of our research have appeared in *Nine: A Journal of Baseball History and Culture*.[1]

The focus of this study is on "baseball" in a rather strict sense. For example, while we have included some fatalities resulting from baseball-derived games such as stickball, pepper, and one-a-cat, we have not included softball-related fatalities. The same is true of ball and bat games played prior to the "New York Game," formalized in the mid–1840s when Alexander Cartwright listed the rules governing his New York Knickerbockers, an event which most baseball historians consider the foundation of the game as we know it today. Therefore, we have excluded deaths like that of young George Goble who, in 1834, died a day after being struck by "a ball club" while he was "playing ball" near Wilkes-Barre, Pennsylvania. There is just no way of knowing if these types of deaths are truly "baseball"-related.

A definition of what we mean by "game-related" fatalities is also in order. If the death occurred as part of the game in some fashion or within the grounds (stadium, field, parking lot) where a game was being played, we considered it a game-related death. This criteria seems obvious if one is talking about a beaning or a collision. But what about the fan who has a heart attack or is murdered at the ballpark?

Fan deaths, regardless of cause, are included if they occurred on the grounds. A death that occurred outside the playing field after a game is not included unless it was a carryover

1

from the game itself and occurred on the grounds. Therefore, fans who died outside the play-ing field grounds while celebrating their team's victory will not be found in these pages. Mur-ders that occurred during a game are included, while homicides that are baseball-related, such as those resulting from an argument over a team or play, but occurred outside the playing field grounds, even if the argument began there, are not. Hence, we will not recount deaths resulting from bar or street fights over a baseball issue. Finally, deaths that happened during practice or warm-up are included.

The book is divided into three main sections by victims: players, field personnel, and fans. Players include not only those participating in a game on the field but also those sitting on the bench or on the sidelines if they were a member of one of the participating teams. Field personnel include umpires, owners, managers, coaches, bat boys, stadium employees, and reporters. Fans include anyone watching a game, even those who were killed while pass-ing by a game in progress.

Each section is further divided into chapters by cause of death. The players section will include an additional chapter on fatalities widely reported to have been baseball-related, but upon further investigation turned out to be incorrect or entirely fictional.

Within each chapter we grouped fatalities by level of play: major league, minor league, black baseball, and amateur. Major league fatalities are those that occurred at the highest level of organized professional baseball, while minor league fatalities would be at the level just below that of the major leagues. We decided to include a separate listing for black baseball fatalities because of the historical interest in the game as played in a segregated America. This category includes Negro League teams (existing from about 1920 to the early 1960s) as well as all African American teams—professional, semi-professional, and amateur—that played before the demise of the Negro Leagues. The amateur level includes semipro teams, indus-trial league teams, and college and high school teams; Little League and American Legion teams; and organized youth league games, sandlot games, and unorganized pick-up games occurring on streets, schoolyards, church grounds, recreation parks, and other such venues.

Within each chapter, deaths are presented in chronological order.

Mention should be made of the sources used to document these fatalities. We depended heavily on newspaper accounts for most of the deaths, finding some in national publications such as the *Sporting News, Baseball Magazine, New York Times, Boston Globe, Atlanta Consti-tution, Chicago Tribune, Washington Post,* and *Los Angeles Times,* but many in the local papers where the deaths occurred. We made every attempt to acquire copies of the local newspaper to verify a fatality under the assumption that these local sources would have the most com-plete and accurate accounts. If the local and national papers disagreed over specifics of inci-dents such as names, dates, ages, or circumstances (all of which could vary widely from account to account), we went with the details reported in the local sources.

Part of the problem we encountered was determining the accuracy of news reports, espe-cially those from nineteenth and early twentieth century newspapers. Papers from this era often did not disclose their sources and overly dramatized accounts or fabricated details from sketchy telegraphic messages to make them more interesting for their readers. We developed a nose for the apocryphal and thus took every measure possible to verify the credibility of suspect reports before including the fatalities in our book.[2]

To further complicate matters, some accounts reported something to the effect that the victim was not expected to recover or had no hope of survival or that he was fatally injured. In many of those cases we later discovered that the individual had indeed survived. Therefore, we do not list an incident unless the source stated definitively that the individual was dead.

A typical example serves to illustrate the point. In July 1897, the *Chicago Daily Tribune* stated that a Jefferson Brown was killed while watching a sandlot game near some railroad tracks in Portsmouth, Ohio. According to this brief account, he was stretched out under a freight car and "became so interested that he did not notice a switch engine enter the siding to move the string of cars, and was cut in two by the wheels," a gruesome ending to a pleasant afternoon. Closer to the scene of the tragedy, the *Columbus Dispatch* reported on the incident, except in its version the victim's name was Jefferson Reed and he was "sitting on the end of a tie, leaning against a wheel" when "a sudden jar from a shifting engine threw him beneath the wheels, cutting off his right arm at the shoulder, and terribly lacerating his chest." The paper implied Reed had died when it declared categorically that he was "fatally injured." But the story that appeared in the victim's hometown newspaper, the Portsmouth *Daily Tribune*, provided yet a third variation. The injured man was Jefferson Bower, not Brown or Reed. He was indeed under one of the stationary freight cars watching the game when it was struck by a locomotive. The sudden jolt caused the wheels to "run over his arm, crushing it above the elbow, making amputation necessary." Most important, he was hospitalized, surgery was performed, and he survived.[3]

Fortunately, most libraries were generous in lending microfilm copies of newspapers when they existed. We also contacted local history groups and individuals knowledgeable about the incident in question, consulted the player files and other sources available in the A. Bartlett Giamatti Research Center at the National Baseball Hall of Fame and Museum in Cooperstown, New York, and acquired primary source materials such as death certificates when needed and available. Finally, online indexes and databases such as ProQuest Historical Newspapers, NewspaperARCHIVE.com, The Baseball Index, Academic Search Premier, Academic OneFile, Physical Education Index, Health Reference Center — Academic, Health and Wellness Resource Center, Medline, and WorldCat were immensely helpful in either providing or identifying sources of information. We have used endnotes to document the sources used to confirm a death.

This study is as comprehensive as we were able to make it. But while hundreds of fatalities were identified, we assume that there are others we did not uncover. Even though there are several excellent online newspaper databases, coverage, especially of smaller newspapers, is still somewhat spotty. Many of the fatalities we found in local papers were never reported in the national press.

Introduction

"Baseball Is 'Deadliest Sport,'" proclaimed the *Chicago Daily Tribune* in 1920. "Most Dangerous Recreation Is Found to Be Baseball," asserted the *New York Times* ten years later. "Baseball Tops Deaths in New York Survey," announced the *Los Angeles Times* in 1951. And "Baseball Deaths Outstrip Football, 2–1," reported *Collegiate Baseball* in 1984.[1]

Baseball "deadly"? Have people actually been killed while playing or observing the National Pastime? Could these findings possibly be correct?

These headlines are indeed accurate. Literally hundreds of players, officials, and fans have died at baseball games since the mid–nineteenth century. While the exact number of fatalities will in all probability never be known — coverage of deaths, especially in the past, was sporadic at best — it is clear from even the most cursory research that baseball can be a deadly sport.

The first comprehensive study of game-related fatalities was completed in 1917. Dr. Robert E. Coughlin, a New York physician, identified 943 sports fatalities nationwide from 1905 to 1915. Of these, 284 (30 percent) were baseball-related, more than any other sport. His year-by-year breakdown found 11 in 1905, 19 in 1906, 13 in 1907, 42 in 1908, 32 in 1909, 53 in 1910, 29 in 1911, 14 in 1912, 24 in 1913, 27 in 1914, and 20 in 1915.[2]

Subsequent studies confirmed what Dr. Coughlin had discovered — baseball is sometimes lethal. In 1951, Dr. Thomas A. Gonzales of the New York Office of the Chief Medical Examiner reported on a 32-year (1918–1950) longitudinal study of sports fatalities in the New York City area. He was able to confirm 104 deaths with baseball accounting for 43 (41 percent) of them.[3]

This second study went even further than the Coughlin report. Necropsies were performed on 73 of the fatalities to determine cause of death. Dr. Gonzales found that most baseball-related deaths were due to the ball being thrown, pitched, or hit. Of the 43 total baseball fatalities, 25 (58 percent) were due to blows to the head. Dr. Gonzales concluded that "the efforts to reduce the incidence of non-fatal accidents in the various branches of athletics by revision of rules, by better medical supervision and coaching, and by the introduction of protective equipment have met with some measure of success."[4]

More recently the United States Consumer Product Safety Commission has conducted studies of sports deaths among children between the ages of 5 and 14. In a 1984 report covering the years 1973 to 1980, the commission identified 40 baseball-related fatalities among children in this age group. In comparison, football suffered 19 fatalities, half as many as baseball even though about as many children were estimated to play football (4.2 million) as baseball (4.8 million).[5]

In a 1996 follow-up report on the same age group from 1973 to 1995, the commission analyzed 88 reported baseball fatalities. Blunt trauma to the chest (*commotio cordis*) by the ball was the cause of 38 of the deaths, with ball-related head injuries causing 21 deaths and bat injuries causing 13. The report concluded that improved safety features such as softer balls, chest protectors for all batters, and face guards on batting helmets would reduce injuries and, ultimately, fatalities.[6]

All of these studies point to the fact that baseball can be a dangerous sport. But how does it compare to other sports? The answer to this question varies depending on factors such as time period, age of participant, and whether the victim is a player or a fan.

At one time, baseball truly was the "National Pastime," played in every town and hamlet in the country. Other competitive sports, such as football and basketball, were much less popular prior to the Second World War and the advent of television. Consequently, it is not surprising that because baseball has more participants, fatalities are also more numerous.

Sports-related fatality statistics were not kept in any organized way until recently. Earlier, interested individuals would sometimes track and report on deaths, but mostly what was available was spotty and often inaccurate. The 1917 Coughlin report mentioned above was the first comprehensive comparative analysis of sports fatalities. Ranked by number, some of the 943 deaths he identified from 1905 to 1915 are as follows: baseball (284), football (215), auto racing (128), boxing (105), cycling (77), horse racing (54), wrestling (15), golf (14), bowling (9), and basketball (4). Coughlin provided no estimates as to the number of participants in each of these activities.[7]

In the 1951 Gonzales study in the New York City area, baseball was the most deadly sport. Out of 104 fatalities from 1918 to 1950, baseball accounted for 43 of them, followed by football (22), boxing (21), and basketball (7). Gonzales, like Coughlin, did not indicate how many participated in these sports.[8]

Football has done a much better job of tracking fatalities than baseball, partly because in its early history football was seen by many as too violent and harmful, especially for young people. In response to this perception and as a means to improve the safety of the sport, the American Football Coaches Association issued its "Annual Survey of Football Fatalities" beginning in 1931. These reports have continued under the auspices of the National Center for Catastrophic Sport Injury Research at the University of North Carolina at Chapel Hill. Now titled the "Annual Survey of Football Injury Research," the latest report covers fatalities from 1931 through 2005. During these 75 years, there were 1,001 fatalities at all levels of play directly due to football. There were 658 fatalities indirectly due to football.[9]

The NCCSIR also issues an annual survey covering injuries and fatalities for all sports at the college and high school levels. The most recent report, covering the period from 1982 to 2004, categorizes fatalities according to direct and indirect causes. For football there were 94 direct and 144 indirect fatalities at the high school level and 9 direct and 34 indirect fatalities at the college level. During this same period, baseball experienced 8 direct and 11 indirect fatalities at the high school level and 3 direct and 2 indirect at the college level. Clearly football is now the more dangerous of the two sports, at least at the high school and college levels.[10]

In the pages that follow, we look at fatalities among baseball players, field personnel, and fans in the United States. We analyze the causes, discuss what steps were taken to reduce fatalities (there are far fewer today than there were a century ago), and describe how the number and type of fatalities have changed over time. We also explore specific incidents and provide necrologies for all the cases we have been able to identify and verify.

I

Players

1. Beaning Fatalities

Chin music. Brushback. High hard one. High and tight. Knockdown. Bean ball.

Ever since pitchers began throwing overhand, batters, rather than the plate, have occasionally been the target. While hitting a batter is usually not done on purpose, pitching close inside is an act of intimidation, an attempt to instill fear in the batter. For the art of pitching is more than just messing with a batter's timing; it is the art of messing with his head as well. "The confidence will seep out of most batters if they've just been occupied in ducking a high fast one inside that whistles past his head or neck. And without that confidence he isn't as dangerous a hitter," opined renowned *Washington Post* sports columnist Shirley Povich.[1]

In the early game, there were restrictions on how the ball was to be delivered to the batter. As Peter Morris explains in *A Game of Inches*, "the pitcher's role was to give the batter something to hit" by propelling the ball with "a straight-arm motion and a release from an underhand position." Pitchers, of course, had an entirely different take on the matter and used every means necessary — both legal and illegal — to get the batter out. While the game's rulemakers attempted to dictate and control how pitching was to be done, the pitchers struggled mightily to free themselves from these constraints. By the early 1870s, pitchers were allowed to bend their arms and to release the ball at hip level, a significant change which enhanced the throwing of the curveball. And when a full overhand delivery was allowed in both professional leagues in the mid–1880s, pitchers were able to develop a full arsenal of pitches.[2]

Throwing inside or even directly at the batter began in earnest once the rules changed. A new regulation established by the American Association in 1884 (followed by the National Association in 1887) giving first base to a batter who was hit by a ball helped control the situation somewhat, but pitchers quickly found that making batsmen afraid by plunking one on occasion paid big dividends. "The ball players are being killed off so fast now that the race will soon become extinct if the pitcher's box is not moved from half to three-quarters of a mile further back," warned the *National Police Gazette* half facetiously in 1888, just a few years after the introduction of overhand pitching. "The present style of pitching is about equivalent to standing fifty feet from a cannon and trying to hit the ball as it is shot out. The fact is that it is a hundred per cent more dangerous, as the cannon ball would come out straight, while the pitcher keeps the batter dancing a hornpipe by throwing every other ball or so directly at him, in order to scare him out of making a hit," the editorial concluded.[3]

Many players, officials, and observers of the sport complained about the often deadly consequences of throwing at or near a batter's head. In 1913, Harry A. Williams, future president of the Pacific Coast League, declared that he was "opposed to the 'bean' ball simply because I am opposed to murder on general principles." Any pitcher who intentionally "bounces the ball off the batter's knob," he argued, should "be plastered with some sort of penalty every time he does it." Columnist Edward Burns agreed, referring to bean-ball pitchers as "kid bullies at heart."[4]

But not everyone disapproved of the practice. Povich, for one, thought that throwing a brushback was perfectly acceptable. "Baseball is a rugged sport," he contended. "The fact that only one man has been killed by a pitched ball in the long history of big league baseball testifies that bean balls are not an extreme hazard. The bean ball is a misnomer, anyway. What the pitchers throw is a brush-off ball, rarely aimed at the head and comparatively harmless when it hits any other part of the anatomy." What Povich apparently did not know was that beanings at one time were the major cause of player fatalities.[5]

While only one major leaguer died as a result of a beaning, nine minor league players have been killed that way. In addition, more than 100 amateur players of all ages have died from beanings since 1888, the year the *National Police Gazette* editorial appeared. Most of these deaths could have been prevented if a very simple protective device — the batting helmet — had been accepted as standard baseball equipment earlier than it was.

The delay in adoption certainly was not from lack of awareness about the dangers of the bean ball. Over the years, baseball attempted to eliminate intentional beanings by various rule changes that punished the offenders, trying everything from fines to ejections of pitchers and managers. While these policies may have cut down on intentional beanings, they did nothing to prevent the far more prevalent unintentional variety. So, considering all the serious injuries and fatalities from blows to the head and baseball's awareness of such dangers, why did it take baseball so long to require the helmet?

Most of the opposition, oddly enough, came from the players themselves. For many, it was an issue of *machismo*. "For some quixotic reason most ballplayers refuse to don helmets," wrote New York sports columnist Arthur Daley in 1955. "Some are afraid that it will make them look like sissies. For that flimsy excuse they risk their lives day after day," he concluded. Warren Giles, president of the National League, gave a similar explanation the following spring when he made helmets mandatory in his league: "In the past, a lot of players thought it was a little sissified to go up to the plate wearing helmets. They just didn't like the idea; they thought the fans might razz them."[6]

For others, though, it was a question of comfort and the concern that helmets would obstruct the batter's vision. When Will Harridge made helmets mandatory in the American League in early 1958 and decreed that no batter could step up to the plate without head protection, the biggest opponent was Ted Williams. The Red Sox slugger claimed that wearing a helmet "interferes with my timing," and during spring training that year, he refused to don a helmet. Boston general manager Joe Cronin supported Williams' position on the matter. "Williams won't wear a helmet, but helmets aren't necessary," claimed Cronin. "All the rule demands is some protective plate. Williams has been practicing with one the past ten days, and thinks it's perfectly all right." Once it became known that the Splendid Splinter wore a fibre lining under his cap, the confrontation was resolved.[7]

While today's modern helmets, such as the Rawlings "Cool-Flo" model, are designed for comfort as well as safety, it took over a century of trial and error before they reached this stage. The A. J. Reach Company, for example, developed an inflatable device known as the Pneumatic Head Protector in 1905. This headgear, which had to be placed on the head before inflating, required the assistance of a teammate who blew into a small tube. It was first used in the majors in 1907 by future Hall-of-Fame catcher Roger Bresnahan after he had suffered severe injury from a beaning. Needless to say, it was never widely accepted.[8]

Even after the beaning death of major leaguer Ray Chapman in 1920, batting helmets remained primitive and unpopular. In 1937, the Des Moines (IA) Demons of the Class A Western League used polo helmets in a May 30 game against the Cedar Rapids (IA) Raiders. Players and managers found the helmets "too heavy and cumbersome" and they were not used again after that one game. Some major leaguers attempted to improve on protective devices. In 1939 Skeeter Newsome, shortstop for the Philadelphia A's, began using an aluminum liner under his cap when at bat.[9]

By the 1940s, though, many team officials were moving toward requiring use of protective headgear of some sort. The National League was the first to act when they

An early example of headgear, this one sold by Spalding, ca. 1920. Protective devices such as this football-type helmet were not popular in part because they were so cumbersome to wear.

passed a resolution in early 1941 stating that "clubs will experiment with helmets in their Spring training camps. The helmets, weighing between three and five ounces, fit into the regulation caps and are calculated to minimize the danger to batters from wild pitches." The league left it to the individual clubs to decide whether their players would wear helmets. Brooklyn general manager Larry MacPhail moved quickly, decreeing in March 1941 that every team in the Dodgers organization would use protective headgear. MacPhail felt compelled to act after serious beaning injuries to Pee Wee Reese and Ducky Medwick the year before. The device used was still crude by today's standards: "Zippered pockets are cut in each side of a regulation baseball cap. Into one of these pockets, on the side he faces the pitcher, the batter will slip a plastic plate which is about a quarter of an inch thick and little more than an ounce in weight. The plate, about the width and length of a man's head, covers the vulnerable area from the temple to about an inch behind the ear." This liner was designed by two Johns Hopkins surgeons, Dr. George E. Bennett and Dr. Walter E. Dandy, at the urging of National League president Ford Frick. A major advantage as far as the players were concerned was that it wasn't "cumbersome and so conspicuous that everybody could see it."[10]

Other organizations followed the Dodgers' lead. The Class B Interstate League became the first in organized ball to require head protection when it passed a resolution during its 1941 winter meetings ordering the eight member teams to purchase helmets. Players, though, were not required to use them: "We can't force the players to wear them, but it is compulsory for the clubs to buy them," stated league president Arthur Ehlers. Lee MacPhail, son of Larry MacPhail and manager of the Dodgers' Reading club, was behind the move.[11]

Individual major leaguers began using head protection as well. The prototype of the modern batting helmet was introduced by Branch Rickey, general manager of the Pittsburgh Pirates, in 1952. The American Baseball Cap Company, in which Rickey had a financial interest, developed a six-and-a-half-ounce fiberglass and polyester resin cap worn in place of the felt hat when a player was at bat. Players referred to them as "bowlers," "skullers," or "miner's caps." By 1954, four National League clubs (the Reds, Phillies, Giants, and Cubs) and two American League clubs (the Indians and White Sox) encouraged, and in some cases required, their players to use the helmets developed by Rickey's company.[12]

With the advent of the plastic cap, pressure increased on organized ball to require the use of them. In a 1953 editorial titled "Make Safety Caps Mandatory," the *Sporting News* called on league presidents Warren Giles and Will Harridge to do just that. If "humanitarian factors" weren't sufficient grounds for mandating caps, the paper argued, then owners and officials should consider the financial aspect of head injuries: "The players represent investments, more valuable than usual in this day of shrinking talent pool. Sheer economic common sense should move the owners to insist that their players wear the helmets." Sports columnist Arthur Daley stated it more bluntly. "A baseball is a lethal weapon," he asserted. "The main thing is for the authorities to make the wearing of helmets mandatory."[13]

The time was right for baseball to finally act. In 1956 head protection for batters became required in the National League. The American League followed in 1958. Players were allowed to use inserts and liners until 1971, when the helmet was mandated in the major leagues. That same year all Class A and Rookie League batters were ordered to wear helmets with ear flaps. This rule was expanded in 1974 to include all minor leaguers and all major league rookies. Eventually helmets were required for all players.[14]

While major league players were still debating protective headgear, organized Little League baseball moved more quickly to protect batters. In the late 1950s, Dr. Creighton Hale, director of research for Little League baseball, conducted extensive studies of pitch speed and batter reaction time. Because of his research, the pitching mound was moved back and batters were required to wear plastic helmets with ear flaps that protected the temples and back of the head years before they were required in the major leagues.[15]

While helmets have not entirely eliminated deaths from beanings, they have dramatically reduced the number of fatalities. Clearly, as the following discussion of specific incidents and the necrology which follows will indicate, helmets were the most important piece of offensive protective equipment to be developed.

Major League Fatalities

As mentioned previously, **Ray Chapman** is the only major leaguer to have died from a beaning. At the Polo Grounds on the afternoon of August 16, 1920, Chapman, shortstop for the Cleveland Indians, stepped into the box at the top of the fifth inning for his third at-bat against Yankees pitcher Carl Mays. On the very first pitch, Mays, a submariner and notorious headhunter, threw an inside fastball. Chapman, who appeared to be crouching over the plate, never even moved as the ball struck him on his left temple. The impact was so loud that many thought Chapman's bat had struck the ball. "I would have sworn the ball hit the bat," said fan D. L. Webster the next day, "for it rolled out to Mays, who threw it to first base." As umpire Tom Connolly yelled for medical assistance, Chapman slumped dazed at the plate. Several moments later he revived enough to be escorted off the field. At first unable to speak, he appeared to improve somewhat later at that day. In fact, Cleveland manager Tris Speaker initially felt that Chapman would survive. "I was hit on the head in 1916 in a manner similar to this," he explained, "and I am hopeful that Chappie will be back again soon." Sadly, such would not be the case. Late that night he took a turn for the worse and, with his life hanging in the balance, emergency surgery was performed. It was all in vain, for the 29-year-old player died early the next morning.[16]

Mays claimed then, as he did throughout his life, that the beaning was unintentional. He blamed it in part on the ball itself, asserting that a "rough" spot on the ball caused it to sail in toward Chapman. He also felt that Chapman either failed to see the ball or that he was "hypnotized by the ball," standing frozen as it hurled toward him. Chapman's death was "a recollection of the most unpleasant kind which I shall carry with me as long as I live," he wrote months after the event. At a hearing shortly after the incident, New York assistant district attorney John F. Joyce declared it to be "purely accidental." And while Tris Speaker did "not hold Mays responsible in any way" for Chapman's death, such was not the case with some umpires and more than a few players.[17]

Members of the Detroit Tigers and the Boston Red Sox in particular reacted strongly to the Chapman incident and tried unsuccessfully to get Mays "suspended from organized baseball." They sent a telegram to that effect to American League president Ban Johnson, who, for his part, refused to act immediately. "I will make no definite statement regarding Mays' future status until I have more complete and definite reports," he informed the press. In the meantime, American League umpires Billy Evans and William Dineen added their two cents' worth, insisting that "no pitcher in the American League resorted to trickery more than Carl Mays in attempting to rough a ball to get a break on it which would make it more difficult to hit." Several days later, though, Johnson announced that he would take "no official action" against Mays, in part because he felt Mays was so distraught by his role in Chapman's demise that "he may never be capable, temperamentally, of pitching again." In addition, with feeling running so high against Mays, "it would be unadvisable for him to attempt to pitch this year at any rate." Yankee owners Jacob Ruppert and T. L. Huston objected strenuously to Johnson's implication that Mays was "a broken reed." Indeed, they maintained that Mays "will go along and follow his regular means of livelihood as a strong man should. He will take his regular turn in the pitcher's box and we expect him win games as usual." And win, he did. On August 23, less than a week after Chapman's death, the Yankee hurler was again on the mound, pitching his team to a 10 to 0 victory. He ended that season with a 26 and 11 record and would remain in the majors for the next nine seasons.[18]

While this incident has been widely reported, few are aware of the nine minor league players who met the same fate. For Chapman was not the first, nor would he be the last, beaning fatality.

Minor League Fatalities

Herbert M. "Whit" Whitney has the sad distinction of being the first professional player killed by a pitch. Whitney, 27-year-old star catcher and leading hitter for the first-place

Burlington (IA) Pathfinders of the Class D Iowa State League, was in his first season of professional ball after several years of playing in semipro leagues in Montana. A native of Winchendon, MA, the young player was a favorite among teammates and fans. "His work while fielding as a catcher was easily superior to any other catcher in the league," eulogized the local newspaper. "His presence at bat was always a signal for applause from the stands. He was never afraid of working too hard, and went after every ball that came his way."[19]

Whitney was struck in the head during a Sunday afternoon game on June 24, 1906, in Waterloo, IA. He was facing Fred Evans, of the Waterloo Microbes, who threw a ball that fractured Whitney's skull. The young catcher, who collapsed unconscious at the plate, was rushed to a nearby hospital. Late the following night, doctors decided that surgery was necessary. While preparing to remove a section of the skull to reduce pressure, Whitney suddenly began hemorrhaging from the nose and ears. Efforts to staunch the flow of blood proved futile and Whitney died at 3:30 A.M. that Tuesday. His body was shipped home to Massachusetts for burial.[20]

Pitcher Fred Evans was devastated by the news of Whitney's death. No one blamed the Microbes hurler, but that did not lessen Evans' sense of responsibility. The two players were friends, which made it even harder on Evans. Teammates prevented the pitcher from viewing Whitney's body out of concern for Evans. Clearly, as in most accidents of this sort, there are two victims, the one who died and the one who was the agent of his death.

On August 9, 1906, less than two months later, a second fatal beaning occurred. **Thomas F. Burke**, 26, left fielder for the Lynn (MA) Shoemakers of the Class B New England League, was batting in the home half of the sixth inning against the Fall River (MA) Indians. Indians pitcher Edward Yeager threw a ball that broke in on Burke, striking him on the temple. The home plate umpire caught Burke as he fell unconscious. He was quickly carried to the dressing room where he was attended to by a Dr. C. D. S. Lovell. Shortly thereafter he was transported to the Lynn hospital with a fractured skull.[21]

Burke, a former player with Boston University and a law student in the off-season, remained unconscious in the hospital. Even though surgery was performed and doctors initially held out hope for his recovery, Burke never regained consciousness. He passed away shortly after noon on August 11, two days after the beaning.[22]

A distraught Yeager attended the Lynn players' funeral on August 15. Three days later Yeager was arrested and charged with manslaughter. According to the police chief, the pitcher was arrested "in order that the police and local court might have a complete record of Burke's death." Nonetheless, an anxious Yeager had to post $500 bail and wait two days until his hearing. Several witnesses to the event, including the hearing judge, testified that Yeager did not intentionally bean Burke, that the batter simply failed to get out of the way of the breaking pitch. Charges against Yeager were dropped and he was immediately released.[23]

Three years later, second baseman **Charles "Cupid" Pinkney**, 20, of the Class B Central League Dayton (OH) Veterans, was killed in a game against the Grand Rapids (MI) Wolverines. In the late afternoon of September 14, 1909, Pinkney was at bat in the bottom of the seventh for the last-place Veterans in the second game of a doubleheader. In the stands was Pinkney's father, who had traveled to Dayton from Cleveland to see his son play. Pinkney had performed well that day, even hitting a home run in his first at-bat in the first game. But because the day was growing late, making the ball difficult to see, both teams agreed that the seventh would be the final inning even though the Veterans were down two runs. With one on and one out, Pinkney stepped in against Wolverines pitcher Kurt "Casey" Hageman, a four-year veteran of the minor leagues.

This was not the first time that day the two had faced each other. In fact, Hageman was the starting pitcher in the first game as well and had given up the home run to Pinkney in the first inning of that game. Hageman was removed in the second inning of that first contest after allowing four runs on four hits (including a double, a triple, and Pinkney's homer), a walk, a wild pitch, and a passed ball, and committing an error.[24]

The first three pitches to Pinkney in his final at-bat were balls, and Hageman, "who had been troubled with wildness all afternoon ... sent up a terrific shoot, which Pinkney could not dodge in time, and the best second baseman that has worn a Dayton uniform for many days was felled to the ground." The inside fastball struck Pinkney behind the left ear. Pinkney's father rushed down from the stands as his son was carried off the field. "While standing at his son's side the aged father suddenly succumbed and restoratives were required to bring him to consciousness."[25]

Hageman was "completely unnerved" after hitting Pinkney and had to be removed from the game. "He locked himself in his room ... refusing to see even his teammates, although everyone absolves him from all blame in the accident. From early in the morning [September 15] he kept the phone to the hospital in constant use, asking particulars of Pinkney's condition."[26]

Emergency surgery was performed, but Pinkney died the next day without regaining consciousness, his father by his side. As Pinkney's body traveled back to his native Cleveland, Dayton and Grand Rapids canceled their games for the remainder of the season. In the words of a poetic tribute that appeared in the Dayton newspaper, "The Umpire of the Game of Life, Has called a fav'rite player out, And stilled with grief is ev'ry Voice, That yesterday was wont to shout."[27]

In 1912 and 1913, **John L. "Johnny" Dodge** had a brief major league career, appearing in 127 games as a utility infielder for the Phillies and Reds during those two years. His best season was with the 1913 Reds when he batted .241 in 94 games, hitting 4 home runs and driving in 45. In early 1914, however, the weak-hitting Dodge was released from the Reds to the Louisville Colonels of the American Association. Dodge would never make it back to the majors, and in 1916 the 27-year-old player was covering third base for the last-place Mobile (AL) Sea Gulls of the Class A Southern League. On June 18, 1916, his career came to a sudden and tragic end.

The Sea Gulls were playing the first-place Nashville (TN) Volunteers that Sunday afternoon. The year before, Dodge had been a member of the Nashville nine. In the home half of the seventh inning, Dodge came to the plate to confront his old Nashville teammate, Tom Rogers. An inside breaking ball from Rogers caught Dodge square in the face. According to the *Sporting News*, "at the time it was not thought Dodge was seriously injured. Examination by physicians, however, showed that his face was crushed in such a manner that complications might result and he was taken to a hospital, but nothing medical aid could do would save his life." Dodge died around 7:30 the following night. The third baseman was the sole support of his younger sister, so the Sea Gulls held a benefit game for her on August 11, raising some $1,500.[28]

As for Tom Rogers, his pitching did not suffer because of the incident. On July 11, less than a month after beaning Johnny Dodge, he pitched a perfect game against the Chattanooga (TN) Lookouts. His opponent that afternoon pitched one-hit ball, losing 2–0 because of two errors in the seventh inning. The following season Rogers was in the majors pitching for the St. Louis Browns. He compiled a 15–30 record over four major league seasons with three clubs.

In one of those odd twists of fate, in 1921 he was briefly a teammate of Carl Mays, the pitcher who had killed Ray Chapman the year before.[29]

The Base Ball Players' Fraternity was deeply disturbed by Dodge's death, however. While not accusing Rogers of intentionally throwing at Dodge, the organization's president saw the fatality as "an object lesson." Dodge's demise "should forcibly impress every player with the inherent dangers of the game, and with the fact that each one owes to his fellow players the duty of exercising reasonable precaution to prevent accidents." A letter of condolence was sent to Dodge's sister by members of the organization's advisory board.[30]

Jesse "Jake" Batterton, 19, was an outstanding prospect in the St. Louis Cardinals organization. In 1933 he was playing second base for the Springfield (MO) Cardinals in the Class A Western League. In the top half of the second inning of the second game of a July 2 doubleheader against the Omaha (NE) Packers, Batterton came up for his first at-bat. On the mound was Omaha's Floyd "Swede" Carlsen. The moment the right-hander released his fastball, he knew it was heading straight for Batterton. He yelled at the batter to duck, but instead of moving away from the pitch, Batterton bent directly into the path of the ball. It caught Batterton squarely on the head, causing a five-inch skull fracture.

Oddly, though, the second baseman did not lose consciousness. After falling to the ground, he sat up and announced, "Just let me sit here a few minutes. I'm all right." After a quick examination by the Omaha team physician, Batterton rose and walked back to the bench. A few minutes later, he went into the clubhouse, where he was examined again. In spite of his protestations that he was all right, he was sent to an Omaha hospital. Later that evening his condition worsened and surgery was performed. He died of a cerebral hemorrhage the following morning. An inconsolable Swede Carlsen stayed by his side, proclaiming over and over, "I'm sorry, I'm sorry." Batterton's body was sent home to Los Angeles the following day.[31]

Winnipeg, Manitoba, Canada, was the scene of the next two minor league beaning fatalities. In the late evening gloom on August 27, 1936, the visiting Superior (WI) Blues of the Class D Northern League were at bat in the first inning against the hometown Maroons. At the plate was Superior's 21-year-old second baseman, **George Tkach**. On the mound for Winnipeg was one of the team's star pitchers, Alex Uffelman.

With an 0 and 2 count, Tkach crowded the plate. Apparently thinking the next pitch would be delivered outside, the second baseman stepped into the ball. The ball slammed into the batter's left jaw, fracturing it. Although Tkach "dropped like an ox" from the blow, at first no one thought the injury was fatal. He was transported to the hospital for treatment and observation. Arthur Morrison, manager of Sherburn Park where the game was played, visited Tkach the next day in the hospital. Morrison asked Tkach what he thought had happened and the second baseman replied simply, "I guess I forgot to duck."[32]

Two days later, paralysis of the face began to occur. Surgery was performed the following day to remove a large blood clot on the brain. Still, physicians thought he would make a complete recovery. His condition declined steadily, though, and shortly after noon on September 2, nearly a week after the incident, George Tkach died. At an inquest held two days later, a coroner's jury declared the incident to be accidental.[33]

Tragedy struck again at Sherburn Park on July 16, 1938, less than two years after the Tkach fatality. During the night half of a doubleheader on that Saturday, the Maroons were playing the Grand Forks (ND) Chiefs, both teams struggling in the second division of the Class D Northern League. **Linus "Skeeter" Ebnet**, the Maroons shortstop, was the third batter up in the bottom of the first. As Ebnet strode to the plate, Chiefs pitcher Vince "Dutch" Clawson had already recorded two quick outs. Ebnet, who had gone two for five in the first game but had committed two errors, stepped into the box. Accounts as to what happened next differ. Scott Young, covering the game for the *Winnipeg Free Press*, reported that Clawson's "first pitch to Ebnet was inside, and as Ebnet ducked back to avoid the pitch, the ball broke in sharply, hitting the Maroon infield ace with a dull, ominous thud." Clawson had a different recollection: "There were two balls called on Skeets at the time, and my only thought on the third pitch was to get the ball over the plate, but it broke inside and Ebnet ducked into it."[34]

Regardless of the specifics, Ebnet was severely injured. "Players of both teams crowded around the prostrate, twitching figure at home plate," wrote Young. "Johnny Mostil, Grand Forks manager, forced them back, asking for air. Water was brought, and towels. Skeeter, a favorite with fans and players alike, regained consciousness for a fleeting instant, then again his head fell back, and he went limp. Four of his teammates carried him from the field to a waiting ambulance, called less than a minute after the accident."[35]

Ebnet was transported to Grace Hospital, where a number of x-rays were taken. Doctors diagnosed a concussion, but could find no fractures. His condition was reported as "fair." The game continued with Gaylen Shupe, losing pitcher in the first game, taking Ebnet's place at shortstop. The Maroons won, 8 to 4.

Over the next five days, the 23-year-old struggled for his life. On July 18, emergency surgery was performed to relieve pressure on his brain. He continued to deteriorate, and at 7:20 P.M. on July 21, with his parents by his side, Skeeter Ebnet died. He was sent home to Albany, MN, for burial.[36]

In 1947, his first year of professional baseball, **James "Stormy" Davis**, 20-year-old outfielder with the Ballinger (TX) Cats, was showing great promise in the Class D Longhorn League. Although he had started the season at a slightly higher level with the Tyler (TX) Trojans of the Class C Lone Star League, he was performing very well for his new club. In just 48 games, he was batting over .300 with 17 home runs, 57 hits, and 64 runs batted in to his credit.

Then in mid-season, everything abruptly ended for the talented young star. During a July 3 game against the Sweetwater (TX) Sports, Davis was beaned by pitcher Stan "Midnight" Wilson. The Mobile, AL, native was immediately taken to the hospital in Sweetwater, where emergency surgery was performed. Although physicians found no blood clot or hemorrhage, the tissue in the brain was severely swollen. The operation appeared successful and for a week Davis showed improvement. Then, at 2:00 P.M. on July 10, a conscious Stormy Davis suddenly died of a brain hemorrhage.[37]

While helmets and protective headgear were slowly being introduced in organized ball, sadly these devises had not made their way to the Class D Alabama-Florida League in 1951. As a result, another beaning fatality occurred in the minor leagues. It would be the final one.

The Dothan (AL) Browns outfielder, **Ottis Johnson,** was one of the league's best hitters. In early June, the 24-year-old married father of one led the league with 10 home runs and was fifth in batting average with an impressive .384. He also led his team with 48 hits, 38 runs batted in, 11 doubles, and 28 runs scored. Clearly he was the Browns' biggest offensive threat.

On the evening of June 2, 1951, in Headland, AL, the Browns were being handily defeated by the Dixie Runners pitching ace, lefty Harry "Jack" Clifton. Clifton, who would win 22 games that season, was working on another gem of a game when Johnson stepped in against him in the top of the fifth inning. Always an aggressive pitcher, Clifton came right after the Browns bomber. When the dust had settled, Johnson lay unconscious at the plate, a victim of a Clifton beanball to the temple. One person in attendance at that game later said the blow "cracked like a shot. This was before the protective helmet. He hit the deck and was unconscious before he hit the ground." After Johnson was removed by ambulance, Clifton stayed in the game, winning it, 5 to 1.[38]

X-rays showed a fractured skull. For a week, Johnson floated in and out of consciousness, even talking at one point, although he had no memory of the incident. Even as late as June 7, the outfielder was listed as "serious but satisfactory." The following day, though, emergency decompression surgery had to be performed, and by Saturday, June 9, he was in very serious trouble. At 5:00 A.M. on June 10, Ottis Johnson died.[39]

The Alabama-Florida League was nearly a victim of the beaning as well. On the evening of June 12, one day after Ottis Johnson's funeral, the Browns were scheduled to face Jack Clifton again, this time in Dothan. Team members and officials were furious about this turn of events. Browns owner Charles Smith threatened to leave the league if Clifton pitched. Although Smith did not accuse Clifton of intentionally beaning Johnson, nonetheless the owner proclaimed, "Clifton will never pitch against Dothan as long as I am paying the bills." Smith defended his position, saying, "One accident has happened and I don't want another one to happen. I'm merely trying to protect our players." To add to Smith's concerns, Clifton was known for going after batters, leading the league that season in both strikeouts and batters plunked.[40]

Ottis Johnson's widow disagreed with the position taken by the Browns ownership. She said her husband told her that the he was sure the beaning was unintentional, that Clifton "couldn't help the accident." She asserted that "Ottis would want Jack to continue to play." Clifton had even visited with Johnson in the hospital shortly before the outfielder's death.[41]

Nonetheless, Smith withdrew his team when it was confirmed that the southpaw would pitch. It cost the Browns a forfeit and the owner a fine. Clifton's reputation preceded him at his next start against the Panama City (FL) Fliers. Apparently the Fliers batters were skittish in the box, for Clifton pitched a no-hitter, striking out 11 and walking 7. The final score was 19 to 2, the Fliers' runs resulting from three walks, an error, and a hit batter. With that kind of wildness, no wonder opponents were nervous about facing the southpaw.[42]

The Browns were scheduled to face Clifton again on June 24, and once more Smith pulled his team from the field, forfeiting a second game. In addition, the owner announced he was withdrawing the Browns from the league. League president G. D. Halstead said he hoped Smith would reconsider, but if he insisted on withdrawing, then another city would be found to replace Dothan. The matter became even more complicated when three other league teams — Panama City (FL), Enterprise (AL), and Ozark (AL) — stated that they, too, would not play unless Clifton and Headland manager Bubba Ball were removed from the league. League president Halstead announced his resignation in response to this threat.[43]

An emergency meeting of the clubs was called for July 1 in Dothan. Halstead reconsidered his resignation and chaired this meeting. An apparent truce was called when Headland president A. D. Walden agreed not to pitch Clifton against Dothan the rest of the season. Although Clifton continued to pitch against other teams, he played the outfield when Headland and Dothan met July 3 and 4. As the summer wore on, the situation seemed to cool down some. In fact, Dothan won the post-season playoffs that year.[44]

As for Jack Clifton, he ended the season with a record of 22–11, tied for the league lead in wins. Early in 1952, though, he announced his retirement from baseball. One can only wonder what effect the beaning death and resulting turmoil had on him. Certainly no one who causes an accidental death emerges from the event unscathed. When Ottis Johnson's hometown of Evergreen, AL, held a memorial tribute to him on April 22, 1995, one of the former players in attendance was Jack Clifton.[45]

Black Baseball Fatalities

Brooklyn resident **George Fleischman**, 24, catcher for the Stapleton Baseball Club on Staten Island, NY, was beaned during the fifth inning of a game in Stapleton on August 23, 1908, against the Brooklyn Royal Giants, an African American team. He continued to play in spite of his injury. Collapsing later while dressing in the clubhouse, he was taken to an area hospital, where a physician determined he had a blood clot on his brain. He died late the next morning without regaining consciousness.[46]

The one black baseball and nine minor league fatalities discussed above were only the tip of the beaning iceberg. The amateur player necrology which follows indicates the full extent of the problem which resulted from the late adoption of protective headgear.

Amateur Fatalities

Otto Bronson, 18, was struck behind his left ear while ducking out of the way of a wild pitch during a game in Hamilton, NY, on August 21, 1887. He died moments after being hit.[47]

Edward Pousch, 18, was struck in the temple by a fastball during a morning pick-up game in Columbus, OH, on July 22, 1888. He died later that day of a concussion.[48]

Michael Murray, 24-year-old brakeman with the Buffalo, Rochester and Pittsburgh Railway, played shortstop for the amateur Ontario Baseball Club in Rochester, NY. On the afternoon of August 19, 1888, he was killed when a pitched ball broke his neck.[49]

Thomas J. Godfrey, 25-year-old member of the Castleton (Staten Island) Club, was struck in the temple by a "hot ball" (fastball) in a game against the Staten Island Athletic Club on September 22, 1889. Godfrey died at 9:00 that night.[50]

John Walters, 20, was hit by a wild pitch under his left ear in a game in Richmond, IN, on September 29, 1889. He was stunned by the blow, but remained conscious. After resting a short while, he attempted to continue playing. Growing steadily worse, though, he left before the end of the game and walked home on his own, where he collapsed shortly after arrival. He died of a brain hemorrhage about 8:00 that evening.[51]

Thomas E. Mandery, 17, died in New York City on October 24, 1889, a year after being struck between the eyes by a fastball. The blow caused immediate "discoloration" in both eyes. Eventually he became blind and suffered from periodic convulsions. An autopsy determined the cause of death to be "an abscess on the brain."[52]

Ralph B. Stanley, 20, was struck in the neck by pitcher Charles Eitle in a game in Carson City, NV, on September 20, 1891. According to one account, "He dropped to his knees, arose, started to run and stopped, saying: 'Run bases for me,' and pitched forward on his face, dying in three minutes." Apparently, Stanley had a congenital "weak spot" on his neck which the ball hit, causing his death.[53]

Max Meindel, 25, player-manager of the Defiance, PA, baseball team, was beaned near the left temple during a game in Altoona, PA, on June 17, 1893. He died the following day from a skull fracture and ruptured blood vessels in the brain.[54]

Peter Hyland, 23-year-old employee of the Carson, Pirie, Scott, and Company of Chicago, IL, played for the retail store's baseball team. In an intersquad game on August 20, 1893, a wild pitch was delivered by fellow employee Ed Carter. With the ball coming straight for his head, Hyland ducked the wrong way in an attempt to get out of the way. Hyland fell unconscious at the plate when the ball struck him on the back of the head. Even though a physician was in the stands and rushed to his side immediately, the unfortunate player died within the hour. Although Carter was immediately arrested for killing Hyland, a coroner's jury determined it was an accident and Carter was released the following day.[55]

S. C. Griffith, a young businessman, was struck on the temple in a game on June 12, 1894, in Tampa, FL. He died shortly after the accident.[56]

George Cowan, 22, was attempting to make the Oberlin College, OH, varsity baseball team on the afternoon of April 16, 1895, when he was struck by a fastball pitched by fellow student Cy Voorhees. When Cowan turned his head to avoid the ball, it hit him behind the ear. He fell, but was able to walk home even though he was bleeding from the nose and mouth. He collapsed after walking only a short distance and was carried to a nearby home. Cowan soon became unconscious and died about 7:00 that evening.[57]

William C. Dewees, a paperhanger, was beaned by a policeman named McDonald in a pick-up game on June 29, 1895, in Philadelphia, PA. He died the next day.[58]

Morris Davis, 13, was killed on June 30, 1895, in Taylor Bottoms, KY, when he was beaned earlier that day.[59]

Austin Smith, 18, died almost instantly when struck below the ear by a curveball delivered by Edward McGinnis in a game on June 20, 1897, in Sandy Hill, NY.[60]

Charles Dial was beaned above the right ear in a game on April 9, 1899, in Grass Valley, CA. While at first the injury appeared not to be serious, his condition declined steadily, and two days later emergency surgery was performed. The doctors discovered that the skull had been dented inward at the point of impact and that blood clots had formed. Dial never recovered from the operation and he died on April 13.[61]

George Lakin, 19, was struck behind the ear on June 23, 1900, in Baltimore, MD. He died the next day.[62]

Elmore Silvers, 23, a member of a Bainbridge, GA, city team, traveled to Quincy, FL, for a game on August 27, 1901. While at bat in the seventh inning, he was hit on the ear after he turned his head to avoid the incoming ball. Stunned briefly, he remained in the game, staying until its completion. He went to his hotel room afterwards, where he began to show signs of distress. A physician was summoned, but despite treatment, Silvers died at 3:00 the next morning.[63]

Walter L. Myles, 18, was struck behind the left ear during a game in West Chester, PA, on May 10, 1902. He died the following afternoon.[64]

Hiram Williamson, 22, was a pitcher for the Providence, MD, baseball team. During the fourth inning of a game at Cherry Hill, MD, on July 9, 1904, Williamson was hit on the back of the head while at bat. He remained in the game, but fell unconscious when he returned to his home afterwards. He died July 11, his bride of four weeks at his bedside.[65]

Verne Lowe, 19-year-old member of the Coshocton, OH, team, was struck in the head during the second inning of a game in Dresden, OH, on August 6, 1904. He continued to play, getting two hits and driving in the winning run. In his hotel room soon afterwards, though, he fell unconscious. He remained comatose throughout the night, dying the next day.[66]

Henry Diehl, 20, was beaned over his right ear as he attempted to duck out of the way of a curve thrown by Bert Thorne during a game on June 10, 1905, in Wooster, OH. He was knocked down, but got up and started toward first. Before he reached the bag, he asked to be removed from the game, commenting in a joking manner, "I've got it on the noodle." He then collapsed unconscious, dying an hour later from a fractured skull.[67]

Lloyd C. Grout, 15, was struck on the back of his head near the left ear when he turned to avoid an errant curveball during a church league game on July 28, 1905, in Cedar Rapids, IA. He was stunned briefly, but was not knocked to the ground. He stayed to watch the rest of the inning before walking home unassisted. Later that evening he was examined by the family physician as a precaution, but he still showed no signs of being seriously injured. About 11:00 that night he took a sudden turn for the worse, and the physician was again summoned. It was apparent that the youngster was suffering from a brain hemorrhage, but the doctor could do nothing to save him. Grout died early the next morning about six hours after the beaning.[68]

Joseph McDonald was struck on the left temple during a game between town teams in Mount Holly, NJ, on September 2, 1905. Later that evening his condition worsened, so he was taken to a local hospital. Surgery was performed when physicians discovered he was suffering from a brain hemorrhage. He died on September 4, a day after the operation.[69]

Jesse Robertson, a member of the U.S. Navy, died from a fractured skull received during a game at a naval training station in Norfolk, VA, on May 24, 1906.[70]

Edward P. Dillon, a dispatcher with the Pittsburgh, Fort Wayne, and Chicago railroad, was struck on the left temple by a curveball during a June 21, 1906, game at Conway, PA, against a team of railroad telegraphers. He died early the following day.[71]

Charles McDonald, 17, center fielder for the St. Joseph's baseball team, was struck on the temple during a game in Philadelphia, PA, on July 1, 1906. His death a few hours later was one of two that occurred in Philadelphia that day.[72]

John Aulting suffered a fatal skull fracture during a game in Fleetwood, PA, on July 4, 1906.[73]

William Steth, 20, a player with the Swanville, MN, town team, was knocked unconscious by "a swift in-shoot" during a game against Grey Eagle, MN, held in Little Falls on May 31, 1907. When the ball struck him on the ear, he collapsed, but came to quickly and finished playing the game. Shortly after the contest's conclusion, he again fell unconscious, dying a few moments later.[74]

Charles L. Clemons, a semipro player from Brooklyn, was killed almost instantly on August 24, 1907, while playing in a game between Oyster Bay and Glen Cove, NY. According to his parents, they had had a premonition about his accident and had asked him not to play. Frank McKenna, who threw the fatal pitch, was overcome by the accident. A coroner's jury cleared McKenna of any wrongdoing.[75]

August Senecae, 18, was struck on the head at Bridgeton, RI, on June 21, 1908. He died at his home in Woonsocket, RI, on June 22.[76]

Harry "Elmer" Cole was at bat for the Benton, PA, town team in a July 4, 1908, game against a team from nearby Divide, PA, when a ball pitched by Howard Shannon struck Cole behind and slightly above the left ear. Cole was heard to exclaim, "Gee! that was a dandy," before trotting down to first base. A pinch runner was sent in and Cole returned to the bench, where he lay down briefly. Saying that he was not feeling well, Cole began the mile-and-a-half walk home. Upon reaching his house, he collapsed on the front porch, where he was found by a neighbor. He was taken by train to a hospital in Wilkes-Barre, PA, where he died of a cerebral hemorrhage at 4:00 A.M. on July 6.[77]

George C. Franklin, 26, was struck on the temple by a "moderately fast pitch" during the early innings of a game in Imperial, CA, on February 22, 1909. He was knocked unconscious, but after reviving, played the remaining seven innings of the game, including hitting a triple in one of his at-bats. He went home after the game, where he was found paralyzed and unconscious later that night. He never regained consciousness, dying shortly after 11:00 the following morning.[78]

Walter Schwartz, 13, was struck on the temple by a wild pitch during an afternoon sandlot game in Saginaw, MI, on July 4, 1909. A fractured skull caused his death later that night.[79]

Rudolph Ruhling, 15, was beaned playing street ball in New York City on April 10, 1910. He felt fine at first, but later that day began to complain of pain. Surgery was attempted, but he died early the following morning.[80]

Frank Burns, freshman center fielder for the Troy, NY, high school baseball team, was hit on the left temple by an inside fastball in a game against Rensselaer Polytechnic Institute in Troy on April 16, 1910. Burns was felled by the pitch, but revived and said he wanted to continue playing. His teammates forced him to sit on the bench, where he watched the game to its completion. Shortly after the game, he was examined by a physician. His only complaint at the time was that he had a headache. When he returned home, doctors examined him again but could find no apparent damage. Later that night, though, he suddenly made a turn for the worse. He died around 3:00 A.M. on April 17. William O'Reilly, the pitcher who delivered the fatal blow, was a childhood friend of Burns.' O'Reilly suffered a nervous breakdown because of Burns' death.[81]

Frank Kostchryz, 15, was the first batter in a game between his Standard Car Wheel Company team and the Standard Sewing Machine Company team in Cleveland, OH, on May 29, 1910. With the count full, Kostchryz swung wildly at the next pitch. The ball struck him on the right temple, knocking him unconscious. A bone in his neck snapped when his head hit the ground. Kostchryz was rushed to a local hospital, but was dead on arrival. It was one of two game-related deaths in Cleveland that day (*see* **Walter J. Garson**).[82]

Leonard R. Massengale, 27, had not pitched since his college days at Mercer University, but friends convinced him to play for the Warrenton, GA, team against a team in nearby Thomson on June 27, 1910. An attorney and former member of the Georgia House of Representatives, Massengale was struck above his left ear in his first at-bat. He fell unconscious at the plate with a fractured skull. Attending physicians determined that surgery was necessary, and he was sent by train to a hospital in Augusta. The operation was performed on June 29. While the surgery was successful, his lungs began to fill with fluid and he died at 2:00 A.M. on July 4, a week after the beaning. He was survived by his wife and six-week-old son.[83]

Howard Layer, 12, was struck behind the ear in a game at Cornfield Point, MD, on August 10, 1910, where he was attending a summer camp for members of the boys' choir of the Church of the Good Shephard. The blow caused a brain hemorrhage.[84]

Wayne Hinkle, a 19-year-old student at Ohio State University, died on August 20, 1910, shortly after being hit on the head in a game at Rye Beach on Lake Erie.[85]

Frank P. Lawrence, 21, a member of the San Fernando High School team, was struck on the temple during a game against Santa Paula High School team in Santa Paula, CA, on April 15, 1911. When Lawrence was hit by pitcher John Munger, he fell unconscious for a short time, but revived quickly and continued to play for two more innings. Lawrence fell unconscious again and died about an hour later.[86]

Bertrand Frick, 17, suffered a skull fracture in a high school game between Cuyahoga Falls and Ravenna, OH, on May 6, 1911. Although he was unconscious for a few moments, he came to and stayed in the game. The following morning he suddenly fell unconscious again and died half an hour later.[87]

John H. King, 17, fell unconscious and died two hours after being struck on the temple in a game at Bridgeport, CT, on June 25, 1911.[88]

Chauncey Olliner, 12, died on July 6, 1911, as the result of a beaning suffered days earlier in a game in Guilford, CT. At first he appeared to be unhurt even though he was knocked unconscious by the blow. Several days after the event, though, he began complaining of a severe headache, then suddenly lapsed into unconsciousness. He died a few hours later.[89]

Herbert Turner, 13, had his skull fractured by a blow to the back of the head received during an evening pick-up game on August 10, 1911. Turner had been coming home from work in Hillyard, WA, when he joined some friends in the impromptu contest. Shortly after being struck, he began to feel shooting pains and fell unconscious while telling his parents of the accident. He never recovered consciousness before he died on August 13.[90]

William Schmidt, 21, was struck on the right temple during a game among employees of the Chicago Telephone Company in Chicago, IL, on September 17, 1911. He died at home a few hours after the beaning.[91]

George S. Hiett, 27, a member of the Sherwood team in the Sunday School League in Washington, DC, was beaned on May 4, 1912, by Charles Kelly, pitcher for the rival Church of the Nativity team. The ball stuck Hiett on the temple, causing a brain concussion. Hiett fell after being hit, but arose and sat on the bench watching the remainder of the game. He fainted while dressing to go home and was rushed to the hospital. Although he came to briefly and was even able to talk, he fell unconscious again and remained so until his death later that night.[92]

Albert Bohen, 15, was struck on the head by a fastball during a game on June 30, 1912, in Rockford, IL. Two days after the accident he became seriously ill and was taken to a local hospital. He died early on July 9, ten days after being hit.[93]

Harry Kerr, 20, died the afternoon of September 19, 1912, after being beaned during a game in Orient, IA, the day before.[94]

Vance Faught, 19, a player on the Cozad, NE, high school team, died on May 26, 1913, after being struck behind the ear during a game against a rival team from Grand Island, NE.[95]

William Wiggins, 22, fell unconscious at the plate after a beaning fractured his skull on May 30, 1913, in Kearny, NJ. He died June 2, never regaining consciousness.[96]

Paris Smith, 18, of Anacortes, WA, died June 1, 1913, after being hit on the head while batting in a game the day before. Milo Stock, 23, lost an eye as a result of a beaning during the same game.[97]

Bill Hammer, a 21-year-old school teacher, suffered a ruptured blood vessel in his brain when he was beaned on May 31, 1914, in Tompkinsville, KY. He died the following day.[98]

Frank Boucher, 22, had his skull fractured by a blow to his forehead on May 31, 1914, in Rockville, CT. He continued playing, but later that night fell ill. He died early the next morning.[99]

Leo Levestue, 25, died the night of June 28, 1914, in Fall River, MA, due to a brain concussion received during a game the day before.[100]

Walter Sanders, a farmer from Salisbury, MO, died September 7, 1914, after being struck on the temple.[101]

William Downing was beaned in a game in Needham, MA, on April 24, 1915. He returned home on his own, but soon collapsed. He died the next day.[102]

Lewis Wasson, 26, was struck on the left side of his head by the first pitch thrown during a church league game in Indianapolis, IN, on May 1, 1915. He died later that evening.[103]

William E. Crawford, 15, died May 13, 1915, in Hanover, PA, a few minutes after being struck on the temple.[104]

Walter Jannusch, 18, of Des Plaines, IL, died from a brain concussion on May 17, 1915, after a beaning the day before.[105]

Guy W. Ommert, 17, suffered a skull fracture during a game in Palmyra, PA, May 22, 1915. He died at a hospital in Harrisburg, PA, the following day.[106]

George Wesley, left-handed pitcher for the Mohrland, UT, city baseball team, was struck above the ear during a first inning at-bat on May 23, 1915, against the Castle Gate, UT, team in a contest held in Price, UT. Wesley, who had pitched briefly for the Helena Senators of the Class D Union Association the year before, scored later that inning. In the sixth inning, he hit a home run and collapsed immediately after touching home. He was taken to the Utah Fuel Company hospital, where he died early the next morning.[107]

A. J. Waller, 23, of Kansas City, MO, was beaned in an amateur league game in Dearborn, MO, on July 5, 1915. He died at his home early the next day.[108]

Percy E. Williams was injured in a game in San Francisco, CA, on July 11, 1915. Shortly after being hit in the head by a pitched ball, he started to feel ill and went home, where he lived alone. His family called on him the following morning, finding him dead from a cerebral hemorrhage.[109]

Edward Hafferkamp, a 34-year-old attorney, died August 1, 1915, in St. Louis, MO, from a brain hemorrhage after being struck the day before.[110]

Roy Dean was struck on the forehead during a game in Covington, OK, on August 8, 1915. Dean, from Fordland, MO, was in Enid working on a threshing crew. His parents were contacted, but Dean died August 11, before they arrived.[111]

George Cox, 13, was hit on the temple during a game in Philadelphia, PA, on August 17, 1915. He died two days later.[112]

Karl Vollmer, 11, was beaned on the right temple during a sandlot game near his home in Baden (St. Louis), MO, on the afternoon of September 23, 1915. After being hit he went home, where his mother found him conscious, but on the floor. He died at 6:00 the following morning.[113]

Russell Kistler, 29, was beaned during a railroad league game in Marysville, PA, on September 18, 1915. He died in a Harrisburg, PA, hospital on September 23, six days after the accident.[114]

Martin Meyer, 24, of Jamaica, Long Island, NY, was beaned August 5, 1916. He continued to play, but collapsed 15 minutes later and was carried off the field. He died on August 7.[115]

Robert Wacker, third baseman for a semipro team in Milwaukee, WI, was beaned on August 8, 1916. He completed the game, but collapsed afterwards and was taken to a local hospital, where he died shortly after arrival.[116]

Robert Wagner, second baseman for a semipro team in Allentown, PA, died from a blow to the temple received in a game in Danielsville, PA, on May 30, 1917.[117]

Andrew Dammer, an elevator operator for Franklin MacVeagh and Company, died an hour after being struck in a game among wholesale grocery workers in Chicago, IL, on July 14, 1917.[118]

Lester Frye, first baseman for an amateur team from Freeport, ME, was beaned on the side of his head by an inside fastball delivered by Lewis Woodcock at Lisbon Falls, ME, on August 6, 1921. He died from a skull fracture on August 9.[119]

Earl Heuer, 25, an accountant for Guggenheim and Company in Manhattan, died April 30, 1922, after an operation for a brain concussion received in a game on Staten Island the day before.[120]

Arno Schmeiser, a teacher from Rockville, WI, was hit on the left temple by a curveball in a game at Osman, WI, April 30, 1922. He died an hour after the game ended.[121]

Leon Scanlon, 19, in a September 9, 1922, game in Rosemont, PA, between employees of the Philadelphia and Rosemont factories of the Durham Carriage Works, was struck on the temple after stepping into a curveball. He died moments after the beaning.[122]

Michael Donohue, 26, third baseman for the Robertsdale, PA, baseball team, suffered a skull fracture during a game in Coaldale, PA, on July 23, 1923. He died from his injuries on July 26.[123]

Thomas Hanley, 32, was beaned on the left side of his head in Jersey City, NJ, on July 17, 1925. When hit by pitcher Walter Donlon, Hanley collapsed at the plate and was rushed unconscious to Jersey City Hospital. After reviving, he returned to the game and continued to play shortstop. He became ill the following morning. An examining physician discovered that the left front of his skull was fractured. Hanley died shortly afterwards.[124]

Orville Allen, 31, a semipro player, was beaned during an afternoon game at Morrisonville, IL, on July 11, 1926. He was taken to St. Vincent's hospital in Taylorsville, where he died later that night.[125]

Frank Rigler, 22, a star player with the East Helena, MT, baseball team, suffered a fractured skull from a beaning that occurred during the final inning of a July 15, 1927, game against the Prints, another local team. He fell unconscious at the plate and was rushed to a local hospital where an examination, including x-rays, failed to reveal the extent of his injuries. He died about 11:30 P.M. that same day without regaining consciousness. The young player was so popular with the fans and his teammates that a series of benefit games to raise money for a special headstone were held over a several-week period following his demise.[126]

William A. Tierney, 18, a member of the Bergenfield, NJ, town team, was beaned on the back of the head during a game against a team from Hackensack, NJ, on June 10, 1928. He fell unconscious briefly, but came to and continued to play. At home later that evening he began experiencing severe pains in his head. An examination at an Englewood, NJ, hospital determined that his skull was fractured. He died later that night.[127]

Frank Janik, 24, a member of the New York Central Railroad Athletic Club baseball team, suffered a fractured skull from a ball pitched by Joseph J. Szary, 19, during a game on the afternoon of September 15, 1928 in Buffalo, NY. Janik died the next night.[128]

Edward Kusiak, 20, a semipro player, died of a skull fracture in Ludlow, MA, shortly after midnight on May 13, 1929. He had been beaned on the left temple in a game the preceding afternoon.[129]

Norman Evans, 35, had his skull fractured when he was struck behind the ear after failing to get out of the way of an inside pitch during a game in Lando, SC, on June 6, 1931. He was taken to a hospital in nearby Rock Hill, SC, where he died on June 9.[130]

Anthony Judiniewicz, 20, collapsed unconscious after receiving a brain concussion during an early afternoon game in Milwaukee, WI, on April 17, 1932. He died two days later.[131]

Frank Logan, II, 26, a star student-athlete at Haverford College, played third base for an amateur team in the Upper Darby (PA) League. He was beaned during practice before a game between teams from Stonehurst and Highland Park, on June 14, 1932. He played the entire game, but fell ill the next day. He died at the Temple University Hospital in Philadelphia on June 16, two days after being struck.[132]

Balzer B. Klein, 26, an outfielder on the Bismarck, ND, city team, suffered a fractured skull and brain hemorrhage during the second inning of a game in Wilton, ND, on the evening of July 13, 1932. According to testimony given at an inquest the next day, Klein appeared to freeze after stepping into an inside pitch delivered by Fred Michel. The ball struck the batter over his left ear, knocking him unconscious. After reviving, the injured player remained to watch the rest of the game in spite of a physician's recommendation that he go home and apply ice packs to his head. Shortly afterwards, however, he had lapsed into unconsciousness and was taken to a local hospital. He remained in that state until his death the next day around 5:30 in the morning.[133]

Philip Azarella, Jr., 13, was beaned May 31, 1933, in Dunkirk, NY, and died June 2.[134]

Kenneth A. Meehan, 28, captain and second baseman of the Orange, MA, city team, suffered a fatal beaning on June 4, 1933.[135]

Howard McBeck, 16, was an outfielder on the St. Peter's High School team in Poughkeepsie, NY. His skull was fractured by a wild pitch in a game against Staatsburg (NY) High School on May 1, 1934. He was able to walk toward the dugout, but collapsed before reaching the bench. He was taken to the hospital where he died on May 3.[136]

Theodore Wager, 30, was struck on the head during a game in Dansville, NY, on July 8, 1934. He was taken to a local hospital, where he died the following day.[137]

Raymond Ater, shortstop for the Pampa (TX) Roadrunners, a city team, was beaned in the bottom of the fifth inning of a night game against Shawnee, OK, on July 21, 1934. He died in a Pampa hospital the next day. Ater, a former minor leaguer who had played for the Tyler (TX) Governors of the Class C Dixie League in 1933, had been struck in the same part of his head when he was with the Fort Worth Cats of the Class A Texas League two years earlier. Doctors speculated that this earlier injury contributed to his demise.[138]

Boyd Loendorf, 26, was struck behind the right ear during the sixth inning of a game in Richey, MT, on October 5, 1935. Although he was knocked unconscious by the blow and removed himself from the game after he recovered, he appeared not to be seriously hurt. On the way home, though, he lapsed again into unconsciousness, remaining so until his death early the next day.[139]

Harry Kronenberg, 24, was struck on the temple during a sandlot game in Brooklyn, NY, on June 27, 1936. He felt ill afterwards, but was able to complete the game. About 2:00 the next morning, his parents became alarmed at his condition and rushed him to the hospital. Soon thereafter he lapsed into a coma. Although emergency surgery was performed to stop a brain hemorrhage, he died the afternoon of June 28.[140]

George Knotts, 18, was playing in a sandlot game in Corning, AR, on April 17, 1937, when he was hit on the head. He took first and continued to play for awhile, but did not finish the game. Shortly after walking back to town at the conclusion of the contest, he complained of a severe headache, then fell unconscious moments later. He died of a skull fracture and a brain hemorrhage around midnight that same day.[141]

George McCarthy, 19, was beaned by a high school teammate during a recreation league game in Oswego, NY, on August 25, 1938. He died early the next morning.[142]

Nicholas Mongero, 21, was struck on the left temple during the fourth inning of a game near Yorktown Heights, NY, on September 25, 1938. He finished the game before returning home. Later that evening he complained of dizzy spells and was taken to the hospital, where he died of a brain embolism on September 29, five days after the accident.[143]

Robert Siberry, 13, died March 5, 1939, shortly after being struck during a sandlot game in Greenville, OH. Some thought he failed to duck because the sun got in his eyes.[144]

John Noga, 16, was fatally beaned by his friend, Chester Serzen, during a local park game in Chicago, IL, on August 15, 1939. Noga attempted to get out of the way of the errant pitch, but the ball struck him behind the left ear. He dropped unconscious and never recovered.[145]

Albert R. Davidson, Jr., 19, a freshman on the Ohio State University baseball team, was beaned during practice on April 9, 1941. He died the following evening without regaining consciousness.[146]

Valentine C. Hoelzer, Jr., 21, was hit on the left temple during a game between athletic clubs in Jamaica, NY, on May 25, 1941. When he regained consciousness a few minutes later, his parents drove him to Jamaica Hospital only to be turned away because no rooms were available. They then drove him to Queens General Hospital, where emergency surgery was performed. He was on a respirator until his death the following afternoon at 5:15.[147]

William Fahy, Jr., 17, was beaned in a sandlot game in Jersey City, NJ, on June 21, 1941. He died from a skull fracture on the evening of June 24, four days after being injured.[148]

Richard J. Mulcahy, Jr., 18, was struck below the left ear during the second day of spring practice for the Hingham (MA) High School team on March 22, 1948. The high school senior was facing a substitute tryout pitcher who, in the same at-bat, had just nicked Mulcahy on the side with a wild pitch. Mulcahy, a star athlete and the team's starting left fielder, threw his hands up and walked a few steps before collapsing. He died about an hour later after efforts to revive him failed. According to the postmortem, the ball struck the laryngeal nerve, "causing paralysis of respiratory muscles."[149]

John S. Argo, Jr., 19, was beaned while practicing near his home in Memphis, TN, for a night game on June 1, 1948. He began lapsing in and out of consciousness soon after the accident. His condition deteriorated over the next two days and he was taken to a hospital about 9:30 A.M. on June 4. He died about two hours later.[150]

Norman Latare, 16, left fielder for his Oxford Junction (IA) high school team, was beaned during a game in Wyoming, IA, on September 21, 1948. Clifford Dirks, the Wyoming pitcher, slipped just as he was delivering the ball. The pitch sailed directly at Latare, striking him on the left temple. The batter appeared to be uninjured, but his coach benched him for the rest of the game as a precaution. At home later that evening, Latare complained of a headache and went to bed. The next morning he was examined by a local physician who found that the young man was suffering from a mild concussion. Although the doctor believed that Latare would recover quickly, he died in the early morning hours of September 23. Tragically, Clifford Dirks would fatally injure another player the following spring (*see* **Glen Rhoads**).[151]

Kenneth Maxfield, 39, player-manager for the Arthur Murray team of San Bernardino, CA, a semipro team, died on November 23, 1948, two days after he was beaned during a game against the visiting Redlands (CA) Eagles.[152]

Donald Walrath, 19, was knocked unconscious during the seventh inning of a game in Hopedale, OH, on July 26, 1953. The Marine Reservist and former high school basketball star was rushed to the local hospital, where he died the following Saturday, August 1.[153]

Terry Dickey, 8, was struck behind the ear in a sandlot game in Fairfield, IL, on June 27, 1955. The youngster immediately went home and fell asleep. His parents later found him unconscious. They rushed to the local hospital, but he died of a brain hemorrhage shortly thereafter.[154]

Donald Jolk, 23, playing for his company's team during a game in Renton, WA, on May 30, 1956, was beaned behind the ear by an inside pitch as he turned to get out of the way. He died moments after being struck.[155]

Charles L. Greenlief, 15, was killed instantly when struck on his neck during practice with his high school baseball team in Normantown, WV, on April 29, 1964.[156]

Steve Hutchison, 20, a member of the Northeast Missouri State University baseball team, was struck on the left side of his head below the helmet during the seventh inning of a Ban Johnson League championship game in Kansas City, KS, August 16, 1975. He stayed in the game, but was taken to the hospital that night. He died on August 22, six days after the beaning.[157]

2. Other Pitched-Ball Fatalities

While beanings were the most frequent cause of player fatalities prior to the adoption of the batting helmet, pitched balls striking other parts of the anatomy have resulted in deaths as well. In most cases, these non-beaning deaths were due to sudden cardiac arrest caused by the ball (or other blunt object such as a bat) striking the chest area over the heart, a condition known medically as *commotio cordis*, or concussion of the heart. It is a relatively rare event, mainly because the blow must occur at the exact moment between heartbeats for death to occur.

These blows are non-penetrating, often leaving no visible contusions, abrasions, or broken bones. Often times they appear to be relatively minor: the ball, for instance, does not have to be thrown with great velocity to cause death. And the victims are usually healthy in every other respect, showing no signs of preexisting heart disease. Sadly, most of these blunt trauma deaths occur among young people, mainly because a child's musculature and rib cage have not developed enough to absorb the shock from the blow. In fact, *commotio cordis* is the most common cause of fatalities among young baseball players ages 5 to 14, according to a study released by the United States Consumer Product Safety Commission.[1]

In addition to batters, catchers have been especial victims of pitched balls striking the head or chest. And, as we shall see in later chapters, thrown (non-pitched) and batted balls have killed position players and base runners as well.

Minor League Fatalities

Raymond "Pete" Mann, third baseman for the Macon (GA) Peaches of the Class B South Atlantic Association, is the only minor league player to die after a pitched ball struck him on the chest. His death occurred in an afternoon game against the Asheville (NC) Tourists in Macon, GA, on July 13, 1927.

Mann, 20, from Terre Haute, IN, was in his second year with the Peaches. He had played a few weeks the previous season with the Raleigh (NC), Capitals of the Class C Piedmont League before coming to the Peaches. The pitcher, Tom Farrell, in his third year of professional ball, was considered a major league prospect. In fact, according to sources close to the Tourists, an undisclosed major league team had contacted the Asheville team the day before about acquiring the young hurler.[2]

Macon catcher Tom Angley led off the bottom of the third inning with a single. As he took a wide lead off of first in the scoreless game, Mann stepped up to the plate. The Asheville catcher, noting Angley's lead, called for pitches on the outer half of the plate in the hopes of picking him off. After two such outside fastballs, Mann stepped into the third, some thought in an attempt to sacrifice Angley to second. Unfortunately, the ball "took a funny, twisting curve," and, although he tried to jump out of the way, the pitch broke in and struck Mann just below the heart "with a dull thud." The young Macon infielder fell where he stood.[3]

The Asheville catcher immediately began yelling for assistance. Players and officials, including a doctor who was attending the game, rushed to the fallen player's side. The doctor worked on Mann for a couple of minutes before declaring him dead. As Mann's body was carried to the clubhouse, the umpires called the game and fans solemnly filed out of the stadium. Farrell, "in an almost hysterical state," locked himself in his hotel room after the game. He remained by himself until the Tourists had to leave for Augusta later that night. In a public statement released the next day, he expressed his deep sorrow. "All that I can say," he wrote, "is that I am sorry — and heartbroken."[4]

The following day, a coroner's jury exonerated Farrell, calling the death accidental. Mann's body was returned home accompanied by Macon pitcher Pat Stamey. Peaches players wore black armbands the rest of the season in honor of their fallen teammate.[5]

While Mann is the only professional player to have died as the result of being struck over the heart, scores of amateur players have been killed in similar accidents. In addition, a number of catchers have died from blows to the head or chest from wild pitches and passed balls.

Amateur Fatalities — Batters

William J. Williams, 14, was killed instantly in Minneapolis, MN, on June 1, 1897, after a pitched ball struck him over his heart.[6]

Hugh Cavanagh, 22, was batting with an 0 and 2 count in the seventh inning of a game between athletic clubs in Montclair, NJ, on May 6, 1899, when he swung and missed an inside curve. After the ball struck him over the heart, he stood dazed for a few seconds, then rubbed his chest and started toward first. When he collapsed a few feet from the bag, he was carried to the team bench, where he died a few moments later.[7]

Eldrakin Potter, 14, was struck over his heart on the third pitch delivered by Lighty Reed in a sandlot game in Suffolk, VA, on August 26, 1899. Potter doubled over, then collapsed at the plate. He was dead 20 minutes later.[8]

Punch Arnold, 15, died shortly after a blow to the chest in a game in Newnan, GA, on April 13, 1903. Initially stunned, he got up to resume play, but collapsed again. Physicians were unable to revive him.[9]

Calvin Phillippi, 26, was killed during an industrial league game on July 25, 1903, in Jonestown, PA, after a pitched ball hit him on the jugular vein.[10]

Jesse Strode, 22, died immediately after a blow above the heart on a pitch thrown by his best friend, Oscar Champion, in a game in Gillette, AR, on May 1, 1905.[11]

Walter Buchanan, 14, was struck in the abdomen by a pitched ball during a game in Elida, OH, on August 31, 1905. He ran to first, but fell dead as he reached the bag.[12]

Howard Newton, 17, was hit over the heart during the sixth inning of a game between company teams on May 26, 1906, in Kansas City, MO. According to witnesses, he stepped into a 3 and 2 inside pitch, dropped the bat when struck, then ran to first base, where he immediately collapsed and died. The pitcher, Jefferson Wise, was arrested but later released.[13]

Casper R. Musselman, 19, was catcher for the Catasauqua, PA, town team in a home game against a team from Philipsburg, PA, on the evening of August 28, 1906. In his fourth inning at-bat, he was struck over the heart on the second pitch. He stood dazed for a moment, threw his bat aside, and started toward first. He collapsed unconscious a few feet before reaching the bag. He was carried home where he was attended by two physicians, but he died shortly thereafter.[14]

William Thomas King, 26, was struck over the heart at the top of the third inning during a game between Relay and Newark, MD, city teams in St. Denis, MD, on May 26, 1907. He made a step toward first base, but then collapsed. Physicians were unable to revive him.[15]

Harry Randall, 16, died immediately after being struck on the chest by a wild pitch in Derby, CT, on June 8, 1907.[16]

Charles Lempka, 14, was hit over the heart by a fastball during a YMCA contest held at Riverview Military Academy in Poughkeepsie, NY, on May 28, 1908. He ran a short distance toward first base before collapsing and dying.[17]

Paul Morgan, 21, died a few minutes after being struck over the heart in a game near Springfield, SC, on July 4, 1908. Grover Cannon, the 15-year-old pitcher, was distraught at having killed Morgan.[18]

Alfred Vollmer, 17, was hit on the chest during a Sunday school baseball game in Ecorse, MI, on May 31, 1909. He ran halfway to first base before collapsing. He died before anyone could reach him.[19]

Harry Rubes died instantly after being stuck over the heart in a game in Spencer, IA, on July 26, 1909.[20]

Eugene Swinbank, 17, was at bat in the third inning in a game between athletic clubs in Chicago, IL, on September 26, 1909. His team was down 4 to 0 when he came to the plate with the bases loaded. With a count of 0 and 2 on Swinbank, the catcher called for an inside pitch. The ball struck the young batter over the heart. As Swinbank ran toward first, he exclaimed, "I'll force one run in, anyway." He collapsed a few feet from first. He was rushed to the hospital in an automobile, but died on the way.[21]

William Schmidt, 28, first baseman for a team in Freeburg, IL, was killed almost immediately after being stuck over the heart in a game against a team from St. Louis, MO, on April 17, 1910. He stepped toward first base before dying.[22]

George Campbell, 6, was struck on the instep of his right foot during a game on July 14, 1912, in Kearny, NJ. Afraid that the friend who hit him would get in trouble, Campbell told his parents that he had stepped on a rock. While a local physician could find no apparent damage or even see a cut on the foot, he applied a poultice to reduce the pain. By the following Saturday, he was so ill his parents rushed him to the hospital. According to the hospital physicians, blood poisoning had set in. Campbell died July 21, a week after the injury.[23]

Roy Mimms, 30, died a few minutes after being hit over the heart during a game in Fort Worth, TX, on May 31, 1914.[24]

Joseph Snyder, 21, first baseman for a city team from Berea, OH, was stuck over the heart during a July 4, 1914, game in Medina, OH, against that city's team. He turned toward first before dying.[25]

Mike Bellevic (or **Bellabich**), 13, was cut on the knee by a pitched ball while batting during a pick-up game in Litchfield, IL, on July 12, 1914. The wound became infected and Bellevic died of blood poisoning early the morning of July 17, just five days after being injured.[26]

Charles Seymour, 16, was killed instantly in Payson, IL, after being struck over the heart during a game between Payson (IL) High School and Hull (IL) High School on May 22, 1915. Seymour was a player for Payson.[27]

Oscar Genter, 17, stood with his back to the diamond, waiting his turn to bat, during the bottom of the third inning of a sandlot game in Evansville, IN, on May 30, 1915. The first pitch sailed high over the catcher's mitt, striking Genter on the back of the head. The blow stunned him, but he insisted that he was not injured. After a few minutes, though, he was escorted home. The next day he experienced severe head pains and a doctor was summoned. He remained conscious, but his condition worsened and he died the evening of June 1.[28]

Shirley Phillips, 16, was hit over the heart by a pitch from J. E. Slaughter, 22, during a game in Belington, WV, on April 23, 1916. Phillips started walking toward first base before he collapsed and died.[29]

George White, 22, was the first batter in the first game of the season between married and unmarried employees of the Michigan Lubricator Company in Detroit, MI, on May 21, 1916. The first pitch from John Schultz, 22, struck the newlywed over the heart, killing him instantly.[30]

James D. Irwin, 15, died immediately after being hit over the heart in a game in Oil City, PA, on May 24, 1916.[31]

Peter McManus, 18, captain of the Stamford (CT) High School baseball team, died on first base after being struck over the heart while at bat on May 30, 1917, in a game at Stamford.[32]

Charles Baldwin, 19, was hit directly over the heart on the second pitch during an at-bat in a game between athletic clubs in Chase, MD, on May 27, 1922. After being struck by Roy Earle's pitch, Baldwin stood dazed for a moment before running toward first. He fell unconscious, and efforts to revive him failed.[33]

Grady Ard, 18, died October 7, 1923, two weeks after being stuck in the stomach during a game in Pace, FL. He did not survive the emergency surgery that was performed on him.[34]

Eugene McGrath, 34, first baseman and a former player with the Newark (NJ) Bears of the Class AA International League, was struck near the heart during a semipro game in Linoleumville, NY, on June 14, 1925. McGrath was the first batter up in the bottom half of the first inning. Victor Branconi, pitcher for the Clover Athletic Club from Perth Amboy, NJ, threw a first-pitch brushback to McGrath, who was crowding the plate. Over 2,000 fans watched in horror as McGrath collapsed unconscious in the batter's box. He died upon reaching the hospital. Branconi, shaken by the incident, refused to continue pitching, so the game was suspended. A coroner's jury the next day cleared the pitcher of any responsibility for McGrath's death, declaring it to be accidental.[35]

Stanley A. Nelson, 27, captain of a team in the Twilight League in Utica, NY, died 10 minutes after being hit over the heart on June 24, 1927.[36]

William Nicklaus, 16, died a few minutes after being struck over the heart during batting practice for the Butler (NJ) High School baseball team on April 20, 1933. The attending physician diagnosed "paralysis of the solar plexis" as the cause of death.[37]

Robert Lewis Perry, 16, was struck over the heart by a curve that failed to break during a sandlot game in Westmoreland, TN, on August 28, 1938. Perry collapsed at the plate, but got up and ran a short distance toward first base before dying.[38]

Thomas Kantos, 24, an outfielder for the Ahepa All-Stars of Chicago, IL, was struck just below the heart during a sixth inning at-bat in a Chicago park on May 18, 1941. After being hit by pitcher Walter Gadowski, Kantos took a few steps toward first before collapsing.[39]

Drew Thomas, 12, of Haynesville, LA, was struck below the heart during a sandlot game in Athens, LA, on the afternoon of August 18, 1951. He died within a couple of minutes after being hit.[40]

Samuel Edward "Eddie" Tharpe, 12, died immediately after being struck over the heart in a game during morning recess at Varnville (SC) Elementary School on April 19, 1955.[41]

Halvis Martin Fletcher, 13, died July 31, 1956, after a pitch hit him on the chest during a junior league championship game in Baton Rouge, LA.[42]

Timothy McDoniel, 16, was killed after being struck over the heart when he missed a bunt during a sandlot game in Newark, AR, on May 22, 1960. He took several steps toward first before collapsing.[43]

Barry B. Babcock, 9, was in just his third Little League game in Temple City, CA, on May 17, 1961, when he stepped into a slow curve. Barry, who had been the team bat boy the previous two seasons, fell into the umpire's arms after being stuck on the chest by the pitch. As his father and the umpire attempted without success to resuscitate the youngster, the pitcher, Michael Hanes, 10, collapsed in hysterics on the mound. Over 500 attended Barry's funeral three days later, including members of his third-grade class and five teams from the Temple City Little League. His death was reputedly the first to occur during an official Little League game.[44]

Carl William Knutson, Jr., 13, of South San Gabriel, CA, was the star pitcher for his Temple City PONY League team. He had just struck out the first three batters he faced when he stepped up to the plate during the bottom half of the first inning on June 16, 1965. An inside fastball hit him squarely on the chest. Carl collapsed at the plate, and efforts to revive him failed. His parents and siblings arrived just as he was being lifted into an ambulance. Over 300 attended his funeral on June 19.[45]

Kurt Salha, 9, was killed after being struck on the chest during his Little League team's batting practice in Los Banos, CA, on May 18, 1970. The team coach was pitching four balls to each child in turn, two to hit and two to bunt. Salha was struck when he turned to bunt his second ball. The teammate who was catching put his arm around Salha and asked if he was okay. The youngster responded that he was, then collapsed as he turned to walk away. The coach applied artificial respiration while another coach ran to call an ambulance. The child was pronounced dead on arrival at a local hospital.[46]

David Piritano, 12, died after being hit on the chest by an inside fastball during a game in Chicago, IL, on June 25, 1970.[47]

Gerald Piotter, Jr., 9, a member of a Miami County (IN) Little League team, was at bat in the second inning of a late afternoon game in Macy, IN, on June 14, 1980, when a pitched ball hit him over the heart. According to witnesses, the ball was not thrown hard, and at first it appeared that Piotter "just had the wind knocked out of him." When he failed to improve, medical help was summoned. He was transported to a hospital in nearby Peru, IN, and then flown to Methodist Hospital in Indianapolis. He died on June 18, four days after being struck, "due to the accident and undisclosed complications."[48]

William Ryan Wojick, 10, was at bat during the bottom of the fourth inning on March 18, 1990, with his Citrus Park (FL) Little League team trailing 8 to 6. As he tried to jump away from a wild third pitch, he inadvertently turn into it instead. He was struck under his left armpit. Ryan, as he was known, collapsed at the plate, gasping for breath. Paramedics were called and efforts were made to revive him. A helicopter transported him to a nearby hospital, where he was pronounced dead 45 minutes after the accident.[49]

Michael Marano, 12, was killed after being struck in the chest by a ball shot from a pitching machine during evening batting practice for his Bensonhurst (NY) Little League team on June 28, 1994. His coaches indicated that he had overextended his swing, thus exposing his chest, in what was to be the last batting practice pitch that day. Efforts to revive him failed.[50]

David Cadena, 17, played outfield for the J. W. Nixon High School baseball team in Laredo, TX. He was struck over the heart while attempting to lay down a bunt during a February 26, 1998, tournament game against rival Uvalde (TX) High School. He was rushed to a local hospital, where he was pronounced dead shortly before 10:00 that evening.[51]

Corey Smith, 13, was at bat during a Northern Columbus (OH) Athletic Association baseball game on the evening of May 25, 1999, when he was struck above the heart. He was taken to a local children's hospital, where he died shortly after arrival.[52]

John Ashmore, 13, suffered a blow to the left side of his chest during a Fayette County (GA) Youth Baseball Association game the evening of May 9, 2003. Fans used cell phones to call for medical assistance, and the youngster was flown to a children's hospital in the area, but he was pronounced dead on arrival.[53]

Justin Saccone, 15, was struck on the chest while he was attempting to bunt during a recreation park game in Melbourne, KY, on September 21, 2003. As he lay on the ground, he told his coach, "I'm OK, I'm OK, just let me lay here a minute." He was pronounced dead upon arrival at a local hospital.[54]

Black Baseball Fatalities — Catchers

Ben Myers, 19 or 20, catcher with the Southern Star Baseball Club, an African American amateur team, was struck in the neck by a passed fastball during a picnic game in Montgomery, AL, on May 26, 1890. He died instantly from a broken neck. According to bystanders, he was standing close to the plate and not wearing a mask.[55]

Amateur Fatalities — Catchers

Frank C. Wilcox, 19, was struck near the temple after he turned his head while catching for a city league team in Auburn, ME, on June 16, 1905. He finished the game, but fell unconscious a short time later. Although he drifted in and out of consciousness over the next two days, he died from a ruptured blood vessel in the brain on June 18.[56]

W. H. Williams, died immediately after being struck on the chest while catching during a game in Soperton, GA, on July 25, 1906.[57]

Benson Smith, 14, was catching for pitcher and team captain Thomas Mitchell during a game in Chicago, IL, on August 16, 1909. Mitchell felt Smith was becoming tired and told Martin Baley, another player, to substitute for Smith. As Smith turned to leave, Mitchell threw another pitch, striking Smith on the right ear. He was helped home by Mitchell and Baley, but he died before a physician arrived.[58]

Percy Damon, 26, was struck on the side of his head behind his catcher's mask during the eighth inning of a game between fire stations in Hanover, MA, on July 24, 1915. He finished the game, returned to his home, and, after eating, went to bed not feeling well. He was found dead early the next morning.[59]

Franklin Hoen, 18, was killed on May 18, 1916, in Mount Airy, PA, after a pitch glanced off his catcher's mitt, striking him in the head. He was not wearing a mask.[60]

Anthony Esposito, 13, was catching pitches from Frank Mulvihill, 20, who stood on the opposite side of a Brooklyn, NY, street at twilight on May 9, 1927. Mulvihill threw a curve that missed Esposito's catcher's glove, striking him over the heart. He died immediately after the blow. Mulvihill was arrested and spent the night in jail before being cleared of all charges when the death was declared to be accidental by the assistant district attorney the next day.[61]

Peter Denock, 16, catcher for the DePaul Institute for the Deaf (now the DePaul School of Hearing and Speech) in Pittsburgh, PA, was struck in his stomach during a game on June 12, 1927. He died a few minutes later.[62]

3. Thrown Ball Fatalities

In his seminal work, *The Physics of Baseball*, renowned physicist Robert K. Adair states that the maximum velocity of a pitched ball occurs at its point of release. According to his calculations, drag causes a drop in speed of about 1 mile per hour for each 7 feet of travel, thus resulting in an approximate loss of 8 miles per hour by the time the ball reaches home. Even then a ball released at 98 miles per hour would cross the plate — or hit the batter — at a speed of about 90 miles per hour. This velocity is certainly sufficient to cause considerable damage when it strikes the human body, as has been shown in preceding two chapters.

Do position players, though, release the ball with as much velocity as pitchers? Adair believes that in most circumstances they do, even though he has no hard data to support his assumption. If Adair is correct, then it is not surprising that thrown baseballs can be just as deadly as those delivered by a pitcher. In fact, at least two dozen players — including baserunners and fielders — have died over the years as a result of errant throws.[1]

Minor League Fatalities

Just three weeks after the beaning fatality of Ottis Johnson in Alabama — the last to occur in the minor leagues — 19-year-old **Richard "Dick" Conway** became the only minor league position player to die from a thrown ball. This tragedy occurred the evening of June 29, 1951, during infield practice before a game in Ogden, UT, between Conway's Twin Falls (ID) Cowboys and the Ogden Reds of the Class C Pioneer League.

Conway, in just his first year of professional ball, was already a significant offensive threat, leading his league in home runs with 12 at the time of his death. Normally the 6-foot, 3-inch resident of Lynn, MA, served as the team's starting catcher. However, on a physician's advice, he had not started in recent games because he had been suffering from fainting spells caused by poor nutrition. That evening, though, he was scheduled to play first due to an injury to the regular first baseman, so was taking fielding practice in preparation for the game. He was not unfamiliar with this position, as he often liked to spend warm-up time at first even when catching because it allowed him to limber up and to concentrate on his footwork.

Covering second was the Cowboys' player-manager, Don Trower, who, after receiving a throw, pivoted toward first to complete a practice double play. Conway, unfortunately, was distracted, one report said because he was pursuing a pop fly, another because he was picking up a loose ball. In any event, he was not aware that the ball was hurling toward him. Trower yelled a warning to the young catcher. Sadly, Conway turned into the ball, but did not get his glove up in time. He was struck just above his heart.[2]

Trower and other players rushed toward Conway as he bent over in pain. He waved them off and resumed his position at first. Within seconds, he collapsed unconscious on the field. Although an ambulance arrived quickly to take him to Ogden's St. Benedict's Hospital, he was pronounced dead on arrival. An autopsy by Dr. Ralph Ellis confirmed that Conway had been killed by the throw alone; that there was no preexisting heart disease.[3]

Black Baseball Fatalities — Position Players

An **unnamed African American convict** at a prison farm near Valdosta, GA, was playing ball with other black convicts on August 27, 1899. He was not paying attention to the play as one prisoner threw to another. The ball struck the victim on the head, causing him to be knocked unconscious. He died the next day.[4]

Amateur Fatalities — Position Players

George Lassette, 7, was playing tag baseball with his friends on a vacant lot near his home in New York City on May 23, 1885. Charles McCormick, another child playing in the game, threw the ball high in the air. It plummeted downward, striking Lassette on the chest. He fell unconscious and was carried home by McCormick and Jacob Lassette, his brother. He was dead by the time a physician arrived.[5]

Robert L. Shannon, 23, was an experienced baseball player, having served one year as captain of his Washington, DC, high school team. Nonetheless, he no longer enjoyed playing the game because, as he told friends, "I have been hurt every time I have gone out." So it was with great reluctance that he agreed to play for the Chesapeake and Potomac Telephone Company, where he was employed as a stenographer. The company team was scheduled to play another team on the Georgetown University campus the evening of June 24, 1903. When they arrived, the other team failed to show, so they decided to split into two squads. As pitchers for the two teams began to warm up, Shannon and his friend, Walter Ward, stood talking on the sidelines. Suddenly, Ward spotted a wild throw heading their way. He dodged out of the way, but Shannon failed to move, apparently not seeing the ball. It struck him on the neck near his ear. Ward caught Shannon as he fell to the ground. A physician who was playing on the telephone company's team and another who happened to be playing on a team nearby, rushed to Shannon's side. Although he was quickly carried to the university hospital, Shannon was dead upon arrival.[6]

Stach Wisnoski, 20, was fielding in a sandlot game in Houston, TX, on May 27, 1906, when he was struck by a ball thrown by another player attempting to get a baserunner. Although Wisnoski picked the ball up and completed the play, he died after making the throw.[7]

Attillio Marino (in some accounts his name is spelled **Tella Marianna**), 12, was catching during a game in Philadelphia, PA, on July 1, 1906, when the first baseman threw to Marino to stop a baserunner from stealing home. The ball slipped through Marino's fingers and struck him over the heart. He collapsed unconscious at the plate and died on the way to a local hospital. His death was one of two in Philadelphia that day (*see* **Charles McDonald**).[8]

S. H. Smith, a student at Alabama Polytechnic Institute (now Auburn University), was fatally injured in a game in Auburn on the afternoon of March 18, 1908. A throw from the catcher to second base struck Smith on the back of the head, causing a brain hemorrhage. He died later that night.[9]

Albert Stephenson, 15, was playing the infield during a game in Camden, NJ, when a throw to him bounced off a rock and hit him on the knee. The blow caused an earlier sore to reopen and begin bleeding again. A serious infection resulted several days later because Stephenson failed to properly clean the wound. When he finally went to a local hospital, physicians decided that blood poisoning had set in and his leg needed to be amputated. He was so weak at this point, though, that they could not perform the surgery. He died on July 27, 1910, about a week after being injured.[10]

Edward W. Hoge, 12, was playing catch with his older brother, Cecil, before a game in Washington, DC, on the afternoon of September 7, 1910. He was struck on the right temple after he missed the throw from his 14-year-old sibling. His brother carried him home and a physician was summoned, but he was dead by the time help arrived.[11]

John Veal, 9, was playing baseball in a friend's yard in Santa Ana, CA, on April 13, 1924, when he was "struck a light blow on the chest" by a "soft ball." He died shortly afterwards.[12]

Rudolph Solomon, 20, a pitcher for a semipro team from Cobleskill, NY, was struck above the right ear by an errant throw from first baseman Louis Myers during a game against a team from Delanson, NY, on August 22, 1925. Just before the inning was to begin, Myers was tossing the ball around the infield when his throw to the third baseman hit Solomon as he stood on the pitcher's mound. He sat briefly on the sidelines before collapsing, unconscious. He was taken home and, when he grew worse, was transported to a local hospital the following afternoon. Emergency surgery was performed, but he died from a fractured skull early on the morning of August 24.[13]

William A. Estergreen, Jr., 15, suffered a fractured skull while playing catch with a friend in Atlantic City, NJ, on March 23, 1926. He walked home, but fell unconscious three hours later. He died that evening in the hospital.[14]

Jack Smith, 12, was covering third during a sandlot game in Amityville, Long Island, New York on June 27, 1934. The 11-year-old second baseman threw to Smith in an attempt to get a baserunner, but the ball slipped through his hands, striking him in the stomach. A bystander, seeing Smith collapse in pain, carried the child to a local hospital, where he was pronounced dead on arrival.[15]

Mikel Davis, 6, was playing catch with some older boys on the street in front of his Los Angeles, CA, home on May 22, 1949. When he attempted to catch a high fly thrown by one of the other children, the ball slipped through his hands, striking him on the chest. He died on the way to the hospital.[16]

Robert M. Klingler, 10, was sitting on the bench during practice before a game in Emlenton, PA, on June 11, 1951. Two teammates were tossing the ball back and forth when it glanced off the catcher's mitt used by one of the children, striking Klingler on the base of the skull. He died half an hour later.[17]

Gary Eldon Moore, 16, was throwing balls during pre-game drills with other members of his Comanche, OK, high school baseball team on April 2, 1952, when one of the tossed balls struck him over the heart. He died on the field when attempts to revive him failed.[18]

Chad Pickens, 16, played second base for the Weirton, OH, high school team. During an intrasquad game on May 10, 1955, his skull was fractured by a ball thrown as part of a double play. He died in the hospital on May 14.[19]

Kim McCarren, 7, was playing in a sandlot game with friends in Silver Spring, MD, on April 18, 1957, when he was struck at the base of the neck by a thrown ball. His mother carried him to a nearby neighbor's house, where paramedics were unsuccessful in their attempts to revive him.[20]

Johnny DiMiceli, 7, was struck on the back of the neck when he ran between two older friends as all three were playing catch in Smithtown, Long Island, NY, on July 25, 1958. He died a few minutes after being hit.[21]

Henry Verzyl, 19, was at home in Middle Village, Queens, NY, on leave from the U.S. Navy. He was playing catch with his 17-year-old cousin on May 5, 1962, when he missed one of the throws. A youngster walking nearby tossed the ball back, striking Verzyl on the right temple. He died a few minutes after reaching the hospital.[22]

John Adams, 11, was warming up at first base before a Little League game in Escondido, CA, on the evening of June 16, 1971. A ball thrown by a teammate ricocheted off his glove and struck him over the heart. He was rushed to a local hospital, but physicians were unable to resuscitate him.[23]

Andrew Cook, 5, was catching returned balls for his coach, who was pitching during a coach-pitch league game in Omaha, NE, on June 26, 1999, when the safety soft-core baseball used by the league struck him on the chest. While the ball had been thrown by an adult who was helping the team's young catcher, it was not thrown hard. Cook collapsed and efforts to revive him failed. He was flown by helicopter to a nearby hospital, where he was pronounced dead about an hour after the accident.[24]

Caleb Slaton, 11, was warming up by throwing a ball back and forth to a friend prior to a pickup game in a park in Russellville, KY, on April 22, 2002. One of the throws hit him just above the heart. He collapsed and went into cardiac arrest. Local paramedics were able to restart his heart, but he remained unconscious. He was transported to a local hospital and then was flown to Vanderbilt Children's Hospital in Nashville, TN. He died May 5 without regaining consciousness.[25]

Amateur Fatalities — Baserunners

William Higgins, 20, was running from second to third in a game in Fontana, KS, on August 13, 1903, when a throw to second struck him on the temple. He died two hours after being hit.[26]

Reuben Walt, 30, was running to first after hitting a ground ball during a game on June 12, 1906, in Herndon, PA. The throw to first accidentally struck Walt in the head, killing him.[27]

Michael Ruth, 26, was at bat in Jasonville, IN, on June 24, 1913, when the runner on first made a break for second as the pitcher began his delivery. The catcher's throw struck Ruth on the head. He fell unconscious in the batter's box and died later that night from a brain concussion.[28]

Harry C. Posz, 16, and several neighborhood friends were playing a modified game of baseball they called "one-a-cat" on a vacant lot in St. Louis, MO, on February 20, 1915. In this particular game, there were three players at bat and a pitcher, catcher, and first baseman in the field. A run was scored each time a batter reached first and returned home safely. In his at-bat, Posz hit a single. The batter after him bunted, and Posz raced for home. The catcher, Clifford J. Rimmey, fielded the ball and threw to first in hopes of a double play. The ball struck Posz below the right ear, knocking him unconscious. A doctor was summoned, but Posz died before he could arrive.[29]

Glen Rhoads, 17, second baseman for his Lisbon (IA) High School team, was taking a lead off second during a home game on May 3, 1949. On the mound for visiting Wyoming (IA) High School was Clifford Dirks who, during a game the previous September, had fatally beaned a batter (*see* **Norman Latare**). After receiving a pitched ball back from the catcher, Dirks quickly turned and made a snap throw to the Wyoming second baseman in an attempt to pick off Rhoads. As the baserunner rushed back to second, the ball struck him on the base of the skull, knocking him unconscious. Rhoads was revived on the field, then sent home. When later that evening he began to have difficulty breathing, Rhoads' parents, with the assistance of the family physician, drove their injured son to the hospital, where he died shortly after arrival.[30]

Jerry Lynn Dodson, 13, was caught in a rundown during a game of tag with two friends in Louisville, KY, on July 15, 1961. When one of the fielders attempted to throw to the other, the ball struck Dodson on the left side of his neck. He collapsed and attempts to revive him failed. An autopsy concluded that he died of a heart attack resulting from paralysis of the carotid sinus nerve.[31]

Ray Eaton, 32, hit a single with a runner on base during an amateur league game in Hopkinsville, KY, on May 9, 1965. When the outfielder threw home in an attempt to get the baserunner, Eaton took off for second. The catcher threw to second, striking Eaton at the base of his skull as he neared the bag. He collapsed and died moments after being struck.[32]

Charles Dowd, Jr., 18, was a member of the Essex Catholic High School (Newark, NJ) baseball team. In a game against St. Joseph's High School in Metuchen, NJ, on May 18, 1967, Dowd hit a grounder to the shortstop. As he was running to first, the shortstop's throw struck him on the head, splitting his batting helmet. Dowd died at Perth Amboy (NJ) General Hospital early on the morning of May 20.[33]

Stuart Schechtman, 15, was standing on third during a PONY League game in Queens, NY, on the evening of July 5, 1967, when a wild pitch got past the catcher. As Schechtman dashed toward home, the catcher's throw struck him on the head, killing him instantly. An autopsy found that the blow caused heart failure due to a sudden drop in the youngster's blood pressure.[34]

Robert Roggatz, 10, was a star player on his Lincolnwood, IL, Little League team. In fact, he was the Illinois "hit, run, and pitch" champion for his age group and was scheduled to compete against the Indiana state champion during a Chicago White Sox game. But on June 21, 1978, just four days before he was to appear at Comiskey Park, he was taking his lead off third during a game that evening. His coach called for a delayed steal, so when the catcher threw the ball back to the pitcher, Roggatz ran toward home. The pitcher's return throw struck him on the chest just as he was sliding across the plate. He dusted himself off, and as he reached the dugout, he collapsed. His entire family watched in horror as his father, a Chicago fireman, rushed to his side and began mouth-to-mouth resuscitation. Paramedics arrived, attempted to defibrillate his heart, then took him to the hospital, where further efforts to revive him failed. He was buried in his team uniform on June 24, 1978.[35]

Shawn Barnes, 15, was headed to second after getting a hit during a Madison (IN) High School practice game on March 27, 2000. A fielder's throw struck him on the chest. Barnes rounded second as the ball rolled away, but collapsed on the way to third. Attempts to revive him failed, and he died shortly after being hit.[36]

4. Bat and Batted-Ball Fatalities

"The pitcher has got only a ball," Hank Aaron once reflected. "I've got a bat. So the percentage in weapons is in my favor and I let the fellow with the ball do the fretting." Of course, Aaron is speaking figuratively, not literally. With a single swing of this "weapon," he, and countless other sluggers, have destroyed many a pitcher's best efforts.[1]

Tragically, though, the bat sometimes does become a weapon in the literal sense, especially when a batted ball slams into another player or the bat hits the catcher or a teammate. Indeed, dozens of pitchers, catchers, position players, and baserunners have been killed by a screaming liner, a foul tip, or the back swing of a bat. And, as will be discussed in later chapters, umpires and scores of fans have been victims as well.

While batted balls have always been potentially hazardous, the danger increased markedly with the development of aluminum bats. Introduced at the youth, high school, and college levels in the early 1970s, aluminum bats, which are more durable than wooden ones, helped cash-strapped baseball programs save money. They are also a greater risk to safety.

The threat lies primarily with the significant increase in batted ball speed resulting from aluminum bats, which gives pitchers and infielders much less time to react to a line drive. A 2001 study of two wooden bat models and five aluminum models illustrated this problem. Researchers found that the maximum batted ball speed reached for the two wooden bats was 101 miles per hour whereas the maximum speed reached for the five aluminum bats was 106 miles per hour. In addition, the difference in ball speed between the best performing aluminum bat and the two wooden bats was 9 miles per hour. They also discovered that all 19 players at the levels they studied (high school to professional) could bat a ball over 100 miles per hour and that batted ball speed increased with the skill level of the batter.[2]

The flip side of batted ball speed is player reaction time. Studies have found that a pitcher needs about 0.4 seconds to react to a batted ball, which gives him enough time to field a ball traveling approximately 92 miles per hour. While balls batted from wooden bats sometimes travel at velocities greater than that, more often than not the speed is within the margin of safety. But given that even a high school player with an aluminum bat can routinely propel a ball in excess of 100 miles per hour, one can readily see that pitchers simply do not have enough time to protect themselves.[3]

Catchers have been especially victimized by a specific type of batted ball, the foul tip. Squatting just a few feet behind the batter, many a catcher has been injured or killed by a ball to the head or chest. There is good reason why catcher's equipment is often sardonically referred to as "the tools of ignorance."

Considering how vulnerable catchers were even in the early days of the game, it is curious that it took time for protective devices to be developed and accepted. As with batting helmets, players often resisted this new gear because it would seem "unmanly." While catchers were among the first to use a glove, the only form of protection initially was a rubber mouthpiece to prevent damage to the teeth. The mask (without the use of a helmet) did not arrive on the scene until the 1870s, followed by the chest protector in 1883. And while various types of shin protection were tried sporadically in the nineteenth century, use did not become widespread until future Hall-of-Famer Roger Bresnahan of the New York Giants adopted them during the 1907 season.[4]

Amateur Fatalities — Batted-Balls — Pitchers

Benjamin Shorrock, 23, was pitching a game in Haledon, NJ, on September 5, 1881, when the batter hit a line drive that struck Shorrock on the chest. He was able to pick up the ball and throw the runner out before collapsing on the mound. A physician was summoned, but he was unable to revive Shorrock. The cause of death was "paralysis of the heart."[5]

Charles Harrington began the spring of 1902 as a pitcher for the Dallas (TX) Griffins. Early in the season, though, he was released by the Class D Texas League team. He soon connected with an amateur team in nearby Midlothian. In an afternoon game on July 5, he was struck in the stomach by a batted ball. He was able to field the ball and throw the runner out at first, but when he resumed his position on the mound, he fell over dead.[6]

Eugene Harris, 15, was throwing batting practice to a 25-year-old player before a game in Asheville, NC, on April 8, 1905, when a "terrific liner" struck him on the back of the head. He died 15 minutes after the accident.[7]

Harry Becker, 14, was a pitcher for the Townsend Harris High School team in the Bronx, NY, in 1909 when he was severely injured by a batted ball. The injury ended his high school baseball career, but he continued to pitch in sandlot games. In an afternoon game on May 19, 1910, he stood on the mound with two outs and a full count on Andrew Towart, captain of the opposing team. Towart connected on the next pitch and the ball, which was made of intertwined rubber bands covered by leather, "whizzed at comet speed" toward Becker. Even though Becker was able to get his hands up in time, the ball broke through and struck him in the stomach. He recovered in time to throw Towart out, then fell unconscious to the ground. Becker died before help could arrive.[8]

Leonard Hand, 21, a pitcher for a semipro team in Cincinnati, OH, was struck simultaneously on the head by both a thrown and a batted ball while warming up before a game in Dayton, KY, on June 25, 1910. At the exact moment the batter hit the ball, someone else threw another ball at the pitcher. He attempted to dodge out of the way, but both balls struck him, one behind an ear and the second on the right temple. He died from his injuries later that night.[9]

John Freeman, 14, dreamed of joining the Navy when he grew up. He particularly enjoyed talking with the seamen connected to the Navy Medical School Hospital near his home in Washington, DC. He was pitching to a group of sailors during a game on July 28, 1911, when a ball hit by Joseph Mayotte, a 20-year-old patient at the hospital, struck Freeman behind the right ear. Although hospital staff immediately came to his assistance, he was dead before they could get him inside for treatment.[10]

James Audrey Ensor, 11, was pitching on June 6, 1921, during a game among students attending the elementary department of the Maryland State Normal School (now Towson Uni-

Spalding's Trade-Marked Catcher's Mask.

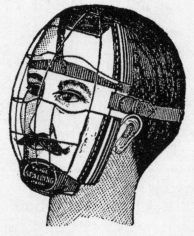

The first Catcher's Mask brought out in 1875, was a very heavy, clumsy affair, and it was not until we invented our open-eyed mask in 1877 that it came into general use. Now it would be considered unsafe and even dangerous for a catcher to face the swift underhand throwing of the present day unless protected by a reliable mask. The increased demand for these goods has brought manufacturers into the field who, having no reputation to sustain, have vied with each other to see how *cheap* they could make a so-called mask, and in consequence have ignored the essential qualification, *strength*. A cheaply made, inferior quality of mask is much worse than no protection at all. for a broken wire or one that will not stand the force of the ball without caving in, is liable to disfigure a player for life. We would warn catchers not to trust their faces behind one of these *cheap* made masks. Our trade-marked masks are made of the very best hard wire, plated to prevent rusting, and well trimmed, and every one is a thorough face protector. We shall make them in three grades as described below, and with our increased facilities for manufacturing, are enabled to improve the quality, and at the same time reduce the price.

Beware of counterfeits. *None genuine without our Trade Mark stamped on each Mask.*

No. 00—**Spalding's Special League Mask**, used by all the leading professional catchers, extra heavy wire, well padded with goat hair, and the padding faced with the best imported dogskin, which is impervious to perspiration, and retains its pliability and softness .... Each $3 00

" 0.—**Spalding's Regulation League Mask**, made of heavy wire, well padded, and faced with horsehide, warranted first-class in every respect .... Each.. 2 50

" 1.—**Spalding's Boys' League Mask**, made of heavy wire, equally as heavy in proportion to size as the No. 00 mask. It is made to fit a boy's face, and gives the same protection as the League Mask .... Each 2 00

CHEAP MASKS.

To meet the demand for good masks at a low price, we have manufactured a line of cheap masks, which are superior to any masks in the market at the same price. We do not guarantee these masks, and believe that our Trade Marked Masks are worth more than the difference in price.

No. A.—**Amateur Mask**, made the same size and general style as the League Mask, but with lighter wire, and faced with leather (we guarantee this Mask to be superior to so-called League or professional masks sold by other manufacturers) $1 50

" B. **Boys' Mask**, similar to the Amateur Mask, only made smaller to fit a boy's face .... Each 1 25

☞ Any of the above masks mailed postpaid on receipt of price.

By the late 1870s, full face protection for catchers became available. This model was sold by Spalding in the 1880s.

versity) in Towson, MD. When fellow student Edgar Lightcap hit the ball, Ensor turned his back, thinking it was a fly to the outfield. The ball struck Ensor behind the right ear, knocking him unconscious. He died from a brain concussion several minutes later.[11]

Alvert Muzzio, 8, was interested in forming a team of boys about his own age. Joseph DeVito, a 14-year-old who lived in the same New York City apartment building as Muzzio, agreed to meet with the younger children to help them organize and

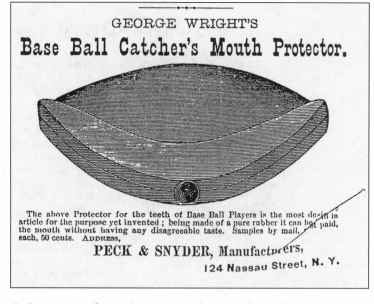

Early protection for catchers was rudimentary at best. This mouth protector, marketed in the 1870s, carried the endorsement of the Cincinnati Red Stockings' superstar, George Wright.

to instruct them in the fundamentals of the game. During an evening practice game on June 11, 1932, DeVito hit a ball pitched by Muzzio, which struck the youngster on the chest. He fell unconscious and died before help could arrive.[12]

Morris E. Stanley, 35, was pitching in a family sandlot game in Florissant, MO, on May 21, 1950, when his 15-year-old nephew hit a line drive back to the box. The ball struck Stanley on the back of the ear as he attempted to get out of the way. Knocked unconscious by the blow, he was rushed to a local doctor's office, where artificial respiration was attempted. When treatment failed to revive him, he was then taken by ambulance to a nearby hospital. He was pronounced dead on arrival from a fractured skull.[13]

Lawrence Bulanek, 7, was pitching to his 39-year-old father, Antone, and several of his friends in the backyard of their Houston, TX, home on July 3, 1950. When it began to get dark, the senior Bulanek said they would have to stop. His young son, though, asked to throw one more pitch. Antone Bulanek hit the ball, striking his son over the heart. Lawrence Bulanek died before they could reach the hospital.[14]

Julius Riofrir, 17, a recent graduate of Glendale (CA) High School, was pitching batting practice to teammate and fellow graduate Fernando Rios before an American Legion Baseball League game on the evening of June 22, 1997. Rios, who had just been drafted by the Cincinnati Reds, hit a ball which ricocheted off the concrete curbing around the batting cage. Although Riofrir was standing behind protective screening, the ball managed to break through and strike him on temple, fracturing his skull. Riofrir fell unconscious and was immediately rushed a local hospital, where he was put on life support. He was declared brain dead late the following afternoon. In the early morning hours of June 24, his parents decided to donate his organs, and all life support was discontinued.[15]

Brandy Mitchell, 9, was pitching during a street ball game with several other children near her Michigan City, IN, home on August 12, 1999. A ball hit by her 9-year-old male cousin struck her in the face, knocking her down. She stood up, but then fell backwards, hitting the back of her head on the asphalt pavement. The fall dislocated a vertebrae in her neck, causing spinal cord compression. A neighbor called 911, but the child died without regaining consciousness.[16]

Brandon Patch, 18, pitcher for the Miles City (MT) Mavericks, was struck on the head by a ball hit off an aluminum bat during the fifth inning of a tied American Legion Baseball League game in Helena, MT, on July 25, 2003. When his parents rushed to their son's side, they found he was still conscious. "I've got a migraine headache, Dad," the young player said before passing out. He lay on the field for nearly 30 minutes before being taken to the hospital. Later that evening he was flown to Great Falls, MT, where he was put on life support. He died the following morning. Patch's parents spent the next two years attempting to get aluminum bats eliminated in the state. In early 2005, the Montana legislature passed a resolution calling on the American Legion to prohibit aluminum bats after a legislative committee deadlock on an outright ban. Montana governor Brian Schweitzer signed the resolution in April 2005.[17]

Ryan Nielsen, 17, third baseman for Cooper Hills High School team in West Jordan, UT, was pitching batting practice to a friend about 4:30 P.M. on August 27, 2004. Even though he was throwing from behind a protective screen, a line drive struck him on the neck. His friend called 911, then performed CPR until paramedics arrived and put him on life support. He was flown to a hospital in Salt Lake City. Nielsen died several hours later from a ruptured carotid artery.[18]

Chris Gavora, 17, was standing behind a protective screen, pitching to a friend during pre-game warm-ups in one of the batting cages at his Grapevine, TX, high school on February 22, 2007. A teammate in a cage directly behind him "hit a line drive that went through an opening in the net, across an open area, and through the other batting cage's opening." Unfortunately, the batting cage Gavora was using did not have the second layer of netting that was supposed to have been installed behind the pitcher. Gavora was struck on the back of his head by the batted ball. He was rushed to a local hospital, where surgery was performed later that night. He died on the afternoon of February 24. As a result of this fatality, the local school board passed a requirement that anyone entering a batting cage — including pitchers and coaches — must wear a batting helmet. In addition, the board instituted regular safety inspections of all batting cages.[19]

Amateur Fatalities — Batted-Balls — Catchers

Eddie McDade, 15, caught for the Mount Vernon Baseball Club, one of several amateur teams in Manayunk, PA. During a game against the rival Liberty Baseball Club on July 9, 1887, a foul tip off the bat of Mickey Curley struck McDade on the neck. Gasping for air, he remained conscious and even staggered around the field as several hundred fans rushed to him. Billy Carlin, a friend, came to McDade's assistance. According to Carlin, McDade was able to whisper, "Billy, get me a doctor. This is my last game." He then fell unconscious and was taken to his home. Two doctors arrived and found that his windpipe was broken. Although they inserted a tube below the break, the surgery was unsuccessful and McDade died about four hours later.[20]

John Dean, catcher for a team from Spring Green, WI, was injured by a foul tip during a game on September 20, 1895, in Boscobel, WI. The ball broke through his mask, striking him on the forehead. He died the next day.[21]

Edward Conner was struck over the heart while catching during a game in Lawrence, MA, on May 30, 1899. He died within moments of being injured.[22]

Ward M. Snyder, 23, was the starting pitcher in a game between athletic clubs in Homewood, PA, on August 4, 1900. Local newspaper accounts differ in the specifics of what happened next. One reported that he was ineffective and was moved to the shortstop position in the second inning. Another stated that he began feeling ill about the middle of the game and left to stand on the sidelines next to his father. In any event, both agreed that he eventually became the team's catcher. During the course of the game, a foul tip struck Snyder over the heart, killing him almost instantly.[23]

Estel Payton, 16, was hit over the heart by a foul tip during a game near Ottumwa, IA, on July 30, 1905. He died immediately after throwing the ball back to the pitcher.[24]

Robert W. Pierce, 15, was struck over the heart while catching for his North Kingston, RI, high school team in a game in Wickford, RI, on May 27, 1908. He died moments later from "paralysis of the heart."[25]

John Wulkotte was catching during a tie game between amateur teams in Cincinnati, OH, on May 31, 1908. A foul tip struck him on the forehead. Wulkotte died before an ambulance could arrive.[26]

Edward Ballard, 20, died instantly after a foul tip struck him over the heart during a game in Wisner, MI, on September 4, 1910.[27]

Harry Greenhood, 12, was struck on the neck by a foul tip while catching during a game with friends on August 15, 1911, on the diamond at Central High School in Philadelphia, PA. He gave out a cry before collapsing at the plate. His terrified friends carried his body to a local drugstore, where the druggist called a physician. The doctor arrived, but found that the child was already dead.[28]

Homer Norris, 10, was struck over the heart by a foul tip during a game in Wellston, OH, on June 9, 1912. He caught one more ball before collapsing over home plate.[29]

Leo Clair Cummings, 12, was catching in a sandlot game in Pittsfield, MA, on May 10, 1913. The children were using a golf ball in place of a regulation baseball. A foul tip drove the golf ball though the wire netting on Cummings catcher's mask, striking him on the forehead and fracturing his skull. He died May 16, seven days after being hit.[30]

Fritz Greenwald, 21, was struck below the right ear by a foul tip during a game in Holland, NY, on May 30, 1913. The blow fractured his skull. The next day, he was placed on a train to be taken to a hospital in Buffalo, NY, but died along the way.[31]

Clarence Bender, 22, was killed April 23, 1919, by a foul tip that struck him over his heart during a noontime game at his place of employment, the Pressed Steel Car Company in McKees Rocks, PA.[32]

Raymond Blackburn, Jr., 14, was struck in the stomach by a foul tip during a sandlot game in Gloucester, NJ, on May 23, 1938. He died in a doctor's office shortly after the accident.[33]

Norman Ingram, 14, was catching his 12-year-old brother, Willard, during a sandlot game in Burlington, IA, on July 13, 1939. The younger brother threw a fastball which the batter fouled off, striking Norman near his heart. He died moments after being struck.[34]

Dennis Wucki, 13, was catching during a practice game at a Chicago, IL, park on June 20, 1978, when a foul tip struck him in the head. "The ball hit him in one of the few places unprotected by his helmet or catcher's mask," said the boy's father, John Wucki. The elder Wucki, a coach on the team, rushed to help his son, who stood up, took off his mask, and complained of not feeling well before collapsing unconscious. The youngster died on the evening of June 23 without regaining consciousness.[35]

Jose Martin Solis, 15, was killed by a blow to the heart during practice with his high school varsity team before a game in Dallas, TX, on December 9, 1981, even though he was wearing a chest protector. After being struck, he took several steps before collapsing on the field. The school nurse saw the accident and rushed to administer CPR, but Solis was pronounced dead on arrival at a local hospital.[36]

Amateur Fatalities — Batted-Balls — Other Position Players

Joseph Stendenbard, 15, was playing shortstop during a sandlot game in San Antonio, TX, in March of 1891. A line drive off the bat of a larger man slipped through Stendenbard's hands. The ball struck him on the right temple, knocking him momentarily unconscious. He came to after a few minutes and resumed playing his position. After the game he was taken home, where he again became unconscious. He died shortly thereafter.[37]

Joseph Kercher, 13, of Kutztown, PA, was struck over the heart and killed after failing to catch a line drive during a schoolyard game on October 27, 1894.[38]

Reade Jarman, 24, playing shortstop for his Charlottesville, VA, baseball club in a game on June 10, 1902, was struck in the throat by a ground ball that took a bad hop, causing the opening between the vocal cords to swell. Jarman, who threw the runner out at first before collapsing, died moments later.[39]

Albert Edward Johnson, 32, second baseman for an Oak Park, IL, athletic club, was taking infield practice before a championship game in River Forest, IL, on September 17, 1904. Someone hit a liner which Johnson failed to catch, the ball striking him just above the heart. Although momentarily dazed, he picked the ball up and threw it back in. Several minutes later he fell to the ground unconscious. Several doctors, including one who was also a teammate, ran to his assistance, but they were unable to revive him.[40]

Frederick Whittaker, 19, was hit over the heart by a line drive while playing shortstop in a game in Hamilton Terrace near Trenton, NJ, on July 29, 1905. He continued to play, but fifteen minutes later he collapsed unconscious. He died in an ambulance on the way to the hospital.[41]

Leander "Goosey" Holmgreen, 19, first baseman for a company team from McKeesport, PA, was struck over the heart by a line drive during infield practice before a game in Ellsworth, PA, on May 15, 1909. Holmgreen, who was preoccupied catching a ball thrown by the shortstop, did not see the ball heading toward him. He died about three minutes after being hit.[42]

Paul Murphy, 9, attempted to catch a fly ball hit by his 13-year-old brother, Joe, while playing in Walton, MI, on April 14, 1913. He missed and the ball struck him on the chest, killing him instantly.[43]

John Nelson, 18, was playing first base during the seventh inning of a game in Brooklyn, NY, on April 11, 1914, when a missed line drive struck him on the forehead. When he came to about 15 minutes later, he continued to play. He began experiencing severe head pains about 3:00 the following afternoon. A doctor was called, but Nelson died two hours later of a ruptured blood vessel.[44]

John Hardy, 17, was playing the infield during a sandlot game in Philadelphia, PA, on May 16, 1914, when a sharply hit ground ball took a bad hop and struck him on the head as he bent to field it. He was taken to a local hospital where he died May 25, 10 days after the accident.[45]

Charles Wellman, 13, was hit behind the right ear by a liner while he was playing third base in a street game in Chicago, IL, on June 7, 1914. He died about 10:00 that evening from a brain concussion.[46]

Binks Alton, 30, was struck on the temple by a foul ball while waiting to bat during a game in Mineral Point, WI, on June 30, 1914. He continued to play, but became ill after the game. He died the next day.[47]

James Savio, 22, had his wrist broken by a batted ball during a semipro game in Fort Wayne, IN, early in the summer of 1914. Because he did not seek immediate medical attention, an infection set in. In mid–September he was taken to a local hospital for surgery, but it was found that the infection was systemic and physicians were unable to save his life. He died on September 21, 1914, several months after the initial injury.[48]

William Davidson, 13, was playing with his father and a neighborhood friend near their home in Thompson, OH, on May 25, 1915. When the elder Davidson threw to the neighbor child at bat, the youngster hit a line drive which struck the younger Davidson squarely between the eyes. Knocked unconscious, the child died early the next morning.[49]

Roy Plymell, 22, was struck behind the right ear while playing the infield in a game in London, OH, on July 10, 1915. He died later that night.[50]

William Lewis, 14, was struck on the knee by a ground ball while playing the infield during a game in St. Clairsville, OH, in early March 1919. He developed blood poisoning from cuts caused by the blow and died March 19, two weeks after the initial injury.[51]

Michael Levy, 14, was chasing a fly ball during a schoolyard game on March 16, 1933, in Baltimore, MD, when he tripped and fell. The ball struck him on the back of the head. While at first it did not appear that he was severely injured, he died on March 19 from the blow.[52]

Joseph Stefanelli, 14, was struck on the right temple by a line drive while playing shortstop for a sandlot team in East Orange, NJ, on March 24, 1950. He walked home immediately after the accident. When he began to experience pain, he was taken to Columbus Hospital in Newark. He died later that night.[53]

Pat Blackwell, 10, was taking infield practice as a shortstop for his Little League team in Valsetz, OR, on June 6, 1957. A ground ball took a bad hop, striking Blackwell on the left temple and knocking him unconscious. He died late that night without regaining consciousness.[54]

Carl Allman, 15, was running in from the outfield to take his turn at bat during batting practice with his Burleson High School team before a district playoff game in Wilmer, TX, on May 13, 1958, between Wilmer-Hutchins High School and Burleson. According to the Wilmer coach, Allman "was between third base and home plate and looking away from the plate" when a line drive off the bat of a teammate struck him on the back of the head. He was rushed to a local clinic, but was pronounced dead on arrival.[55]

Louis J. Lise, 18, was standing near the foul line during tryouts for the New Rochelle, NY, High School team on March 17, 1966, when a line drive struck him on the head. He died later that day.[56]

James E. Kimball was struck on the chest by a pop fly during a Portland, OR, Little

League game on May 7, 1968, the same day as his 10th birthday. He was pronounced dead on arrival at a local hospital.[57]

Bruce Edgerley, 16, was playing shortstop during batting practice before a county recreation department game in Beaufort, SC, the evening of May 30, 1990. A line drive off a teammate's bat struck him on the chest. "I think he just wasn't looking. He was pretty agile and would have been able to move if he had seen it," commented the team coach after the accident. The coach and his son performed CPR, but Edgerley was dead by the time paramedics arrived.[58]

Jason Smyly, 6, was playing tee-ball with his family at a park in Saraland, AL, on April 16, 1995, when a ball glanced off his glove, striking him on the chest. He died in a local hospital later that night.[59]

Jacob Watt, 6, was struck in the chest by a line drive while he waited to take batting practice before a Lexington, IL, Jaycee-sponsored baseball game on the evening of June 4, 1998. All attempts to revive him failed, and he was pronounced dead about 90 minutes after the accident.[60]

Ryan Blanco, 7, collapsed immediately after being struck on the chest by a ball batted by his 11-year-old brother as they played in the backyard of their Centereach, Long Island, NY, home around 5:00 P.M. on June 11, 2000. A neighbor performed CPR before paramedics arrived. The child was rushed to a local hospital, where he was declared dead about an hour later.[61]

Nader Parman II, 7, was batting a ball around with a 15-year-old neighbor in the front yard of his East Cobb, GA, home on the evening of May 17, 2002. The older child threw the ball up and swung at it in an attempt to hit a pop fly. Instead he hit a line drive that struck the youngster on the chest, killing him almost instantly.[62]

Amateur Fatalities — Batted-Balls — Baserunners

Frank Duncan, 20, died from a brain concussion shortly after being struck on the head by a line drive as he ran from first to second during a May 1, 1904, game in Baltimore, MD.[63]

Roy Duncan, 18, was struck in the head while running from second to third in a game on March 26, 1910, in Kittaning, PA. He died almost instantly from the blow.[64]

Frank Breitweiser, 18, was standing on second base during a Central Park game on April 28, 1910, when a ball batted in a nearby game struck him on the temple, killing him within moments.[65]

Howard J. Collins, 18, was struck on the left temple as he ran from first to second during a high school game in Chadds Ford, PA, on June 17, 1930. He died two days later at a West Chester, PA, hospital.[66]

Amateur Fatalities — Batted-Balls — Self-Inflicted

Edward Likely, 23, was batting during a practice game in Lincoln, NE, on June 13, 1887. When he swung at an inside fastball, it glanced off the handle and struck him in the face. Falling unconscious at the plate, the top of his head hit the ground. He was taken to a nearby hotel, but he died about 10 minutes after the incident. Attending physicians speculated that death was due to head trauma caused by a combination of the ball injury and his head striking the ground.[67]

Joseph Marsh, 23, was batting with two out in the second inning of a game in Dalton, MA, on September 3, 1900, when a first-pitch inside fastball glanced off his hand and bat handle, striking him below the right ear. Marsh collapsed a few feet from the plate. A physician attending the game rushed to his side, but was unable to revive the player. His death ten minutes later was caused by "paralysis of the heart."[68]

Allan Munro Newman, 25, formerly a Brown University player, was the second man at bat during the top of the first inning of a city league game in Pawtucket, RI, on August 21, 1903. After taking a couple of pitches, he swung at

A Death on the Field.

This illustration from the *St. Louis Globe-Democrat* depicts the death of Edward Likely from a self-inflicted foul tip in Lincoln, Nebraska, on June 13, 1887.

a high, inside fastball. The ball ricocheted off his bat, striking him on the right temple "sufficiently loud to be heard in the grand stand." He fell, but remained conscious. He continued to play until the third inning, when he complained of a headache and removed himself from the game. At the end of the game, his teammates found him lying down in the dressing room, still in his uniform. Although conscious, he could not move because of the severity of the pain. He was carried outside to await an ambulance. Physicians at the hospital found that he was suffering from a brain hemorrhage, and emergency surgery was performed. He died around 7:00 that night.[69]

Clarence Thomas was at bat during a late afternoon game near Black Creek, VA, on August 20, 1909, when he fouled off a fastball, striking himself above the heart. He fell at the plate and died a few moments later.[70]

William Harrison Zimmerman, 17, was taking batting practice with a pitching machine at Miraleste High School in Rancho Palos Verdes, CA, on November 30, 1976. He hit a liner to the ground which bounced back at him, striking him on the knee. According to doctors, Zimmerman, who had a history of heart problems, suffered a heart attack caused by the pain of the blow. He was rushed to a local hospital, where he was pronounced dead less than two hours after the accident.[71]

Amateur Fatalities — Batted-Balls — Unknown Position

James C. Allen, 14, was struck on the head by a fly ball in Reading, PA, on March 28, 1910. He died a few hours later.[72]

Samuel James, 30, was struck on the temple by a batted ball during a game in Dana, IN, on October 23, 1910. He died the next day.[73]

Thomas Gilpin died immediately after being struck by a foul ball near the heart during a game in Sparks, OK, on June 8, 1914.[74]

Eddie Gray, 10, died instantly after being struck over the heart during a schoolyard game in Riverton, ID, on October 13, 1914. The ball was batted by his teacher.[75]

Robert Jackson Howison, 10, was hit on the head and knocked unconscious during a game in Ashland, VA, on April 17, 1915. "Such was the force of the blow that the sound of the impact was heard in the grandstand," a local newspaper reported. He revived a few moments later and was taken out of the game. As he left the field on his way home, he collapsed. He was transported by car to a Richmond, VA, hospital, where surgery was performed to remove a large blood clot. He never regained consciousness and died early the next morning.[76]

Lamar Carn, 24, suffered a fractured skull when he was struck by a batted ball during an afternoon game in Tutwiler, MS, on July 9, 1915. Only after finishing the game and returning to his home in Clarksdale, MS, did he fall unconscious. He was taken to a hospital in Memphis, TN, where emergency surgery was performed. Carn died the morning of July 13.[77]

William Biersdorff, 21, died immediately after struck above the heart by a foul ball during a game in Grant Park, Chicago, IL, on June 5, 1920.[78]

Russell W. Pierson, Jr., 14, was playing in a park game in Maplewood, NJ, on March 27, 1937, when he was struck on the head by a batted ball. He finished the game, but collapsed later that night. He was taken to a hospital in Orange, NJ, but died the next day from a cerebral hemorrhage.[79]

Leo Fitch, 19, was struck on the left ear by a batted ball during a night game in Mechanicville, NY, on July 21, 1938. In spite of the injury, he continued to play and even drove himself home afterwards. When he did not show up to work the next morning, his employer became concerned. He found Fitch unconscious in his bed. Fitch was rushed to a hospital in Albany, NY, where emergency surgery was performed, but he died the morning of July 23.[80]

Amateur Fatalities — Bats

Harry Bernstein, 10, was catching during a game in Philadelphia, PA, in mid–April 1874 when the batter struck him on the head while swinging at a pitch. Bernstein died on April 30, about two weeks after being injured.[81]

James J. Crowley, 14, was standing to the left of his 12-year-old friend, William Hamilton, as the younger child stood at the plate, waiting on the pitch in a sandlot game outside a "juvenile asylum" in New York City on the morning of July 9, 1878. Just as the pitch was delivered, Crowley called for the young batter to "hit it a good one!" When Hamilton swung and missed the ball, the bat flew out of his hands and struck Crowley on the lower jaw below the right ear. On impact, he raised his hands, yelled "Oh, my," spun around, and fell dead to the ground. A physician at the juvenile home determined that the blow from the bat "paralyzed a bundle of nerves communicating with the boy's brain."[82]

John Campbell, 12, was struck in the stomach by a bat while playing in a game in Providence, RI, on July 12, 1879. He died later that day.[83]

Harry Brown, 19, died an hour after a bat that slipped from the hands of a teammate struck him during a game in Salem, MA, on May 30, 1888.[84]

Arthur E. Miller, 12, was killed by a bat during a game in Glen Cove, New York, on June 11, 1889.[85]

Frank Wesan, 14, was on third when his friend, John Hague, hit a double during a game in Philadelphia, PA, on May 26, 1906. As Wesan ran toward home, Hague threw his bat aside, striking Wesan on the head. He died later that night from a brain concussion.[86]

Harold Brown, 15, suffered a "cerebellar abscess" several days after being struck on the head by a bat during a game with friends in Rutledge, IA. He continued to play immediately after the accident, but over the next few days began "slowly losing his mind." His parents committed him to a Mount Pleasant, IA, asylum, where he died the morning of June 14, 1907.[87]

Arthur Burroughs, 9, was catching in a game in Central Falls, RI, on May 20, 1909, when batter Earl Paine swung at a pitch, missed the ball and stuck Burroughs over the heart with the bat. The young catcher died within seconds.[88]

Charles E. Moran, 23, was struck on his side while catching in a game in LaPorte, IN. He died during emergency surgery performed the morning of June 18, 1910.[89]

H. D. Edwards was standing close to home plate in a game in Montclair, NJ, on July 4, 1910, when his teammate hit a home run. As the batter started running toward first, he threw the bat aside, striking Edwards on the head. He died on July 25 from "cerebral inflammation."[90]

Nicholas Fernicola, 26, a medical student at the Hahnemann Medical College in Philadelphia, PA, was injured during a student game at the college in 1913 by a bat which struck him on the head. When he came home to Newark, NJ, during Thanksgiving break later that year, he began to experience severe pain in his head. A week later he lost his ability to speak and by early December was completely paralyzed down his left side. He was taken to a Newark hospital on January 11, 1914, but failed to improve, dying on February 6, 1914, from what his physicians diagnosed as "abscess of the brain." Interestingly, Fernicola told his family that he had been originally injured by a fellow student who struck Fernicola on the head with a book, while his hospital records list the cause of his injury as a blow to the head with a bat.[91]

Paul Zeigler, 16, a sophomore at Grass Lake, MI, high school, and Leonard Wolff, a friend, were hitting fly balls to some other boys before school on April 15, 1915, when Zeigler dropped his ball. Just as he bent to pick it up, Wolff swung his bat, striking Zeigler on the left temple. Zeigler seemed to be uninjured. He went on to school, but later that afternoon, he went home complaining of a severe headache. Mrs. Nellie Kelly, the woman who ran the boarding house where he lived, gave him some aspirin, and Zeigler lay on the couch. Kelly left to run some errands. When she returned several hours later, she found Zeigler unconscious. An examining physician discovered that Zeigler was suffering a ruptured blood vessel in his brain. He took Zeigler to a local hospital, but the teen died shortly after arrival.[92]

Lloyd Kennedy, 20, was struck on his right side when a teammate's bat slipped from his hands during a game in Fargo, ND, on May 23, 1915. Although a physician who was attending the game rushed to help Kennedy, he died a few minutes later.[93]

Lawrence G. Sumner, 20, a student at Virginia Polytechnic Institute, was struck over the heart when a bat slipped from the hands of his friend and classmate, Otis Forbes, during a game in Blacksburg, VA, on March 27, 1921. He was rushed to the university hospital, but died about 15 minutes after the accident.[94]

Philip J. Harris was killed and Arthur Delaney was seriously injured when a bat slipped from the hands of another teammate during batting practice before a game in Delmar, NY, on August 7, 1927. The bat struck Harris on the head, then bounced and hit Delaney on the jaw. Delaney recovered, but Harris lost consciousness and died August 9.[95]

Floyd Miller, 12, was struck on the head when a teammate swung at and missed a pitched ball during a game in Wahpeton, ND, on April 25, 1932. Miller died the same day.[96]

James Linde, 11, was cut on the lip when a bat struck him during a game in Cincinnati, OH, on May 5, 1933. The child, a hemophiliac, died from "an uncontrollable hemorrhage" on May 7.[97]

Donald Weber, 13, stepped in front of a classmate swinging at a ball during a schoolyard game in Redlands, CA, on March 27, 1934. The bat struck him on the head, causing a concussion. He died several hours later.[98]

Ralph Musick, 18, was hit on the head when a bat slipped through his cousin's hands as he swung at a pitch during a schoolyard game in Roanoke, VA, on October 21, 1936. According to his family physician, his death the next day was due in part to a weak heart in addition to the head injury.[99]

Richard Leahy, 17, in a game between Jersey City, NJ, baseball clubs on the evening of June 14, 1939, was struck on the head when a bat slipped from the hands of an opposing batter. He died in the hospital a few hours later.[100]

Russell Liller, 9, was hit on the back of the head during a sandlot game in Keyser, WV, on May 13, 1945, when the bat slipped from the hands of a batter swinging at a pitched ball. The blow broke his neck, causing his death shortly thereafter.[101]

Walter Gibbs, Jr., 6, was catching during a pick-up game with two friends at Newark, NJ, playground on June 19, 1947, when the batter swung and struck Gibbs behind the left ear. He died from a skull fracture before help could arrive.[102]

James Feilen, 11, got an extra-base hit during a schoolyard game in Chicago, IL, on March 15, 1949. As he headed toward second, he stopped and returned to first because he had failed to touch the bag. A batter on the sidelines hitting balls to the outfield swung just as Feilen reached first, striking him on the top of the head with the bat. He died at home several hours after the accident.[103]

Mark Bogenholm, 7, was on third during a sandlot game in Chicago, IL, on July 11, 1955, when he attempted to steal home. The batter swung just as Bogenholm reached the plate, striking him across the chest with the bat. He died immediately after being hit.[104]

Arnold Barrett, 23, was catching during a park game in the Bronx, NY, on July 29, 1962, when the batter swung and missed the ball, striking Barrett with the bat. He died shortly after being hit.[105]

5. Collision Fatalities

While baseball is supposed to be a non-contact sport, collisions between players occur regularly and, in most cases, are considered a legitimate and expected part of the game. The runner on first goes in hard at second, knocking over the second baseman or the shortstop in an attempt to break up a double play. The baserunner on third barrels into the catcher who is blocking home, hoping to jar the ball loose and score the winning run. Two outfielders run hard after a fly ball, neither seeing nor hearing the other's presence, only to smash into each other and crumple to the ground dazed and injured. A fielder rams into a wall or fence in pursuit of a foul or a ball heading for the bleachers.

Renowned sports columnist George Vass, in fact, referred to baseball as "mayhem on the grass" because, as he observed, "severe injury and baseball walk hand in hand." Scores of players have suffered broken bones, concussions, and internal injuries as a result of collisions. The prime example is Pete Reiser who, as a result of playing with such reckless abandon, shortened his major league career because of many grievous injuries resulting from collisions with walls.[1]

Sometimes such collisions even result in death. In a study of high school and college players from 1982 to 2002, the authors identified 41 cases of catastrophic injuries, 10 of which were fatalities. Collisions between players (fielder to fielder or baserunner to fielder) were the most common cause, accounting for 41.5 percent (17 incidents) of all catastrophic injuries. Sadly, three of these were fatal.[2]

Minor League Fatalities

Louis Henke, first baseman for the Atlanta (GA) Atlantas of the newly-organized Southern League (later known as the Southern Association), was once described as "a grand athlete" who "fielded in fine style, was a slashing hitter, and could throw like a shot from a Mauser." Indeed, Henke was one of the team leaders during the Atlantas' 1885 inaugural season, heading a roster that included star pitcher Tom Sullivan, who led the league in winning percentage with a 22 and 7 record, and sluggers John Cahill and Walton Goldsby, who tied for the league lead in homers that year with six each.[3]

All season long Atlanta vied for first place with two other league powerhouses, the Augusta (GA) Browns and the Nashville (TN) Americans. So when the Americans came to Atlanta for a series in mid–August, everyone thought it would determine the league championship.

In the opening game on August 14, Atlanta quickly jumped out to a one-run lead when shortstop John Cahill smashed a ball between center and left for a home run. The Atlantas added two more in the third when catcher George McVey hit a double, scoring the runners on first and third. Atlanta had the game well in hand when tragedy struck in the fourth inning.[4]

Henke came to bat with one out and Atlanta third baseman, Elmer Cleveland, standing on third after a hit and an error. Playing first was Nashville's Charles "Lefty" Marr, who was generally in left field. He was covering this unfamiliar position because Leonard Sowders, who had started the game in his usual position at first, had asked to be moved to left after the first inning because he was suffering from a sore thumb injured in a game a few days previously. Had the switch not been made, a fatality might have been avoided.

Henke hit a sharp grounder to Nashville third baseman James Hillary. The fielder initially turned toward home, hoping to gun down Cleveland at the plate. Changing his mind, he threw quickly to first. Marr was standing on the bag, but bobbled the throw. As he bent to pick the ball up, "Henke came thundering down to the base. He was the swiftest and most daring base runner on the Atlanta nine, as well as one of the heaviest and most muscular of its players." Marr began to straighten up just as Henke reached the bag. Marr's "head struck Henke's side with fearful force. Both players were stunned, but Marr recovered in a moment, and seizing the ball which had rolled a few feet away, threw to the pitcher."[5]

The injured Henke lay gasping for breath for several minutes. When Henke was able to stand, Gus Schmelz, Atlanta's manager, removed him from the game, sending him first to the clubhouse and then to the hotel where he boarded. Initially showing improvement, by late that night Henke was in severe distress. Attending physicians discovered that Henke's "liver had been torn from its ligaments and had never ceased to bleed since the fatal shock." Henke lapsed into unconsciousness by mid-afternoon on August 15. He died around 6:00 that evening surrounded by his teammates.[6]

Henke's body was sent to Cincinnati, OH, his hometown, for burial. The Atlantas continued to pay Henke's salary to his widow and only child for the remainder of the season, and several benefit games were held to help support his survivors. A minor controversy arose when someone sent a wire to the *Cincinnati Enquirer* implying that the accident was the result of "bad feelings" between the two teams. The *Atlanta Constitution* denied that there was any truth to this rumor. "Nothing could be more unjust," wrote the paper. "Henke's injuries were purely accidental and were so recognized by himself, by every member of both teams and by the audience. The personal friendship between himself and Marr was scarcely less than that between himself and [Henry] Bittman [Henke's best friend on the Atlanta team]. They played together last season and were devoted and intimate friends."[7]

A similar fatality occurred 19 years later in a game between the Dayton (OH) Veterans and the South Bend (IN) Greens in the Class B Central League. In the middle of the July 7, 1904, game, Dayton first baseman **Frank "Red" Herbert** hit a ground ball to South Bend first baseman Alva Spangler. Herbert ran hard to first while Spangler cleanly fielded the ball. Spangler stood near the bag with his hands extended to tag Herbert as he came down the line. The Veterans batter ran directly into the Greens fielder at a full run. Spangler's hands struck Herbert with a powerful blow in the pit of his stomach, injuring Herbert and knocking him unconscious. Although Herbert had to be removed from the game, no one at the time thought the injury serious. The Veterans ended up losing the contest 2 to 4.[8]

Herbert's condition began to deteriorate late the following day. The team doctor was summoned when the injured player began to cough up blood and experience intermittent convulsions. Herbert was taken to a local hospital shortly before noon on July 9. He remained conscious and, according to one source, felt that he would get better soon. Sadly, he died later that afternoon.[9]

An autopsy was performed from which doctors concluded that Herbert had been suffering from "ulcerated" intestines caused by an undetected case of typhus fever. The collision with Spangler led to the internal bleeding that resulted in his death. His body was shipped home to Wheeling, WV, for burial. The team and the league raised money in support of his widow and baby.[10]

Even though **Leo Smith**, 19, was playing just his third game of professional ball on May 23, 1909, he was already "mighty near being the star performer" for the Kokomo (IN) Wild Cats of the Class D Northern State of Indiana League. The league itself was new as well, having been organized in the towns of Bluffton, Lafayette, Huntington, Kokomo, Marion, and Wabash earlier that spring.[11]

Smith, a slightly-built speedster from Logansport, IN, was covering his usual third base position during the fifth inning against the Bluffton Babes when batter William Rennard hit a double deep to centerfield. Rennard, in an attempt to put himself in a better position to score in a close game, tried to stretch it into a triple. The relay into Smith was perfect, and he stood there waiting for the baserunner. Rennard "plunged recklessly into the plucky third baseman, who, despite his hurts, held the ball until the umpire had called the runner out. Then he sank to the ground badly injured."[12]

Rennard's head had struck Smith in the pit of his stomach. An ambulance was called and the young player was administered aid before being taken to his room at a local hotel. Later that evening he was transported to a hospital where he initially showed some improvement. In fact, two days after the injury, he was talking of attending the games even though he could not play. But late in the evening of May 25, his condition suddenly began to decline. At 2:30 in the morning on May 26, the Kokomo third baseman died. Under protest from some of the other teams, Kokomo suspended all games until Smith's funeral in Logansport on May 28. William Rennard was kept in town for several days until a coroner's inquest cleared him of malicious intent.[13]

The Pittsburgh Pirates hoped they had a future superstar when they signed **Alfredo Edmead**, an 18-year-old outfield prospect from the Dominican Republic. In fact, the Pirates' signing bonus was the largest they had ever offered to any player from the Dominican, and they had big plans for the speedy youngster. The first step, though, was seasoning, so they assigned him to their Class A Carolina League club, the Salem (VA) Pirates.[14]

And Edmead was proving to be everything the Pirates had hoped for. At one point early in the 1974 season, the outfielder, described by his manager as "a natural hitter," had at least one hit in 20 out of 21 consecutive games. By late August, he was batting over .300, had seven homers, and was second on the team with 59 stolen bases. He, along with roommate and fellow Dominican Miguel Dilone, batted first and second for the championship-bound Salem Pirates.[15]

On the evening of August 22, the Salem team traveled to North Carolina to play the Rocky Mount Phillies. Named to the Carolina League all-star team just two days earlier, Edmead was playing with particular enthusiasm. He was fielding his right-field position with his usual intensity and, early in the game, scored Salem's first run after stealing second and third to raise his total to 61. Then, in the bottom of the sixth inning, a routine pop fly ended his life.[16]

Rocky Mount's pitcher hit a blooper to short right. As Salem second baseman Pablo Cruz went back on the ball, Edmead "was running with his head down and never stopped." The outfielder dove for the ball just as Cruz arrived. Cruz's knee struck Edmead's head with a powerful blow, knocking him unconscious. "Pablo got up but a couple of players ran out and saw Alfredo and called for an ambulance right away."[17]

Edmead stopped breathing as he lay on the field. Salem's trainer revived him, and the young player was transported to a local hospital. He died an hour later from massive brain trauma. The game continued without the players being informed of Edmead's passing. It was only later in the clubhouse after a 10 to 9 loss that they were told. The tragedy was doubly hard for 27-year-old Pablo Cruz. He and Edmead were both from Santo Domingo and, ironically, Cruz was the scout who had signed Edmead to a Pirates contract. "My God. My brother. My little brother," Cruz cried. "He always tried so hard. I didn't see him."[18]

Amateur Fatalities

John Quigley, 19, catcher for the semipro Harlem (NY) Clippers, crouched behind the plate in the bottom of the fifth inning during a July 7, 1877, game at Wappingers Falls, NY, against the local semipro Actives. Standing on third was 6' 2", 200-pound Actives pitcher and first baseman Dennis "Big Dan" Brouthers. When the Actives batter put the ball in play, Brouthers, who was the starting pitcher that day, raced toward home. Quigley, blocking the plate in anticipation of a throw home, never stood a chance. When the much larger Brouthers plowed into the catcher, Quigley "was struck on the left side of the forehead in a terrible manner by Bruther's [sic] knee. He fell over on the ground, but was picked up and stood still for a few moments, but in a short time after was taken [to] one side and laid down on the grass, and then the terrible injuries he had sustained became apparent, blood in large quantities streaming from the wounds." A Dr. Congreve, who happened to be watching the game, raced to Quigley's assistance. The injured catcher was taken to Congreve's house, where he and another physician examined him. The doctors discovered that "the upper portion of the orbit and the frontal bone had been knocked in." They performed surgery, removing several pieces of broken skull. Oddly, Quigley remained conscious and was even able to talk. Brouthers, who visited the fatally injured Quigley regularly, was "completely overwhelmed with grief over the affair."

Quigley lingered near death for over a month. Then, at 4:40 in the afternoon of Sunday, August 12, he died. An inquest held the following day declared the death to be purely accidental and completely exonerated Brouthers. The verdict did nothing to console Brouthers, who was so devastated that he stopped playing for about two months and seriously considered leaving the game. His anguish, however, lessened, and two years later he began what was to be a 19-year major league career as a first baseman, hitting 106 homers, winning a total of five batting titles, and compiling a lifetime .342 batting average. One of the premier sluggers of the nineteenth century, he was elected to the Hall of Fame in 1945, 13 years after his death in 1932.[19]

Benjamin Frank Myers, 20, was fatally injured during practice before a game in early September 1895 between the Pioneer Baseball Club, an amateur team he founded, and another local amateur team in Washington, DC. He was on first after hitting a single when he took off for second in an attempted steal. The throw from the catcher was high, forcing second baseman Michael Connors to jump for the ball. As he came down, Myers ran behind him, causing both players to collide, with Myers landing underneath Connors. When teammates rushed to the motionless Myers, they found that he had been severely injured. He was taken to a local hospital where the attending physician found an incapacitating injury to the player's neck. Although Myers remained conscious and was able to talk, he was completely paralyzed below the waist and partially paralyzed above. He lingered in this condition for a week before dying on Sunday morning, September 8.[20]

Thomas Kelley, 16, was covering third base during an April 23, 1899, game between his Badger Baseball Club and another local team from Madison, WI, when the opposing player on second came in hard at third. The baserunner's head rammed into Kelley's stomach, knocking him down and causing severe internal injury. Kelley was immediately taken home, where he died shortly before 1:00 P.M. the following day.[21]

F. E. Kirkpatrick, in a game in Madera, CA, on April 28, 1901, collided with teammate James O'Mara as both pursued a pop fly. O'Mara's head struck Kirkpatrick under his chin, knocking him unconscious. Two physicians attempted to revive Kirkpatrick without success. He died on the field shortly after the accident.[22]

John Hoge, 21, manager and catcher for the Murphy Baseball Club, broke his finger sliding into home during a game near Bridgeport, WV, on September 9, 1906. The bone protruded from the finger and dirt was ground into the wound. Although a physician immediately cleaned and dressed the wound, tetanus set in a week later. Hoge was sent to a hospital in Martins Ferry, OH, where he improved somewhat. But on the evening of September 18, he began to have convulsions. He died late the following day.[23]

McKee (first name unknown), a member of a team near Rolla, MO, collided with teammate Clark while both were pursuing a fly ball during a game on October 9, 1906. Clark's mouth struck McKee with such force that several of his upper teeth broke off and were embedded in McKee's skull. Clark was knocked unconscious and McKee was killed almost instantly.[24]

Leonard DeLong collided with a baserunner while attempting to catch a pop fly during a game in Lamont, IA, on April 24, 1909. His kidneys and left side were severely injured. He died later that evening.[25]

William MacNamara, right fielder for the Rutherford (NJ) Montereys Athletic Club, hit a single in the seventh inning of a game on July 3, 1909, against the Simpson Athletic Club. During an attempted steal of second, the catcher threw high to the second baseman, forcing him to jump up for the ball. As MacNamara slid under him, the fielder came down right in the middle of MacNamara's stomach. The injured baserunner was carried off the field and transported to his home in Kingsland, NJ, where he died on July 5.[26]

Francis Merithew Jenks, 15, played center field for his Hanover (NH) High School team. In a May 7, 1913, game against rival Lebanon (NH) High School, Jenks tripped while sliding into third during the bottom of the second inning. His head struck the ground and he was knocked unconscious for about 10 minutes. After reviving, he resumed playing his center field position. Two innings later, his head collided with the shortstop's as both were attempting to field a pop fly. Jenks was so severely injured by the combined accidents that he was immediately taken to a local hospital. He died late that night from a skull fracture.[27]

J. Whetstone, 24, broke his neck when he slid into the catcher's legs while attempting to score in the middle of a close game in Woodville, LA, on June 16, 1913. The umpire called Whetstone out, and the next batter was approaching the plate before anyone noticed that Whetstone was unconscious. When attempts to revived him failed, a physician was summoned. The doctor saw that Whetstone had a severe spinal cord injury and recommended that he be taken immediately to New Orleans for surgery. The young player's father hired a special train to transport his son to the Touro Infirmary. While Whetstone survived the trip that took most of the night, he died early the next morning on the operating table before surgery could be performed.[28]

Willis F. Davis, 19, suffered severe internal injuries while sliding into third during a game between teams from Conway Springs and Kingman, KS, in early May 1914. He was taken to a Wichita, KS, hospital for treatment, but peritonitis set in. He died on May 19, about two weeks after being injured.[29]

Gaulando (first name unknown), a youngster in Ladd, IL, was injured internally after a teammate fell on top of him as they both were pursuing a fly ball during a sandlot game on May 31, 1914. He started to walk home, but had to be assisted before he had gone very far. He died a few hours later after being taken to a local hospital.[30]

Thomas Jackson, 20, died while at Arkansas Agricultural and Mechanical College (now the University of Arkansas at Monticello) in Monticello, AR, on May 9, 1915, several weeks after being injured sliding into a base.[31]

Ernest Edwin "Speck" Wyss, 22, was a semipro catcher in Peoria, IL. On May 29, 1915, he caught all nine innings for the Peoria Heights Baseball Club in a game against a rival local team. Following that game, he insisted on catching for the Portman Baseball Club during a second game that afternoon against Peoria Heights, the team he had caught for in the first game. During the second inning of the afternoon game, Orville Gilbert, the Peoria Heights catcher, was on third when a teammate hit a grounder to the shortstop. Gilbert collided with Wyss at home just as he received the throw from the Portman fielder. Wyss dropped the ball when Gilbert's knee struck him a jarring blow on his chest and head. A short time later, a foul tip hit Wyss near the same spot. He tired by the sixth inning and sat on the bench after being removed from the game. Although Wyss seemed in good spirits, he complained of pain in his chest and head. Before the second game was completed, he went into the clubhouse to rest. Wyss was found unconscious when the players entered the clubhouse after the game. He was immediately taken to a local hospital where he died at 7:15 the following morning without regaining consciousness. An inquest later that day concluded that the cause of death was a cerebral hemorrhage.[32]

Mike Davenport was a star athlete who played football and baseball for Georgia Military College in Milledgeville, GA. During a baseball game in Milledgeville on April 8, 1922, against a freshman team from Georgia Tech, the center fielder collided with the shortstop as both went after a pop fly. Both players were knocked unconscious. Although the infielder quickly recovered, Davenport did not. He was taken to a local hospital, where it was found that he was suffering from a severe concussion. While surgery performed on April 11 seemed to help somewhat, Davenport died the morning of April 16 without regaining consciousness.[33]

Leroy Kellogg, second baseman on the Princeton University freshman baseball team, suffered a cut on his left side while sliding into second base during a game in Princeton, NJ, in early May 1923. Although the injury was treated at the university infirmary, he became seriously ill from a septic infection two weeks later. He died from blood poisoning on June 9, 1923.[34]

Frank "Lanky" Caldwell, 18, first baseman for Yorkville High School, York, SC, was fatally injured while sliding into second during an away game against Clover High School in Clover, SC, on May 8, 1924. In the course of his slide, Caldwell suffered a severe blow to the back when he collided with the Clover second baseman. At first, it appeared that Caldwell was not badly injured, but when he collapsed a short while later, he was taken to a hospital in nearby Rock Hill, SC. He died from his injuries on May 12.[35]

Richard Matthews, 14, cut his left foot while sliding into a base during a game in Greenfield, PA, on May 11, 1927. He was taken to the St. Joseph's Hospital in Pittsburgh two days later after falling ill from an infection. He died May 16 from blood poisoning.[36]

John "Johnny Praz" Przeciemski, 22, a semipro right fielder for the Archer Daniels Midland Oil Company in West New York, NJ, suffered a ruptured windpipe when he collided with teammate Harold Curtis while both were chasing a fly ball during practice before a game on October 11, 1936. Przeciemski died a few hours after the accident.[37]

Marvin Carey, 12, was injured while running out a hit during a game between classes at Perry (NY) High School on May 30, 1937. Carey's intestines were ruptured when the fielder's head struck him in the abdomen. Carey died shortly after the accident.[38]

Donald Fromelt, 21, center fielder with the Webster (SD) Baseball Club, was fatally injured in a regional championship playoff game in Bristol, SD, on August 22, 1937, when he collided with Herluf Andersen, the second baseman, as both went after a fly to shallow center. Fromelt died almost instantly from a broken neck.[39]

Robert Rodriguez, 26, serving a sentence at Folsom State Prison in Folsom, CA, for petty theft, died from internal injuries suffered while sliding into third base during a prison game around May 4, 1939.[40]

Harry Newman, 27, died from a broken neck shortly after colliding with another outfielder as both were chasing a fly ball after a sandlot game in Detroit, MI, on May 30, 1939. One of Newman's three brothers, all of whom had left the field just moments before the accident to eat dinner, commented later, "Harry said that he wanted to stay around a little while to catch flies." Lawrence Sweet, the other player involved in the collision, was uninjured.[41]

Howard Swamp, 14, shortstop on the Menasha, WI, Junior Boys Baseball League all-star team, collided with left fielder James Suess as both were pursuing a fly to shallow left during the league's annual all-star game on Sunday morning, August 30, 1942. Swamp dove for the ball, ramming his head against Suess' thigh. He was transported immediately to a local hospital, where he died around 2:00 P.M. that same day. Cause of death was "a basal skull fracture and cranial bleeding." Sadly, the young player's father, Andrew Swamp, 41, had hanged himself in the local police lockup just three days earlier. The elder Swamp had been picked up for questioning concerning the theft of a ring and an electric shaver. He was found with his belt around his neck hanging from his cell bars at 6:45 P.M. on August 27. Joint funeral services were held for father and son.[42]

Daniel Kuechle, 26, a member of the Bettinger's Coal baseball team, injured his right knee sliding into home during a twilight-league game against the Horsehead Ale team in Buffalo, NY, on May 23, 1947. The injury appeared to be minor and Kuechle continued to play the game. Several days later, though, he found that a blood vessel had broken and inflammation had set in. The condition grew so bad that he was taken to a local hospital on May 31, where the attending physician performed two operations in an attempt to save his life. Kuechle died on June 13, three weeks after the initial injury.[43]

Bill Ferguson, 15, was fatally injured when he collided with another outfielder during a league all-star game in Vinita, OK, on June 16, 1969. The head of the other player struck Ferguson above his right eye, causing severe head injuries and knocking him unconscious.

Ferguson stopped breathing and had to be revived by mouth-to-mouth resuscitation by one of the coaches. He died on the way to a local hospital.[44]

Dennis Clement, 15, ruptured his spleen when he collided with another player at second base during a game at Pembroke Academy in Allenstown, NH, on May 7, 1979. After walking off the field, he was taken to a local hospital by his parents. He died on May 17, a week and a half after the accident.[45]

Scott Halbrook, 19, a freshman outfielder for the Oregon State University baseball team, suffered a "basal skull fracture" that damaged his brain when he collided with shortstop Steve Smith as they were chasing a fly ball during practice in Corvallis, OR, on March 2, 1982. Halbrook, who was playing left field at the time, and Smith were at a full run when Smith's nose and forehead struck Halbrook on the temple. Smith suffered a broken nose and a black eye as a result of the accident. Halbrook remained in a coma until his death on March 5.[46]

Kriston Palomo, 16, sophomore first baseman for the St. Bernard High School baseball team, Playa del Rey, CA, was standing near the base line fielding a pop fly during a game on May 3, 1997, in Torrance, CA, when the baserunner from rival Bishop Montgomery High School collided with him. Palomo had his head up as he waited for the ball when the bill of the runner's batting helmet struck him in the throat, crushing his larynx. He went into full cardiac arrest and had to be put on life-support before being rushed to a local hospital. Palomo was declared brain dead the following morning. His organs were donated before he was taken off life support during the early morning hours of May 5.[47]

Brendan Grant, 18, playing left field instead of his usual third base, collided with center fielder Charles Synnott as both pursued a fly ball during the sixth inning of a Belmont (MA) Senior Babe Ruth League night game on June 27, 2001. A teammate noticed that Grant was struggling to breathe as he lay on the ground and yelled for help. Paramedics arrived and stabilized him before he was taken to a local hospital. The young player died a short time later in the hospital emergency room from a fractured larynx and blunt trauma to his neck.[48]

6. Health-Related Fatalities

From the middle of the nineteenth century through the first half of the twentieth, a public debate raged as to the value of competitive sports. It was during this period that the popularity of organized athletic competition grew rapidly in both the United States and Europe, and some questioned the public's obsession with these contests. Baseball, football, basketball, tennis, rowing, cycling, and distance running all had their proponents and detractors.

Much of the opposition centered around fears that the physical health of the young people who engaged in these activities was being compromised. While most physicians and physical educators at the time generally agreed that moderate exercise was beneficial to a population growing more sedentary, some argued that athletes were endangering their lives through the stresses and strains placed on the body during intense athletic competition.

Of particular concern among opponents of excessive "athleticism" was the impact of physical exertion upon the heart. "The athlete's heart is frequently badly strained," claimed University of Illinois president E. J. James in 1905, "and the work tells upon the strongest constitution. In after life, when the body should be the strongest, the undermined system collapses and the athlete fills an early grave from heart disease, consumption, or some other disease induced by overexertion."[1]

It is quite understandable that the heart should attract the most attention. "The heart was the most obviously vital of organs, and the one whose functioning, in the form of accelerated beat, was most clearly affected by exercise," explains biomedical historian James C. Whorton. "Heart attack victims were often stricken while engaged in exercise or work, and even though athletes completing a game or race were not experiencing cardiac failure, their appearance of pained breathlessness and exhaustion aroused an uneasy wonder in the spectator."[2]

In 1899 a Swedish physician studying cross-country skiers before and after racing identified a condition he termed "athlete's heart." As Whorton describes it, "The heart of the trained athlete does present different clinical data than that of the 'normal' person. The athletic heart is larger, beats less frequently, often exhibits murmurs and a diffuse impulse, and is sometimes subject to arrhythmias."[3]

Many at the time thought that "athlete's heart" was the cause of sudden death among competitive sportsmen or the basis for their physical deterioration and early death after retirement from athletic competition. It was only with the advent of modern diagnostic techniques developed later in the twentieth century that this belief was proven to be false. Indeed, as we now know, "athlete's heart" is a perfectly natural phenomena in which "the heart adapts to physical demands by enlarging, especially the left ventricle. Enlargement increases the cardiac output, the amount of blood pumped with each beat of the heart.... Importantly, cases of death occurring during physical activity are not caused by athletic heart syndrome, but by undiagnosed heart disorders."[4]

Even with our current medical knowledge, the public is still shocked when an athlete in prime physical condition dies during or immediately after a game. How could someone so healthy, so vital, suddenly die like that? While such incidents are relatively rare — one study found that the rate of sudden death among high school and college athletes in the United States is less than one in 100,000 per year — these deaths gain wide publicity in part because of their rarity. If such fatalities were an everyday occurrence, they would be much less news-worthy.[5]

As indicated above, the most common cause of non-impact sudden death among athletes is an undetected heart disorder. Less common are sudden deaths due to the rupture of an artery, an asthma attack, or a brain aneurysm. And, among modern-day athletes, drugs and nutritional supplements may be contributing factors as well.[6]

Major League Fatalities

Just 21 years old at the time of his passing, **Jim Creighton**, pitcher for the Brooklyn (NY) Excelsiors, was one of baseball's first superstars. As described by noted baseball historian John Thorn, Creighton, who is credited with being the first pitcher to snap his wrist while delivering the ball, "possessed an unprecedented combination of speed, spin and command that virtually defined the position for all those who followed."[7]

During an October 14, 1862, game, however, Creighton was covering second base, not pitching. It was to be his last contest. As the most widely circulated story goes, he injured himself batting during the middle innings. According to teammate John Chapman, in an account he told years after the fact, "I was present at the game between the Excelsiors and the Unions of Morrisana at which Jim Creighton injured himself. He did it hitting out a home run. When he had crossed the rubber he turned to George Flanley and said, 'I must have snapped my belt,' and George said, 'I guess not.' It turned out that he had suffered a fatal injury. Nothing could be done for him, and baseball met with a most severe loss."[8]

But Creighton was also an avid cricket player, and herein lies a dispute as to his death. Baseball in the 1860s was still vying with cricket as the "national pastime." Even as late as 1881 when professional baseball was well established and the game was being played in every village and hamlet in the country, the *New York Times* argued that "there is really reason to believe that base-ball is gradually dying out in this country. It has been openly announced by an athletic authority that what was once called the national game is being steadily superseded by cricket."[9]

So when Creighton died just days after the October 14 baseball match, some in the base-ball establishment, fearing that the sudden demise of one of its stars would blacken the reputation of the game, quickly pointed to cricket as the source of Creighton's fatal injury. Thus, in a blatant attempt to shift the blame to baseball's chief rival, Dr. J. B. Jones, president of the Brooklyn Excelsiors, claimed later in 1862 that his pitching ace had sustained his fatal injury in a cricket match played several days before the October 14 baseball game.[10]

Quite possibly, Creighton's swing — described by John Thorn as "in the manner of the day, with hands separated on the bat, little or no turn of the wrists, and incredible torque applied by the twisting motion of the upper body" — aggravated what is now believed to have been a pre-existing inguinal hernia. Commonly called a "rupture," the only treatment for a hernia at that time was the wearing of a truss, a belt-like supportive device designed to keep the intestines from protruding though the abdominal wall. Creighton, who was probably warned by his physicians not to engage in strenuous physical activity, collapsed during the October 14 contest and had to be carried to his home. The unfortunate player lingered for several days in great agony before dying of a "strangulated intestine" on October 18.[11]

Sometimes what an athlete puts into his or her body can lead to disastrous results. Such was the case with Baltimore Orioles rookie pitcher, **Steve Bechler**, who, at age 23, died during early spring training in Fort Lauderdale, FL, in 2003.

Bechler had just three major league appearances under his belt when he reported overweight and out of shape to the Orioles' training camp in mid–February 2003. During the final portion of the morning conditioning drills on February 16, manager Mike Hargrove noticed that Bechler was in distress, "looking ashen and leaning against a fence." One of the

Many considered Jim Creighton to be baseball's first superstar. His untimely death at the age of 21 in 1862 shocked the baseball world. The baseball establishment attempted to blame his death on the sport of cricket, baseball's competitor as the National Pastime (courtesy National Baseball Hall of Fame Library, Cooperstown, NY).

trainers sent for a cart to transport Bechler to the clubhouse, where he was given fluids. An ambulance was called when the young right-hander showed no improvement. Shortly after noon he was taken to a local hospital.[12]

His health deteriorated dramatically during that day and night, his temperature at one point reaching 108 degrees. He was also having difficulty breathing, so physicians opened an airway and placed him on a respirator. Various organs began to fail, resulting in Bechler's death at 10:10 the following morning. The initial diagnosis was "multi-organ failure due to heatstroke."[13]

But there were complicating factors in his death. A bottle of a weight-loss supplement containing ephedra was discovered in Bechler's locker, and traces of the appetite suppressant were found in his stomach. Several weeks after Bechler's death, the Broward County, FL, medical examiner, Dr. Joshua Perper, issued an official autopsy report. "It is my professional opinion that the toxicity of ephedra played a significant role in the death of Mr. Bechler, although it's impossible to define mathematically the contribution of each one of the factors in his unfortunate death due to heatstroke," he concluded. These other factors included "abnormal liver function and mild hypertension," his weight problem, and the fact he was not used to south Florida's warm weather, reported to be 81 degrees with 74 percent humidity the morning he fell ill.[14]

Minor League Fatalities

Robert "Bob" Osgood, 19-year-old catcher for the Marion (OH) Cubs of the Class D Ohio-Indiana League, had been with his club only three days when he suddenly collapsed in the visitor's dugout during a rain delay before a game against the Richmond (IN) Braves on May 11, 1948. Earlier that evening he had been running in the outfield during pre-game warm-ups and had returned to the dugout with his teammates when the rain started. According to Lewis Bekeza, the team's manager, Osgood looked ill just before he passed out. Various attempts to revive the young player failed, and he was declared dead about an hour after collapsing.[15]

An autopsy revealed that Osgood had died of heart failure. Apparently he had suffered from heart problems since childhood, a fact that had almost ended his career in high school. As a student in Somerville, MA, he was not allowed to play any sports because of his heart condition until his mother convinced school authorities to allow him to join the baseball team. He became one of the outstanding high school players in the greater Boston area. In addition, Osgood had suffered from the flu shortly before joining the Cubs. He told his roommate that he had been hospitalized and had left his previous team, the Fayetteville (NC) Cubs of the Class B Tri-State League, because of illness.[16]

Herbert Allen "Herb" Gorman, the San Diego (CA) Padres' 27-year-old left fielder, was excited about starting for the first time that 1953 season. Acquired by the Class AAA Pacific Coast League Padres the year before, Gorman, who had one plate appearance as a pinch hitter for the St. Louis Cardinals in 1952, was in his seventh season of organized ball. When legendary Padres' manager Francis "Lefty" O'Doul penciled him in to start in the first game of a doubleheader against the Hollywood (CA) Stars on April 5, the outfielder seized the opportunity given him by hitting one double in the second inning and another in the fourth, driving in the Padres' first run in the process.[17]

Unknown to either player or manager, though, was just how ill Gorman was. The first inkling that something was wrong was when Gorman, without O'Doul's knowledge, went into the clubhouse during the bottom of the fifth inning complaining of stomach pains. The trainer gave him some medication to treat what was thought to be indigestion. Gorman resumed playing and was on deck later that inning when it ended with a teammate being gunned down at the plate trying to score.[18]

When he took his left field position at the top of the sixth inning, though, he suddenly doubled over with severe chest pains. Gorman's best friend on the team, shortstop Buddy Peterson, rushed to the stricken player. Although Gorman protested that he was "all right," he clearly was not. When manager O'Doul learned of Gorman's distress, he halted play and ordered his left fielder to the clubhouse. Peterson and several other teammates started to help Gorman off the field when he "broke away as he neared the bench and jumped over the retaining screen under his own power, walked unescorted through the dugout and into the clubhouse, where he was administered first aid, including oxygen, by Trainer Les Cook." The game continued with the Padres eventually losing 4 to 2.[19]

A physician attending the game was summoned to the clubhouse, where he found Gorman unconscious. Fearing that the Padres player was suffering a heart attack, the physician immediately called an ambulance. Gorman's wife, who sat in the stands unaware of the events taking place, was told by club officials that her husband had taken ill. Bill Starr, the president of the Padres, drove her to the hospital while her husband was being rushed there by ambulance.[20]

Gorman died about 3:30 P.M. on the way to the hospital. An autopsy confirmed that he had suffered a fatal heart attack caused when "a massive blood clot, possibly forming over a period of time ... reached the heart." His teammates voted unanimously to postpone the second game of the doubleheader while nearly 4,000 fans filed out of the stadium in silence when his death was announced over the public address system. Gorman's number 25 was retired by the Padres as a tribute to the fallen player.[21]

A little over a year later, another health-related fatality occurred in the minor leagues when **Charles "Mac" Smith**, 23-year-old utility infielder for the Hagerstown (MD) Packets of the Class B Piedmont League, died shortly after hitting a single and driving in a run during the fifth inning of a home game against the Portsmouth (VA) Merrimacs on July 2, 1954. Smith, who was playing third base that evening, began feeling dizzy immediately after reaching first. He called time before collapsing unconscious on the field.[22]

The ex-Marine, who was awarded two Purple Hearts, a Navy Cross, and a Presidential Citation for his service during the Korean war, died en route to a local hospital. Although Smith appeared to be healthy, he had contracted malaria during his time overseas, and doctors concluded that it, combined "with complications," caused his death.[23]

Club officials decided to delay announcing Smith's death until after the game. The Packets went on to win 8 to 6, with Smith's RBI in the fifth turning out to be the winning run. The game scheduled for the following evening was postponed out of respect for the fallen player.[24]

Millard Fillmore "Dixie" Howell, a right-hander once described by Chicago White Sox manager Marty Marion as "the salvation of our bull pen," languished in the minors for years with just a cup of coffee with the Cleveland Indians in 1940 and another with the Cincinnati Reds in 1949 before being called up by the White Sox in early June 1955. He appeared in 35 games that season, winning 8 and losing 3 with a 2.92 ERA. He remained on the Chicago staff until early 1958, compiling a lifetime major league record of 19 wins, 15 losses, and 19 saves, with one of the defeats occurring during his brief stint with the Reds.[25]

In May 1958, Chicago sent their aging reliever to its Class AAA affiliate, the Indianapolis (IN) Indians of the American Association. Howell spent the next two seasons trying to make it back to the majors. He was still with Indianapolis in early 1960, having gone 6 and 8 with the club the season before. Shortly after workouts on March 18 at the Indians' spring training camp in Hollywood, FL, Howell began experiencing chest pains. Indians general manager Ray Johnston called a doctor, who immediately sent the 40-year-old pitcher to a local hospital. Although initially showing signs of improvement, Howell died of a heart attack about six hours after the onset of his chest pains.[26]

Ronaldo Romero was showing great promise as a starting pitcher for the Gastonia (NC) Rangers of the Class A South Atlantic League. Having gone 5 and 5 with the club in 1989, he was 2 and 0 with a 1.35 ERA in the his first nine games of the 1990 season. So when the 19-year-old right-hander had given up 7 runs on 5 hits in the first two innings of a May 14 road game against the Fayetteville (NC) Generals, it was apparent that something was wrong. Sitting in the visitors' dugout at the top of the third, he began having difficulty breathing and complained that his heart was fluttering. Suddenly, he had a heart seizure. Emergency cardiopulmonary resuscitation was applied on the spot before the young player was transported to a nearby hospital. The attending physician pronounced him dead at 8:45 P.M., about half an hour after he had collapsed in the dugout. Although the game was immediately suspended, fans and his teammates were not informed of his death until the following morning.[27]

Before the start of that evening's game there was no indication that anything was wrong with Romero. In fact, Rangers trainer Tom Tisdale said afterwards that Romero told him "he was the strongest he felt" that season. An autopsy revealed that Romero had suffered from an enlarged heart which, according to Dr. Thomas Clark of the North Carolina Medical Examiner's Office, "is consistent with sudden death." But questions remained as to contributory causes. The medical examiner for Cumberland County, NC, found "four small white tablets" with Romero and sent these off for analysis. Suspicions were aroused.[28]

Team officials speculated that these tablets were Supac, an over-the-counter pain medication containing "a mixtures [sic] of aspirin, acetaminophen and 33 milligrams of caffeine." Although Rangers trainer Tisdale said he had not given Romero any Supac before the game, it was commonly used in the clubhouse. Team manager Orlando Gomez was outraged at the suggestion of drug use. "I think it's a sin to accuse him of drug abuse. He was a clean kid, a very clean kid," he insisted. "I don't think anyone should point a finger toward drug abuse."[29]

Two weeks later, Gomez was proven right. North Carolina Medical Examiner Clark reported that, although "no postmortem tests could determine what caused Romero's enlarged heart," drugs were definitely not involved. While traces of aspirin and caffeine consistent with the consumption of Supac were found in Romero's system, the toxicology test "does not show that he had any drugs present that may have contributed to his death."[30]

Black Baseball Fatalities — Heart Attacks

John Garcia, 28, catcher for the Cuban Giants, died catching a towering pop foul during the bottom of the second inning in game in Jamaica, NY, on October 1, 1904, against a local team known as the Woodhulls. Garcia caught the ball, but it rolled out of his glove when he fell face-first on the ground. His teammates picked him up and carried him to a hospital located across the street from the ball field. The examining physician, seeing that the player was already dead, opined a short time later that "the excitement of the game, perhaps the tension he was under while he was waiting for the ball to land, had killed him."[31]

George Washington, 34, hurler for the Philadelphia Giants, collapsed and died of "heart disease" while dressing in the clubhouse before a game he was to pitch in Winsted, CT, on July 1, 1908. He had complained of not feeling well since pitching in Hoboken, NJ, three days earlier. According to press accounts, Washington's death "cast a hoodoo over the Winsted team," causing them to lose 7 to 1.[32]

Clyde Nelson, 32, utility infielder for the Indianapolis Clowns, was covering first base in the second game of a doubleheader against the Philadelphia Stars at Shibe Park on the evening of July 25, 1949. Having won the opening game 6 to 4, it looked as if the Clowns might take the second as well. The visitors were holding a slim 2 to 1 lead in the bottom of the ninth when Milt Smith, the Stars' second baseman, popped the ball up in foul territory between home and first. Both Len Pigg, the Clowns' catcher, and Nelson raced for the ball. Just as Pigg made the catch, Nelson suddenly crumpled to the ground beside him. He was carried into the clubhouse where a physician worked in vain to revive the fallen player. Nelson was pronounced dead of a heart attack a short time later.[33]

Amateur Fatalities — Heart Attacks

Bob Robert collapsed and died at second base while running out a hit in a game near Dooly, GA, on September 15, 1883. According to one of his teammates, Robert had complained of "a fulness in his breathing or breast" just moments before he batted.[34]

Orlando Poe, 12, son of an Army general, died of heart disease on March 30, 1889, shortly after a game in Detroit, MI. Poe, whose parents were out of town at the time, played in spite of being told not to do so by his physician.[35]

Harvey George, 21, was in the act of pitching in the bottom half of the first inning of a June 30, 1895, city league game in Decatur, IN, between his Marion, IN, team and the local squad, when he suddenly died on the mound. It was the opening game of the season and over 3,000 fans were in attendance. Some felt that his heavy smoking contributed to his death.[36]

Olin Francis, 29, died from "valvular heart trouble" while "executing difficult curves" during a game in Bristol, VA, on May 17, 1905.[37]

Edward W. Johnston, 28, suffered heart failure shortly after running out a ball in a game in Chicago, IL, on May 22, 1905. As he turned toward the bench after being called out, he pitched forward and died a few moments later.[38]

Ben Rice, a student at the Sparks (GA) Collegiate Institute, collapsed and died of heart failure while playing baseball on the school grounds on the afternoon of April 20, 1908.[39]

William D. Schutte, 17, caught during team practice in a park in Knoxville, PA, on the evening of June 17, 1908. Schutte and several other players remained in the park after practice to talk about their play. Realizing that they had stayed after the 10:00 P.M. park closing, they hurried to leave before park officials confronted them. Someone playing a practical joke jumped out of the bushes and yelled at the boys, causing them to run in different directions. Two of Schutte's friends were concerned that they could not find him afterwards and began a search. They found him lying dead several blocks from the park. Schutte, who suffered from heart disease, was believed to have died from heart failure.[40]

John Stauffer, 35, was pitching for his Duquesne Steel Mill team in a game near Pittsburgh, PA, on September 4, 1909. After striking out the last batter in the bottom of the fourth, he walked to the bench, where he collapsed after sitting down. A physician was summoned, but Stauffer died from "heart disease" before help could arrive.[41]

Fred D. Redahan, 16, died immediately after playing in a baseball game in Portland, ME, on the afternoon of March 23, 1910. Apparently he died of "weakness of the heart" caused by a lengthy, debilitating illness.[42]

Walter J. Garson, 34, died from a blood clot in his heart while he was playing ball with his 5-year-old daughter in the front yard of their Cleveland, OH, home on May 29, 1910. Garson, who was under a doctor's care for an undisclosed illness, began feeling ill and decided to go inside the house, collapsing on the way in. A physician found Garson dead when he arrived. It was one of two game-related fatalities in Cleveland that day (*see* **Frank Kostchryz**).[43]

Sherman K. Rott, a Marine bugler stationed at the Charleston Navy Yard, played shortstop for his unit's team in an August 13, 1910, Charleston (SC) City League game against a team from the local Army base. Early in the game, he had doubled and scored his team's first run. At the top of the fourth, with the Navy team down 2 to 1, Rott hit a single to right field. The next two batters advanced him to third. With two out, his teammate hit a ground ball to second. Rott raced home as the fielder threw to first for the final out. Just after crossing the plate, Rott fell to his knees and then crumpled to the ground. The Army team catcher and the Navy's pitcher and manager heard him exclaim, "Oh, my heart!" as he collapsed. A navy surgeon and a physician in the stands rushed to Rott's aid, but the player died about five minutes later. Rott, who had served in the Marines for several years, was scheduled to leave the military at the end of the year due to poor health.[44]

Robert O. Mahaffey, 19, collapsed and died on the pitcher's mound during the fifth inning of a park game in Chicago, IL, on April 18, 1914. With two runs already in and two on, Mahaffey was "pitching hard" according to one account. An inquest two days later concluded he had died of "heart disease."[45]

Charles Clarke, 18, was on second base in the fifth inning of a game between church teams in Harlem, NY, on June 7, 1914, when a teammate hit a line drive to center. Just after scoring on the hit, Clarke collapsed behind home plate. An ambulance was summoned, but Clarke died of heart failure before help could arrive.[46]

William Wine, 25, a soldier stationed at Fort Totten in Queens, NY, was thrown out at first to end the inning during a game against the Whitestone Columbia Club in Whitestone, NY, on June 12, 1915. Walking past the bag toward his position in right, Wine collapsed and died just past the infield.[47]

Louis Fetyk, 22, with his team behind in the sixth inning, hit what appeared to be a home run to the outfield and began racing around the bases during a game in Van Cortlandt Park in the Bronx, NY, on June 11, 1921. Just as Fetyk rounded second, he suddenly collapsed on the base path. A physician called to the scene found that Fetyk had died from heart failure.[48]

A. F. Leeiz, 51, suffered a heart attack while playing in a sandlot game in Chicago, IL, on October 11, 1931. He died in the ambulance on the way to a local hospital.[49]

Michael J. Burke, 50, one of the founders of the semipro California State League and manager of that league's San Mateo (CA) Blues, died of "dilatation of the heart due to over exercise" shortly after a four-inning contest on June 11, 1933, in which he pitched a complete game for his Elks Lodge against a team of San Mateo city hall employees. Burke, who had run hard to first after hitting a single during the third inning, was joking and laughing on the way to the clubhouse after the game when he suddenly became ill. He was able to call out for help before collapsing. Teammates and the city's fire chief administered first aid until a physician arrived. The doctor, after examining Burke, sent him immediately to a local hospital, where he died about 30 minutes after arriving.[50]

Stanley M. Rees, 38, who was 1 and 0 in two games with the Washington Senators in 1918, was taking batting practice with friends in a Lexington, KY, park on the morning of August 29, 1937, when he began feeling overheated. Declaring that he wanted to go home, Rees was helped to his car by a teammate. The former major league left-hander suddenly fainted while seated in his automobile. A friend drove Rees to a local hospital, where he died of heart failure shortly after arrival.[51]

Ralph W. "Paddy" Kreitz, 55, who caught seven games with the Chicago White Sox in 1911, hit a single and was running to first in an annual Old Timers Game in Blue Lake Park, Portland, OR, on July 20, 1941, when he suddenly grabbed his side and collapsed on the base path. He died of heart failure about half an hour later.[52]

Elmer Gene Keever, 17, the starting pitcher in a high school game in Asheville, NC, on May 5, 1958, strode to the batter's box in the top of the fifth inning with the scored tied at two apiece. After taking the first two pitches, he stepped away from the plate and suddenly collapsed. Coaches attempted to revive him without success. Keever was pronounced dead on arrival at a local hospital, "apparently the victim of a heart attack."[53]

John F. Jones, 39, was playing in a game in Central Park, New York, when he died of a heart attack on the evening of June 11, 1958.[54]

Brian Korbin, 9, had a heart attack while playing in a Little League game in Charlottesville, VA, on the afternoon of May 8, 1993. He died while being treated in the University of Virginia Hospital emergency room later that evening.[55]

Nicholas A. Graham, 19, collapsed during a game in Providence, RI, on July 18, 1998. He died later that evening at a local hospital. An autopsy found the cause of death to be "abnormal heartbeat due to an enlarged heart."[56]

Ryan Garrison, 12, who was playing second base in a tournament game in Racine, WI, on the evening of April 21, 2000, suddenly collapsed on the field while warming up between innings. Attempts to revive him failed, and he was transported to a local hospital, where he was pronounced dead. An autopsy revealed that the youngster died of cardiac arrhythmia caused by an enlarged heart.[57]

Jason Malone, 11, was waiting his turn to bat during the sixth inning of a game on June 29, 2002, in Berea, OH, when he told a teammate he needed water. When the young third baseman and pitcher for his Berea Yankees team stood up, he immediately collapsed. A rescue squad from the local fire department worked at reviving him for 25 minutes before taking him to a local hospital. He died of heart failure about an hour later.[58]

Scott Rosenberger, 17, had just finished running during warm-ups with his Elkville, IL, high school team on March 24, 2003, when he collapsed on the field. Paramedics unsuccessfully attempted to revive the third baseman. He was rushed to a local hospital, where he was declared dead later that day. An autopsy revealed that he suffered from cardiomyopathy, a condition in which an inflamed heart muscle does not work as well as it should.[59]

Rudie Bachman, 15, collapsed at the end of an American Legion League game in Stanford, IL, around 7:00 P.M. on June 8, 2004. A first baseman and relief pitcher during that evening's contest, Bachman was transported to a hospital in Normal, IL, where he was pronounced dead later that evening. A preliminary autopsy revealed that Bachman had "scar tissue on his heart" which "could have contributed to an irregular heartbeat."[60]

Matthew Miulli, 17, had just run a mile during tryouts for a Tampa, FL, high school team on January 19, 2005, when he began feeling ill. As he sat in the bleachers, he suddenly collapsed. Coaches and paramedics attempted to revive him. He was taken to a local hospital, where he was pronounced dead later that afternoon. A preliminary autopsy revealed he "died from congenital heart disease that included a narrowing of the valve that feeds the aorta."[61]

Robbie Levine, 9, was running the bases during drills with his Merrick, NY, Little League team, when he collapsed near home plate on the evening of September 27, 2005. His father, the team's coach, rushed to his son's side and attempted to revive him. He was taken to a nearby hospital, where he was pronounced dead later that night. The physician in the emergency room determined that the youngster had died from "cardiac arrest."[62]

Amateur Fatalities — Other Health-Related Causes

John Emmet Crowder, 17, was watching a baseball game in Richmond, VA, on June 11, 1877, when one of the players asked him to take his place on the field. During his at-bat, he hit what other participants said would have been a home run. But while circling the bases, he collapsed suddenly and died a short time later. Death was thought to be caused "by rupture of a blood-vessel in the brain."[63]

Martin Head, 16, was playing the outfield in a sandlot game in Johnston, RI, on May 19, 1878. According to one account, he was in pursuit of a fly ball when he had "to jump into a hole or low place in the field." After throwing the ball back to the pitcher, he resumed his position in the outfield, where he "fell to the ground, expiring instantly.... The cause of death is attributed to the rupture of a blood vessel in consequence of over-exertion at play." Other papers reported that he fell dead while "running to the home base" due to "having burst a blood-vessel."[64]

John Hilton died from heat exhaustion during a game in Huntsville, AL, on March 10, 1905.[65]

A. Harten, a station agent with the Chicago, Rock Island, and Pacific Railroad, was playing first base in a game on July 9, 1905, in Altoona, IA, when he "was stricken with apoplexy" and died.[66]

Orrie McWilliams, 15, was eating a piece of candy while catching during practice before a 1:00 P.M. game at his high school in Deep River, IA, on April 19, 1907. When the pitcher threw a fastball, he inhaled the candy, causing it to lodge in his throat. A teacher standing nearby told him to go to a doctor, but he collapsed on the way and had to be carried to the doctor's office. He died before the physician could dislodge the candy.[67]

John R. Perry, 23, who was playing the outfield for a Knights of Pythias baseball team in St. Louis, MO, on May 24, 1908, collapsed after fielding and then throwing a ball to second base. He died before an ambulance could arrive. One account said he was "overcome with heat," another that it was "overexertion and heart disease," while his burial announcement said he died from "congestion of brain," an archaic term that may have meant meningitis.[68]

Louis Sweetstein, 13, died the morning of May 8, 1914, a day after having played ball with friends for several hours in Detroit, MI. The evening before his death, he was "seized with convulsions." According to the coroner, who decided not hold an inquest, the youngster's death was due to "playing base ball too strenuously and too long."[69]

Landon Bell, 23, pitcher for the Franklin Electric Company team, hit a home run during an industrial league game in Middletown, CT, on July 31, 1915. Just after crossing the plate, he "complained of a stitch in his side, but when advised to rest, laughed it off." He died a few minutes later due to "heated over-exertion" just as he resumed his position on the pitching mound.[70]

Devin Beck, 11, was practicing at first base before a Little League game in Ammon, ID, on the evening of May 24, 2000, when a ball thrown by a teammate struck him on the side of his neck. The youngster took a couple of steps, collapsed, stopped breathing, and soon went into cardiac arrest. Paramedics were able to get his heart beating again, and he was transported to a local hospital where he was declared dead shortly before 10:00 that night. At first it was thought that the blow had crushed his trachea, but no damage or obstruction was found. A physician later concluded that the boy had died from a ruptured aneurysm that may have been coincidental to the ball striking the child's neck. "The aneurysm is clearly one of the likely reasons this happened," said Idaho Falls, ID, pediatrician Dr. Eric Olson, but "this is not the fault of baseball. This is just a freak accident." While the blow may have triggered the event, it could have happened at any time, while "jogging, walking down the street or reading a book."[71]

7. Fatalities from Weather and Field Conditions

Willie Tasby had a problem. A journeyman outfielder with the Baltimore Orioles, Boston Red Sox, Washington Senators, and Cleveland Indians from 1958 to 1963, he was absolutely convinced that lightning would strike him if he wore his metal-cleated shoes during stormy weather. With two out in the top of the ninth inning of a July 19, 1959, game against the Detroit Tigers, the solution suddenly came to him as he sat anxiously in the Orioles dugout during a 36-minute rain delay — no shoes, no lightning strike. Tasby dashed to his center field position when the game resumed. Quickly removing his spikes, he handed them to Albie Pearson, the right fielder, to place in foul territory. Then he stood there expectantly as water soaked his stockinged feet. Fortunately for him, the Tigers' Lou Berberet fouled out to end the game, thus preserving the Orioles' one-run lead and saving Tasby the embarrassment of running shoeless after a fly ball.[1]

Lightning is a very real danger to anyone standing in an open field like a baseball park. In the years from 1959 to 2004, reported deaths from lightning in the United States alone totaled 3,728, with most occurring in the west and south during the summer months. Hundreds have died from lightning strikes while engaged in or watching sports. One survey covering a ten-year period from 1976 to 1986 found that an estimated 245 individuals died during a sporting or recreational event in the United States. Water sports led all other activities with 118 fatalities, followed by golf (32), camping or picnicking (28), hiking (16), baseball or softball (8), and football (8). Other activities accounted for the remaining 35 deaths.[2]

A variety of factors increase the odds of being struck by lightning, including the use of metal objects such as metal bleachers and metal bats. Since the number of lightning strikes is highest before and after the peak of a storm, not during it, and since lightning has been known to strike more than 30 minutes after the last peal of thunder, many athletes and spectators wait too long to seek shelter or retake the field well before all danger has passed. Considering these facts, perhaps Willie Tasby's fear was not as irrational as it might at first appear to have been.[3]

Sometimes the conditions of the playing field itself have contributed to a player's demise. Abandoned lots or open fields often contain rocks, bricks, bottles, broken glass, and other refuse that can inflict injury and death. The ground is usually uneven as well. Occasionally a player has suffered fatal injury falling into a hole or a depression in the earth. And, especially in an urban setting, vehicular traffic presents it own special dangers.

While there are no confirmed deaths due to wildlife, there have been a number of incidents over the years that involve snakes and bees. According to one account appearing in the

New York Times, a game in Long Branch, NJ, on April 24, 1889, was interrupted when a center fielder in pursuit of a fly ball fell head-first into a nest of 32 garter snakes. He lay prostrate on the ground as other players killed 26 of the reptiles with their bats. The game was postponed until the next day. Along the same lines, the *Washington Post* reported on a practice game at the University of North Carolina in Chapel Hill on October 15, 1928, during the course of which outfielder Henry Sinclair was bitten on his finger by "a small brown spotted snake" as he bent to retrieve a home run ball in the weeds. When he returned to the field and began to feel dizzy, the coach ordered him to open his wound and suck out the poison. Sinclair was then sent to the university infirmary, where medical personnel cauterized the wound. The article ends on this hopeful note: "The bite did not prove serious and Sinclair expects to resume practice in a few days."[4]

Finally, an amateur league pennant was determined by a snake. In the Lawrence (MA) Suburban Twilight League championship game in Salem, NH, on July 30, 1949, the Salem Athletic Club was leading the St. Michael's Athletic Club from Andover, MA, 4 to 2 in the seventh inning. At the top of the inning, the Salem coach sent in Bruce Magoon to play shortstop. The substitute player grabbed a glove from under the bench and headed for the field. With runners on first and second after a single and a walk, a routine grounder was hit to Magoon at short. The unfortunate player muffed the play, resulting in a bases-loaded situation. Magoon called time when he felt what he thought was a sponge inside the glove. Instead he found a foot-long black snake curled up in the pocket. The agitated shortstop protested that the at-bat should be done over because the snake interfered with his fielding, but the umpires held that the rules did not permit them to change the play. St. Michael's then proceeded to score four runs, eventually winning the championship 6 to 4.[5]

More recently, a March 24, 2005, spring training game in Tucson, AZ, between the Arizona Diamondbacks and the Colorado Rockies was called after five innings because of a swarm of bees. In the bottom of that inning, the pesky insects began buzzing Rockies pitcher Darren Oliver as he took the mound. The liberal use of bug spray failed to discourage the determined attackers, so after several attempts to pitch over the next 20 minutes failed, Oliver took himself out of the game. Relief pitcher Allan Simpson had to complete the inning for the starter. When the bees returned at the top of the sixth, Diamondbacks general manager Joe Garagiola, Jr., decided to call the game, stating that it was potentially dangerous having "players worrying about [bees] and baseballs flying around the field." For his part, Oliver was convinced that the coconut oil in his hair gel was the source of the bees' attraction. "I guess I must have smelled good," explained the exasperated lefty. "It was kind of funny at first, but after a while I started getting a little nervous and scared out there."[6]

Minor League Fatalities — Weather-Related

Andy Strong of the Crowley (LA) Millers of the Class C Evangeline League was in his first season of organized ball. A high school basketball and football coach from Pittsburg, TX, the 23-year-old father of one had joined the Millers on May 28, 1951, as the team's starting center fielder.[7]

On June 16, just a couple of weeks after Strong's professional debut, the Millers traveled to Alexandria, LA, for an evening contest against the Aces. Although there was a threat of stormy weather and lightning was seen in the distance, officials decided to proceed with the game. Play was halted briefly in the fifth inning when a heavy downpour forced players and officials to scurry for the dugouts. When play resumed a short time later, there was still no lightning in the immediate vicinity.[8]

The game was tied at one apiece in the bottom of the sixth. The Aces had a runner on with two out when Millers pitcher Oscar Johnson went into his delivery. Seemingly out of nowhere, a large bolt of lightning suddenly surged horizontally across the stadium, striking and melting a reflector on a light standard in the outfield. As players raced for safety, a second bolt broke off from the first and struck Andy Strong on the top of his head. A popping sound was heard as the center fielder "crumpled to the ground while a puff of blue-black smoke drifted upward." Teammates, umpires, and a doctor rushed to Strong's assistance. Although the doctor attempted to revive Strong, it was clear that the youthful player had been killed instantly.[9]

The umpires immediately called the game. As an ambulance removed Strong's body, fans and players stood silently in complete shock at what had happened. "Some of them wandered around for over an hour before departing the park," wrote a local sports columnist, "unbelief written all over their faces." Over 2,500 fans flocked to an "Andy Strong Night" held at the Crowley stadium on June 20. Attending the tribute were Strong's widow and one-year-old son, his father, and two of his brothers.[10]

Black Baseball Fatalities — Weather-Related

William Bedford, playing second base for the Cuban Giants, an African American barnstorming team, was killed by lightning while fielding a ball during practice before a game in Atlantic City, NJ, on August 26, 1909. Details vary as to his death. In one account, "his right shoulder was torn to shreds" and his "head was cut and his cap torn to tatters." Other papers reported that "although dead when picked up, Bedford's body carries no burns or other marks of the lightning." All accounts suggest that his metal cleats and the screws that held them in place attracted the lightning. Two of Bedford's teammates, shortstop Walter Gordon and catcher Charles Follie (or Follies), were knocked down but otherwise uninjured by the bolt.[11]

Wilbur McFall and **Charlie Bolden** were killed instantly when hit by lightning as they stood near home plate waiting to bat during a sandlot game between African American teams in Danville, VA, on June 21, 1939. The catcher that stood between them was uninjured, while three other players were knocked unconscious.[12]

Amateur Fatalities — Weather-Related

Nicholas Newmayer, playing in a sandlot game in the gold mining town of Central City, CO, on June 22, 1884, was instantly killed when lightning struck him during an intense hailstorm. James Lick, also a player, was severely injured by the same bolt.[13]

Charles Jeffries, 28, outfielder and pitcher for a team in Johnstown, PA, was practicing before a game in McKeesport, PA, against a steel mill team on July 11, 1904. The day was partly cloudy, but there seemed to be no threat of storms in the immediate area. Jeffries had just reached the infield after catching a fly in the outfield and was in the act of tossing the ball to a teammate when "there was a crash of thunder followed by a vivid flash of lightning."

With over 500 fans witnessing the incident, "Jeffries threw up his hands as if to ward off a blow, then dropped to the ground." Although a physician immediately attended to Jeffries, he had been killed instantly. Two of Jeffries' teammates were slightly injured as well.[14]

Joseph Barrett, 16, playing second base in a game at a railroad roundhouse in Cumberland, MD, on July 11, 1904, was killed instantly when struck by lightning. Barrett "was hurled several feet" and two teammates were "stunned." Barrett and Jeffries (see above) were killed on the same afternoon.[15]

Albert LaPlant, 22, and his teammates were crossing the infield at the end of the sixth inning during a game played under stormy skies in St. Anthony, IA, on June 30, 1907, when lightning suddenly struck. LaPlant, second baseman for the St. Anthony's team, was killed instantly when the bolt hit him on top of his head as he walked past the pitcher's mound. It traveled down his right side, burning off both his shoes. Eight other players were knocked to the ground, but recovered within a few minutes.[16]

Carl King was killed when lightning struck near home plate during a game in Willacoochee, GA, against a team from Nashville, GA, on July 24, 1920. Five other players were injured.[17]

Thomas Cyril "Cy" Long, 24, creator of a racist newspaper comic strip that he was hoping to syndicate throughout the south and northeast, was killed by lightning while practicing before a game in Newton, NC, on July 1, 1922. Long, a recent graduate of Catholic University in Washington, DC, had just returned from a trip promoting his cartoon series featuring "Mose Bones," an African American comic figure based upon "the character and dialect of the southern darky."[18]

Donald Donovan, 17, right fielder for the Lawrence, MA, high school team, died when a bolt of lightning hit the grandstand during an evening game against a visiting team from Nashua, NH, on May 7, 1930. While waiting out a thunderstorm, Donovan and players from both teams were leaning against the protective wire screening in front of the stands. The bolt killed Donovan instantly and knocked down several other players.[19]

Henry Nemetz, 25, playing right field for a team from Gunnison, MS, was struck by lightning as he was throwing the ball back to the infield about 10 minutes into a late afternoon game in Shelby, MS, on May 26, 1932. While his clothing was scorched and burned, he was alive when carried into the clubhouse. He died there a few moments later. Four other players were slightly injured from the strike.[20]

Charles Edward Lee, 18, a member of the Pennsylvania State College freshman squad, was warming up in the outfield before a game against the university's varsity team in State College, PA, on May 29, 1933, when lightning struck him and two teammates. Lee died instantly, and Penrose Miller and Harvey Larson were hospitalized with severe injuries.[21]

Joseph Welch, 16, was a pitcher for the St. Gregory School in Detroit, MI. In a game against the St. Francis Orphan Home on July 19, 1935, Welch was struck by lightning just as he went to the pitching mound. He died a short time after reaching a local hospital. Six other players were knocked down, but were otherwise uninjured by the bolt.[22]

William Simerlein, 16, **Peter Hillstrom**, 14, and team manager **Raymond Phillips**, 40, were participating in an evening practice session with their American Legion team in Butler, WI, on July 31, 1945, when a violent storm suddenly blew up. "There was no warning at all," said one of the other participants later. "We wanted to hurry up and get in some practice, because we thought it was going to rain, but we didn't expect a thunderstorm." In an instant, lightning struck the infield near the shortstop position, tearing the clothing and shoes off of

Hillstrom, who was nearest the bolt; Simerlein, who was about 40 feet away in left field; and Phillips, the team manager, who was standing about 50 feet away. In addition, five other players were knocked down, one of them falling unconscious for nearly an hour. "It was so sudden, I didn't see any lightning at all," explained a teammate. "There was just this awful crack, than a terrible flash that blinded me, and then it rained. That was all there was to it." Townspeople, police, and medical personnel rushed to help the fallen players. Phillips, Simerlein, and Hillstrom died on the field. The other injured players were treated where they lay. Richard Johnson, 15, the most seriously injured of the survivors, was taken to a local hospital, where he came to about 45 minutes later. Dazed and confused, he was unable to talk or see until later at home.[23]

Norman Eschbach, 19, and **Stanford Buck**, 21, were playing the outfield during the first inning of an evening sandlot game on August 12, 1947, in Pennsburg, PA, when a bolt of lightning from a storm five miles away struck Eschbach in the right ear. The charge moved through the center fielder's body, emerged from his right heel, and raced along the ground before striking Buck in left field. The force of the charge melted Eschbach's eyeglasses and left him unconscious, bleeding profusely from the right ear, hip and heel. Buck, after being knocked down, rose briefly before collapsing unconscious. First aid was administered on the scene, then both players were taken to local hospitals, where they died a few hours later. Third base coach Laverne Schwenk, 21, was severely injured by the same strike.[24]

Allen L. Joyner, Jr., 23, **Harry Moore**, 24, and **Joe Taylor**, 20, had just taken their infield positions at the beginning of a game in Baker, FL, on July 31, 1949, when lightning struck the chicken-wire backstop. The bolt traveled around the infield striking Joyner at third, Moore at short, and Taylor at second, cutting a 20-foot trench along the third base line. "There was a loud crack like a big whip and a brilliant line of fire ran down the third base line," left fielder Gordon Walter testified later. "Then came this awful thunder and when I could see again I noticed all our infielders lying on the ground and people started running all over the field, shouting and screaming." Joyner and Moore were killed instantly, and Taylor died the next day. About 50 other people in the crowd of 300 were shocked and burned.[25]

Harold Jensen, 26, was covering first during an August 7, 1949, Miami Valley League semipro game in Urbana, OH, between Urbana and Troy, OH, when it began to drizzle during the top of the first inning. With Troy baserunners on second and third and the visitors leading 2 to 0, a bolt of lightning unexpectedly hit about 50 yards behind the center fielder, then bounced across the field, striking and instantly killing Jensen as he stood about 15 feet from the bag. Also injured were the Urbana second baseman, the left fielder, and a relief pitcher who had just begun to warm up along the right field line. Both umpires were shocked, but required no treatment, while the baserunners were uninjured.[26]

Robert F. Morris, 16, several other players, and an umpire were all knocked to the ground "like they had been poleaxed simultaneously by one giant blow" from the same lightning bolt when it struck as a light rain fell at the end of the first inning during an American Legion game in Helena, MT, on July 2, 1950. The lightning hit second baseman Morris on the top of his head as he ran toward the dugout, tearing his baseball cap and burning him down his right side. Rescuers, including two doctors, worked on him for an hour as fans watched in silent horror and his parents and younger sister stood nearby. He was declared dead about an hour later. Five players and the umpire were briefly hospitalized.[27]

Thomas Graham, 16, was playing in a game with other classmates at a school in Frankford, PA, on August 30, 1950, when a sudden afternoon thunderstorm caused him and about

45 other children to seek shelter under the school's pavilion. Lightning struck the shelter, hitting Graham and destroying a wooden support post. The schoolyard supervisor began to administer aid while sending another child to call the rescue squad. After the squad arrived and began artificial respiration, a police officer was dispatched to find a physician. The officer tried unsuccessfully to reach seven different doctors while an eighth refused to leave his office. Finally, the local hospital sent one of its on-duty physicians, who arrived only to find that Graham had died in the meantime.[28]

Gary F. Klingler, 10, was participating in an Indianapolis, IN, Little League practice game on the afternoon of June 30, 1959, when a powerful thunderstorm suddenly blew up. As the storm flooded the streets with rain and hail, lightning struck Klingler, stationed at third base. A teammate was also injured. "It happened so fast I didn't realize what happened until I looked down and saw the boys lying on the field," an observer said later. "Klingler's clothes were ripped off and I knew he was gone." Both boys were rushed to a local hospital, where Klingler died about an hour later.[29]

John Wade, 19, a pitcher with a semipro team in Lake Havasu City, AZ, was in the midst of his windup during the opening game of the season on May 13, 1973, when a bolt of lightning, described by one witness as a "column of fire," struck him on the head, burning off his hair, clothes, and left shoe. Wade died instantly, while seven of his teammates were hospitalized, two in critical condition. A photographer standing near third said the lightning traveled around the infield, then "exploded directly in front of me and kicked up a huge geyser. At first I thought it was a bomb." The other players who were injured eventually recovered.[30]

Paul Adamansky, 8, and about two dozen other children were playing in or watching a Little League game in Central Park in New York City on June 16, 1975, when a sudden rainstorm caused them to seek shelter. While most of the children were herded to a tunnel, about six others ran under a 35-foot oak tree. "Then the big lightning came," reported a passerby. "It was like spray all around the tree. The kids were lying on the ground and shaking all over, and some were calling for help." Others in the park ran to their assistance and began administering artificial respiration until the police could arrive. Adamansky was pronounced dead on arrival at Lennox Hill Hospital, while a 13-year-old companion was hospitalized with severe burns and four other girls were held for observation.[31]

Kenneth A. Hahn, 18, was killed by lightning while playing in a church league game on a farm near Constantine, IN, on June 1, 1980. The strike tore his clothing and produced severe burns all over this body. Attempts to revive him failed.[32]

Adriano Martinez, 18, nephew of major league pinch-hit legend Manny Mota, was considered one of the best ball players in the Long Island, NY, area. In fact, the coach of his Central Islip (NY) High School team thought he was the "best professional prospect" he had ever had in 25 years of coaching. On the evening of August 7, 1984, as Martinez was playing his usual shortstop position during a Connie Mack League game held at Patchogue-Medford (NY) High School, a light rain began to fall. While there was no lightning in the immediate area, it was becoming too dark to see properly, so the umpire decided that he would call the game at the end of the inning. At 7:50 P.M., five minutes after informing both benches of his decision, lightning struck Martinez as he stood in the field. "The bolt came out of nowhere," said Jim Farley, the left fielder on Martinez's team. "I covered my head. The force drew me back, and I fell back on the ground. I looked at Adriano — you could tell. He was, like, smoking." Umpires and coaches rushed to the fallen player and attempted to revive him. An ambulance arrived and took him to a local hospital where he died about an hour later. Two days later, the Suffolk County Connie Mack League canceled the remainder of the season because, explained league president Sal Filosa, "There's too much heartache in the league."[33]

Ben Jackson, 22, a pitcher at Valdosta State University in Valdosta, GA, was on the mound during an over–40 summer league game in his hometown of Thomasville, GA, on the afternoon of August 8, 1999. The left-hander, who had had arm surgery earlier in the year, was using the game as part of his rehabilitation regimen. As he was about to start the fourth inning, he was struck by lightning. The same bolt felled the first baseman and first base umpire and burned the face of the catcher. Jackson was rushed to a local hospital, where he died about an hour after arrival.[34]

Amateur Fatalities — Field Conditions

An unnamed boy, 16, was in pursuit of a ball during a sandlot game near some railroad tracks between Elizabeth and Newark, NJ, on the afternoon of July 9, 1869, when he stopped on one set of the tracks to avoid a westbound train that was fast approaching. He was unaware of the eastbound train from Trenton which was barreling down the tracks on which he stood. The youngster was killed instantly when the locomotive ran him over.[35]

John Stillane, 12, was running out a single during a street game in New York City on August 7, 1899, when he tripped and fell against a stoop that was serving as first base. His left side slammed against the brick outcropping, knocking him unconscious. He died later that day without regaining consciousness.[36]

W. W. Marsh was chasing a fly ball during a practice game in Rivermont, VA, on April 11, 1902, when he tumbled over an embankment. His fall of about 15 feet ruptured several blood vessels, causing his death a short time later.[37]

Lewis Mould, 22, ran in front of a streetcar while playing in a park game in Pittsburgh, PA, on May 15, 1909. The collision broke his leg and caused internal injuries which led to his death shortly after he was taken to a local hospital.[38]

Wilson E. Losch, 12, was in pursuit of a fly ball during a game in Reading, PA, on July 6, 1909, when he stumbled and fell. His head hit a large rock, resulting in a skull fracture. He died later that day.[39]

Andrew (Louis) Brown, 9, was chasing a ball during an afternoon game in a field near the Allegheny River in Pittsburgh, PA, on July 22, 1909, when he tumbled down the embankment into the water. He drowned before help could arrive. His body was recovered later that night by a local police officer.[40]

Oliver P. Thompson, 13, was playing in a neighborhood game in a field on a hill overlooking a paved street in Washington, DC, on September 24, 1909. When a ball was hit over an embankment at the edge of the field, Thompson ran down the hill in pursuit of the ball. The youngster ran into the middle of the street just as a funeral procession was coming down the road. According to conflicting testimony by witnesses, he either stumbled and fell in front of a horse-drawn hearse or was struck by the wheel of the hearse and knocked down. In either event, the two wheels on the right side of the hearse ran over his back as he lay face-down in the street. Thompson was conscious and writhing in pain when his playmates carried him home. A physician was summoned who, upon examination, recommended that he be taken to a local hospital. Thompson died on the way to the hospital about an hour after the accident.[41]

Louis Rose, 10, was playing in a field near an abandoned railroad reservoir in Jersey City, NJ, on April 24, 1910, when a fly ball was hit in his direction. Rose was intent on catching the ball and did not notice that he was near the water. He fell into the reservoir and was unable to swim back to shore. One of his teammates made several unsuccessful attempts to rescue him as he sank in about 12 feet of water. His body was recovered about 20 minutes later.[42]

William La Lone, 11, stumbled and fell into the path of a "jitney" bus while chasing a ball during a street game in Seattle, WA, on May 1, 1915. The driver was unable to stop in time and the radiator of the bus struck La Lone on the left temple, killing him almost immediately.[43]

Nicholas Dunn, 14, was struck and killed by a car while playing street ball in Brooklyn, NY, on April 5, 1924.[44]

Clement Skidinski, 13, was struck and killed by a truck while chasing a ball during a street game in Chicago, IL, on June 1, 1925.[45]

Edward McKenna, 9, was killed when he ran in front of a train in pursuit of a ball during a street game in Jersey City, NJ, on June 18, 1925. The two friends playing with him were so frightened that they hid in a nearby church. McKenna's body was discovered and identified several hours later.[46]

John G. Carpenter, 10, tripped over a block of wood being used as a base while playing ball with neighborhood friends in the backyard of his home in San Antonio, TX, of March 23, 1927. His headfirst fall broke his neck. A rescue squad from a local fire station and a physician and a nurse attempted to revive him without success. He was declared dead about 30 minutes later.[47]

Raymond Binkowski, 9, was playing street ball near his home in Chicago, IL, on August 12, 1928, when a car turning a corner struck and killed him almost instantly.[48]

James Lageiffe, 10, was legging out a double in a New York City street game on August 27, 1928, when he was hit by a car. He died in a local hospital about an hour after the accident.[49]

Bruno Cia, 6, was struck and killed by a car while playing street ball near his home in Chicago, IL, on March 2, 1931.[50]

Edward Swanson, 15, was in pursuit of a fly ball during a street game in Los Angeles, CA, when he tripped and fell backwards, hitting his head on the pavement. He required six blood transfusions over the next two weeks because of hemorrhaging. When the bleeding finally stopped, he was sent home where, several days later, he began hemorrhaging from his nose. This time physicians could not stop the bleeding and he died on November 29, 1931, nearly three weeks after his fall.[51]

Roy Hinkley, 11, was playing the outfield during a sandlot game near railroad tracks in Rochester, NY, around 7:00 P.M. on May 13, 1936, when a fly ball was hit in his direction. Hinkley, with his eyes on the ball, ran onto the tracks just as the eastbound Baltimore and Ohio Railroad passenger train was passing through. The youngster was struck by the locomotive as he was in the act of catching the ball, the force of the blow knocking him out of his shoes and killing him instantly.[52]

Henry Jimenez, 6, was killed instantly when he ran in front of a car while pursuing a ball during a street game in New York City on August 16, 1939.[53]

Saul Cola, 10, was chasing a fly ball during a sandlot game near his home in the Bronx, NY, on August 24, 1942, when he crashed through a wooden fence surrounding the field and fell down a 20-foot-deep concrete air-shaft belonging to the building next door. He died before help could arrive.[54]

Kenneth Eckman, 12, fell on a piece of broken glass while chasing a ball during a schoolyard game in Oak Lawn, IL, on May 18, 1952. The glass cut through his jugular vein, causing his death about five hours after the accident.[55]

Gene Reynolds, 19, and **Robert Brown**, 18, along with several other members of the Howard County Junior College baseball team in Big Spring, TX, were helping to erect a metal foul pole for a practice game on the afternoon of March 31, 1953, when it fell onto some power lines. An electric charge of 7,500 volts raced down the pole, injuring all those holding onto it. Reynolds and Brown died on the field, while eight other teammates were sent to a local hospital, where they were treated for shock and burns.[56]

Donald Schipani, 14, was pursuing a fly ball to deep center during a sandlot game at Columbia Stadium in Boston, MA, on May 9, 1953, when he ran headfirst into the stadium's concrete outfield wall. The blow fractured his skull, killing him instantly.[57]

Leo Boswell, 12, was killed by a speeding car when he ran into the street while chasing a ball during a sandlot game in Chicago, IL, on July 16, 1972.[58]

8. Fatalities from Violence

"Violence," proclaimed political activist H. Rap Brown (Jamil Abdullah al-Amin) in 1967, "is as American as cherry pie." While it is obvious to even the most casual observer of world affairs that violence is not a uniquely American phenomenon, it is clear that violent behavior is an all too common occurrence in everyday life. And at times this seems to be the case most especially within the context of competitive sports.

Bench-clearing brawls in baseball, fistfights among players and fans during basketball games, deadly hooliganism during soccer matches — these and similar violent events in other sports regularly populate television newscasts and newspaper sports pages. While one may argue whether sports violence is worse today than in the past, no one can deny that it does occur and that it is a serous problem.

The question naturally arises as to why. What is it about athletic competition that brings out the best in some and the worse in others? What factors contribute to the outbreak of a violent event? Why is certain aggressive behavior in athletic competition sometimes accepted — and even encouraged — by participants and spectators as being just "part of the game," while similar behavior in the "real world" would be condemned and subject to legal punishment?

Research over the past several decades has shown that there is a different, often less mature, level of moral reasoning that occurs in sports. Players and fans alike accept competitive sports as "a 'world within a world' with its own unique conventions and moral understandings." In a study of 120 high school and college athletes, sports psychologists Brenda Jo Bredemeier and David L. Shields found that "most of the students clearly perceived a difference between morality in sport and in everyday life." They refer to this less mature level of moral reasoning as "egocentric." According to their findings, "moral norms which prescribe equal consideration of all people are often suspended during competition in favor of a more egocentric moral perspective." This suspension occurs because "the very nature of competition requires that self-interest be temporarily adopted while the athlete strives to win. In everyday life, such preoccupation with self almost inevitably leads to moral failings. But in sport, participants are freed to concentrate on self-interest by a carefully balanced rule structure that equalizes opportunity. Players are guarded against the moral defaults of others by protective rules and by officials who impose sanctions for violations."[1]

Fortunately, most athletes do "use a complex moral logic in attempts to coordinate the goal of winning with the need to respect limits to egocentricity." While aggressive play is expected and rewarded, players usually attempt to draw a line between "legitimate and illegitimate aggression." The difference between the two forms of aggression is determined in part by the rules of the game. Sliding hard into second base to break up a double play, for example, is acceptable, while leaving the base path to intentionally knock down a fielder is a violation of the rules. The problem, though, is that, more than the rules, "less formal criteria ... such as intimidation, domination, fairness and retribution are continuously woven into participants' fabric of thought, providing a changing picture of what constitutes legitimate action. Shifting expectations, created by the fast-paced and emotionally charged action, can readily lead to perceived violations or 'cheap shots.'" Since, as Brendemeier and Shields found, "athletes with less mature moral reasoning accepted a greater number of aggressive acts as legiti-

As this 1860 *Vanity Fair* cartoon illustrates, nineteenth century baseball had an often-deserved reputation as a rough and violent sport.

mate than did their peers with higher moral reasoning scores," it is easy to see why some players resort to violence during the heat of athletic competition.[2]

While research has shown that occurrences of aggressive behavior are more frequent in a high-contact sport like football than in a low-contact one like baseball, the National Pastime is certainly not immune to violence. In a 1995 study, 49 Class A minor league players were administered the "Baseball Aggression Questionnaire" to determine under what circumstances the players felt aggressive behavior was both warranted and acceptable. Participants were also asked to indicate their level of remorse if an opponent were injured by the aggressive act. Of the 14 game situations presented to them, the players agreed that in nine of them "an act of aggression was appropriate and expected to be performed. These acts ranged from the pitcher hitting an opposing batter, to sliding hard at the baseman's knees to break up a double play, to running over the catcher if the plate is being blocked, and to leaving the bench and heading onto the field when a teammate charges the mound." While the respondents felt there were limits to the level of an aggressive response (none, for example, thought it appropriate for a pitcher to intentionally throw at a batter's head), in no situation did the players indicate they "should feel remorse if an opposing player was injured." The researchers concluded that "justifying acts of aggression is common among athletes because aggression is seen as acceptable in sports.... This, coupled with the lack of significant consequences for aggressive actions, helps make aggression seem legitimate and aids in relieving the athletes of personal responsibility for their actions."[3]

There appear to be a variety of other factors contributing to violence in sports. Of par-

Fights and brawls among players were not uncommon in the nineteenth century, as depicted in this 1870 *Punchinello* editorial cartoon.

ticular significance to baseball is the relationship between temperature and aggression. A study of batters hit by a pitch (HBP) during major league games from 1986 through 1988 found a direct linear relationship between temperature and HBP incidents because "higher temperatures lead major league pitchers to become more aggressive in pitching to batters." Statistically, the researchers found, "there is approximately a two-thirds greater chance of a batter's being hit in a game played when the temperature is in the nineties or above than in a game played when the temperature is in the seventies or below."[4]

Also at play may be "the point differential between two teams, with the highest degrees of aggression arising when teams are separated by a wide scoring margin. Furthermore, players on winning and losing teams exhibit different patterns of aggression as a game progresses." Aggression increases at a constant rate throughout the game for the winning team whereas the losers' level of aggression tends to drop off about midway through the game presumably because "athletes in the unsuccessful teams conclude that their aggressive actions are not effective and, consequently, switch to less aggressive strategies in an attempt to perform better." In addition, "possibly because of frustration, a team's position in the overall league affects the degree of individual player aggression. Indeed, teams that come first tend to exhibit lower amounts of aggression than the frustrated teams who have to be content with second place and those who come last and who find it hard to justify to themselves their overall poor performance."[5]

Clearly, then, there are a myriad of causes of sports-related violence. While most of these events do not result in death, there are times when, sadly, they do.

Black Baseball Fatalities

In the early innings of a game between African American amateur teams near Brenham, TX, on August 18, 1895, catcher Charlie Randle, in attempting to pick off a baserunner, struck **Joe Richardson**, the batter, with the ball. About 20 minutes later, the roles were reversed with Richardson catching and Randle batting. During the at-bat, Randle was struck in the back of the head when Richardson threw to second during an attempted steal. An enraged Randle turned and "drawing back the bat he stuck Richardson in the head with force enough to knock a home run and felled him senseless to the ground, where he remained inanimate for about ten minutes." Richardson was carried home, where he died early on the morning of August 20. Randle was arrested and charged with murder.[6]

A melee between African American teams in Brooks, GA, during an amateur championship game on August 28, 1910, resulted in a reported three fatalities and several serious injuries. The two teams began fighting in the bottom of the ninth inning over a disputed call that allowed the local Brooks team to score the winning run. When members of the losing team from Hartford, GA, charged the umpire, the Brooks players rushed to protect him. The umpire escaped unharmed as fans soon rushed the field. Guns and knives were pulled and baseball bats were used as clubs. All the fatalities occurred among the Brooks players. **Kid Iverson** and **Harvey Mayes** were killed instantly and **Jim Barrett** died from gunshot wounds on September 5.[7]

Amateur Fatalities

During the afternoon of August 16, 1876, a dispute over the use of a farmer's field near Holly Springs, MS, for a baseball game resulted in tragedy. Marsh Walker, 20, captain of a local team, had gained permission from the farmer to use his field for a game. By the time the team arrived, they found another team led by **Willis Jones**, 22, already occupying the same field. Rather than set up a new playing area, Walker's team claimed the right to use the section marked off by Jones' team. When Walker's team began interfering with the play of the other team, Jones ordered Walker and his teammates to leave. During the ensuring fight between the two captains, Walker struck Jones over the head with a baseball bat, resulting in Jones' almost instantaneous death.[8]

Two brothers got into a fight during a game in Great Bend, PA, on the evening of August 15, 1877, which resulted in the death of one of them several days later. According to one account, **Addison Banker**, 24, was at bat when his younger brother, Walter, 19, struck him with the ball. The two brothers began arguing with each other, and at some point Addison slapped Walter on the face. Walter threatened to shoot his brother if Addison slapped him again. Responding to this challenge, Addison slapped Walter a second time, and the two began to wrestle. While Addison had his younger brother in a headlock, Walter drew a pistol and shot Addison in his right side. The bullet pierced Addison's lung, causing massive internal bleeding. Walter, who had been in trouble with the law previously for theft, turned himself in to the local police. Addison lingered near death for several days before expiring on August 22. He was reported to have blamed himself for the incident and expressed the desire that his brother not be punished.[9]

A group of about 40 boys was gathered in a schoolyard near Atlanta, GA, on July 8,

1878, when a fight broke out between two of the young men. **Willie Lawshe**, 22, was batting the ball around before the game began when he missed a high throw back to him. The ball soared close to the head of the Charles Venable, 15, who was seated on the ground near home plate. Venable told Lawshe, "Look out!" and then said something along the lines of, "You are breeding scabs." When Lawshe made a threatening motion toward Venable followed by a cutting remark to the effect that the younger boy was "too pretty to hit," a fight ensued. Lawshe, being older and bigger, easily pinned Venable to the ground and began to beat him. Standing nearby was Venable's friend, Carl Mitchell, 14, who was distressed at seeing Venable in trouble. Picking up a baseball bat, Mitchell struck Lawshe on the back of the head in an attempt to stop the fight. Lawshe was knocked unconscious and stopped breathing for a few seconds. One of Lawshe's friends in the crowd struck Mitchell in the face, knocking him to the ground. After Mitchell's friends intervened, Mitchell fled the schoolyard while Lawshe was carried home.

Later that evening, with Lawshe alive but still unconscious, Mitchell turned himself in to the local police. The following day a grand jury charged Mitchell with assault to commit murder and Mitchell was released on a $5,000 bond. When Lawshe died from a fractured skull shortly after 5:00 P.M. on July 9, a warrant was issued charging Mitchell with murder. Mitchell was released after posting another $5,000 bond.

A grand jury later reduced the charge against Mitchell to involuntary manslaughter and a two-day trial, known as the Base-Ball Murder, began on December 17, 1878. Venable testified for the defense, stating that the more powerful Lawshe had threatened to kill him as they fought: "he was beating and choking me, as I thought, to death." At one point during the fight, according to Venable, Lawshe had bitten him on the ear, causing it to bleed profusely. Mitchell took the stand in his own defense, stating that he thought his friend was being killed by Lawshe. He contended that he hit Lawshe with the bat not to kill him, but to stop him from harming Venable. "I struck him in that belief," he testified, "and I would rather have been killed myself than to have this thing occur." The case went to the jury on the late afternoon of December 18. After a short deliberation, they found Mitchell not guilty. As the jury pronounced its verdict, "nearly one hundred of Carl's school-mates rushed forward to take him by the hand. The scene was quite affecting."[10]

A small gang of boys was playing baseball in an alley near St. Paul's Cathedral in Pittsburgh, PA, on the evening of May 14, 1884, when an argument broke out between two of the players, **John O'Gorman Fortune**, 16, and James Tesch. According to one witness at the inquest, Fortune first hit Tesch after which Tesch threw a large lump of coal at Fortune, striking him behind the ear. Fortune chased his assailant away, then continued playing ball. When he began feeling ill a short time later, Fortune returned home, washed the blood from his face and neck, and went to bed. Early the next morning his mother found him "delirious" and summoned a physician. Fortune quickly lapsed into unconsciousness and died about 9:30 A.M. from a fractured skull.[11]

George Anderson, 12, and about a dozen other boys were playing street ball in Chicago, IL, on May 8, 1891, when an argument resulted in several boys attacking Anderson with baseball bats or a combination of a bat and a ball. Anderson died at home shortly thereafter, and an investigation by the deputy coroner led to the breakup of "a tough gang of youngsters" who, "when they congregate at night, smoke vile cigars, chew tobacco, tell wild West Indian yarns and play cards." Two of the gang members, Joseph Roth and E. L. Jones, were considered the prime suspects. Jones, 16, was eventually charged with murder, but was released on

May 25 after a number of those present at the attack convinced the judge that Jones was not the culprit.[12]

Cal Taylor and Bose Faulkner were opponents in a game near Eufaula, AL, on August 8, 1897, when the two got into an argument. Taylor accused Faulkner of cheating and left the game to sit on the sidelines. Faulkner followed Taylor and struck him on the head with a stick as he sat on the ground. Faulkner immediately ran off after assaulting Taylor, who died early the next morning. Faulkner was eventually found and arrested in Phoenix City, AL, on August 28. He claimed to have struck Taylor in self-defense.[13]

A fight broke out between **Ed Puckett** and Herb Karrick (or Carrick) during a game in Grassy Lick, KY, on June 16, 1906. Brothers of the two combatants soon joined the fray. Herb's brother, John, struck Ed Puckett over the head with a bat; he died within minutes. Charles Puckett, the deceased's brother, knocked John Karrick unconscious with a bat in retaliation. Karrick recovered and stood trial a week later, but was acquitted on the grounds of self-defense.[14]

Shortly after a game in Washington, DC, on April 25, 1907, Delaware Ross, 25, attacked **Arthur Reed**, 19, with a baseball bat over a dispute concerning ownership of the bat. Although the blow fractured Reed's skull, he did not go to the hospital until the next day. His condition steadily declined and surgery was performed on April 28. Reed died on the operating table that morning. Ross was arrested the day following the assault and was initially indicted on a charge of first degree murder. Ross claimed that he had hit Reed because he believed the victim was about to pull a knife. During the course of the trial in October, the prosecuting attorney decided to reduce the charge to second degree murder, then announced that he would reduce it even further to manslaughter. Even though the judge instructed the jury as to the change in the charge, they returned a verdict of "guilty as indicted," which was recorded as murder in the second degree. Ross's attorney announced plans to make a motion for a new trial on the grounds that the jury had exceeded their charge. On December 13, 1907, nearly two months after the trial, the judge overrode the jury and allowed Ross to enter a guilty plea on the charge of manslaughter. He was sentenced to three-and-a-half years in prison and was sent to the federal penitentiary in Atlanta on January 23, 1908.[15]

Rorie Young, 21, and an individual identified only as Hoffman got into a fight during a game in Grovetown, GA, on July 4, 1907. According to one account, Hoffman struck Young with a ball, causing a confrontation between the two players. They decided to settle their disagreement with a fistfight and began walking to the sidelines. Another individual known only as Capers followed the two and got into an argument with Young before the fight began. Young made a motion as if he were about to draw a knife, so Capers pulled a pistol and shot Young in the head, killing him instantly. When Capers started to escape, he was captured and turned over to the Columbia County sheriff.[16]

Best friends William F. Mason, 48, and **Edward Haas**, 27, decided to pull a practical joke at a company baseball game in Brookline, PA, on June 22, 1908. They hatched a scheme wherein Mason, who was scheduled to umpire the game, would make a bad decision against Haas, who was playing center field. Haas would pretend to get angry and then attack Mason who, in turn, would pull out a gun loaded with blank cartridges and fire at Haas. Mason planned to use a Springfield rifle he had purchased two years earlier.

Mason was late arriving at the game and was replaced as umpire. Deciding to continue with the "joke" anyway, Mason sat with his wife in the grandstand between third and home, his rifle loaded with two cartridges hidden under his coat. After misplaying a ball in the bottom of the third, Haas approached Mason in the stands. Mason taunted Haas by calling out, "Why did you muff that fly?" As Haas turned laughingly to respond, Mason pulled his rifle and fired at Haas twenty feet away. Sadly, instead of being blank, the cartridge was loaded with buckshot. Most of the pellets struck Haas in the chest while others hit his forehead or severed an artery in his right arm. Another player was also slightly wounded in the face and foot. While Mason ran for a doctor, Haas died where he lay minutes after being shot. A grieving Mason wandered the streets for several hours before turning himself in to the police later that evening. He repeated over and over, "If only I had been the one shot instead." Fearing he might commit suicide, Mason was kept under observation at the police station until 1:00 A.M. the next day before being released. Haas' wife and family agreed that it was purely an accident and requested that Mason not be prosecuted. *The Pittsburgh Post* used the event to call for stricter gun control, stating in an editorial "that use of a gun as a plaything, as an instrument in perpetuating a joke, is an idiotic idea. The death occurs, either of child passing or intimate friend, mawkish sympathy is expressed, great grief is experienced, and the fool and his gun reappear."[17]

A group of boys, all under the age of 10, were in the backyard of a tenement house in New York City playing ball on the afternoon of March 14, 1909. The noise of the youngsters having fun awoke one of the adult residents sleeping in an apartment above the courtyard. In his anger, he threw a brick at the children, striking **Dominick Cerone**, 6, on the head as he was pitching. He collapsed where he stood "with his head crushed in." The young boy died about four hours later at a local hospital. The police were unable to identify the assailant.[18]

In a dispute over the ownership of a catcher's mitt, **Jesse Sprouse**, 12, and Frederick L. Thompson came to blows during a game near Alexandria, VA, on May 12, 1910. Sprouse struck Thompson on the leg with a bat, whereupon Thompson snatched the bat away from Sprouse and hit him on the head with it. Sprouse died in the hospital early the next day. A jury exonerated Thompson later that afternoon after physicians testified that "young Sprouse had an unusually thin skull, and that the condition of the blood vessels leading to the brain were not normal" and after others who had participated in the game affirmed that death was unintentional.[19]

When **Stanislaw Klich**, 15, and Joseph Alminowicz, 16, got into a fight during a game in East St. Louis, IL, on September 15, 1914, Alminowicz struck Klich over the head with a baseball bat, fracturing his skull. Klich lingered near death for nearly two weeks before passing on September 29. Alminowicz disappeared, and his father was arrested after a coroner's inquest on September 30 for failing to bring his son with him.[20]

A dispute over five dollars in gate receipts after a game in New York City on June 21, 1917, resulted in the death of **Henry Ayres**, 16. The victim and Timothy Moynihan, also 16, were rival gang members and captains of the respective baseball teams. When they began to argue over which team should receive the money, Moynihan pulled a gun and fatally wounded Ayres. Moynihan was arrested and charged with first degree murder after confessing. At his trial shortly before Christmas, Moynihan maintained his innocence and testified that he had confessed only after being beaten while in police custody. A doctor who examined the boy after his interrogation confirmed that Moynihan was "suffering from loss of memory." Nonetheless, after seven hours of deliberation, the jury convicted Moynihan of first degree manslaughter, a compromise verdict after the jury split eight to four for first degree murder. On December 28, Moynihan was sentenced to Sing Sing Prison for from 10 to 15 years.[21]

Joseph G. Nieberding, 16, and about a dozen of his friends were playing ball in a park near their homes in Pittsburgh, PA, on June 27, 1930, when William Hartlep, 54, the park supervisor, instructed the boys to stop playing because "the game endangered motorists and pedestrians." Even though the children had been warned before against playing baseball in the park and in spite of the fact that there was a recreation center about four blocks away, they ignored Hartlep and continued playing. When Hartlep began to gather up their equipment with the intention of holding all the bats and gloves in the park office until he could contact the players' parents, the boys began following him, protesting loudly. At this point, according to Hartlep, several of them "made threatening remarks and became menacing." Hartlep turned and shoved one of the boys.

Upon this provocation, Nieberding approached Hartlep. Fearing for his safety, Hartlep stated later, "I only protected myself—I swung the bat." The blow fractured Nieberding's skull, knocking him unconscious.

Several of the players offered a different version of the events. Hartlep "came and picked up three of our bats and gloves," proclaimed George Davis, 16. "I heard him yell something. I don't know what it was. Joe [Nieberding] and I followed him and kept asking him for our bats. We were closest to him. He started to swing the bats at us and in doing so dropped two of them. Joe stopped to reach for the bats and the man swung, striking him on the head." Paul Gallagher, 16, who owned the bat in question, said that Hartlep "swung the bat with both hands, knocking Joe to the ground. He swung the bat just as though he was swinging at a baseball." At least one adult confirmed the children's accounts.

There was general agreement that Hartlep attempted to assist Nieberding after striking him. He and another man tried to revive the injured boy. When it became apparent that Nieberding was severely injured, they carried him to a nearby hospital. In spite of all efforts, Nieberding died the following day.

Declaring Hartlep's behavior to be "unjustified" and "one of the most disgraceful and cowardly [acts] I ever heard of," Nieberding's father swore that he would "see the matter through to the finish." For Hartlep, that meant his arrest for manslaughter. He was released after posting a $5,000 bond. He also took a leave of absence from his position with the parks department. In response to this event, the Pittsburgh city council passed a resolution calling for more police patrols to prevent baseball playing in city parks because it "is a menace to pedestrians and motorists and destructive to grass and shrubs."

Hartlep went on trial at the end of October. He asserted that the death was accidental, not intentional, testifying in his own defense that Nieberding "had been swinging his bat at me. I lifted my hand with the bat up over my head as I stopped suddenly and turned around to face the crowd that was following me, and Joe banged into me. The bat struck him." The jury, after five hours of deliberation, convicted the father of five of voluntary manslaughter, a verdict which carried a potential 6 to 12 year prison sentence. He was released on bond of $5,000 pending an appeal by his attorney. On February 27, 1931, Hartlep was sentenced to two years' probation and was ordered to pay court costs and a fine of $500 and to cover all the hospital and burial expenses incurred by the victim's parents.[22]

During a school baseball game in Chicago, IL, on September 16, 1930, **Joseph Czorniak**, 15, was called out while attempting to steal second base. An argument with classmate Frank Krygowski, 15, over the decision ended in a fistfight between the two students. Krygowski punched Czorniak in the face, knocking him down. Czorniak's neck was broken by the force of his head hitting the ground. He died later that day.[23]

Cal Wilson, 32, was batting during a game in Stantonville, TN, on August 10, 1935, when he got into an argument with umpire Grady Walls over a decision Walls had made. During the course of the disagreement, Walls picked up a bat and struck Wilson over the head, fracturing his skull. Wilson was taken to a hospital in nearby Corinth, MS, where he died August 13 without regaining consciousness.

Walls was immediately arrested and charged with second degree murder. At the trial which began on June 29, 1936, the state contended that the attack on Wilson was unprovoked; that, in fact, Wilson had turned to leave when Walls struck him. "He never knew what hit him," claimed two witnesses, "nor where the blow came from. He made no effort to strike Walls and made no demonstration whatever, against him." Walls testified that he struck Wilson in self-defense, fearing that Wilson held a knife in his clenched fists. The jury deliberated for over 48 hours before declaring they could not reach a unanimous decision. Ten of the jurors were in favor of conviction, two were not. The presiding judge discharged the jury and set a new trial date for mid–October. At this second trial, Walls was convicted of voluntary manslaughter and was sentenced to three years in prison.[24]

On May 20, 2001, in Rochester, NY, two young brothers, one 6, the other 3, were playing baseball with other children in their neighborhood when the 3-year-old threw a rock at his older brother. The older sibling retaliated by hitting his brother with a brick, then striking him repeatedly in the stomach with a full-size wooden baseball bat. The two children returned home, where the 3-year-old refused dinner and fell asleep on the couch as his 22-year-old mother's 17-year-old boyfriend babysat the two children. Later they were bathed and put to bed together. The younger child was found dead the next morning, a victim of "blunt trauma to the abdomen, which caused internal bleeding."

At first, policed focused their attention on the boyfriend. But further investigation which showed no signs of abuse in the home and the testimony of the 6-year-old and a 16-year-old girl who witnessed the fight convinced them that the older child did indeed kill the younger one. "I've been a police officer for 25 years," commented Rochester police chief Robert Duffy, "and I've seen nothing like this in my career." Being too young to understand his actions, no murder charges were filed against the 6-year-old. "In the mind of that child," explained Police Chief Duffy later, "I'd think it's difficult to comprehend. There were no immediate results to his actions because when they were done they both went back home, had dinner, a bath and went to bed. The victim did not go unconscious. They went home and everything was fine." The 6-year-old was placed in foster care and administered mental health tests.[25]

9. Erroneously Reported Player Fatalities

Over the years, there have been a number of player fatalities that were incorrectly attributed to game-related incidents. In some of these cases, assumptions were made and conclusions drawn out of ignorance, while in others false, but more socially acceptable, explanations were given to the public to protect the privacy of the players' surviving families. Sometimes newspapers mistakenly reported the details of a death even when the true cause was made public, a problem that was more prevalent before the advent of radio, television, and nationwide telephone service. And, in a few cases, reports of deaths were fabricated out of whole cloth as a joke or to tell a good tale. Apocryphal stories in particular seem to have a long shelf-life, in part because it is nearly impossible to disprove them and because they are such fun to tell and retell.

Major League Players

Over six feet tall and "lean as a bean pole," **James E. "Grasshopper Jim" Whitney** was one of the premier pitchers in the majors during the decade of the 1880s. Signed by the Boston Red Caps in 1881, he appeared in 66 games his rookie year, pitching 57 complete ones. His record of 31 wins and 33 loses led the National League in both categories that season. A noted batsman as well, Whitney often played center field or the infield on days he was not pitching. In 1882, in fact, he led his team not only in wins (24), but also in home runs (5), batting average (.323), and slugging percentage (.510). Called the "Grasshopper" because of his "hop, skip, and a jump" ball delivery, the right-hander had his best year in 1883 when his 37 and 21 record helped lead the Beaneaters, as Boston was then known, to the National League championship.[1]

Whitney's pitching effectiveness began to decline the next season, and after going 18 and 32 in 1885, he was released by Boston. For the next several seasons, he played with a number of teams including one year with the Kansas City Cowboys and two with the Washington Nationals. Suffering from deteriorating health, Whitney retired in the middle of the 1890 season to return to his home in Binghamton, NY. He passed away at this father's house on May 21, 1891, at the age of 33.[2]

All local and national obituaries at the time reported that his death was due to "consumption," an archaic medical term usually applied to persons suffering from tuberculosis, an infectious bacterial disease. But in 1897, pitcher Al Maul, a contemporary of Whitney's, claimed that a batted ball was the underlying cause of Whitney's death. According to Maul, Whitney, who was playing for Washington at the time, was struck in the chest by a line drive off the bat of Bill Kuehne during a game against the Pittsburgh Alleghanys in that city. "Before Whitney could step aside or duck," recalled Maul, "the ball crashed into his chest, and he fell forward prone on his stomach. He was carried off the field, and a few days later hemorrhage of the lungs set in. Jim, though deep-chested and a man of steel, never recovered from that blow and died a few years later." While Whitney may or may not have been struck so severely by a ball, this event would not have resulted in his contracting tuberculosis. TB, as it is commonly known, is caught through inhaling or ingesting the droplets of an infected person, which are most often transmitted by sneezing or coughing. Maul's conjecture is medically incorrect.[3]

Breaking in with the Louisville (KY) Colonels of the American Association in 1886, **Hubert B. "Hub" Collins** played seven seasons in the major leagues, primarily as a second baseman and left fielder. He quickly established himself as one of game's elite players, feared for his hitting ability and base-running prowess. In late 1888, Collins was traded to the Brooklyn Bridegrooms, where he helped lead his new team to consecutive pennants in 1889 and 1890. It was there that he had an on-field accident that some wrongly speculated may have contributed to his death less than a year later.[4]

In a July 20, 1891, National League game against the New York Giants, Collins was playing second base when, in the top of the eighth, a pop fly was hit to short right field. As Collins ran back with his eyes on the ball, Brooklyn's Tom Burns roared in from right. Violating a safety rule instituted by manager John Montgomery Ward, neither player called for the ball. Ward did yell for Burns to make the play, but a train passing near the park prevented Collins from hearing him. The two collided face first just as Collins reached for the ball. With both players lying unconscious on the field, the batter raced to third before the center fielder retrieved the dropped ball and relayed it in. The fallen players, "their faces covered with blood and both insensible," were carried to the clubhouse. Burns was the first to revive, but Collins remained motionless. Eventually he came to, and both injured men were taken back to their homes, accompanied by a physician.[5]

By the next day, Collins and Burns had recovered from the collision. Burns received two stitches on his forehead and Collins, with the more severe damage, received eight stitches for a cut running from his forehead to his eye. Fortunately, neither suffered a concussion, although Collins was out of action for several weeks. He also seemed to be adversely affected by the collision. He played in only 107 games that year and his offensive production was down from previous seasons.[6]

The following season, Collins, because of the accident, was assigned exclusively to left field. After playing in 21 games, on May 14 he suddenly took ill on a western road trip and was sent back to Brooklyn to recover. He was diagnosed with a mild case of typhoid fever, but the condition grew worse, and on May 21, 1892, he died at home at the age of 29. His teammates, family, and friends were stunned to learn of his sudden passing. A benefit game was held between Brooklyn and the St. Louis Browns on May 29. Over 7,000 fans attended the unusual Sunday contest, generating nearly $3,000 in gate receipts for Collins' widow and young child.[7]

Some newspaper reports of his death implied that his collision the year before left him more vulnerable to typhoid because "he has never been strong since" the accident. "Many people," concluded another, "attribute the recent death of Hub Collins of the Brooklyn Baseball club to the effects of his collision with Burns last season." A 1908 article on baseball accidents promoted this view, stating that "Collins was so badly hurt that he never got over the effects of the blow he received on the head, and died not a great while afterward." And by 1910, even the reference to typhoid fever had disappeared, with some falsely remembering that Collins died immediately after the collision with Burns.[8]

Apparently his death less than a year after the collision with Burns connected the two events in people's minds, even though Collins was healthy at the start of the 1892 season, showing no ill effects from his accident. His batting average stood at .299, second highest in his career, and he had scored 17 runs and had driven in another 17. These are certainly decent statistics for someone supposedly not fully recovered. In fact, the *Brooklyn Daily Eagle* reported that he was "doing phenomenal work" in left until his illness began on May 14.[9]

In reality, Collins' death from typhoid fever had nothing to do with any injuries he suffered the previous year. Typhoid fever is an infection caused by a bacterium, sometimes passed through contact with an infected individual's stool or urine. Failure to wash one's hands after using a toilet can be one way the illness is spread. On other occasions, a carrier can pass it along through food preparation or water. Since players in the nineteenth century often drank from a communal water bucket, Collins could have contracted the disease this way. Whatever the source of his case of typhoid fever, Collins' 1891 collision did not leave him susceptible to the disease.[10]

In between tours with a variety of minor league clubs, journeyman infielder **James I. "Jimmy" Say** spent parts of three seasons in the majors, playing third and short for such teams as the American Association's Louisville Eclipse and Philadelphia Athletics (1882), the Union Association's Wilmington Quicksteps and Kansas City Cowboys (1884), and the cellar-dwelling Cleveland Blues of the American Association (1887). Sporting a lifetime .266 batting average and .789 fielding percentage, it is readily apparent why Say appeared in only 57 games in his big league career.

When the 32-year-old player died of consumption on June 23, 1894, in Baltimore, MD, some speculated that his death was hastened by a baseball injury that had occurred when he played for the Jersey City (NJ) Jerseys of the Eastern League in 1886. During a game against the Newark (NJ) Little Giants, according to one obituary, "Say tried to steal from second to third base, and in failing to slide, he struck his left side on the baseman's knee, receiving internal injuries." His official death certificate, however, makes no mention of this supposed accident. The primary cause of death is listed as "phthisis," an archaic medical term meaning "a wasting," most often as the result of tuberculosis. Secondary cause was indicated to be "exhaustion," a general diagnosis that coincides with the primary cause. The certificate also states that Say had been ill for seven months. Clearly the contention that a 6-year-old injury left him susceptible to a highly contagious bacterial disease like tuberculosis is medically incorrect.[11]

Utility infielder **James F. "Jimmy" Rogers** had considerable minor league experience before being acquired by the Washington Senators in the spring of 1896. The 24-year-old "scrapper," penciled in at second for the team's home opener on April 17, played well that day, going one for three at the plate and turning a double play as his team won 6 to 3 over the New York Giants. Although Rogers committed one error, he and his fellow rookie shortstop Gene DeMontreville were described as "active, alert young players who promise to develop rapidly." But in the case of Rogers, apparently his development was not rapid enough, for in early July he was "dumbfounded" to learn that he had been traded to the lowly Louisville Colonels, a team that would finish the season with 38 wins and 93 loses.[12]

The quality of leadership he displayed while playing regularly at second and short led the Colonels ownership to offer him the position of player-manager and team captain for the following season. At first Rogers demurred, writing former teammate DeMontreville that he was "a shy and retiring chap, and would prefer to obey orders rather than giving them." After getting married during the off-season, though, he changed his mind and in early January 1897 it was announced that he would take over the on-field management of the Colonels. While the season started well with Rogers at second and the team winning, by early June Louisville was in an extended losing streak. Tired of being the "anvil," Rogers offered his resignation and asked for his release, sarcastically commenting that he would "go to a physician and have him examine me to see how many hammer marks he can find on me."[13]

Rogers was not out of the game long, as several minor league teams pursued his services. He quickly signed with the Springfield (MA) Ponies of the Eastern League, playing there for the remainder of the 1887 season before being cut early the following

Former journeyman player Jimmy Rogers died in 1900 from a bacterial infection of the brain, not from an earlier beaning as reported in obituaries at the time.

year. As his skills diminished, Rogers fell even lower in the minor league system. His release by the Eastern League's Providence (RI) Clamdiggers in late May 1899 brought what was at one time a promising baseball career to an end.[14]

While playing for Louisville in 1896, Rogers came down with malaria, a mosquito-borne illness that may have played a role in his untimely death. On January 22, 1900, the baseball world was shocked to learn that Rogers had passed away the evening before in his hometown of Bridgeport, CT. Obituaries reported that he "had been suffering for several months from brain trouble, due, so his physicians believe, to a blow on the head from a pitched ball while playing in the major League." If that were the case, then he had to have been suffering from this beaning-based brain injury for at least two and a half years. Interestingly, his official death certificate makes no mention of this accident. Instead, the primary cause is given as "manngo encephalitis," in all probability a misspelling of the term "meningoencephalitis," which is "an inflammation of both the brain and the meninges [the membranes that enclose the brain and spinal cord], usually caused by a bacterial infection." Since encephalitis is sometimes transmitted by mosquito, it stands to reason that his death was more likely rooted in his 1896 illness than in any game-related head injury. In any case, a blow to the head does not result in encephalitis.[15]

Because of his death at the age of 30, some have speculated that an old baseball injury may have been the root cause of the untimely demise of pitcher **James A. "Jimmy" Gardner** on April 24, 1905. A right-hander whose five-year major league career was spent mostly with the Pittsburgh Pirates, Gardner was plagued with reoccurring arm problems that sometimes relegated him to the minors in between stints in the majors. When he was released by the Chicago Cubs in early June 1902, he signed with the Toronto (CA) Maple Leafs of the Class A Eastern League where he helped lead the club to a first-place finish. At the beginning of the 1903 season, he was appointed player-manager of the Eastern League champions. In early August, Gardner requested that Arthur Irwin, former manager of the Rochester (NY) Bronchos of the same league, be hired to replace him as manager. Instead, Irwin was brought in "as agent to secure players and strengthen the team in any way he could." While the Maple Leafs directors planned on Gardner remaining in his position for the remainder of the season, Irwin took the helm before season's end. The club finished in second place with a record of 82 and 45.[16]

According to some sources, in 1904 Gardner was "compelled to give up baseball on account of ill health." He returned to his hometown of Pittsburgh, PA, where he managed the sporting goods department for a large department store. In the spring of 1905, an abscess suddenly developed in his ear. When the infection spread to his brain, surgery was performed. Although he appeared to be recovering, several days after the operation he began to decline rapidly. Gardner died on the morning of April 24, leaving behind a wife and small child.[17]

Two months after his death, Gardner's former teammate, pitcher Frank Killen, said he had learned from an undisclosed source that "the cause of his [Gardner's] demise was a fractured skull received by being hit by a pitched ball seven years ago. The poor fellow lived all that time with the fracture." Clearly this was speculation on the part of Killen. None of the local accounts of Gardner's illness and subsequent death ever even implied that his abscess was beaning-related. Certainly if that had been the case, it would have been included in the stories about his death. And in 1898 when this injury supposedly occurred, Gardner was pitching for the Pirates, going 10 and 13 with 19 complete games that year. The following year he was 1 and 0 in three games before being released by the team. He played in the minors until the beginning of the 1902 season, when he was acquired by the Cubs. Even after his release by this organization, he continued to pitch effectively in the minors. It seems highly unlikely that a player with a severe skull fracture would perform at the level that Gardner did. In addition, an abscess forming years after an injury is medically improbable. Killen, like others who knew Gardner, was shocked at his death at such a young age and probably needed an easily understood explanation for his friend's passing.[18]

When later that same year **William H. "Billy" Taylor** passed away, some papers reported it was due to "being struck on the head by a ball." While incorrect, this was a much kinder explanation than what really happened. Taylor, who played in nine games in 1898 for the Louisville Colonels of the National League, primarily at third base, spent most of his professional career in the minors. Being a volatile personality who was decent at bat but inconsistent defensively, Taylor moved from team to team, at one time or another playing in Atlanta, GA, Spokane, WA, and Harrisburg, PA. By 1905 he was with the Little Rock (AR) Travelers of the Class A Southern Association when he suddenly bolted the team in early September to head to his home in Pittsburgh, PA. For some reason, he left the train in Cincinnati, OH, and began drinking, one of his favorite pastimes. On September 12, a policeman found him suffering from *delirium tremens* and attempted to take him to a hospital. But "a terrible encounter ensued and not until nearly all his clothing had been torn off was Taylor subdued." Two hours later the 25-year-old player was dead from alcoholism, not a beaning as reported.[19]

Michael R. "Doc" Powers, 38-year-old catcher for the Philadelphia Athletics, was behind the plate during the April 12, 1909, inaugural game in the newly-constructed Shibe Park when he suddenly began experiencing severe abdominal pains in the seventh inning. A practicing physician who had been in the starting lineup when the Athletics were formed eight years earlier, Powers, as the team's leader, was determined to complete the game. Shortly after the Athletics' 8 to 1 win over the Boston Red Sox, the grizzled veteran collapsed in the team clubhouse. He was immediately rushed to a local hospital.[20]

Initial reports indicated Powers was suffering from "acute gastritis." But when his condition worsened overnight, attending physicians realized that something more serious was at play. Surgery was performed at 1:00 A.M. on April 14 to alleviate what his physician diagnosed as "intussusception of the intestines," a condition in which a section of the intestine is wrapped around itself or folded into itself like a telescope. Fearing that gangrene was setting in, nearly 12 inches of Powers' bowel was removed.[21]

When signs of peritonitis appeared nearly a week later, a second surgery was performed. Sadly, this, too, failed to improve his situation and, as he steadily declined, a desperate third surgery was required

Philadelphia Athletics catcher Doc Powers' death on opening day 1909 was not baseball-induced as many believed at the time (courtesy National Baseball Hall of Fame Library, Cooperstown, NY).

several days later. By April 25 it was apparent that the popular player was approaching death. With his wife at his side, Powers, in great pain and aware that he was dying, was administered last rites. He passed away at 9:14 A.M. on April 26, two weeks after initially falling ill.[22]

At the time, a number of interesting and widely-divergent theories for the cause of Powers' intestinal condition were suggested. One held that Powers had eaten a cheese sandwich shortly before or during the game, resulting in acute indigestion that was the catalyst for his eventual death. Another argued that Powers had run into a wall while in pursuit of a pop foul. Several weeks after Powers' death, the trainer for the Athletics asserted that the uniform belt buckle was the source of Powers intestinal injury. In all likelihood, none of these theories is correct.[23]

The confusion as to cause is complicated by the fact that the diagnosis of "intussusception" as the basis for his eventual death is an unusual one. While it does on rare occasions occur among adults, it is much more commonly found among infants and children under the age of 2. Apparently no autopsy was performed, so it is impossible to prove absolutely if this was a correct diagnosis. And, according to one authority, his death certificate lists the cause of death as heart failure, which is often given when the physician is uncertain as to the specific cause. But if it was intussusception, then there had to be some underlying pathology that caused it. It certainly would not have been brought on by a cheese sandwich or banging into a wall or a belt buckle. So while Powers' sudden onset of illness during the game and his death shortly thereafter led some to conclude it was game-related, it is highly improbable that his playing that day had anything to do with his tragic demise.[24]

Fleet-footed outfielder **Edward "Danny" Green** began his major league career at the age of 21 with the Chicago Orphans (Cubs) in 1898. During his four years with the National League club, he batted over .300 and stole 89 bases. In 1902 he was enticed to break his contract and jump to the American League, joining the cross-town rival White Sox when offered more money by Charles Comiskey. While fast and a decent fielder, Green sported a notoriously bad throwing arm. Teams rarely hesitated to send the runner from third if Green fielded a fly ball. So by 1905, with his arm bothering him and his offensive production in decline, it was apparent that his major league career was about to end.[25]

In early 1906 the somewhat volatile player — in a 1903 game he provoked umpire John Sheridan to the point of physical violence — was given an opportunity to manage a White Sox split-squad during spring training. As manager, Green introduced a rather curious conditioning technique: he had his players roller skate instead of run. This practice irritated Comiskey, and when Green's squad failed to produce a winning record, he was sent to the Milwaukee (WI) Brewers in the Class A American Association. For the next two years, he led the league in runs scored with 119 in 1906 and 107 in 1907.[26]

After spending three years with Milwaukee, Green continued to knock around in the lower minors in a vain attempt to make it back to the big leagues. In the summer of 1912, ominous reports began circulating that Green was seriously ill in a Chicago hospital with an undisclosed illness. In fact, according to these same accounts, he had been in "poor health" for two years. Apparently he was suffering from some mysterious malady, for in November 1913 a dispatch from Camden, NJ, indicated he was in a "sanitarium" with "but a short time to live." This report asserted that "Green began to slip five years ago when his wife died. He was shunted to the minors the same year and went from bad to worse. Worry and grief caused him to begin drinking and he could no longer play baseball." Money was being raised to support "his little girl, his only child."[27]

By January the following year, Green's problems were being blamed on a serious beaning he supposedly had suffered years before. This curious shift from alcoholism to a baseball-related cause soon became the accepted version. While all reported that he was institutionalized in a ward for the "insane" or "feeble minded" in the Camden County hospital in Blackwood, NJ, details as to the cause varied from account to account. One stated that he "was struck on the head with a pitched ball in a game in 1912 and for several days his life was in despair. When he did recover, softening of the brain and partial paralysis of the lower limbs set in. The dashing base runner and heavy hitter of the Cubs and White Sox is a mental wreck." Some reported the beaning occurred when he played for the Des Moines (IA) Boosters of the Class A Western League in 1912, while others said it happened in Milwaukee in 1908, his final year with the team. "His career was practically ended," contended this version. "He was in the hospital for some time. Later he played in several minor leagues, but his health failed him completely two years ago [1912] and he was removed to the Blackwood hospital." When Green died on November 8, 1914, all newspapers reported that his death resulted from an old baseball injury.[28]

All these accounts and the variations and conflicts as to the details raise some interesting questions. First, did Green really suffer a severe head injury during his minor league career? One would expect to find a contemporary newspaper report of such a life-threatening injury to a former major league star. The fact that the authors could not locate one for either 1908 or 1912 or for any of the years Green played ball does not prove that it did not happen, but it certainly makes the assertion suspect. Assuming that in fact a beaning did occur, would such an accident result in insanity and death two to six years later? While the deleterious effects of a concussion do not always show up immediately, it is unlikely that a single severe blow to the head would prove fatal years after the event.

There may be another explanation for Green's death. While the primary cause of death listed on a recently-acquired copy of his death certificate was excised for reasons of privacy, a researcher who contends he has seen the complete death certificate insists it lists "locomotor ataxia (paralysis) due to advanced syphilis" as the cause of Green's death. If this researcher is correct, this diagnosis would certainly account for all the variations in the facts surrounding Green's death and explain why Green was institutionalized for "insanity." And it would be understandable if Green's surviving family members wanted to withhold this information from the public. Death due to injury is certainly more socially acceptable than one resulting from a sexually transmitted disease.[29]

Right-hander **Laurence "Larry" Pape** was a much-touted pitching prospect when he broke into the big leagues with the Boston Red Sox in July of 1909. After spending several years in semipro ball and the first part of 1909 with the Milwaukee (WI) Brewers, Pape was ready for his major league opportunity. Appearing in 11 games that season, he compiled a record of two wins and no losses with a 2.01 ERA. Pape was on the Red Sox roster in early spring 1910, but was sent to the Brockton (MA) Shoemakers of the Class B New England League. Although pitching for a last-place club, Pape established himself as one of the dominant pitchers in the league, even winning one mid–August game 1 to 0 after hurling 14 innings of 5-hit ball. His performance ensured him a place with the Red Sox for the entire 1911 season. There he went 10 and 8 in 27 games with a 2.45 ERA, tenth best in the American League.[30]

The following season proved to be a disastrous one for Pape. He was hit so hard that he was relegated mainly to relief appearances, appearing in just 13 games for a 1 and 1 record and an ERA that had mushroomed to an unacceptable 4.99. When Boston indicated at the end of the season that they were planning to release their hurler, the Cincinnati Reds expressed interest in acquiring him. For some undisclosed reason, Boston refused to sell him to the National League club. Instead they sent him to the Buffalo (NY) Bisons of the Class AA International League for cash. The unhappy player spent the next two years bouncing back and forth among minor league clubs before leaving baseball entirely in 1915.[31]

After baseball Pape returned to his home in Swissvale, PA, a small town near Pittsburgh, where he resumed his trade as an electrical draftsman. Sadly, on July 21, 1918, the former Red Sox pitcher passed away on his thirty-third birthday, survived by a wife and two children. Obituaries that appeared in the local papers reported that his death was due to a game-related injury. "Several years ago," began one account, "he was hit by a batted ball which caused a painful injury and he never recovered." The national media, following the lead of the Pittsburgh press, also reported that he died from "complications resulting from an old injury received while playing ball." The reality was something entirely different. According to his official death certificate, the primary cause of death was "adenocarcinoma of scrotum and left testicle." In addition, he suffered from "pulmonary tuberculosis," which was listed as a contributory cause. In other words, Pape was a victim of a combination of testicular cancer and tuberculosis, not a baseball-related injury.[32]

A career minor leaguer, pitcher **Lynn J. "Lefty" Scoggins** did have a cup of coffee with the Chicago White Sox in 1913, pitching and losing his only major league game on August 26. The next year, the Killeen, TX, native was pitching for the Lincoln (NE) Tigers of the Class A Western League, leading the league with a 2.58 ERA. While the southpaw was given another shot to make the White Sox during spring training in 1915, he spent the remainder of that season with the Los Angeles (CA) Angels of the Class AA Pacific Coast League. He remained with the Angels the following season before moving on to the Dallas (TX) Giants in the Class B Texas League in 1917. It was while with this team that Scoggins became very ill with what was feared to be tuberculosis. Reports indicated that he "probably will never pitch another game," so he was given a job selling tickets for the Giants. Whatever was bothering Scoggins, he did recover and in 1919 appeared on the roster of the Columbia (SC) Comers in the Class B South Atlantic League. On September 1, he was certainly fit enough to clinch the league championship for his team by defeating the Charlotte (NC) Hornets 5 to 0 in front of a hostile Charlotte crowd. After the season, he moved out West, where he attempted ranching. In 1923, he returned to Columbia in an attempt to again play professional ball.[33]

Because of rheumatism in his pitching arm, he was not successful in his comeback bid. When the team moved to Gastonia, NC, in late July, Scoggins remained in Columbia. It was during this summer that the 32-year-old former player became fatally ill, dying in a Columbia hospital on August 16, six weeks after becoming incapacitated. While a cause was never publicly stated, some believed he was the victim of a beaning or a batted ball that supposedly occurred when he played for Columbia in 1919. In actuality, though, he suffered from a "cerebral tumor," a diagnosis confirmed by an autopsy shortly after his death. A baseball-related head injury would not have resulted in a brain tumor.[34]

Many baseball aficionados consider **Jacob E. "Jake" Daubert** to have been one of the finest first basemen of the Deadball Era. Not only was he an excellent defensive player, he was also quite proficient with the bat, winning back-to-back batting titles (1913 and 1914) and maintaining a lifetime batting average slightly over .300. After breaking into the majors with the Brooklyn Superbas (Dodgers) in 1910, he soon became a team leader, helping his team capture the National League championship in 1916. In early 1919 Brooklyn owner Charles

Ebbets, in a fit of pique, summarily traded Daubert to the Cincinnati Reds after the first baseman was successful in an off-season salary dispute with the legendary owner. Unfazed by this action, Daubert, as the Reds' captain, led Cincinnati to the world championship his first year with the team.[35]

By 1924, it was apparent to both the 39-year-old veteran and others that his playing days were numbered. Even the season before he had been plagued by illness, missing most of spring training that year because of severe bronchitis and "la grippe" (influenza). While the 1924 season began well enough, on May 28 his career nearly came to an abrupt end when he was severely beaned by St. Louis Cardinals pitcher Allan Sothoron in the bottom of the first inning. He was out for a week before coming back prematurely on June 3. Although he completed the game, he "was unable to stoop for a ball without becoming dizzy and losing his balance." Team doctors, fearing that a "nerve in the head was affected," sent him home to rest for two weeks. The prognosis a week later was not good. He complained of constant headaches, giving rise to speculation that he might not return at all. "The injury was much more severe than was at first thought," it was reported, "and the veteran is feeling it deeply." But recover he did, reporting back to the team on June 17 for extended practice. Returning to the lineup on June 25, he played both ends of a doubleheader against the Cardinals. And, in a scenario seemingly scripted in Hollywood, he won the second contest with a game-winning double in the bottom of the ninth off of Allan Sothoron, the pitcher who had beaned him the month before.[36]

While having difficulty sleeping after the beaning, Daubert continued to play the rest of the season. In early September it was rumored that he would become player-manager for the Portland (OR) Beavers of the Class AA Pacific Coast League in 1926. In the meantime, Daubert remained in his position at first and made plans to barnstorm after the season. After missing the Reds' final game of the season on September 27, several days later it was learned that he was suffering from "indigestion and stomach trouble." Ominously, on October 1 team physician Dr. Harry Hines announced that surgery would be performed the next day to remove his appendix and what were thought to be gallstones. Initially it appeared that Daubert would recover quickly, but by October 7 "complications" following the surgery left the Cincinnati captain barely clinging to his life. Dr. Hines blamed his condition on the "insomnia" he had been experiencing since his beaning on May 28. "He has not been able to obtain enough sleep," claimed the physician, "and his vitality is low." In desperation, attending physicians tried a blood transfusion on October 8. Even this extreme measure failed to help and early on the morning of October 9, Jake Daubert died.[37]

While Daubert's death certificate listed as primary causes "acute gastric dilatation" and "acute appendicitis," listed as a contributing cause was "cerebral concussion — accidentally struck by ball while playing." This secondary cause was widely circulated in news reports of his death and served as the basis for a later unsuccessful lawsuit by Daubert's widow to secure financial compensation from the Reds. But did this May 28 beaning really contribute to Daubert's death over four months later? Certainly Daubert suffered greatly for several weeks after the beaning, but he did recover and continued to play well. In a September 17 doubleheader against the New York Giants, for example, Daubert played in both games, going 1 for 4 in the first and 2 for 4 in the second, including hitting a triple in the later contest that helped the Reds win. As for his insomnia, this could have been due to any number of causes, including the "indigestion and stomach trouble" that fully manifested itself in late September. And while it may not be possible to know for sure what role the May 28 beaning played in his death, it is interesting to note that years later Daubert's son, suffering from a hereditary spleen condition, displayed symptoms similar to the ones his father had. If Daubert was suffering from this same illness, one can only speculate as to the impact, if any, it may have had on his survival.[38]

When right-hander **James "Roy" Crabb** died on March 30, 1940, in Lewistown, MT, at the age of 49, the local paper reported that "he was dealt a severe chest blow from a line drive, while pitching in the majors, and this he [Crabb] credited with contributing to his illness which proved fatal." Crabb, who played just one year in the majors, going 0 and 1 in two games for the Chicago White Sox and 2 and 4 in seven games for the Philadelphia Athletics in 1912, may have been hit by a line drive and may have suffered from it, but it did not contribute to his death 28 years later. In fact, Crabb continued to play baseball after 1912, including spending the 1913 season with the Los Angeles Angels of the Class AA Pacific Coast League and several years with semipro teams in Cleveland, OH, and Montana. Clearly this reported baseball injury did not prevent him from playing the game he loved nor from working as a painter for nine years after his baseball career had ended. His death certificate lists "haemorrhage [sic] of lungs" due to "bronchigenic [sic] ca of left lung" as the cause of death. In other words, Crabb's death was due to his lungs hemorrhaging because he had been suffering from "bronchogenic carcinoma," or lung cancer, since July 1938. A baseball injury could not have caused this illness.[39]

Minor League Players

Though just 25 years old and in only his second year with the team, no one was surprised when catcher **John McDonough** was appointed player-manager of the Fort Wayne (IN) Hoosiers at the beginning of the 1884 season. The Hoosiers, one of the shakier members of the financially-strapped Northwestern League, needed a respected, mature field captain to anchor the team, and McDonough was the unanimous choice of players and management alike. A widower with a small child, McDonough threw himself into the game, often playing in spite of reoccurring bouts of respiratory illness and nearly incapacitating headaches. Because of this dedication, he had the undying respect of all who played for him. And some thought later that it may have cost him his life.[40]

Throughout that spring and early summer, McDonough caught nearly every game. But as the season wore on, the catcher's health began to deteriorate. The team itself was suffering its own difficulties, mainly of a financial nature, with rumors rife that the Hoosiers would disband or that McDonough would be sold to raise cash. Before any of this could occur, though, McDonough suddenly took ill. In late June he was out of the lineup, reportedly suffering from "the ague," an illness often associated with malaria that causes waves of fever, chills, and shivering. By July 8, McDonough was in Mount Clemens, MI, taking a mineral bath cure for what by then was believed to be "consumption" (tuberculosis). Clearly no one knew what was really wrong, but whatever it was, it was serious. McDonough stayed in Mount Clemens for several weeks. Suddenly, on July 23, his teammates were shocked to learn that "one of the squarest managers and captains that ever stepped on a diamond" had died the day before.[41]

While the cause of death was hotly debated in the local press, all concurred that it was at least in part baseball-related. The *Fort Wayne Sentinel* pronounced McDonough's death "a queer one in which [e]xposure and hard foul tips disabled him." The attending physician, according to the paper, said "he did not have consumption or any necessarily fatal disease, but that he made up his mind he would die" and that this attitude "hurried his untimely end." The Fort Wayne *Daily Gazette* had a slightly different take on the matter, asserting that he had suffered in silence for at least two years. "From the time of his first appearance in this city last season," according to this version, "his most intimate friends were aware of the fact he was not strong. Whilst seemingly enjoying good health, he was a constant and silent sufferer from apparently an affliction of the chest or lungs. Later he complained of a constant headache, which was at times very violent, causing him untold suffering." Never identifying the "fatal disease" that ended his life, the paper stated he had been "struck in the chest by a ball and congestion of the lungs resulted." In addition, unidentified friends contended that McDonough had "a premonition of some impending fatal occurrence, and frequently made the statement that he thought his days were numerically numbered" and that "he had played his last game of ball." Fort Wayne's third newspaper, the *Journal*, was somewhat more specific, reporting that his death "was probably caused by quick consumption, and was attributable in some degree to frequent hard knocks in the chest by the ball."[42]

If McDonough was suffering from ill health all season long, it certainly did not show in his playing. He caught regularly and was an offensive threat as well. In late May, for example, he hit a triple in a one-run loss to the St. Paul (MN) Apostles. And in a home game just a week before he became ill, he hit a home run "over the fence," the first that season and a rarity in the age of the dead ball. Curious behavior for someone supposedly beaten to near death by foul tips and wild pitches. So what did kill McDonough? If it was tuberculosis, the most commonly reported cause, then ball trauma would not be a factor since this contagious disease is bacteria-based. What was listed in Michigan's "Record of Death" may offer a clue. Recorded there a year after his death is "brain fever," an outdated medical term for any inflammation of the brain or the meninges that surround the brain and spinal cord which, in most cases, is caused by an infection. Meningitis and encephalitis are the most common types of "brain fever," and blows to the chest would not have resulted in either. So whether it was tuberculosis or "brain fever," neither would have resulted from a baseball-related injury.[43]

In the fourth inning of a July 28, 1895, game in Fort Worth, TX, between that city's Panthers and the Galveston (TX) Sand Crabs of the Texas-Southern League, Galveston catcher **George Dean** was guarding the plate when a throw from the outfield forced him into the path of Charley Elsey, the Fort Worth baserunner. The ensuing collision knocked Dean unconscious, injuring him severely and causing a delay until he could be carried off the field. By the end of the game, though, Dean was up and moving around and there was every expectation that he would be out only a couple of days. Instead, he became seriously ill, and two weeks later was "confined to his bed" with what was thought to be "typhoid fever, caused from a blow to the head received in Fort Worth." His health continued to decline and by August 18, he was reported to be "almost unconscious" and "very near crossing the great divide." Indeed, when the 26-year-old player died at his sister's home in Galveston later that night, the papers reported that it was due to "a combined attack of typhoid malarial fever and what is supposed to be concussion of the brain." For whatever reason, the press was convinced that the collision three weeks earlier was a major factor in his death. The attending physician was in total disagreement with this journalistic diagnosis and refused to sign the death certificate until the controversy was settled. Two days later, "to prevent any further discussion and a possible disinterment," an official autopsy was held. Finding no evidence of a brain concussion, the coroner concluded that Dean had died from "malarial typhoid fever" and that his baseball injury was not a contributing cause.[44]

One of the more persistently misreported fatality legends involves **James C. "John" Bender**, younger brother of Hall-of-Fame pitcher Charles "Chief" Bender. John, who was not as talented as his more famous brother, never got his shot at the big leagues. Instead, he spent his entire trouble-plagued career moving from team to team in the minors, desperately attempting to stay in the game. Like his older sibling, Bender was a student at the Carlisle Indian Industrial School in Carlisle, PA, but for some undisclosed reason was expelled before he graduated. In 1905 he was acquired by the Charleston (SC) Sea Gulls of the Class C South Atlantic League to play the outfield. From there, he moved on to teams in Jacksonville, FL, Charleston, SC, Augusta, GA, Omaha, NE, Columbia, SC, and various other towns. It was while he was playing in Columbia that he was involved in an incident that resulted in his temporary suspension from minor league baseball by the National Association. While returning to Charleston, SC, by steamer from Jacksonville, FL, on July 19, Bender, who had been drinking heavily, got into an argument with Columbia manager Win Clark. During the ensuing struggle, Bender pulled a knife and stabbed Clark several times on the left shoulder, near the heart, and in the stomach. Clark lived, but Bender was blacklisted throughout professional ball.[45]

The ban was eventually lifted and Bender attempted to make a comeback in 1911. Toward the end of the season, be signed on as an outfielder for the Edmonton (Alberta) Eskimos of the Class D Western Canada League. He proved ineffective and was cut from the team shortly before the last game of the season on September 2. Although Bender resided in Charleston, he remained in Edmonton for several weeks after the season. On the morning of September 25, he entered Lewis Brothers Café in Edmonton to eat breakfast. After consuming what was later described as a "hearty" meal, he left the restaurant, but returned shortly to meet some friends. As he spoke to them, he suddenly "threw his hands above his head and fell at length on the floor." A physician was summoned, but Bender, who had experienced heart problems earlier that year, died from heart failure before help arrived ten minutes later.[46]

Oddly, what should have been a straightforward story was distorted by the press from the very beginning. His hometown Charleston newspaper reported he "died suddenly of heart failure during the progress of a ball game at Edmonton, Canada, Monday afternoon." The paper in Carlisle, PA, where he attended school stated he died during a game "due to heart failure, brought on by excitement." And while Bender was an outfielder who never pitched in the minor leagues, *Sporting Life* added another twist to these erroneous reports by referring to him as "the Indian pitcher," clearly confusing him with his illustrious brother. Even today, misinformation reigns, with some recent accounts describing him either as a pitcher who died during a game or an outfielder who met the same end.[47]

Sporting Life was the prime contributor to another lingering baseball myth, the pitcher who died from throwing a curve. According to this publication, **William Craig**, 24, formerly a pitcher with the Steubenville (OH) Stubs of the defunct Class C Ohio-Pennsylvania League, died on August 15, 1912, "from injuries sustained while pitching a curveball. The swing of his body broke one of his legs and caused internal rupture." Curiously, there is an element of truth to this story. In 1911, a year before his death, Craig "snapped his right leg" while demonstrating a pitch to a coworker at the pottery where he was employed. But this is where the similarities between reality and fiction end. Craig died at 5:00 A.M. on August 15, two weeks after contracting pneumonia. His earlier baseball injury did not play a role in his death.[48]

Amateur Players

On May 30, 1874, the *Atlanta Constitution* reported the murder of **Luther Thrasher** by Lucius "Pink" Price, another youth, during a baseball game in Farmington, GA, several days earlier. According to this account, the two players got into "an angry dispute about the game" when Price "struck him [Thrasher] over the head, fracturing his skull and killing him in a short while." This version was picked up by the magazine *Forest and Stream*, where it entered the national consciousness. The reality, though, is quite different. While Price did strike Thrasher (whose first name was Andrew) over the head with a bat, the dispute arose over a game of marbles, not baseball, on May 26. Thrasher died about eight hours after the assault.[49]

The most enduring of all baseball myths is the one about the dead baserunner who was carried across home plate by the runner behind him to score a run. Now over a hundred years old, the corpse-who-scored tale has been repeated in books and articles time and again, usually in one of two versions. The most common storyline has the game being played in Willmar, MN, on or around July 14, 1903, between town teams from Willmar and nearby Benson. With Willmar down by a run in the bottom of the tenth, the exhausted starting pitcher **Thielman** (no first name is ever given) hits a single. Next up is O'Toole (again, no first name is ever given) who, on an 0 and 2 count, proceeds to hit the ball past the outfielders. With O'Toole hot on his heels, Thielman stumbles rounding second, only to collapse at third. The ever resourceful O'Toole picks up his fallen comrade and races home, touching Thielman's feet on the plate first before crossing it himself, thus scoring the tying and winning runs. At this point, everyone is shocked to find that Thielman has died, supposedly from heart failure. The umpire, versed in even the most arcane of baseball rules, allows both runs, giving Willmar the victory it so richly deserved and its deceased pitcher eternal fame. This version has appeared many times down the years, including in John Hix's "Strange as It Seems" syndicated column in 1933, "Baseball Centennial Oddities" in 1939, *Collier's* magazine in 1947, and *The Saturday Evening Post* in 2000.[50]

A variation on this tale first appeared in *Baseball Magazine* in 1914. While the basic story structure remains the same, the names, locales, and some of the details are changed. Now the game takes place in New Brunswick, Canada, between teams from the town of Chatham and the University of St. Joseph in Memramcook. With two out and the college team down by two runs in the bottom of the ninth, the weak-hitting **O'Hara** hits a double. After teammate Robidoux then smashes a ball to the outfield, O'Hara, like his doppelganger in Minnesota, falls at third. Once again, our quick-thinking hero picks up the prostrate figure and scores the tying runs. After the umpire allows both runs in the face of vociferous protests from the Chatham team, "now came the most dramatic scene of all," continues the story. "Young O'Hara was dead. Awed with the announcement the crowd stood around with bared heads, while the village doctor worked hard to restore, if possible, the young player to life." O'Hara, of course, does not survive, having "sacrificed his life that his team might win. He had scored a run while dead, and thus made what ... seems to be the most solemn, most dramatic, and greatest play that baseball has ever seen." Indeed. This version, too, has appeared in print a number of times, most recently in *Baseball Digest* in 2006.[51]

While this legend clearly has the smell of the apocryphal about it, both versions contain elements that lend them an air of credibility. Willmar, Benson, Chatham, and the University of St. Joseph, for example, are real places. And it is always difficult, if not impossible, to prove the negative, that an event did not happen. But further digging and additional research do support the contention that the story is pure fiction. The authors searched the *Willmar Tribune* and the *Willmar Republican-Gazette*, the community's two newspapers at that time, but could find no reference to the incident in any of the 1903 issues even though the results of local baseball games were regularly reported. In addition, a 1970 centennial history of Kandiyohi County, where Willmar is located, states categorically that "the story was a figment of the imagination of a railroad man here who got together with an umpire and concocted the story sending it out on the telegraph wire. It was told so many times that even the people in this county started to believe it."[52]

Who was this umpire? It appears to have been Umps Anderson, a real life umpire in the Wisconsin State League. In a newspaper account that first appeared in print in 1907, Anderson claimed to have officiated at a doubleheader in Benson on July 4, 1903, in which the unfortunate Thielman (sometimes spelled "Theilman") died at third and was carried across the plate by his teammate during the second game. "I decided that the two runs counted," he proudly proclaimed four years later. Anderson offers no further proof or additional details and, when reading his account, one senses that his tongue is planted firmly in his cheek. There is little doubt that Umps Anderson aspired to be the baseball version of Hans Christian Andersen.[53]

As for the later Canadian version of this story, it is simply a slight variation of the Minnesota-based account. The very structure of the 1914 *Baseball Magazine* article is that of a tall tale. Instead of beginning "Once upon a time...," however, it opens with, "They were sitting around the lobby of the Russel House in Ottawa one rainy evening recently, discussing modern baseball..." before launching into the story as told by a "young man from down by the sea."[54]

On April 26, 1907, similar stories appeared in both the *New York Times* and the *Washington Post* about an incident in Rayville, LA, near Monroe in which **Benjamin Harris**, "star outfielder of the Rayville baseball team," was bitten by a "deadly moccasin" while fielding a ball. Although his "marvelous catch" saved "the game on which a good deal of money had been wagered," it "cost him his right leg, and may possibly cost him his life." It seems that after Harris had been carried off the field on the shoulders of his teammates during an impromptu victory celebration, "his leg commenced to swell to twice its normal size, and amputation was necessary." There was no follow-up on this story. Then, slightly over two years later, Rayville was again the site of a deadly snake attack. As in the previous incident, **James Phelps**, Rayville outfielder, "had just made a phenomenal catch of a long fly, which helped save the game for his team, but in chasing after the ball he backed into a bog. He felt a sharp pain and waded out of the way of a water moccasin. His leg swelled so that he finished the last inning with difficulty, but death ensued 24 hours later." And, in an obvious reference to Harris, the Phelps story concludes with the statement, "By a strange coincidence a player was bitten in the same manner on the same grounds a few years ago, with fatal results." Not only did the Phelps version appear in newspapers throughout the country at that time, it has been repeated in at least two recent baseball books.[55]

Like the legend of the corpse-who-scored, these stories appear to be pure fabrication. For one thing, snake bites are rarely fatal. It is estimated that for every 7,000 bites that occur in the United States annually, only about 10 to 15 result in death. So what are the odds that two players from the same small town in Louisiana would die after being bitten while fielding a fly ball in a baseball game? In addition, the authors did a thorough search through the 1907 and 1909 issues of the *Richland (LA) Beacon-News*, the only newspaper published at that time in Richland Parish where Rayville is located, but could find no references to any baseball-related snakebite fatalities. The *Monroe (LA) News-Star*, the *Times-Democrat* and the *Daily Picayune* out of New Orleans, LA, and the *Vicksburg (TN) Evening Post* were also searched, to no avail. Certainly these newspapers, which regularly ran stories about weird events, would have had an article about the bizarre deaths of two baseball players in nearby Rayville. It is also interesting to note that the stories appearing in the *Washington Post* and the *New York Times* all carry the tag, "Special to," an indication that someone unconnected with either paper was the source of the stories. Could it be that this unidentified individual, probably someone in the Rayville area, was having a little fun with these august "Yankee" publications? Again, while it is nearly impossible to prove that an event did not happen, one can only conclude that the Rayville snake incidents are prime examples of baseball's many "urban" legends.[56]

Harold C. Trainor, 10, was injured while waiting his turn to bat during a sandlot game in Ithaca, NY, on March 28, 1910. He was sitting near home plate when the batter tossed his bat after getting a hit, striking Trainor on the forehead. Although he was stunned momentarily, he recovered and continued playing. Shortly after the game he began complaining of pain and a physician was summoned. He soon became unconscious, dying on April 3, a week after being struck. The attending physician reported the cause of death to be of "cerebrospinal meningitis," a bacterial or viral infection of the membranes of the brain and spinal cord. A blow to the head would not have caused this condition.[57]

In a rather curious case of delayed cause and effect, **William H. Jones** was reported to have died a year after initially being injured in a church picnic baseball game in Camden, NJ. Jones, who was at bat during the game on June 10, 1909, was struck on his elbow by a wild pitch. The blow caused a cut which supposedly became infected as a result of dirt being ground into the wound during a slide into second base later in the game. The following October surgery was performed to remove a tumor that developed on the injured elbow. Jones recovered fully from this operation, but in late April 1910 he became ill with tetanus. The unfortunate father of four died "in horrible agony" on June 2, 1910. As found in one study, while in rare instances the incubation period for tetanus can be up to several months (one case occurred 112 days after the initial injury), nearly 95 percent of the tetanus cases under review showed their first symptoms within a month of the initial injury. The average incubation period, in fact, was seven days. Therefore, it is highly unlikely that Jones contracted the illness six months after his October surgery. His tetanus must have been due to an event unrelated to the June 1909 baseball game and the resulting October 1909 surgery.[58]

A case of probable medical misinterpretation involved **Gregory Darcey**, 28, a police officer who played catcher for the New Brighton Police Station departmental team in Staten Island, NY. During a game against the Union Market Police Station on June 8, 1910, he was struck in the stomach by a passed ball . The blow knocked him unconscious, but he quickly revived and continued playing even though in some pain. Two days later Darcey became gravely ill, dying on June 22, just two weeks after being injured in the game. His physicians diagnosed his death to be from erysipelas, a bacterial infection of the skin resulting from a scratch or other skin wound which, if untreated, can spread through the lymphatic system. While it is rare — though possible — for an individual to die from erysipelas, it would take much longer than two weeks for death to occur. If Darcey did indeed die from this infection, in all likelihood it was from a previous undisclosed injury, not the blow to his stomach.[59]

Fifteen-year-old **George Hayes** died on November 28, 1912, in Philadelphia, PA, reportedly from an earlier game-related injury that resulted in "a fractured kneecap." At first it was thought that the youngster had died from "heart disease," but an autopsy found a "sliver of bone" in his heart, which was attributed to the injury to his knee. This diagnosis is highly questionable since kneecaps, while they do shatter, do not cause bone splinters. Clearly there is some other factor involved in the boy's death.[60]

Curtis Callear, 7, was diagnosed with "tuberculosis of the bone" resulting from a blow to the arm during a game (date not given) in Yelm, WA, in the spring of 1915. He died at home on May 7, 1915. While tuberculosis, an infectious bacterial disease, can spread to the bone marrow, it is not caused by trauma to the body.[61]

The passing of **Ira L. Ostrander**, 25, in South Bend, IN, on June 24, 1935, was attributed to "a streptococcic infection on his arm contracted last week when he was hit by a ball while playing baseball." This diagnosis is medically impossible, since an infection resulting from any of the streptococci bacterium would not have been caused by a baseball striking an arm.[62]

II

Field Personnel

10. Play, Health, and Field-Related Fatalities Among Field Personnel

Field personnel — managers, coaches, bat boys, scorekeepers, reporters, grounds crew — because they are usually close to the action, are often subject to the same dangers visited upon the players. Foul balls, bad throws, weather, poor playing conditions, and other play-related incidents have resulted in a number of fatalities among these individuals. In addition, some field personnel and other employees have died as a result of health issues or stadium construction-related activities.

Major League Play-Related Fatalities

Calvin Troy "Cal" Drummond, 52, was calling balls and strikes in a game between the Baltimore Orioles and California Angels on June 10, 1969, at Baltimore's Memorial Stadium when, late in the game, a foul tip struck a hard blow against his mask. The ten-year veteran completed the game without interruption, but later that night he had to be taken to a local hospital. There he remained unconscious for nearly a week with a concussion before showing signs of improvement. On June 22, he was flown to his home in Greenwood, SC, where, several days later, he again became gravely ill. Surgery was performed on June 30 to remove a blood clot in his brain. Remaining unconscious for about two weeks, he made a slow recovery.[1]

Drummond, overcoming his debilitating head injury, attempted a comeback in the spring of 1970. After successfully umpiring at the college and major league spring training levels, he felt sufficiently recovered to seek reinstatement as a major league umpire. American League president Joe Cronin agreed, and plans were made to assign him to a crew in early May. Prior to that, though, he was sent to Des Moines, IA, to umpire two Class AAA American Association games between the Oaks and the visiting Oklahoma City (OK) 89ers. It would end in tragedy.[2]

Drummond, experiencing "dizziness and numbness on the right side of his head" during the second inning of the May 1 contest, had to leave the game. Feeling better the next day, he assumed his duties behind the plate on the evening of May 2. Everything seemed to be going well until the seventh. At the end of that inning, he walked to the visitors' dugout complaining of dizziness. He suddenly collapsed unconscious and had to be carried into the clubhouse. He was revived briefly, but lapsed back into unconsciousness as he was rushed to a local hospital. During the early morning hours of May 3, 1970, Cal Drummond passed away. An autopsy revealed the cause of death to be "a cerebral infarct," a stroke resulting from a decrease in the blood supply to that area of his brain injured the year before.[3]

Minor League Play-Related Fatalities

While not officially a bat boy, 13-year-old **Gerald "Jerry" Highfill**, who regularly attended Wenatchee (WA) Chiefs home games, had befriended several of the players and was often allowed on the field during pre-game warm-ups. During early batting practice just before the start of a July 30, 1964, game against Class D Northwest League rivals, the Lewiston (ID) Broncos, Highfill was standing behind the batting practice pitcher helping retrieve balls thrown in from the outfield. At bat was the youngster's favorite player, catcher Danny Breeden. Highfill was positioned to the third base side of the pitching screen facing toward the outfield just as Breeden swung at a pitch. The ball rocketed off his bat, striking his young friend on the back of the head. Breeden and others rushed to prostrate child who, though badly injured, remained conscious. Highfill was taken by car to a nearby hospital where he died later that evening due to "hemorrhaging at the base of the brain." Breeden and two other players were so distraught that they were unable to play in that night's game, which Wenatchee lost 10 to 0. Many of the Chiefs attended Highfill's funeral on August 2, with several of them serving as pallbearers.[4]

The Tulsa (OK) Drillers were down 7 to 3 in the top of the ninth in a Class AA Texas League game against the Arkansas Travelers in Little Rock on the night of July 23, 2007. With the Drillers' Matt Miller on first after a single, first base coach **Mike Coolbaugh**, 35, appeared to be concentrating on the baserunner, the first baseman and the pitcher, not the Drillers' batter, Tino Sanchez. With three balls and one strike, a hitter's count, Sanchez, batting left-handed, scorched a liner directly at Coolbaugh, striking him on the left side of his neck just below the ear. "We immediately knew it was serious," said Gene France, a Little Rock physician who was seated near first.[5]

As medical personnel and team trainers rushed to the stricken coach, it was clear that nothing much could be done to save him. CPR was administered before Coolbaugh was rushed by ambulance to a local hospital. There he was declared dead at 9:47 P.M., about an hour after he was injured. An autopsy revealed that the blow had caused a "severe brain hemorrhage as a result of an injury to his left vertebral artery."[6]

A death erroneously reported as play-related was that of Class D Cotton States League umpire **Edward Cermak**. The 29-year-old former outfielder and first baseman had played in one game for the Cleveland Bluebirds in 1901 before spending several years in the minors. Eventually he drifted into umpiring. Sometime during the 1911 season, he was struck on the neck by a foul tip, an accident which apparently destroyed his ability to speak. The following winter he became gravely ill, and when he died on November 22, 1911, his hometown newspaper reported that the injury he had suffered earlier that year was the cause of his death. In fact, Cermak died from pulmonary tuberculosis, an infectious disease cause by a bacterium. Since there was no contributory cause listed on his death certificate, one can only conclude that his throat injury was not a factor in his death.[7]

Amateur Play-Related Fatalities

William Morrissey, 22 (in some accounts he is identified as **Charles Larrabee**), was serving as an umpire in a game in Medford, MA, between town teams from Hingham and Medford on August 14, 1886, when a foul tip struck him over the heart. He staggered a few feet before collapsing face-first near home plate. He died before a physician arrived. Morrissey's twin brother was in the stands and fainted when he saw his sibling fall.[8]

Also in 1888, Samuel Stainbrook (sometimes reported as Samuel Hainbrook as in the *National Police Gazette*) was killed by a foul tip to the neck while umpiring in Kincaid, Kansas, on August 29.

William Grainey, 21, was struck in the neck while he was umpiring a game in Brockton, MA, on the afternoon of June 30, 1888. He left the game for about 15 minutes, but returned to complete his duties. Still in pain, he was helped home, where he became unconscious and died later that night. A postmortem discovered that his hyoid bone, which sits at the base of the tongue and helps support the muscles there, was broken and the swelling had caused him to strangulate. Because of the rarity and nature of the injury, authorities suspected that there might have been other causes for his death. A formal inquest concluded that the blow from the pitched ball was indeed the sole cause of his demise.[9]

Samuel Stainbrook (in some accounts he is identified as **Samuel Stambroak** or **Samuel Hainbrook**) was umpiring a game in Kincaid, KS, on August 29, 1888, when a foul tip off a fastball struck him on the neck, killing him instantly.[10]

Daniel V. McKeon, 22, captain of the Franklin Athletic Association team from Newark, NJ, had just called his team in after practice before a game in Chatham, NJ, on August 17, 1907. As McKeon walked along from first toward home, the last batter up hit a line drive which struck the manager on the mouth just below his nose, killing him almost instantaneously. An autopsy revealed that the blow "had driven the roof of the mouth through the brain into the skull at the base, fracturing it."[11]

John Donaldson, 36, was umpiring a game in Millvale, PA, on May 29, 1909, while his brother, Frank J. Donaldson, was at bat. A foul tip off of Frank's bat struck John on the bridge of his nose, causing a nosebleed. John continued to umpire the game once the bleeding had stopped. The following Monday John umpired two more games before going to his sister's home in nearby Zelienople later that evening. While talking to his sister in the early morning hours of June 1, he suddenly died. An autopsy revealed that the earlier blow to his head had caused a blood clot on his brain.[12]

Harvey C. Harned (in some accounts he is identified as **Harry Harned** or **Harry C. Harved**), 21, was keeping score during a game between branches of the Junior Order of United

American Mechanics in Jersey City, NJ, on June 21, 1913, when an errant throw (in some accounts it was a foul ball) late in the game struck him on the left side of the head. He was helped home, where he died the next day.[13]

James Chapman, 19, was umpiring a game among some boys in Bisbee, AZ, on May 22, 1915, when a foul tip struck him on the forehead. Chapman, who was not wearing a mask, left the game to watch from the sidelines. After the game, he went

The *National Police Gazette* depicted the death of amateur umpire William Grainey in Brockton, Massachusetts, on June 30, 1888.

home where he helped his mother with some chores. Later that evening he complained of a headache. Stating that "it was different from any headache he had ever had," Chapman went to bed. His mother checked on him several minutes later, finding him in a deep sleep. After running an errand, she looked in on him a second time only to find that he had died.[14]

Victor E. Craig, 36, was chosen to score a church Sunday school game in Wilkes-Barre, PA, on June 1, 1915, when he was struck on the side of the head by a foul ball as he sat on a bench just a short distance from home plate. Knocked unconscious, participants revived him after several minutes by pouring water on his head. He completed the game, then walked the two miles back to his home. About thirty minutes later, Craig complained of a severe headache before falling unconscious. A physician was called, but Craig died of a skull fracture later that night.[15]

John Salo, 38, an officer with the Passaic, NJ, police department, was struck in the head by a pitched ball while handling security during a game at the Third Ward Ball Park in Passaic on the afternoon of October 4, 1931. Though in pain, Salo remained at his post, even directing traffic at the end of the game. Shortly afterwards, he collapsed and was rushed to an area hospital. Although he regained consciousness briefly, he died at 9:30 that evening. Ziggy Mayo, the pitcher who threw the fatal pitch, was unaware that he had seriously injured Salo until the next morning. He was cleared on any legal responsibility for Salo's death. A long-distance marathoner known locally as the "Flying Finn," Salo had achieved national fame in 1929 by winning a New York to Los Angeles foot race in 526 hours, 57 minutes, and 30 seconds. The year before he had come in second in a similar race from Los Angeles to New York.[16]

Robert Preston Pitts, 12, was helping shag flies during practice before a Tri-County League amateur game in Centreville, VA, on September 14, 1958. As he ran in from the outfield between second and third, a ball being thrown around by some of the infielders struck him on the left temple. He collapsed unconscious between the two bases. Pitts was immediately taken to a nearby medical facility, where he was pronounced dead from a fractured skull.[17]

George McCormick, 10, was not allowed to play in the Park Ridge (IL) Boys Baseball League because of poor eyesight. The youngster was offered the position of bat boy instead, which he accepted because of his love for the game. During practice on May 24, 1961, McCormick was standing next to the coach retrieving balls as the coach pitched batting practice. A line drive off the bat of one of the boys struck McCormick on the right temple. The coach sat him on the bench, bathed his head with water, then sent him home. He also called the boy's father to let him know what happened. Two days later, the father showed up at practice to inform the team that his son was suffering from a concussion. On May 28, McCormick was taken to a local hospital when his condition worsened. In spite of emergency surgery, he died from a brain hemorrhage at 1:20 A.M. on May 29.[18]

Leonard "Len" Handel, 34, sports editor for the *Anaheim (CA) Bulletin*, was covering the first game of a Connie Mack League doubleheader on July 23, 1965, when a high foul ball struck him on the right temple as he sat at a table behind the backstop. Handel appeared to be unhurt and stayed for both games. Shortly afterwards, though, he became ill and was taken to an area hospital, where he underwent nearly three hours of surgery early the next day. He died from a brain concussion and blood clot on the evening of July 26 after suffering a stroke the day before. Handel's widow sued the city of Anaheim and six other parties claiming that there was not enough protective screening. The suit was dismissed on April 1, 1970, due to lack of evidence showing any negligence on the part of the parties involved.[19]

Major League Health-Related Fatalities

An hour and a half before the New York Yankees home opener against the Washington Senators on April 18, 1952, **Thomas L. Cummiskey**, 54, sports editor for Fox Movietone News, had a heart attack while standing in the New York Yankees dugout with players and other reporters. As ceremonies honoring the recently retired Joe DiMaggio were about to begin, Cummiskey suddenly slumped on the dugout steps. Yankee catcher Yogi Berra, who caught Cummiskey as he fell forward, helped carry the stricken newsman into the Yankee clubhouse. Dr. Bobby Brown, Yankee third baseman, and the team physician, Dr. Sidney Gaynor, attempted to revive Cummiskey without success. He died in the clubhouse without regaining consciousness.[20]

With temperatures in the eighties, Washington Senators 65-year-old first base coach **Clyde Milan** had a heart attack shortly after hitting fungoes to the infielders during afternoon drills on March 3, 1953, in Orlando, FL. Milan walked into the team clubhouse asking for assistance, stretching out on a bench as an ambulance was summoned. He was rushed to an Orlando hospital, where he died two hours after being stricken. Milan, who had played for Washington from 1907 through 1922 and was Walter Johnson's roommate during that time, was considered one of the premier outfielders in the Deadball Era. In 1912 and 1913, he beat out Ty Cobb as the top base stealer in the American League. He managed Washington briefly in 1922, his final year with the team, before beginning a career as a minor league manager. A coach with Washington for the previous 15 seasons, Milan had apparently been suffering chest pains for awhile without reporting them. The cause of his heart attack was diagnosed as "coronary occlusion," a blockage in the arteries supplying blood to the heart.[21]

With over 53,000 excited fans attending opening day for the National League Central champion Cincinnati Reds on April 1, 1996, Riverfront Stadium was rocking as umpire **John McSherry**, 51, took up his position behind home plate. Starting his twenty-sixth year as a major league umpire, crew chief McSherry was considered one of the fairest and most personable officials in the game, someone who could listen to a player's gripes or a manager's protests without taking it personally. But at 328 pounds, he had a long history of obesity and health-related problems. A number of times over the previous few seasons he had been forced to leave games, including game 7 of the 1992 National League championship, because he had been overcome by illness, usually as a result of the heat or dehydration. In fact, he was suffering from an irregular heart beat and had postponed treatment until April 2 so he could umpire that day's game.[22]

As opening day ceremonies concluded, no one was aware that anything was wrong. McSherry seemed to be feeling fine, telling Reds catcher Eddie Taubensee shortly before first pitch, "Eddie, you can call the first two innings." Shortly thereafter, though, tragedy struck. Reds pitcher Pete Schourek had made short work of the first two Montreal Expos batters, getting Mark Grudzielanek to fly out and Mike Lansing to strike out swinging. Then on the second pitch to Rondell White, McSherry stood, said, "Hold on, time out for a second," motioned to second base umpire Steve Hallion, and turned to walk toward the clubhouse. When he suddenly collapsed face-first near home plate, players and officials ran to his assistance. "Once we rolled John over," stated umpire Jerry Crawford later, "he never regained consciousness. I don't think he heard me talking to him." Physicians worked on him for 15 minutes until he could be taken to the hospital. He was pronounced dead about 20 minutes after arrival, a victim of "sudden cardiac death." The game itself was called off after players decided collectively that they could not continue. "Nobody wanted to play after seeing something like that happen," explained Reds manager Ray Knight afterwards. "We didn't feel right about playing."[23]

Minor League Health-Related Fatalities

Michael "By Thunder Mike" Finn, 61-year-old co-owner of the Omaha (NE) Buffaloes of the Class A Western League, was seated in the owners' box with family and friends during a thrilling home game against the visiting Tulsa (OK) Oilers on May 6, 1922. Finn, who had managed in the minors for several years before serving as a major league scout, had been seriously ill with heart problems at his home in Little Rock, AR, for the previous two months and was warned by his doctor not to go to the game. But go he did, insisting, "It will do me good." With the Buffaloes leading 2 to 1 in the third, Tulsa was at bat with one on and one out. When the Oilers' right fielder, Yank Davis, parked one over the right field fence to give his team a one-run lead, Finn became very agitated. "Don't get excited, Mike," remarked a concerned friend seated next to Finn, "I think we had better get out of here." As a double immediately followed Davis' homer, Finn "with a shudder ... grasped the arms of his seat, swayed a second, slipped foreward [sic] on his face, striking his forehead on the arm of a chair as he fell." A physician ran to assist the owner, who had suffered a heart attack, but there was little that could be done. Finn was still breathing as he was taken beneath the grandstand for further treatment. Along the way, he suffered a second attack, dying as last rites were being administered.[24]

A career minor league player and manager, 51-year-old **Ray Brubaker** was in his second year at the helm of the Terre Haute (IN) Phillies of the Class B Three-I League in 1947. Early in the season, everything seemed to be going well for Terre Haute. After placing fourth the year before, they were a much better team this season, running neck and neck for first place with four other contenders. In early May the Phillies traveled to Iowa to take on one of their chief rivals, the Waterloo Hawks. Throughout the day of May 3, Brubaker had been complaining of indigestion. Although the Phillies were scheduled to play the final game of the series that evening, his players urged him to stay away from the park. Realizing the importance of a Phillies win, he refused to do so. His one concession, though, was to remain in the dugout while he sent one of his pitchers out to his coaching position at third when the Phillies were at bat. Down by two runs in the top of the ninth, Terre Haute staged an exciting rally to tie the score on a two-run homer. With one out in the bottom of the inning, Brubaker suddenly had a heart attack and collapsed in the dugout. The attending physician pronounced the manager dead shortly after he was carried into the clubhouse.[25]

Amateur Health-Related Fatalities

William M. "Pinky" Hargrave, 44, played professional ball for 22 seasons at both the major and minor league levels. For 10 years he caught for the Washington Senators, the St. Louis Browns, the Detroit Tigers, and the Boston Braves, ending his major league career after the 1933 season with a lifetime .278 batting average in 650 games. He continued to play minor league and semipro ball for the next several years, even after becoming an employee of the Fort Wayne, IN, utilities department in 1935. When his playing days ended in 1938, Hargrave kept his hand in the game by umpiring amateur and semipro contests in the area. At 9:40 on the morning of October 3, 1942, Hargrave was at Dwenger Park in Fort Wayne helping to convert the baseball diamond into a football field for the fall season, when he suddenly collapsed, dying before help could arrive. An autopsy revealed that the former catcher had suffered a massive heart attack.[26]

Emmit J. Goodbody, 53, was coaching third base during an industrial league game in Chula Vista, CA, on November 9, 1958, when he collapsed on the field about 4:20 P.M. One of the umpires, a medical corpsman at the nearby naval hospital, administered CPR until an ambulance could arrive. Goodbody, who for the previous five years had been under treatment for a heart condition, was declared dead-on-arrival at the hospital about 25 minutes later. Two of Goodbody's sons were members of the two teams playing that day.[27]

Walter "Pard" Pearce, 78, who was quarterback for the Chicago Bears under George Halas and who had played college and minor league baseball, was a much-sought-after umpire and football referee in spite of his advanced age. He was serving as home plate umpire during a high school game in Newport, RI, on May 24, 1974, when he collapsed in the bottom of the first inning. EMTs from the fire department across the street from the school worked on Pearce for several minutes before transporting him to the local hospital, where he was declared dead of an apparent heart attack.[28]

Vincent Ceceri, 56, a volunteer assistant baseball coach at Ponaganset High School in North Scituate, RI, suffered a heart attack during the team's first day of outdoor practice on March 17, 1997. He had just finished hitting grounders and was about to begin fielding instruction when he collapsed about 3:30 P.M. Other coaches in the area administered CPR until a rescue squad arrived. Ceceri was taken to a nearby hospital, where he died about 30 minutes later.[29]

Rick Conyers, 49, a coach on his 11-year-old son's Norcross, GA, Dixie Youth baseball team, was teaching another child how to hit during evening practice on September 23, 2003, when he became ill and returned to the dugout, where he collapsed. CPR was administered by another coach and a player's mother until Conyers could be taken to the hospital. He died later that night, the victim of a heart attack.[30]

Lyle Greunke, 63, an umpire for more than 30 years, was calling balls and strikes during a college game in Blair, NE, on October 5, 2003, when he suffered a heart attack. He was transported by helicopter to a hospital in Omaha where he died on October 8, four days after being stricken.[31]

Harry Udvare, 58, an umpire with the Muskego, WI, Athletic Association, always arrived about an hour before games to help set up the equipment. On the evening of July 9, 2004, Udvare, known affectionately by the parents and children of the league as "Low Ball Harry," was found lying on the field, the equipment arranged neatly around him. Udvare, who suffered from both severe back pain and heart disease, had died from a heart attack.[32]

Scott Marangi, 47, was behind the plate at a high school game on April 14, 2005, in Villa Park, IL, when, in the bottom of the second inning after calling a strike, he had a heart attack and collapsed onto the catcher. One of the coaches administered CPR while a player ran to the school to retrieve a defibrillator. Marangi died later that day at a local hospital.[33]

Des Hamilton, 53, assistant baseball coach for Florida Community College in Jacksonville, FL, collapsed after throwing batting practice before a game on March 17, 2007. "He threw his 35 minutes of BP," said head coach Chris Balquiere, "then when he got to our time limit, he stepped off the portable mound and just fell down." Two trainers and a nurse administered CPR until an ambulance arrived a few minutes later. He died in a local hospital shortly after noon of what was suspected to be a heart attack.[34]

Major League Field-Related Fatalities

During construction of Miller Park, home of the Milwaukee Brewers, three construction workers, **William DeGrave**, 39, **Jerome Starr**, 52, and **Jeffrey Wischer**, 40, were killed on July 14, 1999, when a giant crane known as "Big Blue" collapsed as it was lifting a 450-ton section of the dome roof. When the 567-foot crane fell, it and/or its load smashed into the basket of a smaller crane which was holding the three men who were to attach the roof section. The operator of "Big Blue" and four other workers were injured in the accident. The collapse was caused in part by high wind gusts, which sometimes approached 30 miles per hour, and the size and weight of the load. The structure of the crane itself and the activities of the crane operator were not involved in the accident. The widows of the three victims initiated a lawsuit later that summer. After several trials and appeals, a settlement was reached in early 2006 which awarded the families nearly $60 million in total compensatory damages.[35]

Minor League Field-Related Fatalities

The Memphis (TN) Chickasaws, 1921 champions of the Class A Southern Association, were in need of a new grandstand for Russwood Park, their home field. Shortly after the close of the season, the old wooden section, which had been condemned, was torn down and work was started on a safer, concrete-supported grandstand. On December 19, **Dace Smith**, 25, and about nine other laborers were digging a large, seven-foot-deep, unsupported trench that was to be used as the foundation for the stands when a thirty-foot section suddenly caved in on them. Smith and five other workers were trapped under several tons of soil and loose cinders that had been used with the old stands. Hearing the screams of the few who had escaped, several dozen other workmen rushed to their assistance, laboring for over an hour to free their comrades. While three of the trapped laborers were severely injured, everyone was rescued except Smith, who was found at the bottom of the trench, dead from a broken neck. The contractor overseeing the project claimed that "the vibration of street cars and other vehicles" caused the cave-in.[36]

A workman was killed on February 12, 1928, during construction of the baseball park in Monterey, CA, a facility that the San Francisco (CA) Seals of the Class AA Pacific Coast League intended to use as their spring training site. With the dedication of the facility planned for just ten days later, **James Fancker** was electrocuted when an iron pipe he and two others were lifting fell on power lines carrying 22,000 volts of electricity. In spite of the death, dedication ceremonies went off as scheduled on February 22 with over 3,500 fans in attendance.[37]

Fifty-year-old park caretaker **Sam Neal** was lowering the American flag in center field immediately following a 12 to 2 Longview (TX) Cherokees loss to Class B Big State League rivals, the Wichita Falls (TX) Spudders, on April 21, 1952, when a sudden gust of wind blew the metal chain holding the flag into nearby power lines. In what some later described as "a flash of light," Neal, who was standing on rain-soaked ground at the time, was knocked down by the jolt of electricity as the flag caught fire. Hundreds of horrified fans looked on as paramedics spent over an hour trying to revive Neal. He was declared dead-on-arrival at a local hospital.[38]

Amateur Field-Related Fatalities

John George Schutz, Jr., the young manager of the Erminie club of the Syracuse, NY, city league, was electrocuted on May 4, 1902, when he grabbed the protective wire screen in front of the grandstand behind home plate just before the start of the opening game of the league's season. Schutz had approached the screening to ask the official scorer seated behind it not to use the name of one of his teammates because the player's family did not want him playing on a Sunday. Not hearing warnings from some of the 200 spectators that others had received shocks when they touched the wire, he placed both hands on the screen. Upon contact, he "sank without a quiver or a sound. Lifeless, he hung until his body was snatched away by a friend, leaving charred pieces of flesh smoking upon the wire which he had clutched in his death grasp." Attempts to revive him were futile and a half hour later when a physician arrived, he was pronounced dead. An investigation into how the screening had become electrified was held two weeks later. It was found that an unused Western Union telegraph wire, which was wrapped around one of the poles holding up the screening, had dropped down upon some power lines outside the baseball park. The coroner's report charged Western Union, the Syracuse Lighting Company, and the Syracuse Construction Company, which owned the park, with negligence.[39]

Arthur Moody, 19, and four fans were killed by the same bolt of lightning that struck at the conclusion of a game between company teams in an open field near Mobile, AL, on May 27, 1906. As a light rain began to fall, Moody, who had been acting as umpire, was just handing the prize money to the winning team's captain when the bolt struck the official on the left side of his head. The lightning ran down Moody's right leg, out his right foot, then spread among the crowd around him. Fans Donald Touart, Stephen Touart, John Green, and Charles Thomas were killed by the same blast, and about 15 other fans and players were injured.[40]

George Halabe, 26, a private stationed at Fort Slocum in New York, was struck and killed instantly by lightning on July 22, 1925, as he and two companions picked up trash strewn around the camp baseball field by storms that had flooded the entire post. He was seated on a garbage wagon pulled by two

JOHN GEORGE SCHUTZ JR.

HOW SCHUTZ MET HIS DEATH.

George Schutz, Jr., young manager of a city league team in Syracuse, NY, was electrocuted on May 4, 1902, when he grabbed the protective screening behind home plate shortly before the start of a game.

mules when he was thrown to the ground by the force of the blow. One of the mules was also killed, while the two soldiers walking with the wagon were knocked down. Though stunned briefly, they were otherwise uninjured.[41]

Raymond Phillips, 40, manager of an American Legion Team in Butler, WI, and two team members, William Simerlein, 16, and Peter Hillstrom, 14, were killed instantly when lightning stuck the infield during an evening practice session on July 31, 1945. Five other players were knocked down by the blast.[42]

Daniel Rice, 47, served as coach on his 12-year-old son's baseball team in Buffalo Grove, IL. On June 3, 2002, after rain delayed the start of a game for more than an hour, Rice and the coach of the opposing team went onto the field to check the playing conditions. As they stood in the outfield, a bolt of lightning suddenly struck Rice on the head. The other coach was only slightly injured. Rice, suffering from severe brain injury, died at 1:11 P.M. on June 5.[43]

11. Violence Against Field Personnel

Baseball has had a long, but not so glorious, history of umpire-baiting. It seems from the earliest days of the sport physical and verbal abuse of the men in blue has been an expected — and sometimes encouraged — part of the game. Going toe-to-toe with an umpire was a sign of manhood in some quarters and was often used as a tactic to intimidate and to get the fans into the game. Many owners, in fact, believed that fans wanted such rows and did what they could to exacerbate fan rowdyism against baseball's diamond cops.

In the nineteenth century, baseball was a rough and, on occasion, a vicious game for players and officials alike. Many owners, like Chris Von der Ahe of the St. Louis Browns, were convinced that misbehavior increased gate receipts. Under manager Charles Comiskey, the team was notorious for using obscene verbal insults as a way to distract and dominate its opponents and the umpires. Financial penalties did nothing to deter such behavior since Von der Ahe simply paid the fine whenever a player or coach incurred one.[1]

By the 1890s, abuse of umpires had gotten completely out of hand. As described by eminent baseball historian Bill James, "the game of the nineties was criminal.... Players shoved umpires, spat on them, abused them in every manner short of assault. Fans hurled insults and beer bottles at the players [and umpires] of opposing teams." The Baltimore Orioles epitomized this ugly approach to the game. John Heydler, an umpire during the period and later president of the National League, described the team as "mean, vicious, ready at any time to maim a rival player or an umpire, if it helped their cause. The things they would say to an umpire were unbelievably vile, and they broke the spirits of some fine men." And, of course, if one team could get away with such conduct, others were sure to follow. "Other clubs patterned after them," Heydler contended, "and I feel the lot of the umpire never was worse than in the years when the Orioles were flying high."[2]

As bad as it was for major league umpires, it was even worse at the minor league and amateur levels. Veteran American League umpire Clarence "Brick" Owens received his sobriquet earlier in his career while umpiring a game in Pittsburg, KS. "A close decision against the home boys at Pittsburg sent a mob at me," he recounted years later. "In the crowd was either one remarkable sharpshooter well supplied with bricks, or several. For in rapid succession three bricks crashed against my head and even now [1928] I bear scars as testimony to the accuracy of aim." Owens' experience was not a unique one. Turn-of-the-century industrial league umpire Mike Simpson claimed that "a man is taking his life in his hands when he undertakes to umpire one of those amateur games." One time in Chicago, he had to declare a forfeit after fans and players became threatening. Fortunately, friends in the crowd surrounded him and helped him escape, but not without incident. With bricks and rocks flying about, he made a slow exit toward a nearby firehouse. Suddenly, "a man with a knife made a lunge at me that would have ripped me clean open. I dodged, but a friend of mine got it in the arm and it ripped a slash six inches long up his forearm. He had to have 18 stitches taken in it." And the danger did not end there. Once inside the firehouse, the angry fans "pulled down the shutters," forcing those inside to call the Chicago police for help. "I was pretty glad to get out of it the way I did, I can tell you."[3]

A change for the better began when the American League was established by Ban Johnson in 1901. He took whatever measures necessary to end rowdyism among players and fans, most especially toward umpires. "There must be no profanity on the ball field," he declared in a 1901 directive to

EXPERIENTIA DOCET.

Mrs. H.: WHAT ON EARTH ARE YOU DOING? ARE YOU CRAZY?
Mr. H.: NO. IT'S ALL RIGHT, MY DEAR. I AM GOING TO BE UMPIRE AT A BASE-BALL MATCH, THAT'S ALL.

In the nineteenth century, umpires were often the victims of assaults from players and fans alike, as humorously portrayed in this 1884 *Life* magazine cartoon.

American League owners. "The umpires are agents of the League and must be treated with respect. I will suspend any Manager or player who uses profane or vulgar language to an Umpire, and that suspension will remain in force until such time as the offender can learn to bridle his tongue." A man of his word, Johnson suspended several players that year, including future Hall-of-Fame pitcher Joe McGinnity of the Baltimore Orioles for spitting twice in the face of an umpire and Chicago White Sox shortstop Frank Shugart for attacking another. As the public responded positively to this cleaner type of ball, the popularity of the American League grew, forcing the National League to change as well.[4]

It was a slow process, however. When umpire Billy Evans was nearly killed by a glass bottle thrown by a 17-year-old fan in a September 15, 1907, game between the St. Louis Browns and Detroit Tigers, Ban Johnson ordered owners to suppress rowdyism in the stands or face heavy fines. He even considered banning sales of all liquids in glass containers at American League parks. Further progress to suppress hooliganism aimed at players and officials occurred in 1921 when National League president, and ex-umpire, John Heydler instituted a plan to have vendors report any egregious fan misbehavior they saw to the league for possible prosecution.[5]

While the life of the umpire has improved considerably over the years, he is still subject to aggressive and physically threatening behavior even today. In a 1994 statewide survey of baseball and softball umpires in Ohio, 84 of the 782 respondents reported that they had suffered physical assaults at least once in their careers. While 44 percent indicated the confrontations were minor ("pushing and shoving"), about an equal number reported more serious attacks ("choking or hitting with a bat"). Interestingly, coaches were most often the assailants in

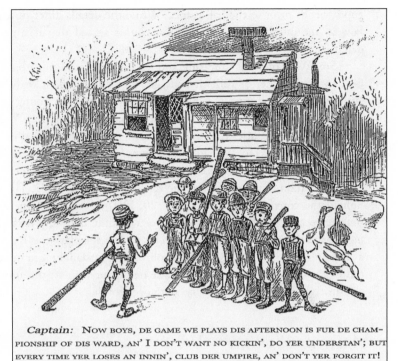

Captain: NOW BOYS, DE GAME WE PLAYS DIS AFTERNOON IS FUR DE CHAMPIONSHIP OF DIS WARD, AN' I DON'T WANT NO KICKIN', DO YER UNDERSTAN'; BUT EVERY TIME YER LOSES AN INNIN', CLUB DER UMPIRE, AN' DON'T YER FORGIT IT!

An 1889 *Life* illustration shows how player rowdyism was sometimes directed at umpires in order to influence the outcome of the game.

baseball, while in softball assaults came mainly from players. The author of the study concluded that "these assaults are frequent enough and often serious enough to warrant organized concern."[6]

Black Baseball Fatalities — Umpires

Sam Powell, 19, acting as umpire, was killed by Frank McCoy, 18, over a disputed call during a game between African American teams in Lowndesboro, AL, on April 29, 1899. There are at least two different versions of how the killing came about. The most popular one involves a heated contest between the Reds and the Blues, two local teams. Powell was apparently biased in favor of the Reds and interpreted several close plays in their favor. With two on in the seventh, McCoy, batting for the Blues, hit what he thought was a home run. As he reached the plate, Powell informed him that his hit was foul. The enraged player called the umpire a "sneaking thief." At that, Powell knocked McCoy to the ground and "stamped on his face." When McCoy was able to get up, he "seized a baseball bat and hit Powell, crushing his skull and producing instant death." In the second version, McCoy "hit a hot grounder ball to the shortstop, who was slow in fielding it." When Powell called McCoy out on a close play at first, McCoy called him a liar, and a fight ensued. After other players pulled Powell off of McCoy, he grabbed a bat and charged McCoy. The fearful player in turn "seized another bat and brained his antagonist, killing him instantly. Five hundred people witnessed the tragedy," concludes this alternate version, "many women fainting. McCoy and Powell were good friends prior to the ball game." While the details differ, it is clear that McCoy did kill Powell, the umpire, with a bat. All accounts agreed that it appeared to be an act of self-defense.[7]

Son Williams was umpiring and keeping score during a baseball game in Briar Creek, GA, in the summer of 1911 when he got into an argument with Son Young over the score. Williams contended the opposing team had five runs while Young insisted they had only three. As Williams walked toward Young with his hand in his pocket, Young pulled a gun and shot him. During the murder trial that followed, Young insisted that he was acting in self-defense because he interpreted Williams' advancing on him with his hand hidden inside his pants pocket as a threat. Young was convicted of manslaughter and sentenced to five years in prison. He appealed on the grounds that the verdict was not justified. The Georgia Court of Appeals upheld the conviction on November 20, 1911, ruling that "where a baseball player and an umpire become involved in a quarrel over a point in the game, and while the umpire is advancing toward the player with his hand in his pocket the player pulls a pistol and kills the umpire, a verdict finding the player guilty of voluntary manslaughter in not contrary to law, nor without evidence to support it." Or, as one newspaper put it, the appeals court held that it was a "crime to kill an umpire" in the state of Georgia.[8]

Amateur Fatalities — Umpires

Bob Nell, 47-year-old farmer from Bullitt County, KY, and Jack Deacon, young laborer from nearby Nelson County, had a long-standing contentious relationship. Their main area of conflict centered around Nell's widowed daughter, Carrie Craven, whom Deacon was attempting to court against Nell's wishes. Nell, a heavy drinker who was violent when drunk, threatened Deacon at least three times during the spring of 1913. In two of those run-ins, Nell was seen brandishing a knife, at one point promising "to cut [Deacon's] heart out and throw it to [him]" if Deacon did not stop seeing Nell's daughter. Deacon, in turn, swore that he would strike Nell in the head at the first opportunity.

On June 28, 1913, Nell was the field umpire in a sandlot game held in Bullitt County between all-star teams for the respective counties. Deacon was there as well, seated on the sidelines as a reserve player for Nelson County. At a pre-game picnic that day, Nell was seen consuming large amounts of alcohol. By game time, Nell's "intoxication accentuated an already very serious lack of that particular judicial temperament essential to umpiring a ball game." The umpire, in a combative mood, fell to arguing with several of the Nelson County players early on in the contest. Things came to a head in the middle innings over a disputed call at home when the home plate umpire called a Bullitt County player out while Nell called him safe. This dispute soon erupted into a shoving match between Nell and one of the Nelson County players. As players gathered around the combatants, Jack Deacon, holding a 42-ounce bat, approached from the rear. Suddenly, Deacon reached over others in the crowd and struck Nell behind the right ear, fracturing his skull.

As Nell lay unconscious on the sidelines, Deacon wandered around the field in a stupor. When he was warned that some in the crowd wanted to grab him, he made a quick escape. Meanwhile Nell, who regained consciousness only briefly, was carried to a nearby house. Emergency surgery was performed on Nell late that night to relieve the pressure on the brain caused by bleeding, but nothing more could be done for him. Nell died late the next day.

An arrest warrant was issued for Deacon. For the next six months he hid from authorities, before being captured in Hamilton, OH, and brought back to Bullitt County in early 1914. During the six-day murder trial that began on April 20, Deacon argued self-defense. While not denying he had struck Nell, Deacon claimed that when he joined the crowd around Nell, the umpire challenged him, then reached toward his back pocket as if going for a knife. Very few witnesses supported Deacon's version of the event. In addition, the only knife found on Nell was a closed pocketknife. The prosecution contended that it was an act of cold-blooded murder, that Deacon killed Nell to get him out of the way so that he could court Nell's daughter. They provided a number of witnesses who testified that Nell had been struck from behind and did not know who attacked him. Even Nell's daughter spoke against her former suitor.

The jury began deliberations on April 25. While they all agreed that Deacon was guilty as charged, they disagreed as to the penalty. Initially only three favored a life sentence while the other nine argued for the death penalty. After six hours, though, all voted for life in prison. Deacon was subsequently transferred to the state penitentiary in Frankfort.

But matters did not end there. Deacon's attorneys appealed the case on several grounds, both medical and legal. When this appeal was denied on January 15, 1915, his family started a petition drive for clemency on the basis that it was an act of passion, not premeditation, and that there had been previous conflicts between Nell and Deacon in which Nell had threatened Deacon with physical harm. These documents also commented on Nell's drunkenness during the game and Deacon's youth and good reputation. Two of these petitions were signed by over 90 percent of the officials in both Nelson and Bullitt counties, including many of those who had testified against Deacon. A third was sent by members of the jury who convicted him. In addition to agreeing with the sentiments expressed in the other two petitions, the jurors felt they were forced to return the verdict they did because they were not allowed to consider extenuating circumstances such as the defendant's age or his previously unblemished record. This petition was signed by all twelve jurors, nine of whom had initially voted in favor of execution. On June 19, 1916, slightly more than two years after his conviction, Gov. A. O. Stanley granted clemency to Jack Deacon.[9]

Charles Bouzek, 33, a farmer and deputy sheriff in Jefferson County, MO, was umpiring the bases in Fenton, MO, on July 16, 1922, when 16-year-old spectator Charles Woolsey from Valley Park, MO, became angered over a call Bouzek made against his team in the fifth inning. With the visitors losing 5 to 0, Bouzek, standing near first, called a Valley Park baserunner out during a close pickoff play. Several Valley Park players approached Bouzek to protest his call. While they were arguing with him, Woolsey, furious over what he thought was a "rotten" call, joined in the fray. As he drew near the beleaguered umpire, he picked up a bat that one of the players had tossed to the side. Reaching across several of them, he struck Bouzek from behind, over his right ear. The umpire collapsed and Woolsey fled the field with players and fans from both sides hot on his heels. Upon capture, Woolsey said, "I guess I hit him harder that I expected to." Bouzek, meanwhile, was examined on the field by a doctor who immediately sent him to a local hospital. The game resumed at that point, with Valley Park eventually losing 11 to 0.

When Bouzek died from a skull fracture early the next morning, Woolsey was charged with first degree murder. At his trial before a juvenile court the following spring, Woolsey argued that "he was infuriated by an offensive remake of Bouzek and that the killing was done in the heat of passion." According to the defendant, Bouzek was arguing with the player he had called out when Woolsey heard him say, "Well, if you or any other — — from Valley Park don't like it, step up." At this challenge, Woolsey "flew up in the air. I didn't know what I was doing. I started to hit at Bouzek with the bat, but I don't know whether I hit him. The next thing I knew Bouzek was lying on the ground. I got scared and started to run. The crowd caught up and knocked me down and kicked me about the face and body, then the Deputy Sheriffs came and got me." The prosecution did not dispute these facts as stated by Woolsey. Based on this presentation, the judge instructed the jury that if they found Woolsey guilty, it must be for either second degree murder or manslaughter, not first degree murder. After three days of deliberation, the jury returned a verdict of manslaughter and Woolsey was sentenced to four years in a reformatory until he turned 21 on March 29, 1927.[10]

Patrick J. McTavey, 38, worked home plate during a heated semipro championship game on Long Island, NY, on September 26, 1927. With the Centuries leading the Cubs 4 to 1, the losing team was making a valiant effort at a comeback during an eighth-inning rally. The bases were loaded and the Cubs made a daring decision to try a suicide squeeze. When the batter missed the pitch, the Centuries' catcher, Martin "Tip" Carroll, threw down to second, not aware that the runner on third, Cubs pitcher John Bills, was heading for home. But the alert second baseman was and hurled the ball back to the catcher. Bills, seeing that he would be tagged out, reversed course and headed back to third. Diving headfirst into the bag just as the third baseman applied the tag, Bills was not certain if he had made it in time. Umpire McTavey, however, settled the matter, calling him safe. It was the last call he ever made.

Thomas Carroll, 25, a Centuries reserve player and brother to the team's catcher, raced out of the dugout, infuriated at the call. Carroll confronted the umpire by demanding that he "repeat his decision." When McTavey said "safe" again, Carroll struck McTavey on the jaw with his fist. McTavey groaned, grabbed the back of his head, and collapsed unconscious to the ground. Water was thrown on the prostrate umpire in a vain attempt to revive him. "His features became contorted," continued one account, "and his face began to turn blue. Several spectators picked McTavey up and bundled him into a taxicab." The injured man was rushed to a local hospital where first aid was administered. He was declared dead five minutes after arrival. A postmortem determined that "part of [McTavey's] jaw-bone had been driven into the brain" by the blow, causing a brain hemorrhage. Carroll, in the meantime, fled the ball field. The player turned himself in to police the following day. Claiming self-defense, the assailant pled innocent and was released on $10,000 bail. He was indicted on a second degree manslaughter charge a few days before Christmas.

The Carroll trial began in mid–February 1927. Both sides, wanting a jury "familiar with the technical details of baseball," selected a panel of twelve "ballplayers, ex-ballplayers and baseball fans." The basic question was one of self-defense: did McTavey's actions in any way provoke the assault by Carroll? Witnesses for the prosecution attested that there was no provocation on the part of the deceased that would have warranted Carroll striking him. Carroll claimed otherwise. He asserted that when he demanded McTavey repeat his call, the umpire responded by saying, "None of your business; get the hell out of here." Then, according to Carroll, McTavey shoved him. When Carroll shoved back, McTavey swung the umpire's mask he was holding at Carroll. "Then I hit him," the defendant stated. The mask issue was hotly debated, with prosecution witnesses testifying that McTavey had cast the mask aside, while the defense maintained that it was in his hands during his confrontation with Carroll.

The jury began deliberations at noon on February 14, Valentine's Day. For six hours the panel was evenly split, with half supporting a not-guilty verdict, the others wanting Carroll to receive a prison sentence of five to ten years. When they asked to go home at 6:00 P.M., the judge refused to release them, demanding that they reach consensus. "Perhaps that had something to do with" what happened, editorialized one paper, "for it was not long after this that they agreed" on acquittal. Carroll's family and friends present in the courtroom applauded the verdict, while McTavey's widow and children wept nearby. Two of the jurors told Carroll a short time later, "You were guilty, Tommy, but we thought your family needed you."[11]

Minor League Fatalities — Other Personnel

Rising from the ranks of "pop and peanut vendors" to president and treasurer of the New Orleans Baseball and Amusement Company and owner of the Class A Southern Association New Orleans (LA) Pelicans, **Alexander Julius Heinemann**, 52, seemed to have the world on a string. But, alas, such was not the case. Plagued by financial worries after having lost more than $300,000 after the stock market collapse of 1929 and worn down by debilitating bouts of persistent rheumatism, the baseball magnate placed a pistol in his mouth and pulled the trigger as he sat in his office at Heinemann Park on the late afternoon of January 8, 1930.[12]

Most who knew him felt his suicide was due mainly to health issues. Just a few days previously he had told a friend that he had "a good position" financially in spite of his stock losses, adding that "they may tell you I'm broke, but the market crash left me with more than $100,000 worth of stocks." He made no secret of his despondency over his ill health. He frequently said his "physical condition made life a heavy burden." Whatever the final motivating factor, he debated for many days before committing the act. In fact, he rehearsed his suicide in front of the park groundskeeper, Edmond Pohlmann, several days before acting on it. According to this friend and employee, Pohlmann was speaking with Heinemann in his office at the park on January 4 when the team owner suddenly "pulled a gun out of his desk drawer and before I knew it he had shoved the barrel into his mouth." After removing the weapon, he asked Pohlmann what would happen if he had shot himself. "I told him it would blow his head off," explained the groundskeeper later. When Heinemann then inquired as to what would happen if he pointed the gun downward, Pohlmann told him it would have the same effect.[13]

As was his daily habit, Heinemann came to the ballpark on the afternoon of January 8. After speaking with the club secretary, Martin Heitzmann, and the head of concessions, Robert Florissia, in his office about 4:00 P.M., Heinemann was last seen in the upper grandstand, "taking what proved to be his last look at the diamond, as if watching the ghost teams of his memory." Heitzmann, who had left the park briefly, came back and went looking for Heinemann about 4:30, but could not find him. Some felt he may have been hiding in a rarely used room near his office. About 15 minutes later, Pohlmann and an assistant heard "the muffled report of a pistol." It was not until an hour and a half later, however, that Heinemann's body was found on his office floor, the pistol still in his hand. Hundreds attended the January 9 funeral of a man noted for his generosity and his charity toward orphans and the downtrodden.[14]

Matthew G. Laven, 28, a front-office intern with the Arkansas Travelers of the Class AA Texas League, killed himself at Ray Winder Field in Little Rock around noon on August 6, 1992. Laven, a veteran of the first Persian Gulf War, may have been suffering from posttraumatic stress disorder when he shot fellow intern Gregory A. Paddock, 25, three times during an argument in a workroom. After wounding Paddock in the face, arm, and back, Laven wandered onto the infield to sit between first and second bases. As police approached him, he shot himself in the chest with the pistol he was holding.[15]

Amateur Fatalities — Other Personnel

Elbert Osborne, a police officer providing security at a game in Dorchester, VA, on June 26, 1915, got into an argument with Nat Willis when Willis attempted to climb over ropes enclosing the ball field. During the ensuing fight, friends of Willis pinned Osborne's arms to his side. Willis then pulled a pistol and shot Osborne in the forehead, killing him instantly. Willis was arrested for murder.[16]

Erroneously Reported Amateur Fatalities

In his 1953 book, *Lore and Legends of Baseball*, sports folklorist Mac Davis wrote that in 1901 "an umpire named Ora Jennings got into an argument with a player who struck him on the head with a bat — and killed him!" While the assault did indeed occur, reports of Jennings' death, as Mark Twain said of his own, were greatly exaggerated.[17]

On August 20, 1901, **Lewis Orie Jennings**, 24, was umpiring a game near Farmersburg, IN, when he got into an argument with player Marcellus Forbes, 26, over a call Jennings had made. Forbes, who had been imprisoned from 1895 to 1897 for assaulting and stabbing another man in adjacent Vigo County, IN, picked up a bat and struck Jennings over the head. At first it appeared that the umpire would not survive his skull fracture. "Jennings is in a precarious condition and no hope is entertained for his recovery," reported one local paper, while another stated that the "blow will probably prove fatal." But recover he did, dying in 1955 at the age of 78. Forbes served time for the assault and on July 4, 1903, shot and killed himself at his home in Farmersburg.[18]

An equally curious case of misinformation was that involving **William Marshall**, 20, from Wadesboro, NC, and Emile Dargan, 18, son of United States congressman George W. Dargan. On August 30, 1889, Marshall was acting as umpire during a game in Darlington, SC, Dargan's home town, between teams from that city and Wadesboro. Dargan was near home plate waiting his turn to bat when Marshall called the Darlington base runner out at third, ending the inning. The runner immediately began protesting that he had been pushed off the bag by the Wadesboro third baseman. Dargan, bat in hand, and several other Darlington players rushed to their teammate's side. During the course of a heated argument, Dargan struck Marshall over the head with his bat. The severely injured umpire was examined by a local physician, then put on a train to be taken back to Wadesboro for treatment. Marshall remained insensible during the trip home.[19]

As might be expected, players and fans from the respective cities disagreed as to what provoked Dargan to attack Marshall. The Dargan supporters claimed that the player called the umpire a liar and turned to walk away. Marshall, infuriated at the accusation, "rushed toward [Dargan] with his fists clinched as if to strike. Just as he reached Dargan, the latter turned suddenly and seeing Marshall upon him, quick as a thought, struck him upon the head with the bat which he was holding in his hands." In other words, Dargan, "only a boy," was simply defending himself from "a fully developed man of good stature." Marshall partisans, on the other hand, had an entirely different view. According to them, it was Dargan who instigated the violence. He "rushed up with a heavy bat in his hand and struck Umpire Marshall a fearful blow across the head, knocking him insensible to the ground."[20]

Initial reports as to Marshall's condition were optimistic. Two days after being struck, Marshall was reportedly "somewhat improved" with "strong hopes" for his "ultimate recovery." Two days later, however, Charlotte sources reported that Marshall had died at home the evening of September 2 and was buried the following day. Reports of the death hit the national newspapers that same day. But there was only one problem: not only was Marshall not buried, he was not even dead. The young man made a full recovery, eventually becoming president of the First National Bank of Wadesboro, an enterprise co-founded by his family. He died on April 28, 1950, at the age of 81.[21]

Why the confusion and the false reports of his death? Updates as to Marshall's condition were issued to outside newspapers via the King News Bureau, owned and operated by C. F. King of Charlotte, NC. King admitted later that he had not traveled to Wadesboro — about 50 miles southeast of Charlotte — himself, but had relied instead on third-party sources. "I got my information from the conductor and passengers who came in on the train by Wadesboro," he explained, "also wired for further particulars, but received no reply." Not getting any response to his telegraph queries and based "on the strength of half a dozen people who came by Wadesboro" and the fact that "Marshall's death was generally commented on the streets of Charlotte," he incorrectly assumed that Marshall had died.[22]

III

Fans

12. Action-Related Fatalities Among Fans

A line-drive foul screams into the stands at 100 miles per hour. A bat slips from a player's hands, cartwheeling dangerously out of control as it crashes among the fans. A fielder hurries his throw, sailing the ball into the front rows. These, and other action-related events, pose serious safety issues for baseball fans. While there are no hard statistics, baseball, along with soccer and auto racing, is among the most dangerous spectator sports.[1]

The greatest threat is the foul ball. One estimate is that 35 to 40 balls end up in the stands during a typical major league game. While most of these do not cause harm, a few do. How many is not known for sure, but James O. Elliott, attorney for the plaintiff in a 1999 fan injury suit against the Detroit Tigers, argues that his study of Tiger Stadium and Comerica Park found "one significant injury per game," including "lacerations, broken facial bones, dislocated fingers." In addition, the danger from bats entering the stands seems to be on the rise. The author of a 2001 *Wall Street Journal* article contends that "thanks to smaller parks, lighter bats and a new generation of muscle hitters, more bats are flying into the stands than ever before." He identified at least 12 hospitalizations in a three year period as a result of bat injuries to fans at major league games. Consequently, many parks now warn fans about both bats and foul balls. Considering the number of games occurring daily at all levels of play, it is easy to see that the threat to fan safety posed by foul balls and other flying objects is high indeed.[2]

In the formative years of the game, there was not much reason to be concerned for fan safety in this regard. For one thing, the underhand style of delivering the ball that was the rule until the late 1870s meant fewer foul balls. In addition, during part of that time the batter called for the pitch, making it much more likely that he would hit the ball rather than foul it off. As a sidearm delivery began to evolve, followed by a rule change in 1884 that allowed for overhand pitching for the first time, pitched ball velocity and ball movement increased, resulting in more foul balls (and strikeouts). Coincidently or not, it was around this same time that protective screening behind home plate began to appear at ballparks.[3]

Initially, wooden barriers or wire screens known as "catcher's fences" were used behind the catcher to keep a wild pitch or passed ball from getting away from him, not for fan protection. But over time, as fan safety became a concern, these evolved into more elaborate affairs designed to protect fans. The Providence (RI) Grays of the National League were the first professional team to install a screen at their home park, the Messer Street Grounds. These screens were erected in 1878 along the grandstand section directly behind the catcher, an area known as the "slaughter pens" for all the foul ball injuries that occurred there. Similar screens were found in most parks by the turn of the century.[4]

While some parks today have taken further steps to protect spectators from objects entering the stands by installing screening or plexiglass panels in front of field-level seating down the first and third base lines — the most active foul-ball zones — most only provide the typical behind-home-plate netting initiated over 100 years ago. One reason is that many field-level fans do not want screens or other protective devices in these areas because they feel their views will be degraded, foul ball catching opportunities will be decreased, or the intimate feeling derived from sitting close to the action will be reduced. Recent lawsuits, though, may bring about significant changes in the traditional level of fan protection.[5]

For more than a century, ballpark owners have enjoyed nearly automatic protection from injury lawsuits under the legal concept known as "assumption of risk." In most cases courts have held that the dangers inherent in baseball are widely known and that fans therefore assume the risk in attending games. Stadium owners do have a "limited duty" to provide reasonable protective measures in the most dangerous areas of their parks and sufficient seating in the protected areas for those who typically may want to sit there. Usually this has meant screening behind home plate and at least part of the way down the first and third base lines and public reminders about the dangers of foul balls and thrown bats, typically by way of signs, public address announcements, or written warnings on the backs of tickets.[6]

A series of recent court decisions seems to be redefining the stadium owner's liability to some degree. In a 2005 case, the New Jersey courts ruled in favor of plaintiff Louis Maisonave, who had suffered a severe eye injury when hit by a foul ball in 1999 while he was purchasing a drink at a vendor's cart on the concourse of Riverfront Stadium, home of the independent Atlantic League Newark Bears. While the Supreme Court of New Jersey, in a split decision, upheld the long-standing concept of "limited duty" as applied to seating in the stands, it ruled that "public policy and fairness require application of traditional negligence principles in all other areas of the stadium, including, but not limited to, concourses and mezzanine areas." In other words, stadiums are subject to a greater level of liability in those areas where fans are not expected to be paying attention to the game. Similarly, in 1997 fan Heather Reider was severely injured in her right eye by a foul ball as she approached the ticket booth located along the third base line outside the McNeese State University stadium in Lake Charles, LA. In 2005, the Louisiana Third Circuit Court of Appeal upheld an earlier jury decision awarding Reider $485,000 in damages. In doing so, the court found that even though McNeese State was aware that the ticket booth was in an active foul ball area, it did not provide sufficient protection for fans in that area. This problem was compounded by the fact that a decorative fence obstructed the view of the playing field. In addition, Reider's contention "that regardless of the dangers assumed by attending this sporting event, she had not yet entered the field and had not yet assumed any risk associated therein" was upheld by the court. As a result of these cases, one expert suggests "designing and placing spectator support areas, such as concession and restroom areas and ticket booths, away from any danger zones or, if moving them is not possible, installing protective screening around them and placing warning signs."[7]

Another factor at play is fan proximity to the action on the field. As will be illustrated in the following necrology, there were far more fan fatalities in the nineteenth and early twentieth centuries than later on. In part this was due to baseball truly being the National Pastime, with amateur ball played in almost every town and hamlet in the country. Since games at this level were typically played in parks, open fields, and sandlots, there was no screening at all and little if any seating. Fans often drew close to the playing field, many times sitting or standing within feet of the foul lines. Consequently, spectators in these areas had zero protection and virtually no time to duck or dodge a sizzling foul, a wild throw, or a flung bat.

Major League Foul Ball Fatalities

On the evening of May 16, 1970, 14-year-old **Alan Fish**, his younger brother, Stuart, and five other boys attended a Los Angeles Dodgers home game as part of an outing supervised by the assistant director of a nearby recreation facility where the boys played baseball. They were seated close to the action, in the second row along the first base line, when, in the bottom of the third, the Dodgers' Manny Mota hit a line drive foul which struck Fish behind and above his left ear. The youngster remained unconscious for about a minute. He was disoriented when he came to, at first "speaking in an unintelligible fashion" before slowly improving. Someone from the visiting San Francisco Giants' dugout sent up an ice pack, which was applied to the impact area of his head. An usher eventually brought two EMTs who took Fish to the stadium first aid station.[8]

By the time Fish arrived at the aid station, he appeared to be fully recovered. The physician who staffed the station examined the wound area and checked the victim's pulse, reflexes, eyes, ears, and throat. He apparently did not take the young man's blood pressure, nor did he ask if Fish had been knocked unconscious or how he had reacted after being struck. After the five minute examination, the physician gave the youngster two aspirins and told him he could resume normal activities. At no point did he suggest additional treatment nor recommend that Fish be taken to another physician for further examination.[9]

Fish returned to his seat and continued to watch the rest of the game. He even chased another foul and went to the concession stands for something to eat and drink. At the end of the game, the youngster climbed onto the top of the Dodgers' dugout, bending over the edge at one point in an attempt to get autographs. While on the way back to the camper he had come in, Fish suddenly became dizzy and "commenced crying and shaking." He lay down in the camper for the 40-minute drive home.[10]

When the child's parents learned what had happened, they took him to a nearby emergency hospital. There they were informed that it would be an hour before he could be treated. Fearing the worst, they rushed him to another medical facility. His condition was so bad at this point that he had to be brought to the reception desk in a wheelchair, where he vomited as he waited for help. His parents, though, were told that this second hospital could not treat him, so they took him to a children's hospital several blocks away. He was admitted early on the morning of May 17. After he was examined by a neurosurgeon, treatment for cerebral swelling was begun. At first he appeared to improve, but by mid-morning his condition deteriorated rapidly. When x-rays revealed "a mass" on the left side of Fish's brain, the neurosurgeon obtained permission from the parents to perform surgery. The young man suffered a convulsion which destroyed brain function about 9:30 that night before surgery could be performed. Sadly, nothing more could be done for the youngster, and at 1:00 P.M. on May 20, all life support was discontinued.[11]

An autopsy revealed that Fish had suffered a hairline fracture from the blow which forced a portion of the skull into the brain. This resulted in an "intracerebral hemorrhage" which continued from the time of the accident until the convulsion over 24 hours later. Failure to stop this bleeding and "thus to eliminate or reduce the buildup of pressure prior to the time he became decerebrate" led to Fish's death.[12]

The child's parents brought a $1 million suit against the Dodgers for "failure to provide the decedent 'with a safe place to witness the ball game'" and against the Dodgers, the stadium physician, and the first two medical facilities for negligent medical practice. Before the case was brought to a jury trial in 1973, the first allegation against the Dodgers was disallowed and the two medical facilities were dropped from the suit. The case went to trial in September 1973. After three days of deliberation, the jury said it could not reach a decision. When the judge admonished them to continue trying, they returned a verdict in favor of the Dodgers and the stadium physician.[13]

Minor League Foul Ball Fatalities

Dominic LaSala (sometimes reported as **Lascala**), 68, thought a trip to Miami Stadium for a game between the Class AAA International League's Marlins and the Columbus (OH) Jets would be a good way to celebrate his nephew's visit from New York. As a special celebration, he went all out by acquiring third base box seats behind the Marlins' dugout for the August 27, 1960, game for himself, his brother-in-law, his nephew, and his nephew's two children. At the top of the seventh with the Marlins down 2 to 0, relief pitcher Arnie Portocarrero towed the rubber against the Jets' hard-hitting right fielder, Johnny Powers. Powers, a left-handed batter who had scored the Jets' first run after an infield single in the first inning, sent a streaking line drive foul directly into the third base box seats. LaSala, who "didn't have time to duck," was struck on the side of his head. "At first he just seemed dazed, not too badly hurt," explained his nephew later. As a precaution, they took him to the Marlins' clubhouse, where he was examined, before sending him by ambulance to a local hospital. X-rays there failed to reveal a skull fracture, so LaSala was released around 11:00 P.M. and was driven home.[14]

Around 2:00 the following morning, LaSala complained of a headache, then became paralyzed on his left side before losing consciousness. He was taken to another area hospital, where physicians determined that immediate surgery was necessary to stop cerebral bleeding. LaSala died on the evening of August 29 without regaining consciousness.[15]

Black Baseball Foul Ball Fatalities

During a game between a Knights of Columbus team and the Philadelphia Giants in Elizabeth, NJ, on September 6, 1925, Giants second baseman Perry Scott hit a foul that "caromed into the bleachers," striking fan **John Dowd**, 34, in the head. When Dowd died that same day, Scott was arrested, but he was released a short time later when an investigation determined that the death was purely accidental.[16]

Amateur Foul Ball Fatalities

John Gale, 40, was walking through a vacant lot in Brooklyn, NY, on September 3, 1887, when he was struck on the head by a batted ball from a nearby game. At first showing no symptoms of serious injury, he suddenly lost consciousness the morning of September 7, five days after being hit, and died later that day.[17]

David McLaughlin, 24, lost consciousness after being hit on the right side of his head during a game in a Boston, MA, park on August 19, 1893. He was helped home after regaining consciousness. Later that night he went to bed complaining of a pain at the back of his head. He was found dead in bed at 8:00 the following morning.[18]

George Paulson, 14, suffered a brain hemorrhage after being struck on the right temple while watching a game in New York City on September 2, 1895. Dominick Corcoran, 21, the pitcher, and Patrick Stafford, the batter, were arrested two days later for causing Paulson's death. At a hearing on September 6, the death was declared accidental and the two players were released.[19]

Walter H. Gorr, 8, died on June 7, 1897, after having been struck in the stomach by a batted ball three weeks earlier. Gorr was leaving his school in Middletown, NY, when a classmate hit a ball he had bounced off the side of the school building. The blow caused internal injuries which a local physician was unable to cure.[20]

Joseph Collins, 10, was sitting on the ground halfway down the first base line while watching a game in a Boston, MA, park on August 14, 1897. A "swift foul" struck him on the forehead, knocking him unconscious. After being taken home by a police ambulance, he was examined by a physician, who determined that he was suffering from a concussion. He died about an hour after the accident.[21]

Simon Cohen, 11, died immediately after being hit behind his right ear while watching a sandlot game in New York City on June 29, 1901.[22]

Joseph Collins, 13, was watching a group of boys play ball at a dump in Lowell, MA, on September 19, 1901, when one of them hit a foul that struck the child behind his left ear. He was taken home unconscious, where he died a few minutes later from a cerebral hemorrhage.[23]

Ernest Seneiel, 12, was watching a game between intercity teams in Chicago, IL, on May 18, 1902, when a foul ball struck him over the heart during the ninth inning as he stood near the first base line. He fell unconscious and players tended to him as others sought a doctor. The batter who hit the foul picked up the child and began walking toward the home of a teammate. While on the way, a physician arrived and found that the youngster had died. Although only 12, Seneiel was an employee of a can company, working so that he could support his widowed mother and three younger siblings.[24]

Hubert Jones, 14, was killed instantly after being hit over the heart by a foul during a game in Belleville, AR, on July 8, 1902.[25]

Stanton Walker, 20, died in such a bizarre fashion that his death has been the subject of several books and articles. On October 25, 1902, Walker was a spectator at a game in Morristown, OH, between a team from that town and one from nearby Bethesda, OH. He was seated between Frank Hyde, who was scoring the game, and Leroy Wilson, another fan. During the course of the game, Hyde asked Wilson for a knife so he could sharpen his pencil. Wilson opened the blade of his penknife and handed it to Walker to pass on to Hyde. Just as Walker took the knife, a foul ball struck him on the hand and drove the blade into his chest over the heart. When asked by his shocked companions if he was hurt, Walker replied "not much." Suddenly, "blood gushed from the wound," and Walker died a few minutes later.[26]

Gertrude Jaeger, 9, was standing near the catcher watching a game in Elizabethport, NJ, in late July 1904 when a foul tip struck her over the heart, killing her instantly.[27]

Wendell Miller, 12, died at home shortly after being struck on the left temple by a foul while he was seated in the grandstand during a game in Glen Ellyn, IL, on September 5, 1904.[28]

James Miles was slated to play a game with his Brooklyn, NY, team at the Prospect Park Parade Grounds on the afternoon of May 20, 1905. But when he and his teammates arrived, they found that a game was already in progress, so they decided to wait until it ended. While standing with his friends, a line drive foul struck him on the temple. The other players carried him home by street car rather than wait for an ambulance. He died the following afternoon from a brain concussion.[29]

Robert Norton, 12, stood on a street corner watching a sandlot game in Jersey City, NJ, on April 15, 1906, when a foul ball struck him on the forehead. Friends carried the unconscious child to his home a block away. He died before a physician arrived.[30]

Kune Schilling, 13, was standing with others along the third base line during a game between company teams in Milwaukee, WI, on September 16, 1906, when a batter hit a line foul into the crowd. Everyone was able to get out of the way without being hurt. When on the next pitch another foul streaked toward the same area, Schilling, rather than move out of the way, simply turned his back and hunched up to protect himself. The ball struck him on the back of the neck, breaking it and killing him before a physician could arrive.[31]

Edward Bowe, 13, was hit on the head by a foul tip during a game in Troy, NY, on May 12, 1907. He was taken to a local hospital, where he died later that day.[32]

Catherine Murray, 58, was hit over the heart by a foul tip while watching a sandlot game near her home in New York City on April 21, 1908. Although she was knocked down by the blow, she seemed to recover and went home without apparent injury. Later that night, she became seriously ill, and she died early the next day. An autopsy revealed that in the center of her heart, which had "swollen to enormous size," was "a round, red spot as big as a marble, marking the place where the ball hit."[33]

William Bailey Altman, a salesman from Cincinnati, OH, was attending a game in Moorehead, KY, on August 10, 1909, when a foul struck him near the heart, killing him within moments.[34]

John Coffey, 9, and his mother were part of a large crowd attending an amateur game in Manhattan, NY, on September 12, 1909. In the bottom of the ninth, a line drive foul flew past third base, striking Coffey on the temple. His mother cradled his body, thinking that he had been knocked unconscious but would recover. A physician who arrived a short while later, though, said he had been killed instantly.[35]

George Quick, an elderly fan, was struck in the side by a foul tip as he stood directly behind the catcher during a game in Huntsville, AL, on September 1, 1910. Knocked down by the blow, he died a few hours after being injured.[36]

Mary Ludek, 8, was playing near a vacant lot in Chicago, IL, on August 31, 1910, while a game was in progress. A ball batted by one of the players struck her in the stomach. She was hospitalized immediately, but died on September 2.[37]

Edna Thumm, 15, attended a recreation park game in Pittsburgh, PA, on May 29, 1911, with her father. Early in the game, she attempted to duck away from a foul but was struck on the forehead. Her father took her home and put her to bed. Later that evening she became unconscious, remaining so until her death at 7:40 the next morning.[38]

Edward Gabryszak, 10, was struck in the stomach while watching a sandlot game in Chicago, IL, on July 17, 1911, and died later that day. The batter who hit the ball was also 10 years old.[39]

Mrs. John Hosie (or **Hosia**), was sitting on the steps in front of her Harrison, NJ, home on May 17, 1913, when a batted ball from a nearby sandlot game struck her in the stomach.

While initially showing no signs of serious injury, on May 19 she called a physician because she was experiencing intense pain. The doctor examined her and discovered that she was suffering from internal bleeding. She died on May 21, five days after being struck.[40]

James Baneskiewicz (or **Beneskiweicz** or **John Banaskrewicz**), 12, was killed almost instantly while watching a sandlot game from atop a railroad boxcar in Baltimore, MD, on May 25, 1913, when a foul struck him on the left temple. Frank Berg, 18, the batter who hit the foul, was charged with manslaughter, but he was released when the coroner determined that it was an accident. Shortly afterwards, Berg and several other boys who had participated in the game were arrested for "gaming on Sunday." These charges were dismissed by the judge after he "gave them a lecture about being more careful in the future." Sadly, on the evening of May 27, the victim's grief-stricken mother, Agnes Baneskiewicz, 47, suffered a fatal heart attack while she was at the undertaker's parlor arranging her son's burial. The coroner determined that Mrs. Baneskiewicz, who had a history of heart disease, died from "organic heart trouble." A double funeral for mother and son was held on May 29.[41]

Joseph D. Adam, 14, died shortly after being struck over the heart by a batted ball while watching a sandlot game in Chicago, IL, on June 28, 1914.[42]

John A. DeRoche, Jr., 16, was struck on the temple by a foul ball while he stood watching just behind the foul line near third base during a high school game in Freehold, NJ, on April 17, 1915. He died the next day.[43]

Banker Duer was struck in the face by a foul ball during a Knights of Pythias game in Charlotte, IA, on August 29, 1915. The blow tore "one of his eyes from its socket" in addition to causing severe head trauma. He died September 1 in a hospital in Clinton, IA.[44]

Thomas Fisher, 5, was sitting on his father's knee while they watched a game in Gillespie, IL, October 10, 1915, when a line drive foul struck him over the heart, killing him instantly.[45]

John Britton, 60, was struck on the head by a foul shortly after he moved closer to the foul line to get a better view of a game being played by teenage boys on June 23, 1918, at a sporting field known as Jasper Oval on the campus of the City College of New York. He was rushed by ambulance to an area hospital, but died along the way.[46]

Stanley Rivett, 9, died immediately after being struck over the heart by a foul as he sat along the third base line during a game in Streator, IL, on May 15, 1921.[47]

Patrick Lynch, 40, sat on the fence near third base during a game in Wellersburg, PA, in mid–June 1921, when a line drive foul hit him below the ear. The blow dislocated his neck, resulting in his death about five minutes later.[48]

Frank Farriar was watching a game in a Troy, NY, park on May 30, 1924, when a foul tip struck him on the head, fracturing his skull. He died the next day.[49]

Margaret Rudar, 16 months old, suffered a fatal skull fracture when she was struck by a batted ball while being carried by her mother past a playground near their home in Pittsburgh, PA, on June 5, 1925. The two were outside the fence when the ball hit the infant. She died before help could arrive.[50]

Chester Mendizs, 11, was struck on the right temple as he stood near third base watching a game at Camp Warren on Staten Island, NY, on August 2, 1925. He was rushed to an area hospital, but died before he arrived.[51]

Harlan Fogel, 21, died within moments of being hit on the head by a foul ball during a game in Stroudsburg, PA, on August 24, 1925, between town teams from Mount Alton and Albrightsville.[52]

Nick Damore, 12, was hit on the jaw by a line drive foul as he stood near the third base line in a game between companies in Youngstown, OH, on July 4, 1926. The blow broke his neck, resulting in his death before he reached an area hospital.[53]

Margaret Miller, 15, was walking with a friend near the hospital in Prospect, PA, on the afternoon of June 26, 1927, when a batted ball from a nearby game "came whizzing by," just missing the friend and striking Miller on the temple. When she revived, she began to walk home, but fell before she had gone very far. Others in the area helped her home, where she again fell unconscious. Her brother-in-law took her by car to the hospital. She died later that night from a brain hemorrhage.[54]

Mary Novak, 8, was skipping rope during recess on the afternoon of May 10, 1928, at the Union Center, NY, school grounds near where four seventh and eighth grade boys were playing baseball. "A swiftly batted ball hurtling through the air" struck her on the left ear, causing a skull fracture. She was carried into the school building, where the principal and several teachers worked to revive her. A short time later, two of the boys who had been playing ball helped her home. Her mother treated her for awhile before taking her to the nearest hospital. When she again became unconscious, she was rushed to the hospital in Johnson City, NY. She died there later that evening.[55]

William S. Buerger, 51, in spite of persistent ill health caused by a stroke six years earlier, attended a game between the Mohawk Athletics team of Utica, NY, and the Sacred Heart team from Syracuse, NY, at Utica Stadium on September 2, 1928, in order to see his son, Carleton, play. Carleton, with a 3 and 0 count leading off in the first inning, sent the next pitch rocketing directly back toward his father, who was seated close to the dugout just to the right of the plate. The foul slammed into Buerger's left eye, fracturing his skull. The elder Buerger was taken to an area hospital where he was treated, but he insisted on leaving afterwards in order to see the rest of the game. His condition grew steadily worse, and after the game he was taken home and put to bed. He died there early the next morning.[56]

George Francis Tuohey, 17, was struck in the abdomen by a foul during a game in Village Green, PA, on May 31, 1930. Feeling sick for several days afterwards, he went to his family physician, but never mentioned he had been hit in the stomach by a ball. About two weeks later he became gravely ill and was admitted to a hospital in Chester, PA, for observation. During exploratory surgery, the attending physician found that the young man's spleen was ruptured. He died on June 19 several days after his spleen was removed.[57]

Raffaele Massucci, 43, was seated near the third base foul line in a town game between Sterling and Summit, NJ, on May 30, 1932, when he was hit on the temple by a line drive foul. He died in a Summit hospital later that day.[58]

Patsy Cappola, 10, was hit in the head by a batted ball while watching a street game in New York City on the evening of June 24, 1933. When he became ill the following morning, he was taken to an area hospital, where he was placed on a respirator. He died there later that night.[59]

Roger Calvert, 13, was seated near third base watching a game on August 10, 1935, at the Y.M.C.A. camp he was attending outside of Washington, DC, when a foul line drive struck him on the base of the skull. He was rushed to a hospital in Annapolis, MD, but died shortly after arriving.[60]

Norma Jean "Curly" Stewart, 4, an avid fan of the game who was not allowed to play because of her youth, stood on the third base line to watch a sandlot game on the afternoon of May 19, 1938, in Detroit, MI. When the 9-year-old batter connected with a pitch, "the ball streaked for third base on a low line. Too late 'Curly' saw it coming towards her. All her friends saw it." The liner struck the child squarely below the heart, knocking her unconscious to the ground. When a police rescue squad was unable to revive her, she was taken to the office of a local physician, where she was pronounced dead.[61]

Norman J. Macdonald, 52, suffered a fractured skull during a game at the Parade Grounds in Prospect Park, Brooklyn, NY, on July 9, 1938. He was taken to a local hospital, where initially he appeared to be recovering from the blow. The next day, though, he took a sudden turn for the worse. He died on July 14, six days after being injured.[62]

Robert Jures, 11 months, was with his mother outside their home in New York City around 7:00 P.M. on June 4, 1939, when she decided to take the child from his carriage to teach him to walk. Nearby, a group of boys were playing stickball with a "hard rubber ball." When one of the boys hit it, the ball streaked across the street, striking the infant in the face. The child died later that night.[63]

Edith Mae Brooks, 8, was practicing a newly-learned folk dance with her two older sisters and some friends in a Richmond, VA, playground on the afternoon of June 3, 1942. Nearby, a group of young men started playing baseball on the softball field in spite of park regulations that prohibited the use of a hard ball. At bat was Harold Edward "Skeebo" Lucas, 20, who sent a line shot over 225 feet, directly into the group of dancing children. When the ball struck the 8-year-old over the heart, she "gasped, took a faltering step forward and fell to the ground." Attempts to revive her failed, and she died as she lay in the grass. The next day, Lucas was arrested and charged with involuntary manslaughter, partly because the players had ignored park rules by using a baseball and partly as a precaution until the investigation into the child's death could be completed and the case cleared through the courts. Declaring the incident "a pure accident," the judge in the case dismissed the charges against Lucas after a June 5 hearing.[64]

Elmer Rader, 64, a fan of the Norristown, PA, A's of the Perkiomen Valley Twilight League, was seated in the bleachers along the first base line at Latshaw Field during a night game against the Harleysville Hornets on July 18, 1988. In the fifth inning, a line drive foul off the bat of a Hornets player struck Rader on the left side of his head. Rader, bleeding from the left ear, was administered first aid before being transported to an area hospital. He was confined there for the next two weeks until he died on August 1. Rader's widow brought a negligence suit against the borough of Norristown, the baseball league, and the head of the committee that governed the sports complex at which the game was played. Her lawsuit charged that the bleachers were located too close to the playing field and that the three-foot-high fence between the seats and the field was not high enough to protect the fans. As if validating her allegations, officials moved the bleachers back 15 feet and installed an eight-foot-high fence within weeks of the accident. An out-of-court settlement was reached in mid–October 1997, with Rader's widow receiving $45,000, split among the defendants.[65]

Major League Thrown Ball Fatalities

Being the nephew and adopted son of legendary Washington Senators owner Clark Griffith may have done more harm than good for young Sherrard "Sherry" Robertson. For one thing, as the apple of his uncle's eye, he advanced through the minors quickly, perhaps missing an opportunity to round off the rough edges and improve as a fielder and batter as a result. For another, the Washington fans never let him forget it. "A clear case of nepotism," asserted renowned sports columnist Shirley Povich about Robertson's 1943 rookie season, and the fans agreed, making the utility infielder "probably the most booed player in Griffith Stadium history." And while he would go on to a 10-year major league career, mostly with Washington, it was this season in particular that was one of "heartbreak."[66]

Robertson appeared in 59 games that year, but only 28 of those were in the field. And in the 27 games he started at third base, he committed eight errors, for a dismal .897 fielding average. Part of the problem was his strong, but erratic, throwing arm. While he had the speed and power to get the ball across the diamond quickly, he had a tendency to overthrow the bag. This would have fatal results near the end of that season.[67]

On the evening of September 29, 1943, Robertson was covering third in the first game of a twi-night doubleheader against the Cleveland Indians at Griffith Stadium. In the top of the ninth, Cleveland's Ken Keltner hit a routine grounder to Robertson, who fielded the ball, then unleashed a hard wild throw to Mickey Vernon, covering first. The ball flew past Vernon, streaked into the stands, and struck 32-year-old Civil Aeronautics Administration employee **Clarence D. Stagemyer**, seated in the front row near the bag, in the head. The unfortunate fan, who at first appeared to be uninjured, simply shook his head a few times. The Senators' physician checked him over and, fearing a concussion, urged Stagemyer to go to the hospital for further treatment. He did so, but died there early the next day, several hours after being hit. A postmortem revealed the cause of death as a "concussion and fractured skull."[68]

Minor League Thrown Ball Fatalities

Self-named "Art the Great," referred to by contemptuous critics as "Whataman," Charles Arthur "Art" Shires was one of the more flamboyant — and volatile — personalities in the world of Depression-era baseball. The deeply troubled first baseman was loaded with talent, but his inability to control his temper and his outlandish behavior, exacerbated by the use of copious amounts of alcohol, would limit him to only 290 games in the majors over a five-year period.

After playing in just 33 games for the Chicago White Sox by the end of the 1928 season, the brash rookie somehow convinced manager Lena Blackburn to make him team captain in 1929. This was a position he did not hold long, for in spring training that year he got into a fistfight with Blackburn after he was admonished for acting the fool during a practice session. Twice more that year he came to blows with his manager, the last resulting in suspension for the remainder of the season and a $3,000 fine. To pay off this financial punishment, he staged a number of bogus boxing matches with an odd variety of opponents, including George Trafton, center for the Chicago Bears. But when he attempted to arrange a bout with the Chicago Cubs' Hack Wilson, baseball commissioner Kenesaw Mountain Landis stepped in and ordered Shires to desist or be banned from baseball for life. A chastened Shires, vowing that he had changed, complied and returned to the White Sox in 1930. Later that season he was traded to the Washington Senators, with his major league career coming to an end in 1932 after 82 games with the Boston Braves.[69]

Such bizarre activities, though, did not begin with his call-up to the White Sox. Indeed, while with the Waco (TX) Cubs of the Class A Texas League in 1928, Shires' notoriously erratic behavior resulted in a tragedy far worse than anything he did as a major leaguer.

The loquacious first sacker loved bantering with the fans and opposing players. Usually this was all in fun, but during a May 30 doubleheader loss in Shreveport, LA, to the hometown Sports, things got completely out of hand. There was much "ragging" going on between the teams that day. While the specifics as to what caused Shires to overreact are not known, for some reason he hurled a baseball into the section of the stands restricted to African American fans. The ball struck 53-year-old **Walter Lawson** in the head, severely injuring him. While Shires never denied throwing the ball, he claimed later that the act was not racially motivated and that he never intended to hurt anyone. Nonetheless, the damage was done.[70]

According to Lawson's physicians, he suffered "a spinal condition induced by the blow from the ball on the head." Lawson was bedridden for weeks after the injury. He and his wife, Ida, instituted a $25,411 lawsuit for damages against Shires and the Waco Cubs, but Lawson died later that year before the case came to trial. Ida Lawson continued to pursue the suit after her husband's death, while Shires, in the meantime, was promoted to the White Sox.[71]

Lawson officially filed suit in the Dallas, TX, Federal Court on March 27, 1929. On the

Art Shires, self-named "the Great," had a notoriously volatile personality. In 1928 as a minor leaguer, he intentionally threw a ball into the stands during a game in Shreveport, LA, striking a fan. When the fan died later that same year, Shires was sued by the victim's widow (courtesy National Baseball Hall of Fame Library, Cooperstown, NY).

next day, a grand jury in Caddo Parish, LA, cleared Shires "of any criminal connection" in Lawson's death. The suit itself, however, was not dismissed and was scheduled for trial on May 17. For some inexplicable reason, Lawson's attorneys were four minutes late to court on that day, and the case was dismissed for "lack of prosecution." The attorneys asked that the suit be reinstated, and on May 20, Judge William H. Atwell did so, with trial rescheduled for the next term of the court.[72]

In early January 1930, the case came before Judge Atwell. Interestingly, Lawson did not argue that the her husband's death was directly due to the blow to his head, but instead that "he never regained his health after the incident." On January 11, 1930, the court found for the plaintiff, ordering Shires to pay $500 in damages to Mrs. Lawson. Shires, who was represented in court by his cousin Tom Shires, agreed through him to do so, and the case was officially taken off the docket.[73]

Amateur Thrown Ball Fatalities

Thomas Toppin, 17, was watching a game between amateur clubs in Chester, PA, on August 12, 1882, when "a wild throw by one of the players" struck Toppin "on the side of the head, the force of the ball breaking one of his teeth." While in some pain, he initially showed no serious ill effects from the blow. Shortly after arriving at work on August 14, he left to consult a physician because his tooth was bothering him. The doctor referred him on to a dentist, and Toppin returned to work later that morning with "a bottle of toothache drops" that he periodically rubbed on the sore tooth. About mid-afternoon he was in such pain that he was taken home unconscious. He was soon "seized with violent spasms and contortions of the body." When this occurred, a physician was called, but there was nothing he could do for victim. Toppin died about two hours after he was taken home. There was much speculation as to what caused his death. The attending physician thought Toppin had suffered a concussion, and that something in the pain medicine he was taking — perhaps ether — had exacerbated the injury. During the coroner's inquest the next day, the druggist who supplied the medicine said there was no ether in the drops. The coroner's jury concluded that Toppin died from "compression of the brain."[74]

Aaron Sokolski, a key witness in a murder case being conducted in Orange, TX, on April 11, 1903, along with several others who had not yet testified, were given permission by the judge to attend a baseball game that day because it would be awhile before they were called. During the course of the game, Sokolski was leaning against a fence behind the catcher when a wild pitch struck him on the right temple, knocking him unconscious. He died about two hours after being injured.[75]

Sarah Swanboam, 58, was walking down the street near her home in Brooklyn, NY, on June 12, 1905, when she was struck on the head by a thrown baseball just as she passed near a group of boys playing in the street. She was able to make it home, but fell unconscious shortly thereafter. She died at home on June 19 from a brain concussion.[76]

Morgan Doran, 21, was struck on the temple by a wild pitch while he stood close to the catcher watching a street game in New York City on June 17, 1906. He was knocked unconscious for about five minutes before friends revived him and helped him home. There he sat on his front steps for a short while before going inside to his mother. His last words before he collapsed and died a few minutes later were reportedly, "Mother, I am done for. I am dying and I know it. I am sorry. Send for the priest."[77]

Manuel N. Lefkowith, 13, was crossing a vacant lot on the way to music lessons in Roxbury, MA, on April 1, 1908, when another boy playing in the lot threw a ball toward him. The child, who was not paying attention, was struck below the temple. About an hour later at supper, he began complaining of a severe headache. Shortly afterwards he fell unconscious and was taken to a local hospital. He died there about 9:30 that night.[78]

Andrew Luksia, 7 months old, was struck on the head by a thrown ball while he was being held by his mother as they watched the father play in a sandlot game near Pittsburgh, PA, in mid–June 1908. The infant died on July 17 about a month after being injured.[79]

Inez Stephenson, 2, was standing on the street near her home in Indianapolis, IN, on July 24, 1910, when she was struck on the chest by a ball thrown wildly by 26-year-old Albert Mattingly, who was playing catch with two friends. When the child died the next day from "an internal hemorrhage caused by the blow," Mattingly was arrested and charged with manslaughter while his two friends were charged with "playing ball on the street." Mattingly's bond was originally set for $10,000, but when his friends and his employer pleaded with the court to lower the amount, it was reduced to $1,000. His employer then paid the bond, and he was released from jail on July 26 pending the coroner's report and a court decision. On July 28, the coroner found the death to be accidental and recommended that Mattingly be exonerated "from all intent to injure." When the parents of the victim asked for leniency, the judge dismissed the case against Mattingly on July 29, stating that he "had been punished sufficiently already."[80]

Michael Dougherty, an alley inspector with the city of Chicago, IL, was on the job in mid–August 1911 when he was hit in the stomach by a baseball thrown by one of a group of children playing in the alley. He died ten days later on August 25.[81]

J. C. Hays, chief of police in Decherd, TN, was watching a game on April 1, 1913, between a team from the local high school and one from the town, when he was struck behind his left ear by a wild pitch as he walked behind the catcher. The blow killed him instantly.[82]

Bessie Lee Rice, 8, was playing at a Gulfport, MS, schoolyard on February 18, 1914, when a baseball thrown by one of the boy students struck her on the temple. She died the next afternoon.[83]

Paul Vernon McCord, 8, was standing behind first base while watching a game in Mount Kisco, NY, on September 16, 1928, when he was struck above the heart by a wild pickoff throw from the pitcher. He died as he was being carried into the local hospital by the town's police chief.[84]

Dominick Espanela, 14, was struck over the heart by a pitched ball as he stood behind the catcher watching a game in Croton, NY, on April 28, 1929. He died a few moments later.[85]

Joseph Stephenson, 9, was sitting amongst some bats near home plate watching an amateur league game at a park in San Antonio, TX, on April 24, 1932, when Bill Heyne, the first baseman for one of the teams, made a wild throw to the catcher, striking the youngster behind the ear. He stood up for a few minutes, then collapsed unconscious. Stephenson was declared dead on arrival after being taken to an area hospital by another spectator. Heyne was arrested and charged with negligent homicide. The justice of the peace who conducted an inquest the next day determined that the child's death was an accident, prompting the assistant district attorney to announce that he would not prosecute the first baseman.[86]

Howard Prince, 13, was watching some friends throw a baseball around in a Bronx, NY, park on the late afternoon of March 31, 1952, when the ball got away from one of the boys and rolled into the street. The youngster retrieved the ball and threw it back in, striking Prince in the head. He was rushed to a local hospital, where he was declared dead on arrival.[87]

William R. Whitla, Jr., 3 months old, was cradled in his mother's arms as she stood under a shade tree 45 feet from first base waiting to watch her husband, a staff sergeant in the Air Force, play in an amateur league game held at the San Bernardino Valley College baseball field in San Bernardino, CA, on May 18, 1958. As players for the opposing team threw the ball around the infield a few minutes prior to the start of the game, the manager of her husband's team asked her to move to a safer spot. She placed her infant on her shoulder and, just as she prepared to leave, a wild throw from the third baseman flew past the first baseman and struck the baby over his right ear. The parents rushed their child to the Air Force base hospital, where doctors worked for more than an hour in a vain attempt to save the child's life. At 3:00 P.M. the infant died from his head injuries.[88]

Clifford Knight, 8, sat on his bike near first base while watching a night game at a park in Fort Wayne, IN, on June 22, 1973, even though he had been warned about being in that area. A ball thrown wildly by one of the infielders streaked past the first baseman and struck Knight over the heart. He fell off his bike clutching his chest. Other spectators attempted to revive him while they waited for EMTs to arrive. The youngster was transported by ambulance to a local hospital, where he was pronounced dead on arrival.[89]

Cayden Huels, 4, was with his older brother in a park in Wesley Chapel, FL, on the evening of November 1, 2007, when he suddenly broke away from his sibling and wandered in front of a pitch-back net where a 10-year-old Amateur Athletic Union player was pitching into the net. The young pitcher had just released a throw when the 4-year-old moved directly into the flight path of the ball. When the ball struck the child on the chest, he took a few steps, then collapsed. The father of the player carried young Huels home, where EMTs arrived and administered CPR. He was then taken to a local hospital, where he was pronounced dead. The cause of death was later determined to be "ventricular fibrillation."[90]

Amateur Bat-Related Fatalities

Roscoe Conkling, 16, was amongst a crowd gathered around home plate during a game at the Riverhead, Long Island, fair grounds on October 1, 1884. The "striker," with a 0 and 2 count, "struck a third time with all his force at a swift shoulder ball. He hit it a glancing blow, the bat at the same time flying like lightning from his hands into the crowd not ten feet away." The barrel of the bat struck Conkling "squarely in the face and the handle whipped around and broke the jaw of the man standing next to him." Conkling, with his cheek and nose "crushed in," died instantly.[91]

Alfred Moyer, 10, was watching 43-year-old Francis Sterner bat in a game in Allentown, PA, on April 24, 1905. Just as Sterner started to swing at a pitch, Moyer ran toward the plate. The bat struck full-force on the boy's head, resulting in his death a few minutes later.[92]

Harry Exley, 12, was with friends watching a group of boys play a game near his home in Savannah, GA, on July 1, 1905. When the batter swung and missed the ball, the bat slipped from his hand and struck Exley in the temple. The blow fractured the youngster's skull and caused a brain concussion. He died on July 5, five days after the accident.[93]

Edward Scradis, 4, was standing near a group of young men who were playing ball at the end of the street near his home in Pittsburgh, PA, on August 22, 1915. Just as 25-year-old Charles Kleber swung the bat, the child ran in front of him. The bat struck him on the chest, causing him to fall unconscious a short time later. A physician was summoned, but the youngster died while being taken home. Kleber was arrested, then released the next day. Witnesses all stated that the fatality was accidental.[94]

Ursula Thompson, 3, was fatally injured when she was struck by a bat that 21-year-old Herbert Green flung aside after hitting a ball during a game near the child's home in Washington, DC, on April 30, 1931. She died before a physician could arrive. Green was arrested and held in custody pending the outcome of the coroner's inquest.[95]

Edward Drazek, 14, was sitting on the bench near home plate watching an adult league team practice in Amsterdam, NY, on July 18, 1933. When the batter, Theodore Pikul, swung at a pitch, the bat flew from his hands, "hurled through the air," and struck Drazek on the head. The unconscious youngster was taken to a local doctor's office, where he revived and was sent home. He appeared to be fully recovered when he went to bed later that evening. Early the next morning, though, he died from a brain hemorrhage caused by the bat's fracturing his skull.[96]

Victor Weinman, 15, was standing near his uncle while the older man hit baseballs close to their home in Philadelphia, PA, on May 13, 1934. When the bat suddenly broke in two during a swing, the barrel half struck the young man on the head. He died from his injuries two days later.[97]

Paul McMillan, 3, was standing near his older brother and some other children as they played a game near his home in Brunswick, GA, on July 31, 1939. When one of the youngsters swung and missed the ball, the bat struck the toddler on the back of his head, killing him within moments.[98]

Amateur Collision-Related Fatalities

Patrick Cosgrove, 70, was sitting on the grass near first base during a game between town teams from Spring Valley and Peru, IL, in Peru, on June 24, 1905, when a foul ball was hit in his direction. The Spring Valley first baseman, Charles Berg, in pursuit of the ball, ran over the elderly fan, spiking him on the head. The player stopped at that point and helped Cosgrove sit up. The local police chief also came to the injured man's assistance. The only thing Cosgrove complained of at the time was a sore hip. A short time later, he was taken home by car. When he enter his house, he appeared confused and was unable to answer questions from his wife. She helped her husband to a chair, where he fell unconscious. She left to get a doctor, and when she returned, she found her husband unconscious on the floor about 15 feet from the chair, bleeding from the left temple. Cosgrove remained unconscious, dying the next afternoon about 5:30. Physicians were not sure if the brain concussion that caused his death was due directly to the collision at the ball park or to the fall later at his home.[99]

Edward Kloss, 12, was sitting directly behind the catcher during a sandlot game in Detroit, MI, on August 1, 1909. When George Stefanski, the 24-year-old catcher, ran back for a pop foul, his knee struck the young fan on the back of the head. The youngster passed out, came to in a few minutes, and stayed to watch the rest of the game. When he reached home afterwards, he began complaining of a severe headache. At first he refused to tell his parents that anything had happened to cause the headache, only later admitting he had been injured at the game. After becoming unconscious again the following evening, two physicians were called. They were able to revive him, but he soon became "irrational" and died August 3 from a brain concussion.[100]

13. Fan Fatalities from Falls, Risky Behavior, and Violence

It all started with a spiking. In an April 28, 1953, game at Busch Stadium, the hated New York Yankees had eked out a one-run lead in the top half of the tenth inning against the lowly hometown Browns after Gil McDougald crashed into catcher Clint Courtney, causing him to drop the ball. As fate would have it, Courtney, still smarting both physically and emotionally from the play at the plate, was first up in the bottom of the inning. Smashing a ball to the outfield wall, the plodding catcher tried to stretch it into a double, only to be nailed by a perfect throw from right fielder Hank Bauer. While tagging the runner, shortstop Phil Rizzuto was spiked twice in the right leg. When Yankee infielders rushed to his defense, both benches cleared and a *battle royale* ensued. The fans, not to be outdone, started hurling glass bottles onto the field. Soon "the bottles came from all over. Three times Gene Woodling [Yankee left fielder] walked in from left field, refusing to be an open target." It took 17 minutes for order to be restored, the Yankees finally winning by that single run. "But when the final out came the bottle-throwing resumed until [Brown's manager Marty] Marion joined the Yankees walking to the dressing room. Outside, angry fans had to be dispersed by police and special police afforded the New Yorkers' bus protection to their hotel." The New York press had a field day with the incident, calling it "one of the worst exhibitions by a crowd in baseball history." Even the more objective *Sporting News* editorialized that it was "a disgrace of such magnitude that all who participated in it should spend the rest of their careers setting a good example in their future conduct, if only by way of atonement."[1]

Sadly, baseball history is replete with such stories. But unruly sports fans engaging in violent behavior is not a recent phenomenon nor is it unique to the National Pastime. As long as there have been spectator sports — even as far back as ancient Rome — there has been violence, and sometimes death, in the stands. And when compared with other countries, American fan violence is relatively mild. Consider, for example, the number of fan deaths resulting from soccer (football) riots around the world: 320 were killed in Lima, Peru, in May 1964; 66 in Glasgow, Scotland, in January 1971; 99 in Moscow, Russia, in October 1982; 93 in Nepal in March 1988; 94 in Sheffield, England, in April 1989; 40 in South Africa in January 1991; 82 in Guatemala City, Guatemala, in October 1996; and 126 in Accra, Ghana, in April 2001.[2]

This comparison is not meant to minimize the problem of violence and aggressive behavior found among fans at American sports venues, however; nor does the fact that the frequency of fan violence in this country is relatively low when one takes into account the number of sporting events that occur annually at all levels of play. Indeed, even a single incident is one too many and a serious issue for all concerned.[3]

Baseball and rowdyism have a long-standing relationship. The game as played on the field and in the stands in the 1880s and 1890s was rough, dirty, and dangerous. Accounts of fights, bottle throwing, and attacks on players, officials, and fellow fans appeared quite regularly in turn-of-the-century press reports of games. In an editorial appearing in the 1919 *Reach Guide,* Francis Richter railed against the earlier cen-

A "HOME-RUN"—BY THE UMPIRE

Players were not the only ones to assault umpires. Angry fans often took out their displeasure on the unfortunate officials as shown in this 1871 *Life* magazine cartoon.

tury's "rowdy ball," which he described as "nothing less than a continual incitement to willful mutilation of rivals, physical encounters between players on and off the diamond, and riots of more or less violence." Richter laid most of the blame for this behavior on the shoulders of the owners themselves, who operated under the mistaken belief that this type of environment attracted fans to the game. While "some of the magnates could not stand this raw work of the players and protested continually against it," he contended, "the larger number of the magnates condoned and excused every act of rowdyism, no matter how flagrant."[4]

By the turn of the century, things began to improve somewhat. The newly formed American League cracked down hard on players and fans who misbehaved and the National League soon followed suit. But these measures did not eliminate the problem of the miscreant fan entirely. Bottle throwing in particular continued to be a scourge on the game. In the 1910s the situation had become so bad that John Heydler, president of the National League, ordered vendors to keep an eye open for anyone hurling bottles at players and officials. He promised to prosecute anyone identified by a vendor as a troublemaker. Curiously, while some parks (including Busch Stadium after the 1953 bottle riot) banned glass containers, many continued to serve drinks in bottles well into the twentieth century. It was mainly due to the efforts of major league umpires that these dangerous missiles were finally eliminated in the late 1960s.[5]

The question naturally arises of why some fans turn violent. There have been a number of theories advanced as to the causes of fan aggression, including crowd frustration with their team's performance, media glorification of violence, gender differences, and environmental conditions (temperature, noise, crowding, atmospheric ionization). Some speculate that violence among American fans is increasing as a result of such factors as fans' anger over player salaries, a general culture-wide decline in etiquette, a male overreaction to the rise of feminism and female equality, worsening economic conditions that heighten class distinctions, racial animosity, and a desire among some fans to do anything to be seen on television. Individual personality traits are at play as well. In a recent study of fans at major college football games, researchers found that a "dysfunctional fan"(defined as one most likely to be "overly zealous and abusive") was generally "a less educated, lower income, younger, single, with no children at home, male who spends an inordinate amount of time consuming sports media and, presumably, beer." They concluded that "individuals most involved in crowd violence at sporting events have deeper, more troubling, personal characteristics (e.g., chronic anti-social attitudes and behaviors) that emerge not only in the sports setting, but likely elsewhere."[6]

And when you add into this mixture copious amounts of alcohol, which tends to lower inhibitions and increase aggressive behavior, there is the potential for very volatile and dangerous situations. It is a problem that is not going away anytime soon, because beer in ballparks is very big business. By one account, beer sales at games comprise as much as 40 percent of all concession income. So much is consumed, in fact, that "approximately 8 percent of male fans leaving MLB games are legally drunk."[7]

Considering that not everyone who drinks turns violent and, conversely, that not everyone who becomes violent has consumed alcohol, what,

As this 1907 *Chicago Daily Tribune* editorial cartoon shows, newspapers regularly railed against fans who sometimes vented their rage by throwing glass bottles at umpires and opposition players.

then, is the relationship between alcohol consumption and fan misbehavior? A key factor determining when drinking turns violent seems to be situational. In non-threatening situations, there appears to be little difference in the level of aggression between intoxicated and non-intoxicated individuals. However, once an intoxicated person feels threatened, the level of aggression is much greater than that displayed by a non-intoxicated person in a similar situation. Concluded one group of researchers, "physical aggression is a function of the interaction of alcohol consumption and the degree of threat inherent in a particular situation." Therefore, competitive situations in which, for example, one group of fans is taunting another could very well end in a fight if either or both have been drinking excessively. In addition, as the study discussed earlier found, the "dysfunctional fan" is much more likely to believe that "alcohol consumption is a necessary element of the game experience." These fans, feeling "compelled to express *any* frustration via complaining and confrontation with others about anything related to the game," may indeed be using alcohol "to reduce their inhibitions and increase their confidence in acting in a dysfunctional (i.e., confrontational and complaining) manner." Clearly, mixing alcohol with a "dysfunctional" personality type is a prescription for disaster.[8]

Once fans are so aroused, crowd violence sometimes results. Social psychologist Delia Saenz attributes the problem to the "deindividuation" that occurs in a mob: "Arousal leads to a loss of one's sense of control. People do what they wouldn't normally do because the person is no longer an individual, no one person is *responsible* for what everyone is doing. The crowd moves itself along." A condition known as "emotional contagion" occurs, a situation in which "norms are formed rapidly and may be followed in a near spontaneous manner by large numbers of people. Although this does not always lead to violence, it increases the possibility of potentially violent confrontations between groups of fans and between fans and agents of social control, such as the police."[9]

As for fans engaging in risky, sometimes self-destructive, behavior, intoxication is also often a factor. Many of the self-inflicted fatalities listed in the necrology below are alcohol-related. Said Robert Becker, the officer in charge of the police detail around Shea Stadium in the mid–1980s, "Ninety-nine percent of all the problems we have can be traced to alcohol." Research on alcohol use and risk taking support these observations. According to one such study, "alcohol produces a pharmacological effect that may be described as disinhibitory, or in other words, related to an increase in behaviors that, due to environmental context, otherwise normally occur at a low rate. Many of these behaviors may be forms of risk-taking that result in aversive consequences to self or others."[10]

In addition, adolescents and young adults are much more likely to engage in dangerous risk-taking antics than are older adults. Findings over the past few years point to the development of the human brain for why this is so. Apparently, "psychosocial capacities that improve decision making and moderate risk taking — such as impulse control, emotion regulation, delay of gratification, and resistance to peer influence — continue to mature well into young adulthood." As the fatalities discussed below clearly show, many young people have died at ballparks because of risky behavior.[11]

Over the years baseball has done a variety of things to limit fan aggression and the conditions that lead to injury and death. As mentioned previously, glass containers were finally eliminated in the late 1960s. Along these same lines, giveaways at stadiums, especially ones that can cause injury, are sometimes saved until the end of the game so that they do not end up on the field below. As one Chicago White Sox official said, "We're not going to give people hard cubes with eight sharp points and usher them into seats overlooking the playing field." Even then, though, fans still find things to throw, as happened during the 1996 World Series. Atlanta Braves players reported that they were pelted with a variety of objects when playing in Yankee Stadium, including "healthy breakfast food; batteries of all types; a veritable fruit salad; booze bottles, full and empty; and profane invective, a New York specialty."[12]

In terms of alcohol usage, stadiums have introduced alcohol-free seating areas, limited or banned beer sales in the seats, limited the amount of alcohol sold, ended sales during the late innings, and instituted better training of vendors and ushers so that they can more easily spot and deal with drunken fans. And, in the era of the cell phone, some stadiums have encouraged fans to call posted phone numbers to report disruptive individuals. All have reduced, to some extent at least, the problems associated with alcohol consumption.[13]

Other safety and security measures have been introduced as well. More and more, stadiums are hiring additional security to help patrol the stands, some of whom are working undercover. Sometimes changes in stadium infrastructure have been made in response to particular incidents. Three Rivers Stadium in Pittsburgh, for example, added chain-link fences to the four-foot-high walls around the upper deck exit ramps because of two fatal falls in the early 1970s. In both cases, the young men fell while jumping from exit ramp to exit ramp, a practice that was apparently quite common at the time.[14]

Finally, the culture of the game itself has changed over the past century and a half. Whereas during the late 1800s the world of baseball was one of "kicking and wrangling with umpires, fights among players, indecent language, and incidents of rowdyism in general" that were often encouraged by the owners, today's officials, out of both a sense of responsibility and a fear of lawsuits, react quickly and forcefully to the first signs of misbehavior. For serious offenders, such as the New York Mets fan in 1986 who was sentenced to fifteen days in jail for fighting with security guards, criminal prosecution sometimes results. "We don't regard these rowdies as sports fans," commented the Queens, NY, district attorney about this case. "We seek jail against them. There's no sportsmanship to their conduct. They just spoil the game for the rest of us. They deserve incarceration as well as ejection." While baseball will not be able to entirely eliminate violence or senseless self-inflicted injuries at games — the individual, after all, is ultimately responsible for his own behavior — such policies certainly help reduce the likelihood that the massive riots of the past will occur again.[15]

Major League Fatalities from Falls or Risky Behavior

Before Wrigley Field, there was the West Side Grounds. And, even before rooftop seats around Wrigley, there were rooftop seats surrounding West Side. The city of Chicago had a very dim view of these seats situated atop several multistory residences located along South Wood (left field) and West Taylor (right field) streets. For a number of years in the early 1900s the city complained that the "housetop grandstands" were "a menace to public safety in that they were not provided with sufficient safeguards for patrons." Of particular concern was the lack of fire escapes. In 1907 Joseph Downey, Chicago building commissioner, attempted to remove these stands, but the owners secured an injunction that prevented the city from doing so. Over the next several months the issue was argued before Judge Oscar E. Heard, but still it lingered on. Then, on July 17, 1908, during an exciting game between the Cubs and New York Giants, tragedy struck, forcing everything to a head.[16]

One of these stands was situated on top of a three-story building on South Wood Street. When, in the fifth inning, Chicago shortstop Joe Tinker hit a home run off of Christy Mathewson to give the Cubs a 1 to 0 lead (which turned out to be the final score), 14-year-old **Willie Hudson**, in his excitement, tumbled off the edge of the roof to the street 50 feet below. The fall broke several bones and fractured his skull. After the youngster died the next morning, Judge Heard immediately ordered the owners of the stands to stop allowing outside spectators on their roofs. A second order, however, enjoined the city from acting immediately until hearings could be held.

While fans continued to frequent the rooftop grandstands, the case wound its way through the courts. On January 18, 1910, an appellate court sustained a lower court ruling that the strands were "a nuisance," upholding the right of the police to prevent anyone from sitting in these stands.[17]

Several months later, a Cubs-Giants game was the setting for another fatality, this time outside the Polo Grounds during a playoff game that decided the National League pennant race, a confrontation made necessary by the baserunning blunder of Fred "Bonehead" Merkle in a September 23 contest between the two teams that ended in a tie instead of a Giants victory. On October 8, 1908, the Cubs sent to the mound Mordecai "Three Finger" Brown to face Giants ace Christy Mathewson. While "Matty" failed to go the distance, Brown pitched a 4 to 2 gem, sending the Cubs on to the World Series to face the Detroit Tigers, a team they would defeat in five games.

As many as 40,000 excited fans made it through the turnstiles, or scaled the fences, that October day. Outside the stadium, "as many more would-be spectators fought or begged for tickets.... So greatly was the capacity of the grounds taxed that finally the high-pitched roof of the grandstand was reached by hundreds. Toward the sky the crowd seemed to pile, and over the highest fringe of fans reared the 155th Street viaduct and Coogan's Bluff, higher yet and dense with men, women, and children." With people crammed in every available nook and cranny that had a vantage point, the elevated trains continued to disgorge passengers. Later estimates put the crowd inside and outside the Polo Grounds at up to 100,000 people. Many of these congregated along the train tracks, "daring even the third rail." **Henry T. McBride** was one of the multitude stuffed into this area, a 34-year veteran of the New York fire department who should have known better. "Clinging to the top" of one of the 100-foot-high track-support pillars to get a better view, "he lost his grip and fell to the street, striking on his head and dying almost instantly." Immediately upon removal of his body, "his vacant place was quickly filled." Commented the press about the throngs, "It was a wonder that many people were not crushed to death or trampled under foot." Surprisingly, only one other serious injury was reported, that of Edward Wheeler, who fell through the bleachers, breaking his right leg. Cubs player and manager Frank Chance was slightly injured after the game when an irate Giants fan threw a glass bottle at him as he tried to reach the safety of the clubhouse, the blow tearing the cartilage in his neck.[18]

In what was an apparent suicide, 24-year-old **George J. Shramek**, under treatment for some undisclosed medical condition, climbed a 5-foot-high retaining wall along the west side upper deck of Baltimore's Memorial Stadium at 6:40 P.M. on August 5, 1969. The recent college graduate had entered the stadium during batting practice before an Orioles–Kansas City Royals game, then was seen scaling the wall a short time later. According to an usher, Shramek "looked down, looked back at the usher, then jumped." He fell 140 feet, barely missing a mother and son entering the stadium. When the woman saw Sharmek's shoes falling toward them, she "yanked her son out of the way just in time to keep from being hit by the young man's plunging body." Shramek was pronounced dead 15 minutes later from "multiple internal injuries."[19]

In the first of two similar fatalities, **Gary Pettitt**, 22, died on July 22, 1971, at Three Rivers Stadium in Pittsburgh, PA, after he fell while jumping from one exit ramp to another. The following spring, 17-year-old **Joseph Farrell** attended the Pirates home opener on April 18, 1972, with several friends. As they were leaving the stadium, they began using a "short-cut," i.e., climbing up on a four-foot-high railing along the exit ramps, then jumping across a four-foot-wide opening to the ramp below. Farrell's six friends were successful in their attempts, but the high school junior, later found to be "under the influence of alcohol," slipped and fell from the top ramp, landing on his head after plunging 82 feet to the ground below. He was rushed to an area hospital where he was declared dead about 20 minutes later. This second fatality prompted authorities to review what steps they needed to take to stop what was apparently a frequent practice. Eventually tall chain link fencing was installed along the ramps to prevent future incidents.[20]

About 20 minutes after a Philadelphia Phillies game on August 24, 1971, at the new Veterans Stadium, 37-year-old **Glenn Shober**, his brother, and two business associates decided to look for a restroom by walking across a four-foot-wide platform that ran across the pit where the left field scoreboard was lowered when not in use. According to stadium officials, "one of the men removed a plastic-covered wire barrier" in order to gain access to the walkway. As they proceeded along, the first man in line came suddenly to an open hole that "should have been covered by a metal plate." He stopped in time, but Shober continued forward, falling through the opening to the concrete base 27 feet below. His companions yelled for help, and after stadium security arrived, Shober was taken to a local hospital. He died from "multiple injuries" at 12:45 A.M. on August 25.[21]

As part of "a therapeutic measure" recommended by his doctor, **Bruce Winick**, 28, "recently released" as a patient at a New York mental heath facility, attended a July 13, 1980, doubleheader at Shea Stadium between the Mets and the St. Louis Cardinals. He was seated with a friend when the two got into an argument shortly before the 1:00 P.M. start of the first game. Winick left his seat, climbed over a wire barrier, and jumped from the fifth mezzanine level between gates A and B, plunging 100 feet to the street below. He was declared dead on arrival at a local hospital.[22]

Furious that the San Francisco Giants had lost 10 of 11 games, 30-year-old **Anthony Perry** ran down the aisle toward the upper deck railing at Candlestick Park, "yelling obscenities" at the team, just after a 5 to 4 loss to the Atlanta Braves on the afternoon of June 6, 1984. "He was rocking back and forth," said an usher in the area, "and all of a sudden he just flipped over on his head and fell over the side." Perry crash-landed on his head in the box seats 40 feet below, injuring fan William Powers in the process. Powers, who had been seated in this section, was knocked unconscious by a plastic seat back dislodged by Perry's fall. Both were rushed to an area hospital, where Perry was declared dead about an hour after his fall. Powers recovered from his injury.[23]

Shortly after a game at Shea Stadium between the New York Mets and Houston Astros on May 1, 1985, **Mark Leddy**, 21, started sliding down the rubber handrail of a non-working escalator from the upper deck. He slipped and fell from the railing about 25 feet above the mezzanine level, then continued to plummet, hitting a steam pipe before landing on the ground, falling approximately 100 feet in total. Initially taken to the Shea first aid station, he was then rushed to a nearby hospital where he died a short while later from "fatal head injuries and leg injuries."[24]

Edward Joyce, 53, was "straddling the rail" along the first base side of the upper deck during the ninth inning of a May 16, 1986, game at Comiskey Park between the Chicago White Sox and Kansas City Royals when he suddenly fell 40 feet to the walkway of the lower deck below. Although police were not sure what precipitated the fall, they did not think there was any foul play involved. "Unless somebody comes forward and says he was pushed," stated a police spokesman, "he was not pushed." He died from his injuries at a local hospital about 10:00 that same night. Fortunately, no one else was injured in the accident.[25]

Unable to get a ticket to a sold-out March 10, 1988, spring training game between the Detroit Tigers and Pittsburgh Pirates at McKechnie Field in Bradenton, FL, 42-year-old **Daniel McCarthy** was standing outside when a foul ball flew out of the stadium and into the street during the third inning. In hot pursuit of the ball, McCarthy walked into the path of an oncoming car traveling the posted speed of 30 miles per hour. The impact flipped him onto the windshield, causing "massive head injuries." The victim was taken to an area hospital, where he died around 11:00 the next morning.[26]

Calmly walking down the aisle to the railing around the upper deck portal at Royals Stadium during the eighth inning of a April 27, 1989, game between Kansas City and the New York Yankees, **Mike Wurzer**, 20, attempted to do a handstand before anyone could stop him.

According to witnesses, "his momentum carried him forward," causing him to flip over the railing and fall 12 to 15 feet to the concrete walkway below. He was transported by helicopter to the hospital, but was pronounced dead on arrival from a broken neck.[27]

Clifford Toolerton, 75, struck his head after falling down some stairs near his seat at Three Rivers Stadium during a Pittsburgh Pirates–Florida Marlins game on August 13, 1993. He died from his injuries the next day at an area hospital.[28]

Ignoring warning signs not to do so, **Francisco Munoz**, 37, was sitting on an escalator handrail as he rode it to the upper deck on the left field side of Yankee Stadium during the ninth inning of an April 25, 1999, game between the Yankees and the Toronto Blue Jays. He slipped, tumbled backwards off the handrail, and plunged 90 feet between several other escalators and the stands, crashing face first onto the pavement below. He died shortly after arriving at a nearby hospital. The Yankees offered to pay to transport his body back to his native Chile, but his family received contributions from friends and refused the offer.[29]

Leaning over a right field walkway railing in order to retrieve his sunglasses from someone passing below, 35-year-old **Todd E. Adams** tumbled over the railing 25 feet to the sidewalk outside of Pacific Bell Park during the eighth inning of a Giants game on September 17, 2003. Adams had been drinking beer with friends while leaning against the railing when his sunglasses fell off the top of his head. A homeless man passing by picked up the glasses and offered to hold them for Adams. Police speculated that Adams thought he could climb down from the walkway by grasping a light post attached to the wall below him, but fell forward over the railing in a failed attempt to reach the light, landing on his head. "Maybe he thought while hanging from the light fixture that he could jump safely to the pavement," mused the police spokesman. "We still don't know exactly what his intentions were." He died shortly after 10:00 that same night. The police officer who reached Adams first reported that "there was a strong odor of alcohol on him."[30]

James A. Kolata, 48, was sitting on an escalator handrail as he was going from the field level to the second level of Miller Park shortly after the start of a July 29, 2004, afternoon game between the Milwaukee Brewers and the Chicago Cubs when he suddenly fell over the side. The 17-foot plunge fractured his skull and vertebrae and caused a lung to collapse. He was unconscious and not breathing when paramedics arrived. Kolata died from his injuries about 5:00 P.M. the following day.[31]

Glenn Kelly, 66, was fatally injured after being pushed to the ground by two police officers during a confrontation at Miller Park on July 7, 2006. Kelly was attending the game between the Milwaukee Brewers and the Chicago Cubs with his son and daughter-in-law when stadium police came to cite the younger couple for "inappropriate behavior." According to the Kelly family attorney, when the elder Kelly attempted to get on the elevator being used by the police to transport the couple to the security office at the stadium, one of the officers "shoved him with one hand" to prevent him from coming with them. A second officer then pushed Kelly with two hands, causing him to fall and strike his head on the concrete floor. Police stated later they were attempting to stop Kelly from entering the elevator "because no one but police are allowed in the elevator when someone is being detained." Kelly refused medical attention even though he had lost consciousness briefly. On the bus ride back home after his son and daughter-in-law had been released, Kelly became "unresponsive." He was taken to an emergency room in Fort Atkinson, WI, where it was found that he was suffering from "a brain hemorrhage and a subdural hematoma." He was declared brain dead the following day. Kelly died on July 12 after life support was discontinued.[32]

Minor League Fatalities from Falls or Risky Behavior

Fan **Wallace H. Montgomery**, 32, was one of several hundred enthusiastic fans attending a Class C Cotton States League contest on May 3, 1939, between the hometown Hot Springs (AR) Bathers and the Monroe (LA) White Sox. He was seated atop the 15-foot-high right field bleacher fence at Ban Johnson Field when, early in the game, he lost his balance and fell backwards off the fence, breaking his neck. Because he landed on the ground outside the stadium, most fans were unaware that anything had happened. Montgomery was rushed by ambulance to a nearby hospital, where he was declared dead on arrival.[33]

Black Baseball Fatalities from Falls or Risky Behavior

Over 2,000 excited fans were crammed into Washington Park in Indianapolis, IN, on the afternoon of June 2, 1918, awaiting the start of the second exhibition game between a team of Army aviators stationed at the Indianapolis Speedway and one of the premier black baseball teams in the country, the Indianapolis ABCs. The contingent from the Speedway, which had been turned over to the military for the duration of World War I, were no pushovers, however. Among its many fine players were several with professional experience, including Lou North, who had pitched briefly with the St. Louis Cardinals the year before. But the ABCs, led by future Hall-of-Fame center fielder Oscar Charleston, were clearly the better team. They had soundly beaten the flyers 4 to 1 the day before, turning four double plays in the process, so the soldiers were out for revenge.[34]

One of the activities planned for that Sunday game was a flyover by Maj. Guy L. Gearhart, the pilot and commander of the Speedway airbase, and his passenger, **Capt. E. P. Webb**, 46, post adjutant. Just prior to the start of the game, the two were to fly a recently-repaired dual-control Curtiss training plane from the Speedway, swoop low over the stadium, and drop two baseballs with long streamers attached to them, providing spectators "a first-hand example ... how American aviators are dropping bombs onto German lines at the present time in France."[35]

The two teams were warming up on the field about 3:15 P.M. when Gearhart's plane arrived and began circling approximately 500 feet above. The players stopped where they stood to watch when "suddenly the hum of the motor began to have a strange sound and the machine was seen to shoot toward the ground. However, nothing was thought of this, because the large crowd of spectators and ball players thought Maj. Gearhart was only trying some fancy stunts, but when the plane began to shoot to the ground in a spinning nose dive, ball players who were out on the field began to scamper to shelter, not knowing what was going to happen." As the players ran for safety and horrified fans gawped in stunned silence, the plane plowed nose-first into the infield just behind second, "cutting a huge hole in the turf and completely smashing the engine." The plane skidded about 20 feet before coming to rest, the cockpit demolished beyond recognition. "The tail of the machine was about twelve feet from the ground when the plane came to a standstill. Splinters of the wrecked cockpit and some of the parts of the lower plane near the pit were scattered many feet from the spot where the machine fell."[36]

As several women fainted and the crowd poured out of the stands toward the wreckage, police and soldiers attending the game rushed onto the field, surrounding the plane to keep the crowd back. Several of the players helped other soldiers pull the two fliers from the plane. Capt. Webb, who had been experiencing his first plane ride, was killed instantly, dying from "a cerebral hemorrhage resulting from a wound on the back of his neck, evidently where the heavy motor crushed his skull." Gearhart, stunned and badly injured, was rushed to the hospital with a brain concussion, "a fractured jaw and a wound on the chin." He remained in the hospital until June 7, when he was moved to the resident hotel where he lived.[37]

There was much speculation as to what caused the crash. At first it was thought that the streamers on the two balls to be dropped by Capt. Webb had gotten entangled "in one of the upper plane control wires ... causing Maj. Gearhart to lose control of the machine," but this was proven not be the case. Aviators at the game believed that Gearhart "attempted to dive out of an airpocket, but that at his low altitude it was impossible to complete the dive before striking the ground." They thought the air-pocket may have been created by several spiraling maneuvers the plane had done just before it nosedived. Others postulated that the engine had stalled and, with the plane so close to the ground, Gearhart did not have enough time to restart it. The pilot himself was little help in solving the mystery because he suffered memory loss from the blow to his head. "He frequently asked how the accident happened," explained the attending physician, "and where Capt. Webb, his companion in the flight was taken, but he has no knowledge of the accident."[38]

Major League Violence-Related Fatalities from Thrown Objects

As bad as the Yankees-Browns 1953 bottle riot was, the worst incidence of this type of violence in the major leagues occurred in a May 11, 1929, game in Cleveland, OH, between the Indians and the Philadelphia Athletics, a tragedy started by an umpiring decision. Having had only three hits against the A's ace, Robert Moses "Lefty" Grove, the Indians were trailing 4 to 0 when they came to bat in the bottom of the eighth. With one out, the next three batters singled off of Grove to score the Tribe's first run. Up next was first baseman Lew Fonseca who, seeing the infielders playing back in hopes of a double play, laid down a perfect bunt back to the mound. And while he beat the throw and was initially called safe by Umpire Clarence "Brick" Owens, the decision was immediately overruled by Umpire William Campbell. As the crowd of 15,000 began to boo vociferously, Indians manager Roger Peckinpaugh charged out of the dugout. Campbell explained the reason for his decision — that Fonseca had run outside of the base line — but Peckinpaugh was having none of it. When the enraged manager was thrown out of the game, the crowd erupted. "A bottle was thrown, and then another until finally the fans, taking their cue from the bolder fellows, filled the air with flying glass." Athletics shortstop Joe Boley was cut on the back of the head by one bottle, while Umpire Emmett "Red" Ormsby, standing near third, suffered a severe concussion that almost cost him his life. He had to be carried from the field. Unknown to anyone at the time, 28-year-old fan **Lee Porter**, who was also struck on the head by a bottle, was even more seriously injured than Ormsby.[39]

The crowd was totally out of control. Even police entering the field to protect the umpires could not restore order. Not until Indians business manager Billy Evans came out and appealed for calm did the bottles stop flying. Once the grounds crew, aided by Cleveland players, had cleared the field of bottles, the game finally resumed. With two runners on and now two out, center fielder Earl Averill hit a sharp grounder to shortstop Sammy Hale, who threw to second for the force, and the third out. Although the Indians would stage another small rally in the bottom of the ninth, they scored only one other run to lose 4 to 2. The next day, Indians manager Peckinpaugh was suspended for five days for his on-field behavior in protesting Campbell's ruling.[40]

While Umpire Ormsby did recover, such was not the case for Lee Porter, who had remained until the conclusion of the game. Although appearing "merely dazed" at the time, when he returned home to Akron, OH, he became suddenly ill the next evening. His condition deteriorated rapidly and he was taken to an Akron hospital on May 14. An examination revealed that he was suffering from a fractured skull. He died later that night from his head injuries. Declared the *Cleveland Plain Dealer* about the affair, "Any man who will throw a bottle or any other life-endangering object from the midst of a crowd at any official or player is the rankest form of coward. He is a low-down cur that has no place in modern society."[41]

Minor League Violence-Related Fatalities from Thrown Objects

Young fan **William Haverkamp**, 13, and his two friends were happy to get through the gates even though they had to wait until the seventh inning to do so. It was May 1, 1908, the start of the Class B Central League season, and the stands at Loyalty Field, home of the Grand Rapids (MI) Wolverines, were packed. Haverkamp and his companions would have liked to be there at the start of the game, but they could not afford the admission price. So they waited patiently outside the gate until they were allowed to enter without charge at the top of the seventh. Since all seats were already occupied, they scurried down in front of the third base bleachers and sat on the ground. During the course of the game, a dispute arose in the stands behind them, one with "loud talking and angry gesticulations." Unexpectedly, a beer bottle flew out of the crowd and struck Haverkamp "a terrible blow on the back of the head, knocking him forward on his face." Although the child appeared to be uninjured, several fans confronted the assailant, Edward Parks. Bert Lewis, seated near Parks, "remonstrated with Parks and was shoved against the fence by the bottle thrower." Lewis, in turn, punched Parks twice in the face, knocking him down. When the police arrived, they arrested Lewis, thinking him the instigator, thus giving Parks a chance to escape.[42]

While the authorities looked for Parks, young Haverkamp walked home with his friends after the game. He was afraid to tell his mother what had happened since she had not wanted him to attend the game, but he did relate the story to his sister. No one, though, knew how ill he was feeling. Suddenly "dizzy and sick at his stomach," he decided to go to bed before supper. When he did not show up at the table, a brother came to his room and found him "dazed and semi-conscious." A medical exam found that Haverkamp was suffering from a concussion. By this time, though, he had lapsed into full unconsciousness and there was little that could be done for him. He died at home later that night.[43]

In the meantime, the police tracked down Parks and arrested him. After Lewis identified Parks as the individual who threw the bottle, Parks was charged with manslaughter. Bail was set at $5,000. Parks, who had five children of his own, was brought to trial later that summer. When the jury could not reach a unanimous decision, the judge declared a mistrial. The prosecutor, insistent that Parks be held accountable for his actions, decided to retry Parks in mid–December. After a brief deliberation at this second trial, the panel of 12 men decided that Parks had not intended to hurt Haverkamp, returning a verdict of not guilty.[44]

Black Baseball Violence-Related Fatalities from Thrown Objects

A full-blown race riot on "the worst block in Harlem" began on the evening of August 4, 1907, in New York as a result of an incident that occurred at an amateur baseball game. The Olympia Baseball Grounds, located at 136th Street and Madison Avenue, was the site of a match between the all-white Olympia Baseball Club and the all-black Harlem Baseball Club. Residents of both races living in the area attended the game as spectators. As was common during this era, sideline bets were being laid as to which of the two teams would win. At the end of the contest, a fight broke out between a white fan and an African American fan as to the payoff on a wager. When a shoving match ensued, whites at the game charged the black combatant. The latter was able to make his escape to a nearby apartment building, where he enlisted the aid of the African American residents. At that point, pandemonium erupted.[45]

Other African Americans, who had been watching the game from their apartment windows, could see groups of blacks and whites fighting down below. Rushing to their neighbors' defense, some came onto the streets armed with knives, razors, and bats. Several women threw plates, furniture, and scalding water out of their windows, while some men climbed up to the roofs and dislodged bricks from the chimneys to drop on the white assailants. "Within ten minutes more than a thousand white and black people were mixed in a fighting, shouting mass," wrote the *New York Times*. Estimates of the number involved ranged from 1,000 to 5,000, about equally divided between both races. It took nearly 300 police officers over two hours to restore order. Typically, only African American participants were arrested, and blacks alone were forced to stay indoors afterwards. In spite of a strong police presence for several days following, roving gangs of white thugs still managed to attack blacks unlucky enough to be caught outdoors by themselves.[46]

Some 60 people of both races were injured in the melee. The two most seriously hurt were both white participants, **John McCue**, 32, and Matthew Murtha, 55, each suffering from fractured skulls caused from bricks hurled from the rooftops. McCue died in a Harlem hospital early the next day.[47]

Amateur Violence-Related Fatalities from Thrown Objects

Arthur L. "Bugs" Raymond, 30, might have become one of the outstanding pitchers of the Deadball Era were it not for the fact of his uncontrollable alcoholism. A spitball pitcher notorious for his "bughouse" behavior both on and off the field, Raymond was acquired by the St. Louis Cardinals in 1907. Going 2 and 6 that first season, he would compile a 15 and 25 record in 1908, hardly impressive numbers. But those 15 victories were nearly a third of the games won by the last-place Cardinals that year, and Raymond had five shutouts and was fourth in the league in strikeouts as well. John McGraw, the captain of the New York Giants, saw the potential in the erratic pitcher and, in a three-way trade involving the Cincinnati

Reds, acquired Raymond for the 1909 season. It would be the best season of Raymond's professional career, ending with a record of 18 and 12 and an ERA of 2.47. In spite of this success and McGraw's herculean efforts to reform his pitcher, Raymond still could not control his drinking. In 1910 he won only four games and by the middle of the following season, with his alcoholism totally out of control, Raymond was cut from the Giants. Now estranged from his wife and mourning the recent death of his young daughter, he returned to his native Chicago where he pitched semipro ball when he was sober enough to do so. The worst was yet to come.[48]

Tragically, a maid found Raymond dead in his Chicago hotel room on September 7, 1912. At first it was assumed he had died of a heart attack brought on by excessive drinking and the high temperatures gripping the area at the time. The night before he had even remarked on the heat, saying "It's about got me in," and complained of a headache. Since there were no indications otherwise, officials concluded his death was from natural causes. Further examination, however, proved differently.[49]

The following day, stories began circulating that the pitcher was the victim of an assault. Witnesses came forward to testify that Raymond had been in a drunken brawl as a spectator during a sandlot game the week before. Upon further investigation, the coroner discovered that the former spitballer died from a cerebral hemorrhage as the result of a blow to the skull. On September 9, police arrested Fred Cigranz (sometimes spelled Cigrans) for the death of Raymond. He later confessed to being the one who had fought with the pitcher, but argued that it was he who was attacked first. According to him, both were watching a game when someone threw a piece of brick that struck Raymond. He, in turn, "hurled" the brick at Cigranz, an acquaintance of 15 years. "I got mad," Cigranz admitted, "and went out on the field after him. I struck him, knocked him down, and kicked him. It didn't hurt him badly enough to kill him." According to eye witnesses, though, those kicks were to Raymond's head. Afterwards, Raymond went to a hospital for treatment, remaining there several days. Two days later he was found dead. But there was additional information revealed by Frank Raymond, the victim's brother, about a previous event that may have contributed to his brother's death. During a game a few weeks earlier, Raymond had gotten into an argument with an undisclosed individual, during the course of which "the fellow picked up a bat and hit me [Raymond] an awful wallop on the head." Thus twice in a matter of weeks Raymond received severe blows to his head, the combination of which proved deadly.[50]

Roy Wolff, 27, and several other fans, apparently bored with a sandlot game they were watching on May 9, 1915, in Denver, CO, decided the liven things up by having a brick throwing contest. As Wolff, a catcher for his amateur team, stood on the sidelines holding up his hat as a target, others took turns hurling bricks at it. After several had tried and missed, a fourth man, "anxious to register a score," let loose a wild throw, striking Wolff squarely on his head. The injured man collapsed unconscious with a fractured skull. Physicians at a local hospital performed emergency surgery later that evening, removing "a large piece of bone" from his head in the process. Initially showing signs of recovery, he took a sudden turn for the worse around 8:00 P.M. on May 11 and died about an hour later.[51]

Amateur Violence-Related Fatalities from Bats

J. C. Johnson, 21, a student at Chattanooga University, was watching a morning game at the college on February 22, 1888, between school clubs when, about two hours into the contest, he got into an argument with a friend and fellow student, Ben McGill, 21, who was acting as umpire. Johnson, supporting one of the teams, became angry when he thought McGill was allowing the opposing team to quick-pitch his team's hitters before they were set in the batter's box. When he yelled out to one of his team's batters, "they're bulldozing you," McGill, who felt the charge was directed at him, called Johnson "a damn liar" in response. At that the enraged fan rushed onto the field and challenged the umpire, saying, "I dare you to hit me." McGill, by this time equally furious, "raised a hickory bat, and with the muscles of both arms bent in the endeavor, struck a terrific blow upon Johnson's head." The victim, knocked to the ground by the blow, was helped up and carried to his dorm room. While medical assistance was still on the way, Johnson "began to bleed at the nose, and vomit clotted blood, and became unconscious." A doctor arrived about 2:30 that afternoon, several hours after the attack, to find a fracture just above the left ear. It left "a depression in the skull one and a half inches long, and blood flowed from it in a stream, showing that the artery was ruptured." The young man died later that evening.[52]

McGill, meanwhile, told bystanders that he did not mean to

Arthur "Bugs" Raymond's major league career came to an early end because of his uncontrolled drinking. He died in 1912 as the result of head injuries received in two brawls just weeks apart, the second of which occurred while he was watching an amateur baseball game in Chicago (courtesy National Baseball Hall of Fame Library, Cooperstown, NY).

hit Johnson so hard and did not think the blow would be a fatal one. He left the playing field before authorities arrived to question him. A $250 reward was posted for his capture. Some thought McGill had fled the city on the advice of some friends, but he was found at the home of his cousin in Chattanooga about 3:30 P.M. the following day. The assailant, who claimed he had not meant to kill Johnson, was charged with voluntary manslaughter and released after his attorneys posted bond. Trial was scheduled for the next term of the court. McGill was eventually found guilty of felonious assault, a less serious charge, because the jury concurred with his contention that there was no intent to kill. After paying a $500 fine, he was freed.[53]

But the story does not end here. In January 1900, Chattanooga was the scene of a sensational celebrity murder trial. In a case that made national headlines, beautiful actress Julia Morrison was facing conviction for the murder of stage manager and leading man Frank Leiden (or Leidenheimer), on stage just before the curtain rose on an September 22, 1899, evening performance of *Mr. Plaster of Paris*, a romantic comedy. To the horror of all in attendance, she shot the actor three times in the head at close range. The actress claimed self-defense, alleging that Leiden had regularly insulted, threatened, and made improper advances toward her, and that her action was one of temporary insanity resulting from these abuses. The state argued that it was premeditated murder.[54]

The case, which included testimony from the defendant herself "forc[ing] her to utter words that brought the blush of shame not only to women, but to men, and tell incidents that are unfit to suggest in public prints," took nearly a week to complete. Toward the end of the trial, the prosecution discovered, much to its chagrin, that one of the jurors it had allowed to be seated was none other than convicted felon Ben McGill. Arguing that they were unaware of this fact and fearing that he would be biased toward Morrison, they asked that McGill be removed from the panel. The judge refused to do so. On January 10, 1900, after consulting for only two minutes, the jurors, including McGill, returned a verdict of not guilty. Editorialized the Chattanooga paper afterwards, "no sane and impartial mind will discover in it [the evidence presented at the trial] any reason why the accused should not have been severely punished, except for sex and good looks, if those may be called a reason."[55]

John Leak purchased some wine from Will and Tom Little just before the start of a ball game near Wadesboro, NC, on July 4, 1906. Apparently Leak had consumed some of the alcohol without paying for it, causing a violent argument to break out between Leak and the Littles. The two brothers attacked Leak with a baseball bat, striking him four times on the head before cutting him on his back several times with a knife. They were charged with murder.[56]

In an assault probably motivated by racial animosity, a white player identified only as Kendricks struck **Will Whitely**, an African American fan, on the head with a baseball bat during a game near Selma, AL, on July 18, 1909, because the victim "made a scoffing remark" about Kendricks' playing ability. The assailant hit Whitely where he sat, killing him instantly.[57]

Alcohol played a central role in a brawl among fans that resulted in one fatality at a game in Beckwith, CA, on the afternoon on August 15, 1909. Supporters of the visiting Loyalton, CA, team and those from Beckwith had often had verbal disagreements when the two towns played, but never anything that turned violent. On this particular afternoon, however, as several of the fans consumed copious amounts of whiskey, the bantering back and forth grew increasingly nasty. J. C. Jones, 26, of Loyalton, in particular seemed to be itching for a fight, according to some witnesses. He came to the game with an ax handle and was verbally aggressive from the start, they said. When he called Jeff Parish, a Beckwith fan, "a d — — n liar" after the latter confronted him about his behavior, the two quickly came to blows. At one point Jones tried to strike Parish with a beer bottle he had hidden in his pants pocket. Others soon joined in the fray. Several fans, including **George King** from Beckwith, attempted to restore peace. By some accounts, as matters began to calm down, Jones snuck off and grabbed a bat from the playing field. The first man he came to was the unfortunate George King. He raised the bat over his head and hit King on the right side near the crown of his head, striking him "a heavy blow." Jones also took a swing at another individual who ducked just in time, "the weapon whizzing over his head." When the crowd began to disperse, King was found unconscious with "his skull ... badly crushed and his right eye forced out of its socket." While King was being taken for medical treatment, Jones made his escape. He was captured a short while later and, when King died about 11:00 that night, was charged with murder and held without bail. In his possession was the bloodstained bat he used to kill King.[58]

At the trial that began on September 21, 1909, Jones told an entirely different story. He admitted to having consumed several bottles of beer both before and during the game, but said he was not drunk. He also acknowledged that he did have a bottle in his pocket, a full one that he planned to share with the Loyalton players after the game. But he argued that he was the one who was assaulted first; that, in fact, someone had grabbed his arms from behind while another fan struck him in the mouth. He pulled out the beer bottle to defend himself. He claimed to have been struck as many as a dozen blows on the face, head, and neck, the final one of which knocked him backwards out of the crowd onto the playing field, causing him to stumble and fall. When he saw his assailants coming toward him, he grabbed a bat he found nearby. He lashed out with this weapon, striking King who, he testified, was one of those assaulting him. He protested that he was only defending himself and that he had no intention of killing King.[59]

The case went to the jury on September 25, and, after five hours of deliberation, they returned a verdict of second degree murder. Before sentence was passed on October 5, Jones' attorneys asked for a new trial on several grounds, asserting among other transgressions that the jury had been drinking at lunch the day they convicted Jones and that after lunch several had been allowed to wander off before returning to the courthouse. The judge denied the motion and sentenced Jones to 14 years at San Quentin, the state prison. The defendant's attorneys vowed to appeal the case.[60]

On July 13, 1911, the California Supreme Court reversed the lower court and ordered a new trial, in part because "testimony favorable to the defense had been ruled out wrongfully by the lower court." This second trial began on October 17, 1911, two years after the original sentence was passed. At 9:00 P.M. on October 20, the jury, convinced that Jones had acted in self-defense out of fear of being mobbed, returned a verdict of not guilty after deliberating just 20 minutes. In addition, many on the panel felt that alcohol was the real culprit because "most of the parties concerned in the affair had been drinking somewhat, and to this fact more than any other may be laid the responsibility for the unfortunate occurrence." Finally, some believed Jones had been punished enough; that even if he bore a greater share of the blame for King's death, his more than two years in prison "had been sufficient under the circumstances." Jones was immediately released, returning to his home in Loyalton the next day.[61]

The refusal to pay a $1 bet as the result of a disputed umpire's decision during a game in Fort Branch, IN, on July 17, 1927, ended in the death of 35-year-old **Walter Warren** four days later. Fort Branch was hosting the Ermac Radios from Evansville in a contest that drew a large number of boisterous and, according to some accounts, intoxicated fans for both sides. As often happens in these settings, small amounts were being wagered as to who would be victorious. One of these was a $3.00 bet between Russell Jackson of Fort Branch and Clement Frank of Evansville. According to witnesses, when the umpire made a ruling in the middle of the game awarding Fort Branch a run to tie the game, Frank, vigorously disagreeing with the call, paid Jackson $2.00 of the bet he had made, but refused to come across with the additional dollar. "Try and get it," Frank was reported to have said. Jackson, in response, struck Frank with his fists. Of course, the fight soon involved others in the area. One of these was Warren, a resident of Evansville and a friend of Frank. Seeing his compatriot under attack, he grabbed a bat and struck Jackson on the back of his neck, knocking him down. And, according to some, he took swings at others as well.[62]

Several Ft. Branch supporters now rushed to Jackson's defense, including 6-foot, 300-pound Fred "Snaky" Stone, 30, a miner from Fort Branch. Albert Duncan, who was standing nearby, claimed that he saw Stone grab a bat and "raise [it] high in the air, and his face showing the great force he was putting in the blow, bring it down on top of Warren's head. I even saw his neck bulge. Warren staggered and fell in a ditch." Warren's wife ran to her husband and, ironically, with the aid of Russell Jackson, the man Warren had hit on the back of the neck placed the unconscious victim in Jackson's car to take him to a physician living close by. Unfortunately, the doctor was not home, so Jackson took both Warrens back to the ball field. From there another fan drove them to a hospital in Evansville. Warren died of a fractured skull at 9:00 A.M. on July 20.[63]

While Warren was being shunted back and forth, Snaky Stone fled the area. Because many of the witnesses refused to identify him to the Fort Branch police, it took them nearly a week to round him up in spite of his distinctive appearance. He was eventually arrested at the Fort Branch mine, where he worked, and held on a $10,000 bond on the charge of manslaughter. Stone, who could not afford bail, stayed in jail until his trial date on October 18.[64]

While not denying he had struck the fatal blow, Stone pled not guilty to the charges against him, claiming his act was one of self-defense. He asserted that Warren had been drinking when he arrived at the game, carrying with him a small bat. During the scuffle that took place that day, Warren allegedly took a swing at Stone first. Stone, in turn, picked up a bat lying nearby and struck Warren on the head. While witnesses for the prosecution testified that Warren was facing away from Stone when struck, the defense presented a number of others who swore that Warren was the aggressor and that Stone was simply defending himself from attack. The case went to the jury on the afternoon of October 21. After deliberating more than five hours, they convicted Stone of assault and battery, a lesser charge, one just short of full acquittal. The judge immediately sentenced the defendant to 90 days at a state prison and assessed him a fine of $350 plus court costs.[65]

What began as racially-charged "trash talk" at a Little League game in Castro Valley, CA, on May 15, 1993, ended in the death of 17-year-old spectator **Joseph Matteucci** two days later. It was the first game of the season, and the predominantly white Castro Valley Black Socks, comprised of boys 16 to 18 years of age, were hosting the mostly black and Hispanic Ashland (CA) American Indians. Around the fifth inning of closely-fought contest, one of the Castro Valley bench-jockeys began hurling racist insults at one of the African American players for Ashland. The animosity between the teams drew the fans into the nasty heckling and, at the end of the game, a general melee broke out on the field. As tempers flared, 18-year-old Ashland catcher Antonio Messina grabbed a bat and swung it at Castro Valley fan Tommy Poorman, who admitted later that he had "slugged an Ashland player" just before the assault. Standing behind Poorman with his back turned to the events taking place was Matteucci. He apparently was on the field trying to restrain a friend on the Castro Valley team. Poorman ducked as the barrel of the weapon rushed toward him. The back of Matteucci's head took the full brunt of the blow from the aluminum bat.[66]

As Matteucci lay mortally wounded on the field, Messina dropped the bat and ran, pursued by three Castro Valley players. The umpire, who had left the field and had not seen the assault on Matteucci, witnessed the 16-year-old Castro Valley pitcher throwing a stone at Messina, striking him on the head and knocking him unconscious. Messina was hospitalized for several days before recovering. Matteucci, sadly, died on May 17.[67]

Messina was eventually arraigned and charged with murder. The young player's public defender entered a plea of not guilty, arguing that the boy was "acting out of fear for his own safety and his little brother's." His client, he claimed, "essentially stuck up for the kid who was being heckled." Others at his hearing, however, testified that Messina had not been threatened by anyone. Before his trial began in the early spring of 1994, Messina pled "no contest" to a charge of voluntary manslaughter and was sentenced to a 12-year prison term.[68]

Danny Ledezma, 22, a convict at Avenal State Prison in Avenal, CA, was watching other prisoners play ball in the prison yard on April 5, 1996, when a fight erupted between rival Hispanic gangs. In the course of the melee, Ledezma was struck over the head with an aluminum bat by another inmate. The victim, just three months short of his release, died later that night. Another prisoner was seriously wounded when someone shoved "a mechanical pencil through his nostrils, damaging his eyes." It took guards several minutes to stop the fighting.[69]

Thirteen-year-old Palmdale, CA, PONY League pitcher Greg Harris, Jr., upset when he lost the final game of the season on April 12, 2005, his team's only loss that year, struck and killed his 15-year-old friend, **Jeremy Rourke**, with an aluminum bat when the two got into an altercation shortly after the game. Rourke, who had come to the game to see his brother play, was standing in line with Harris at the concession stand when he began teasing the young pitcher about the loss. As the two began to argue, he shoved Harris who then, according to some witnesses, retrieved a bat from an equipment bag near him. Turning to Rourke, he first hit him on the knee, then on the neck, severing an artery. The victim was rushed to a local hospital, where he died about two hours later.[70]

Harris was charged with murder, but because of his age, could not be tried as an adult. In a three-day hearing before a juvenile court in early July, the youngster testified that he was acting in self-defense and that he was not trying to kill Rourke. He was scared of the deceased because he "stood a head taller and weighed 100 pounds more than he did," he asserted. Harris, who was African American, also claimed that Rourke, who was white, used a racial epithet during their argument and that he had a reputation as a bully. Later that month, the judge found the youngster guilty of second degree murder, concluding that "his conduct was malicious and that as a ball player, he should have known the serious bodily injuries that could result by bludgeoning someone with a bat, even if he didn't intend to kill." He sentenced Harris to a youth detention facility until he turned 25, the maximum allowed by law.[71]

Harris' attorney appealed his conviction on the grounds that the judge's sentence was too harsh and, based on the evidence as presented in the case, inappropriate. Harris had acted "in the heat of passion" and out of fear of the older, larger boy, she contended, and a more just finding would have been one of voluntary manslaughter, a lesser sentence. The deputy attorney general disagreed, arguing that since Harris had to walk several steps to get his bat, "he had time to reflect on what he was about to do." On January 22, 2007, the 2nd District Court of Appeal in California ordered that Harris be returned to juvenile court to have his sentenced reduced to one of voluntary manslaughter. "Here, all of the evidence indicated Gregory [Harris] acted in the heat of passion, as the trial court stated," affirmed the appellate court, "and therefore fails to support the finding of second-degree murder," a charge that requires malice on the part of the assailant. Two weeks later the prosecution appealed the ruling to the same appellate court, asking the judges to reconsider their decision. This appeal was denied several weeks later.[72]

Amateur Violence-Related Fatalities from Stabbing

W. R. Staples, Jr., was umpiring a game between mining company teams in Sunbright, TN, on June 15, 1889, when his cousin, **Davidson Hall**, 28, came onto the playing field and began to hurl rocks at him. Staples left the area briefly, but when he returned, he again ran into his cousin, who attempted to strike him on the head with a rock he was holding. Staples ordered Hall to stay away from him, but the assailant continued to attack the umpire. At this provocation, Staples pulled his pocketknife and stabbed Hall three times, including once on his left side and once "just below the breastbone." Hall, who was reported to have been drinking, died on the spot while Staples made his escape. He was arrested shortly thereafter. According to several witnesses examined by local authorities at a preliminary hearing, it was a case of self-defense.[73]

Late on the afternoon of May 24, 1953, **Carmella Olivo**, 32, sat with her younger sister and a small crowd of other fans as they watched a game in New York's Central Park between teams in the Spanish Catholic League. Suddenly, Olivo's ex-boyfriend, Edward Cartagena, 42, came through the crowd and began arguing with her. When Olivo told Cartagena to leave her alone, he pulled a six-inch steak knife and stabbed her near the heart. Olivo's sister attempted to stop the assault, but Cartagena pushed her to the ground and proceeded to stab Olivo several more times, killing her instantly. Others in the crowd, infuriated by what they had witnessed, rushed Cartagena and began beating him. "The slayer was clubbed with baseball bats, pummeled with fists and clawed with fingernails," reported the *New York Times*. By the time police arrived, Cartagena was found unconscious near the woman he had killed. He survived the mob attack only to be charged with first degree murder. The assailant was found guilty and sentenced to a hospital for the criminally insane.[74]

Major League Violence-Related Fatalities from Shooting

Excitement rippled through the crowd of nearly 50,000 as the visiting Brooklyn Dodgers took the field for practice about an hour before the start of a July 4, 1950, doubleheader at the Polo Grounds against the New York Giants. Seated in the upper left grandstand near the 8th Avenue side of the park was 13-year-old Otto Flaig, Jr., who had been brought to the game by a family friend, **Bernard L. "Barney" Doyle**, 56. The unemployed freight sorter, who had once managed future heavyweight boxing champion James Braddock early in the fighter's career, was just turning to speak to his young companion when he suddenly slumped forward in his seat. At that same instant, fans in the immediate vicinity reported hearing "a loud popping noise, like a blown-up paper bag bursting." Thinking Doyle had simply fainted, a spectator seated in front of him turned to lend assistance, only to find that Doyle was bleeding profusely from his head. Help was summoned, but Doyle died before a doctor arrived from Harlem Hospital, the victim of a stray bullet to the left temple.[75]

As the game went on, over 40 police detectives searched the area around the Polo Grounds while others roamed through the stands where Doyle had been seated in search of other bullets. They questioned several boys they found playing in the partially-wooded area of Coogan's Bluff, the rise that overlooked the park from behind home plate. About two hours later they discovered a live .22 caliber cartridge there. After telling Polo Grounds officials not to clear trash from the stands, police suspended their search at 10:00 that night.[76]

The next day a forensic investigation determined that Doyle had been killed by a .45 caliber slug, not a .22 as first supposed. Rifling of the fatal bullet indicated as well that it had been fired from an automatic instead of a revolver. With this discovery, 40 additional detectives were assigned to the case, and the search of the park and the adjacent area continued. When no other shells were found within the park, grounds personnel were allowed to clean it up. Police questioned some 1,200 residents of the apartment buildings along the bluff. They quickly focused their attention on 14-year-old Robert Mario Peebles when they discovered two .22 caliber rifles and a .22 caliber target pistol in his aunt's apartment, where he lived. In addition, shell casings from .22s were found on the roof of the building and a parapet overlooking the Polo Grounds was riddled with bullet holes. Both the youngster and his aunt were taken into custody for violating gun ordinances, but Peebles adamantly denied owning a .45 caliber handgun.[77]

Under persistent police questioning, Peebles admitted the next day that he once had owned a .38 caliber revolver, but that it had been taken from him by his aunt. Detectives, joined by police assigned to the juvenile crimes unit, questioned an additional 1,000 adults and children living nearby. They confiscated six illegally owned rifles during their search. Finally on the afternoon of July 7, Peebles admitted to firing a .45 from his roof at the time Doyle was killed. He told police that he had found the gun in Central Park six months earlier and that it had only one shell in it. On the day of the tragedy, he retrieved it from its hiding place in the basement of his apartment building, took it up on the roof, and fired it at a 45-degree angle over the parapet that surrounded the roof on all sides. The bullet traveled 1,120 feet before striking Doyle. It was an act of careless stupidity, not intentional homicide. The child could not even see the stadium from where he fired the weapon, and the parapet was too high for him to intentionally aim it into the seats. After discharging the gun, he threw the shell casing down his toilet and put the empty weapon back in the basement. About half an hour later he learned that someone had been killed and, in a state of panic, scurried from his apartment to discard the gun behind a public swimming pool several blocks away. Because he was not yet 15, Peebles could only be charged with juvenile delinquency. In addition, the gun was never found, so police were not able to prove conclusively that it was the death weapon. At a hearing two weeks later, he was brought up on two counts of juvenile delinquency. Found guilty of possessing guns illegally, Peebles was sentenced to the state juvenile facility in Warwick, NY, for two years.[78]

An argument over a gambling debt that began elsewhere ended in a fatal shooting on opening day at Busch Stadium in St. Louis in 1970. On the April 10 home opener against the New York Mets, U. D. Earvin, 48, was seated in the bleachers of the Cardinals' stadium. During the fifth or sixth inning, he was joined by **Rufus Mack**, 33, a coworker at a local packing company, who came up to Earvin and began arguing with him about a $5.00 bet allegedly owed him by Earvin. The dispute had begun earlier that day when the two were playing a bowling machine game in a local bar. Witnesses overheard Earvin say he would pay off after the game, but Mack insisted that he pay up immediately. According to Mack's sister, Earvin then enticed his friend to the bleacher restrooms with the offer of a drink. When they arrived there, Earvin insulted Mack, calling him among other things "a river rat." A heated confrontation ensued during which Earvin pulled a gun from his pocket and shot Mack twice, killing him instantly. About 20 men were in the restroom at the time and several rushed out to summon security. When the police arrived a few moments later, Earvin was standing over the dead man, his gun now back in his pocket.[79]

Earvin was arrested and charged with first degree murder. At his trial in October 1971, he claimed that he had shot Mack only after the victim made a move toward his pocket. He thought Mack was reaching for a gun and fired in self-defense. The jury, however, thought otherwise, and sentenced Earvin to a life term. In June 1974, the Missouri Supreme Court overturned the conviction on the grounds that certain prosecution testimony should not have been allowed. The judges ordered a new trial, which occurred in April the following year. This second trial resulted in a second degree murder conviction and a sentence of 10 years in prison. Earvin posted bond and was allowed out pending the results of an appeal on this second conviction. By the time his appeal was denied, Earvin had disappeared and was never found to serve out his sentence.[80]

A Giants-Dodgers game was again the venue for another fatal shooting, and this time it was intentional. **Marc Alan Antenorcruz**, 25, a Giants fan, left Dodger Stadium with his sister, his brother, and a friend during the seventh inning of a game in Los Angeles on September 19, 2003. As they walked through the Chavez Ravine parking lot, they ran into a group of Dodger supporters led by Pete Marron, 19, and Manuel Hernandez, 33. The two groups came into conflict when Antenorcruz, who was arguing loudly with his sister Brandi, thought that Carlos Hernandez, 19-year-old nephew of Manuel, was staring at him. The victim, who had been drinking, confronted the younger Hernandez and tempers flared. Carlos Hernandez, Marron, and Brandi Antenorcruz attempted to calm things down. When he reached their SUV, however, Marron took a .25 caliber semiautomatic pistol from the center console, apparently at the urging of Manuel Hernandez. He then walked toward the rear of the vehicle to where Hernandez was standing. At the same time, Antenorcruz started heading back toward the Dodger fans, "kind of power walking," according to Carlos Hernandez. Just as Antenorcruz made an arm motion for one of his group to join him, Marron shot him twice. He died a short while later at a local hospital.[81]

As Marron and his group fled the scene, a passerby was able to secure the tag number off the SUV. Manuel Hernandez was arrested the following Sunday and charged with murder. When Marron disappeared from his home in South Gate near Los Angeles, officials posted a $25,000 reward for his capture. Marron eluded police for over two months before his arrest at a traffic stop in Rancho Cucamonga, CA, on December 2. He was charged with first degree murder and was denied bail. Just before the jury was selected for the joint trial that was to begin on August 9, 2004, Hernandez pled no contest to the reduced charge of voluntary manslaughter. He was sentenced to 15 years in prison, but the judge gave him credit for the 11 months he had already served and substituted five years of supervised probation for further prison time. Marron, continuing to maintain his innocence, stood trial alone. After three hours of deliberation following the week-long proceedings, the jury convicted the shooter of first-degree murder. On October 26, Marron received a sentence of 50-years-to-life.[82]

Minor League Violence-Related Fatalities from Shooting

Recently estranged from his wife and worried over the health of his six-year-old son, **Stanford B. Twente** shot and killed himself during a live local telecast of a June 11, 1950, Class AA Texas League night game in Houston between the Buffaloes and the Tulsa (OK) Oilers. Just as the last half of the sixth inning was about to begin, Twente walked up to the broadcast booth and told announcer Richard Gottlieb that he had something to say. When Gottlieb motioned Twente away after quietly telling him he was busy, the intruder sat down between the announcer and Lee Bennett, the television engineer. Bennett, in turn, told Twente to leave the booth. Twente stood, pulled a .41 caliber pistol from his shirt, and shot himself behind the right ear, falling onto the engineer as he slumped forward. The camera-man, who had been focused on the Houston dugout, swung his camera around at the sound of the shot. As the camera zoomed in on the body lying there, Gottlieb told his audience, "Ladies and gentlemen, a tremendous thing has just happened. A gentleman has just shot himself, and I return you now to the studio." Several minutes later, the broadcast of the game resumed. Twente, after first being taken to the stadium aide station, where he was given oxygen, was rushed to a local hospital. He was pronounced dead there about two hours later.[83]

Witnesses at the game reported seeing a liquor bottle in Twente's pocket, and one man said he saw that Twente had a gun as he approached the booth and tried to stop him. A wait-ress at a local bar told police that Twente had been in just before the start of the game and suggested she tune in to the broadcast because he was going to kill himself at the bottom of the fifth inning. A brief will dated June 3 was found in his pocket, addressed "To Whom It May Concern." It read, "I leave all my possessions to my boy, Bailey Twente, Anderson, S.C. My wife has my insurance policy." Authorities also found a telegram from his wife dated May 31 reporting on the medical condition of his son, who had suffered potentially crippling injuries when he was hit by a car on May 30. "Bailey had an unrestful night," it began. "Leg in terrible shape; muscle tissue and bone broken in center of leg. Bailey bruised all over. Use own judgment about coming. In Anderson County [SC] Hospital." Fortunately, the child did make a full recovery.[84]

A mentally-ill man given to fits of uncontrollable rage shot three people, killing two of them, between games at Miami Stadium on the evening of August 25, 1980. Jose Tomas, 33, had gone to the Class A Florida State League game between the Miami (FL) Orioles and the Fort Lauderdale (FL) Yankees to confront a man whom he thought had been "making time" with his sister-in-law. As the crowd of 542 fans waited for the start of the second game of a doubleheader, Tomas entered the stadium, walked up to Angel Garcia, 43, who was stand-ing in the aisle way behind home plate, began arguing with him, then pulled a .38 caliber revolver belonging to his father and shot Garcia in the neck. Tomas, who had been "ranting and raving" as he approached Garcia, said later that "he wasn't 100 per cent sure that was the guy he was looking for, but he had to do what he had to do." Fortunately the wound was not severe and Garcia was able to drive himself to the hospital for treatment.[85]

Less fortunate were friends **Edward Huntoon**, 23, and **Charles Matanis**, 24. Yelling at Tomas not to leave, they followed him out of the stadium in an attempt to restrain him. They threw a bucket at Tomas, then rushed him as he stood on the sidewalk outside the park. The gunman shot Huntoon in the chest, killing almost instantly. Matanis, also shot in the chest, managed to crawl back into the stadium entrance, where he collapsed, mortally wounded. He was taken to the hospital, but died there about 45 minutes later. Meanwhile, Tomas walked back to the apartment over his parents' grocery store followed by a security guard who managed to call the police before tailing the murderer. Tomas surrendered to police without a struggle.[86]

Black Baseball Violence-Related Fatalities from Shooting

Albert Green, a 19-year-old African American, got into an argument with white fan Solomon George, 21, at the local fair grounds in Griffin, GA, over the sale of tickets to a game between African American teams from Griffin and Newnan, GA, on June 22, 1925. George, claiming Green had "made ugly threats to which George took offense," fired five shots at the victim as he was getting into a buggy to leave after the game. Green died within moments of being struck. George calmly walked to the local police station to turn himself in, telling the chief of police he had "shot a negro." The assailant pled self-defense at a preliminary hearing held the following month and was held in jail pending the results of a grand jury investigation.[87]

Infuriated at being told to move back from the playing field in a May 20, 1950, game in Bradley, SC, between African American teams from Bradley and nearby Kirksey, fan **James L. Roundtree**, 24, vented his frustration by pulling "a little owl-head pistol" and dry-firing it at James Markem, Bradley's 58-year-old first base coach. Markem, who was officiating under the alias of "James McGowan," had gone to the umpire near first to request that the crowd pressing close to the base line be moved back. The umpire agreed and the game was delayed while he and Markem attempted to do so. Roundtree, refusing to move, pulled his gun, aimed it at Markem, and pulled the trigger several times, but the gun failed to fire. Fearing for his life, the coach grabbed the .38 he had hidden in his coat and fired back, striking and killing Roundtree where he stood. "I meant to shoot him in the legs," Markem claimed later, "but I was looking at that pistol [Roundtree's gun] so hard I couldn't shoot any place else." Markem was placed in jail pending an inquest later that month.[88]

Amateur Violence-Related Fatalities from Shooting

A riot with racial overtones broke out during a baseball game in the greater Pittsburgh, PA, area on May 31, 1903, when white ballplayers and hundreds of white fans attempted to expel six African American gamblers from the ball grounds. As the "crapshooters and chuck-a-luck men" began their games of chance, Samuel "Sandy" Garrett, the team's "negro mascot," led the charge of players against the gamblers. During the ensuing scuffle, one of the gamblers shot and seriously wounded Garrett. This enraged the players and their white supporters, who began throwing stones at the gamblers as they chased them through the city. Two of the pursued, **Charles Kelly**, 25, and William Davis, 35, barricaded themselves inside a chicken coop and began shooting at the howling mob outside. In response, the attackers piled dry brush around the building and set it on fire. At the same time, "volley after volley of bullets was poured into the chicken house." Kelly was found dead with three gunshot wounds to the chest and Davis, who attempted to surrender, was hit over the head by a baseball bat as he emerged from the coop. After someone tied a rope around the neck of the semi-conscious man, he was hauled through the mob to the chants of "Lynch him! Lynch him!" Dragged several hundred yards to a large tree, he was kicked and pelted with rocks and struck again over the head with a bat along the way. One of the participants threw the end of the rope into the limbs of the tree, shouting "Get up there one of you and take this rope, so that we can haul this — nigger on to that branch." Only one lone individual attempted to calm the crowd. Had it not been for the timely arrival of the police, Davis would have been lynched. He was taken to a local hospital, where he eventually recovered from his injuries. Authorities made several arrests for the murder of Kelly, but no one was formally charged.[89]

A baseball game held in conjunction with festivities celebrating the laying of the cornerstone for a new high school in Max Meadows, VA, on July 23, 1910, turned violent, ending in the death of one man and the wounding of two others. Nearly a thousand residents attended the day-long affair that included speeches and a lawn party in addition to an afternoon baseball match between teams for Max Meadows and nearby Ivanhoe. During the fifth inning, fan **Robert Hudson**, either "intoxicated or so disorderly as to give the impression that he was," was confronted by police officer George Alford and told to leave the area. When the two began to scuffle, Robert Walk (or Walke), who had been appointed to serve as a "special officer" for the day, rushed to Alford's assistance. As he began to arrest Hudson, the assailant's 19-year-old son, Ernest, then intervened, asking Walk to let his father go. This further agitated the elder Hudson, who proceeded to assault Walk. The officer pulled his gun and began shooting wildly, wounding Robert Hudson twice, once fatally near the heart. He also shot Ernest Hudson in the stomach and fired a fourth bullet through his own arm. Robert Hudson died on the spot, but his son recovered from his injury. Walk was taken to jail pending the outcome of an inquest.[90]

Lock L. Lann got into an argument with Beuford Wilson over ticket sales at a baseball game in Aberdeen, MS, on July 5, 1915. At some point, the disagreement turned violent and Wilson shot and killed Lann. Wilson, in turn, was struck over the head. He was placed in jail, where he was given medical treatment. He was held there without bail until an inquest could be held.[91]

A baseball game in Island, KY, on August 15, 1915, was suspended for an hour because of a fatal shooting involving two fans. The contest between Island and Poplar Grove was already underway when **Jack Selby**, 43, learned that Ernest Gibbs, 40, a man with whom he had previously fought, was at the same game "laying" for him. In spite of being told that Gibbs was armed, Selby, who carried a "club" for self-protection, went looking for his enemy. Finding each other in the crowd of some two hundred spectators, the two began to argue. Suddenly, Gibbs made a motion toward his back pocket as if reaching for his gun, so Selby struck him over the head with his club. "Gibbs staggered a bit, but stood up. He pulled his gun from his pocket and fired five shots, three of them hitting Selby," killing him on the spot. Louis Hughes, who happened to be standing near the combatants, was wounded in the thigh by a fourth bullet. Play resumed after Gibbs was arrested and Selby's body was taken away.[92]

Joseph Conway, 35, and **Jesse Barron**, 29, died in a gun battle that began at a baseball game in Pittsburgh, PA, on May 30, 1921. Witnesses said that Barron, who had started a game of craps on the sidelines of the game, introduced a pair of loaded dice after he started losing. When his "luck" suddenly changed for the better, other players demanded to inspect the dice. Barron, refusing to do so, pulled two guns and began firing into the crowd. Conway was felled when struck by two of the shots, one on his left side and the other near his heart. The crowd

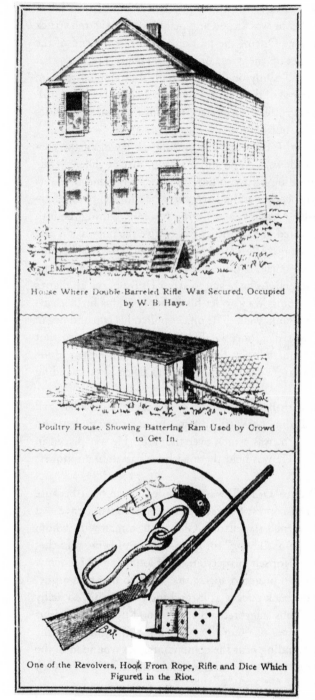

House Where Double-Barreled Rifle Was Secured, Occupied by W. B. Hays.

Poultry House, Showing Battering Ram Used by Crowd to Get In.

One of the Revolvers, Hook From Rope, Rifle and Dice Which Figured in the Riot.

The June 1, 1903, *Pittsburgh Post* ran this illustration of the locations and objects involved in a race riot that resulted in the shooting death of Charles Kelly and the near-lynching of William Davis. The riot resulted from an attempt to expel gamblers from an amateur baseball game.

rushed Barron, who continued to fire his weapons as he backed away from his pursuers, seriously wounding two more spectators. Barron fled the scene while the three wounded men were taken to a hospital. Conway died there shortly after arrival.[93]

Others, meanwhile, chased Barron, finally cornering him at a storeroom near the ball field. Terrified by the threatening mob, Barron fired his pistol several more times, striking two boys and alerting patrolman Howard Ruffner passing nearby. When the shooter stopped to reload, the crowd rushed him, screaming, "Lynch him. Kill the murderer." Ruffner managed to get to Barron first. As he approached the assailant, Barron fired three shots, missing the officer by inches. During the ensuing scuffle, Ruffner pulled his weapon and shot Barron twice in the head, killing him instantly.[94]

In a case of mistaken identity, Louis Olivero, 45, shot and killed **John L. Kallapka**, 21, during a community baseball game in Follansbee, WV, on July 29, 1922. About 4,000 fans were watching Follansbee play a team from Weirton, WV, when Olivero entered the crowd looking for Samuel Basil, Kallapka's brother-in-law. Olivero and Basil had fought several days earlier and Olivero was out for revenge. Spying Kallapka, who "closely resembled" Basil, Olivero pulled a pistol and shot the victim in the heart, killing him instantly. Realizing his mistake, Olivero shouted, "My God! I've shot the wrong man," then sat down and waited for police to arrest him. Olivero was held pending an inquest into his mental condition.[95]

A divorce and child custody battle ended in the murder of two and the suicide of another in the parking lot of youth baseball park in Ozark, AL, on the evening game of May 16, 2000. **Ricky**

Gerald Todd Smith, 35, who had recently lost custody of his two sons after his 14-year marriage ended in divorce, confronted his ex-wife, **Diana Smith**, 32, and her friend, **Edward McQuinn II**, 35, shortly before the game which his children were also attending. Speaking first with one of his sons, Smith walked to his truck to get a shotgun and .22 caliber pistol. After shooting McQuinn in the head with the shotgun, he turned the weapon on his ex-wife. When it failed to fire, he pulled the .22 and shot her several times in the head before shooting himself. Diana Smith and McQuinn were killed on the spot; Ricky Smith died at a local hospital the following morning.[96]

Three people were shot and killed after a youth baseball game in Dandridge, TN, on September 18, 2006, over what police speculated was an ongoing family feud concerning the custody of a 10-year-old boy who had played in the game. **Samuel L. Noe**, 61, the boy's maternal grandfather, confronted **Jerry D. Shands**, 63, and **Ellen D. Shands**, 62, the boy's paternal grandparents, and 39-year-old Jerry Brent Shands, Noe's ex-son-in-law, shortly after the game ended. Noe shot Jerry and Ellen Shands with a .38 caliber revolver before Brent Shands had time to intervene. As Noe and the younger Shands wrestled for possession of the weapon, it discharged twice more, killing Noe and seriously wounding Brent Shands. Jerry Shands died at the ballpark while his wife passed away in a local hospital a short while later.[97]

14. Health-Related Fatalities Among Fans

With all the emphasis placed on the potential danger from foul balls and bats flying into the stands, one might assume that they are the most common threats to the health of fans at baseball games. The reality, however, is actually quite different. In fact, as revealed in a study of all the 2,163 illness and injury cases treated by medical personnel at Riverfront Stadium in Cincinnati, OH, during the 1991 season, foul ball injuries comprised less than five percent of all non-urgent cases (those requiring only "minimal treatment") and less than one percent of all urgent cases (those requiring "immediate medical evaluation with treatment and transport to emergency facility within 20 minutes to 2 hours").[1]

Fortunately, the vast majority (84.8 percent) of health interventions identified in the Riverfront Stadium study were of the non-urgent variety. These included "sprains, strains, minor gastrointestinal disturbances, minor respiratory symptoms, sunburn, and minor wound care (from falls, ball hits, etc.)." Curiously, many such cases involved conditions existing prior to attendance at a game, such as colds and fevers. Of the urgent cases (13.8 percent of all interventions), nearly all (96 percent) were from heat exhaustion, most of which were treated with fluids and rest time in an air-conditioned room. But 1.4 percent of all cases (31 in all) were classified as an emergency, or those requiring "immediate evaluation, therapeutic intervention, and transport to emergency department." These included such events as "cardiopulmonary arrest, cerebrovascular accident, chest pain, arrhythmia, respiratory distress, severe trauma, seizure, altered mental status, and heat stroke." The majority of these emergency cases involved either some type of "respiratory distress" or "seizures and chest pain."[2]

Death in the stands is rare, but it does occur. A survey of all major league clubs covering the 1992 and 1993 seasons found that over two-thirds of them had a least one fan fatality during the two year period. While the percentage is small in comparison to the total attendance during those seasons (30 deaths out of 126,128,730 paid attendees), it is nonetheless a great concern in any public mass event.[3]

Fan fatalities from action on the field and from fan behavior have been covered in previous chapters. What follows are those deaths resulting from health-related factors. Most of these involve some sort of cardiac event and many, interestingly, were reported as having occurred as a result of the fan being overly excited or agitated by what was occurring on the field. While at first blush this diagnosis might appear to be unsubstantiated and not grounded in medical fact, a recent study in Holland concerning heart attacks and strokes on the day of a championship soccer (football) game suggests there may be something to these reports. After reviewing fatalities among Dutch men and women aged 45 and older several days before, after, and on June 22, 1996 — the day Holland lost to France on a penalty shootout in the quarter-final match of the European championship played in England — and comparing the 1996 statistics with those from the same period the year before and the year after, researchers noted a pronounced increase in deaths among men (but not among women) from "myocardial infarction and stroke" on the day of the match. They concluded that "important sporting events may provoke a sufficient level of stress to trigger symptomatic cardiovascular disease." They cautioned, though, that the "triggers induced by a crucial football match may not be due solely to mental or emotional stress. Notably, heavy alcohol use, overeating, and excessive smoking may also play a part."[4]

Major League Health-Related Fatalities

J. W. Maher, 44, died in the stands from "apoplexy, superinduced by the excitement of the game" during the seventh inning of a August 3, 1905, contest between the Pittsburgh Pirates and the New York Giants in Pittsburgh, PA.[5]

Edmond F. Pierdon, 55, collapsed while watching batting practice just before the start of a game between the Pittsburgh Pirates and the New York Giants being held at the American League Ballpark on May 22, 1911. Believing that the fan had fainted from the heat, a groundsman at first attempted to revive him. When the victim did not respond to treatment, the Giants' team doctor came to his aid. Pierdon was pronounced dead at the scene from a heart attack.[6]

Chauncey Martin, 45, was overcome with excitement when Zack Wheat hit an eleventh inning single to drive in the winning run during a June 1, 1915, battle between Martin's beloved Dodgers and the Philadelphia Phillies at Ebbets Field. Seated in the bleachers near third, Martin "gave out one shout and dropped back in his seat" when Wheat delivered the victory shot. The Brooklyn fan died of heart failure before an ambulance could arrive.[7]

William E. Coman, 52, "baseball enthusiast and rooter for the Red Sox," insisted on attending a game between league-leading Boston and the second place Chicago White Sox at Fenway Park on July 28, 1915, in spite of having suffered from serious heart trouble for over two years. During most of the fiercely fought struggle, which Chicago won 1 to 0, the 20,000 fans were at "the raving maniac state," so much so, in fact, that few noticed when Coman collapsed and died in their midst. Little attention was paid as the deceased was carried from the stadium, as most thought he had only fainted.[8]

Alfred Kenning, 65, seated directly behind the Tigers' dugout during a game against the Chicago White Sox at Detroit's Navin Field on May 7, 1922, grew extremely agitated when, during the bottom half of the seventh with the Tigers down 6, Ty Cobb strode to the plate with two on and two out. Just as the Georgia Peach took a mighty swing, Kenning "half rose from his chair, and then sat down, faint and a bit dizzy.... 'Crack' went Cobb's bat and the ball sailed over the right field wall for a home run. But, as the thousands of excited men in the stands rose and cheered, and Lou Blue and Bobby Jones and Cobb crossed the home plate, Kenning was sliding into a crumpled heap on the floor of the box." Play ceased briefly as players on both sides watched while physicians attempted to revive stricken man. He was taken to the clubhouse, but doctors reported later he had died from heart failure "almost as Cobb's bat connected with the horsehide." While Cobb's homer brought Detroit within striking distance, they lost 9 to 7.[9]

H. B. Miltenberger, attending the second game of a Cardinals-Cincinnati Reds doubleheader in St. Louis on May 27, 1924, died of heart failure shortly after the Reds' first baseman, Jake Daubert, hit an eighth inning home run to seal a 3 to 1 Cincinnati victory.[10]

Walter F. Busch, 58, died from a heart attack "brought on" in the sixth inning when Sam West, Washington outfielder, hit a home run in a game at Griffith Stadium between the Senators and the Philadelphia Athletics on a May 17, 1930. With his son by his side, Busch died before he reached the hospital.[11]

Lucien D. Robinson, 74, retired Episcopal minister and seminary professor, enjoyed attending spring training games near his home in Tampa, FL. During a game between the Brooklyn Dodgers and the Cincinnati Reds in Plant City on March 13, 1932, Rev. Robinson suffered a heart attack. He was able to walk out of the park, but collapsed again while being helped to a car. He died before reaching a local hospital.[12]

Herman J. Hoppenjans, 72, suffered a heart attack when Cincinnati's Babe Herman hit a ninth inning home run in a game between the Reds and the Chicago Cubs in Cincinnati on May 20, 1932. He died at his home in Covington, KY, the next day.[13]

Max Zanderer died in his grandstand seat at Yankee Stadium about 4:30 P.M. during a game between New York and the Washington Senators on June 28, 1932. New York City was experiencing a heat wave with high humidity at the time, so physicians concluded that his death was due to "heat and heart disease."[14]

Edward S. Thompson, 67, had a heart attack while watching the first game of the 1932 World Series between New York and the Chicago Cubs at Yankee Stadium on September 28, 1932. The Staten Island resident, who had been suffering from ill health for several years, died before help could arrive.[15]

Frank W. Davis, 63, was seated in the upper deck behind home plate at Griffith Stadium in a game between the Washington Senators and Cleveland Indians on August 25, 1940. With Washington leading 5 to 2 late in the game, Cleveland staged a rally in the seventh. Just as the Indians loaded the bases, Davis suffered a heart attack. He was taken to a first aid station where the physician in attendance pronounced him dead 10 minutes later. Cleveland succeeded in scoring two runs during that inning, but lost the game 5 to 4.[16]

Joseph L. Fielding, 50, died on August 15, 1945, from an apparent heart attack during a game between the New York Giants and the Pittsburgh Pirates at the Polo Grounds.[17]

Emil W. Fehring, 60, recently recovered from a "coronary heart ailment," had a heart attack during the eleventh inning of game 6 of the 1945 World Series between the Detroit Tigers and the Chicago Cubs at Wrigley Field on October 8. Dr. Fehring, a chiropodist who had traveled from his home in Manitowoc, WI, to take in three of the games, was taken from his seat to a first aid station below the grandstand, where he died a few minutes later. While the Cubs won by a run in the bottom of the twelfth, they would lose game 7, and the series, two days later.[18]

James R. McLaren, president of a Brooklyn, NY, bank, died of a heart attack while at Ebbets Field on April 24, 1948, during a game between the Dodgers and the Philadelphia Phillies.[19]

John S. Barry, 70, collapsed and died while in his box seat behind the first base dugout at the beginning of a game between the Braves and the Philadelphia Phillies at Milwaukee County Stadium on May 16, 1953. It was determined later that Barry, a district court judge, had suffered a heart attack.[20]

William Delbert Weeks, 12, suffered a fatal heart attack after a St. Louis Browns–

Chicago White Sox game at Busch Stadium on May 26, 1953. The youngster, who had a congenital heart condition, attended the event with members of his Boy Scout troop. Afterwards Weeks and several other boys raced back to the truck used to bring them to the game. He collapsed and died shortly after reaching the vehicle.[21]

Joseph Eilbacher, 50, had a heart attack during a game between the Chicago White Sox and Detroit Tigers at Comiskey Park on May 27, 1953. Police transported him to a nearby hospital, where he was pronounced dead on arrival.[22]

Una Tumelty, 18, was attending a Brooklyn Dodgers–New York Giants game at Ebbets Field on July 6, 1954, with her father and brother when, during the first inning, she collapsed in her seat after cheering a Duke Snider double. Her father at first thought she was simply looking for something under her seat, but quickly realized she was unconscious. Ushers took the girl to the first aid station under the grandstands, where the physician in attendance tried in vain to revive her. He declared her dead from a heart attack a short time later.[23]

Edward G. Mason, 59, suffered a heart attack while seated in the stands at Ebbets Field in a game between the Brooklyn Dodgers and the Philadelphia Phillies on April 20, 1955. After being treated, he was taken home, where he died later that night.[24]

Francis J. Ahern, 58, chief of police for San Francisco, CA, had a heart attack while cheering a close play at the plate during the fifteenth inning of the second game of a double-header between the Giants and the Los Angeles Dodgers at Seals Stadium on September 1, 1958. With the score tied at 4 and the bases loaded for the second consecutive inning, Ahern, occupying a box seat behind home plate, stood with the crowd to yell as the Giants' Willie Kirkland raced for home. Just as the player was called out on what would have been the winning run, Ahern collapsed to the floor in front of his seat. After being administered last rites by two priests, the police chief was taken to a first aid station, where he was pronounced dead. His wife, who was with him when he died, said later that her husband had been suffering from "a mild heart condition." The 4 hour, 35 minute Labor Day contest ended in the bottom of sixteenth when the Giants scored two runs after giving up a run at the top of the inning, winning 6 to 5.[25]

Vincent F. Haggerty, 50, an attorney from Tenafly, NJ, died of heart failure at Yankee Stadium on October 6 during game 5 of the 1958 World Series between New York and the Milwaukee Braves.[26]

Lucille Larimer, 60, suffered a fatal heart attack at Comiskey Park while attending a game between the Chicago White Sox and the Detroit Tigers on the evening of July 28, 1967.[27]

C. Maynard Nichols, 62, a retired editor for the *New York Times* and an author of three crossword puzzle books, died of a heart attack as he was leaving Yankee Stadium after a game between New York and the Minnesota Twins on July 22, 1971.[28]

John Corbett, 73, was seated down front near third base during pre-game practice at Veterans Stadium in Philadelphia on April 11, 1976, when he suddenly slumped forward in his seat, a victim of his fifth heart attack. The Pittsburgh Pirates' hurler, George "Doc" Medich, was passing by when he noticed the elderly man in apparent cardiac arrest. Medich, a senior medical student at the University of Pittsburgh Medical School during the off-season, jumped the railing and began administering CPR as Corbett's grandson looked on. The pitcher worked tirelessly for over 20 minutes, applying mouth-to-mouth resuscitation and messaging the victim's chest in a vain attempt to save his life. Corbett was then rushed to a local hospital, where he was pronounced dead on arrival. Medich was more successful two years later when, as a pitcher for the Texas Rangers, he went into the stands at Baltimore's Memorial Stadium when he heard a call for help. Fan Germain Languth, seated behind the Orioles' dugout on the evening of July 17, 1978, was having a heart attack. Medich, who was then in his second year of residency at a Pittsburgh, PA, hospital, gave Languth medication and began CPR. He and paramedics worked for half an hour until Languth was stable enough to be taken to a hospital. Thanks to Medich's efforts, Languth survived his attack.[29]

Dennis P. Dunne, 34, a deputy in the Cook County, IL, assessor's office, suffered a fatal heart attack while attending a Chicago White Sox game at Comiskey Park on July 11, 1977. Dunne, who attended the game with his wife and other employees as part of an office outing, collapsed in the lower deck area. He was pronounced dead on arrival at a local hospital. Because he was at the game by virtue of his employment with the assessor's office, the Illinois Industrial Commission ruled a year later that his death was work-related, awarding his widow a monthly payment as a workman's compensation benefit.[30]

Joseph Wagner, 58, and **Minzio Bazarozza**, 75, died within half an hour of each other after suffering heart attacks while attending the same September 4, 1978, game at Baltimore's Memorial Stadium between the Orioles and the Boston Red Sox. Wagner collapsed first about 15 minutes before game time, followed by Bazarozza a short while later. Both were pronounced dead on arrival at the same hospital. Officials said later that both men had histories of heart problems.[31]

Edd Roush, 94, former Cincinnati Reds great and member of the Baseball Hall of Fame, had a fatal heart attack prior to the start of a spring training game between the Pittsburgh Pirates and the Texas Rangers at Bill McKechnie Field in Bradenton, FL, on March 21, 1988. He fell ill as he was walking toward the ballpark pressroom with a friend about 40 minutes before game time. He was immediately taken to a nearby hospital, where he was pronounced dead on arrival.[32]

An unidentified grandfather and his 6-year-old grandson, Antonio Perez, were seated in the right field bleachers at Riverfront Stadium during a game between the Cincinnati Reds and the Atlanta Braves on August 3, 2005, when the grandfather suffered a heart attack. As medical personnel worked in vain to save the man, a security guard took the child to the Reds' bullpen to stay with the relief pitchers for the last two innings of the game. Afterwards, the Reds' Ken Griffey, Jr., escorted the boy into the clubhouse, where the players took care of him until his parents could arrive. The grandfather died later that evening.[33]

Denise Quickenton, 29, was sitting with her husband at Fenway Park on July 29, 2006, watching a game between the Boston Red Sox and the Los Angeles Angels; when she suddenly became ill during the second inning. Her husband took his wife, who was seven months pregnant, to sit at a picnic table in the shade. There she had "some sort of attack." Because they were seated near a first aid station, medical personnel responded quickly and got her on the way to the hospital in minutes. Sadly, she was beyond help, but CPR was continued until her child could be delivered by cesarean section. The day was unusually hot, so many speculated at the time that she had died from heat-related causes, but an autopsy revealed her death to be from "a pre-existing condition."[34]

Minor League Health-Related Fatalities

Gladys Marion Dunn, 58, suffered a heart attack while attending a Class AAA Pacific

Coast League game between the Los Angeles Angels and the San Francisco Seals at Wrigley Field in Los Angeles on June 29, 1957. She was taken to a first aid station, where she died a few minutes later.[35]

Bernie Wanko, 63, had a heart attack during the third inning of a Class A Midwest League game between the South Bend (IN) Silver Hawks and the Fort Wayne (IN) Wizards in South Bend on May 12, 1996. Medical personnel worked on Wanko atop the third base dugout for over 40 minutes before he was stable enough to be taken to a local hospital. The game itself was suspended. Wanko died shortly after 2:30 P.M. on May 14.[36]

Victoria Lampe, 28, had a seizure as she ran across the infield at Walt Disney's Wide World of Sports Stadium near Orlando, FL, as part of a contest held after a game on August 23, 2002, between Class AA Southern League rivals, the Orlando Rays and the Jacksonville (FL) Suns. Lampe was one of 250 women and girls who were searching for a diamond buried somewhere in the infield. "Just as she got to the infield, she collapsed face first," reported a spokesperson for the Rays' parent club, the Tampa Bay Devil Rays. She was not breathing and had no pulse by the time medical help arrived and was pronounced dead on arrival at a local hospital.[37]

Amateur Health-Related Fatalities

King Cherry died of an apparent heart attack while watching a game in Opelika, AL, on July 31, 1885.[38]

Robert Myers, 65, suffered a fatal heart attack while "cheering vigorously" for his favorite player who had just hit a home run during a game in Chicago, IL, on August 29, 1909.[39]

Marcus Goldwater, 48, was attending a game in Los Angeles, CA, with his brother on July 2, 1910, when, during the eighth inning as "excitement had reached fever heat," he began to stand, then slumped forward. He came to rest with his head on the railing in front of his grandstand box seat before falling forward onto the ground. A physician was summoned, but Goldwater died of a heart failure a few moments later.[40]

Julius Van Overmeer died suddenly of "apoplexy" (a stroke) while cheering "a clever play" during a sandlot game in Detroit, MI, on May 7, 1922.[41]

Ulysses Lee, 63, was standing near home plate during a game between teams from Hampton Bays and East Hampton, Long Island, NY, on July 4, 1925, when "he was seen to stagger after urging a base runner to 'come home.'" He fell where he stood as friends rushed to his assistance. Lee died of "heart disease" before a physician could arrive.[42]

John Wells, 54, mayor of Stanhope, NJ, died of "heart disease" while he was watching two of his four sons play baseball against a team from Rockaway, NJ, on July 11, 1925.[43]

Louis M. Rossignol, 44, had a fatal heart attack while attending a game in Macon, GA, on June 26, 1928.[44]

John M. Moore, 56, in his youth a catcher and a football quarterback for the University of Pennsylvania, suffered a heart attack while watching a playground game in Glens Falls, NY, on July 24, 1933. He died later that night at his home.[45]

Michael Lally 70, died of heart failure while watching a game at a local park in Greenwich, CT, on May 31, 1936.[46]

Allen H. Kerr, 49, died of "coronary thrombosis" while attending a game between Harvard and Yale in New Haven, CT, on June 16, 1936. He had suffered several heart attacks during the three years prior to this fatal one.[47]

Horace G. Evans, 66, in his third consecutive term as mayor of Frostburg, MD, died instantly of heart failure while at a local game with two friends on June 24, 1939. He was in the midst of speaking with them when he suddenly collapsed.[48]

Walker Wallace Sanford, 72, suffered a fatal heart attack while attending a high school game in Charlottesville, VA, on the evening of July 26, 1954.[49]

William B. McDonald, 46, mayor of Island Lake, IL, died of heart failure during a Little League game at a local ball field on June 23, 1966. At the time of his attack, he was sitting in the stands with his 12-year-old son while watching two other sons play in the game.[50]

15. Weather and Field-Related Fatalities Among Fans

Stadium design and infrastructure are basic to fan safety. Before the late nineteenth century, most baseball parks were small, simple wooden structures incapable of holding more than a few thousand people. Oftentimes they were hastily constructed affairs with little thought given to fan comfort or safety. If stands burned to the ground, that was not a serious problem, because new ones could be erected in the same spot in a matter of weeks, if not days. And since teams moved around frequently, there was little consideration given to erecting facilities that would last more than a few years. But the growing popularity of the game, the desire among fans for better accommodations, and concerns over public safety created a demand for larger, safer, and more attractive structures. A series of fires in the 1890s, including several at major league parks in 1894, added to this impetus for modernization. As a result, massive concrete and steel stadiums with huge upper decks began to be built.[1]

Larger stadiums meant more fans could attend games and, with tens of thousands of people crowded into a confined space, the need for crowd control became more urgent. Techniques for crowd control have improved greatly over the years. Unlike what occurs in many other countries, U.S. stadiums minimize standing-room-only sections, prevent crowds from gathering and milling around gates and exits, and provide sufficient, flexible means for rapid exit in emergencies. So far such policies have been successful in avoiding tragedies like the one that occurred at a British soccer match in 1989. Nearly 100 people were killed when a huge crowd of additional fans broke through a back gate, crushing the spectators inside against an immovable fence.[2]

Local and statewide fire codes have also become more stringent since the introduction of fireproof construction materials in the first decade of the twentieth century. In fact, stadium officials have "seen a dramatic increase in lawsuits which involve ushers and security personnel being sued for trying to enforce venue and fire laws" as a result of the strengthening of the regulations governing public safety. And, as discussed in an earlier chapter, the numerous restrictions and policies on alcohol sales and consumption in effect at U.S. stadiums today have reduced incidents of crowd misbehavior. In the eyes of many stadium officials, "crowd control is synonymous with alcohol control."[3]

Major League Weather-Related Fatalities

Sometimes injuries and deaths are the result not of rowdy behavior *per se*, but of sheer panic. The May 19, 1929, rainstorm stampede at Yankee Stadium is a classic example of what happens when a crowd gets out of control. About 50,000 fans attended the doubleheader that day against the Red Sox. Over 9,000 sat in the uncovered right field bleachers, an area known as Ruthville because of the number of home runs hit there by Babe Ruth. At the end of the fourth inning of the first game, dark clouds moved in and a light drizzle began to fall. Some of the Ruthville spectators left the seating area, but remained near the southern exit because Ruth and Lou Gehrig were due up at the bottom of the fifth. Just as Gehrig made his way to the plate after Ruth grounded out, the sky opened up and a heavy rain began to fall. Those standing near the exit began making their way down the 14-step stairways leading to the exit passageway eight feet below. Unfortunately, the larger crowd still seated in the bleachers made a mad rush toward the same exit, shoving those in front of them, causing those at the bottom of the stairs to lose their balance. "In an instant, the area at the foot of the stairs, a space about ten feet wide, was a screaming struggling mass of people," reported the *New York Times*. "Men, women, and children — a preponderance of children — were jammed together in a pile so tightly that they could not breathe, let alone work their way out without assistance. The weight of those on the top bore down on those beneath, crushing them before anything could be done, while others continued to fall over them and trample them under feet." Police stationed around the exit reacted quickly and forced the crowd at the top of the stairs back, but not before **Joseph Carter**, 60, and **Eleanor Price**, a 17-year-old Hunter College student, were killed and 62 others injured.[4]

Rumors circulated that other exits from Ruthville were either closed or malfunctioning. Other fans charged that the game had not been called when the weather turned threatening in the fourth inning because stadium officials did not want to have to make good on rain checks. An official investigation the next day cleared the club of all responsibility. New York district attorney John McGeehan determined that the incident was due to "a wild rush of people down a narrow chute without apparent reason" rather than to any negligence on the part of the Yankees.[5]

Two factors seem to have been at play in this incident: crowd control and, to some extent, stadium design. In terms of crowd control, the Yankees fortunately responded quickly with police and medical assistance. Far more fans would have been injured or even killed had authorities not restored order as fast as they did.

But the 1929 tragedy at Yankee Stadium appears to be due in part, at least, to the availability of exits. Although there were other exits from the bleachers, several fans reported that gates for these exits were closed and that a patrolman on duty refused to open them. Quite naturally stadium officials would not accept any culpability for what happened, especially since the club faced multiple lawsuits over the incident. Proclaimed Ed Barrow, then Yankee secretary, "The exits at the stadium have always been considered thoroughly adequate to handle even greater crowds than the one we had last Sunday. Naturally, we are always ready to install improvements, but in this instance I know of no alterations to make. Nothing broke and the exits and runways have always been regarded as ample." The victims disagreed. A multi-party $960,000 negligence lawsuit involving the families of the deceased and 32 of the injured was instituted against the Yankees. A jury verdict in February 1932 found the club "guilty of negligence, but the plaintiffs guilty of 'contributory negligence.'" An appellate court set aside the "contributory negligence" finding, stating that "under the law the plaintiffs could not be held partly responsible, because in a heavy rainstorm it was their natural instinct to seek shelter and they could not be held for the resultant stampede." Later that summer a new trial was ordered to address this issue. At the beginning of this second trial on December 15,

1932, the Yankees settled the claims for $45,000, the money to be divided according to "the severity of the injuries and the sums spent for medical treatment."[6]

Minor League Weather-Related Fatalities

A massive killer tornado struck the town of Sherman, TX, at about 4:30 in the afternoon of May 15, 1896. The storm tore a path 400 feet wide and approximately 28 miles long as it killed 66 men, women, and children in Sherman and severely injured nearly 60 other residents while destroying much of the western half of the town. At the time the storm hit, the San Antonio (TX) Bronchos were playing the Sherman Students in a Texas-Southern League game at the Sherman ballpark. According to one report in the national press, "many of the spectators were killed," but other accounts make no mention of any fan fatalities. In fact, a brief story in the *San Antonio Daily Light* reported on a telegraph message from the San Antonio manager that said "the cyclone never touched the Bronchos and that they were all alive and kicking." The house belonging to Sherman manager Frank Ryan was destroyed, but his wife and two children were not seriously injured.[7]

Severe rain storms forced the cancellation of most of the games scheduled in the Class C Piedmont League on September 2, 1924, including the afternoon contest between the visiting Winston-Salem (NC) Twins and the High Point (NC) Pointers at Welch Park. Several fans were in the stands hoping the game would be played when lightning began striking in the area. While the players and most of the fans sought shelter in the back of the grandstand directly above the ticket booth, High Point fireman **Gilmore Pickett**, 21, stood alone inside the ticket booth office. A lightning bolt suddenly struck the telephone lines leading into the office, causing a loud bang directly below those seated in the stands. At the noise, several rushed to see what had happened beneath them, only to find Pickett dead on the floor. Apparently the fireman had been leaning against the metal box containing the office telephone when the lightning hit.[8]

As part of his 1927 spring tour of the Class B Virginia League, baseball commissioner Kenesaw Mountain Landis planned to spend the day in the coastal town of Portsmouth, VA, home of the Portsmouth Truckers. The festivities slated for that May 25 visit were extensive indeed. Shortly after his arrival by train from Raleigh, NC, he was to tour the Naval Ship Yard at nearby Norfolk and then play a round of golf at the Portsmouth Country Club. After a noontime luncheon, the commissioner was whisked off to the Truckers' High Street Park to attend a mid-afternoon contest against the Petersburg (VA) Bronchos. Expecting a large turnout, the gates were opened an hour before the 3:30 game, at which time fans arriving early were treated to a band concert and "colored dancers in Charleston exhibitions." Even the Portsmouth schools were closed at 2:45 P.M. to allow children to attend.[9]

The pre-game activities ran long and by game time the band was still playing while the players waited anxiously to take the field for practice. Over 2,000 fans were already in the stands with more on the way. Since many that day were concentrating on the activities on the field or were busy finding their seats, few noticed the long line of dark clouds looming out of the west. One reporter in the press box did, however, and, recognizing the threat posed by the impending storm, advised his colleagues to run for cover. Just as they were making their escape, a 72-mile-an-hour gale blew down a section of the left center outfield fence, hurling debris everywhere as it raced toward the grandstand. It gave brief warning to the fans inside the park, many of whom began rushing toward the exits or to the back of the stands.[10]

The storm slammed into the grandstand, ripping the press box into two sections, smashing it like "one crumples a match box in the hand." It rained timber on the crowd below before tearing the roof off the right field side of the grandstand. "There was little lightning, and no more than a crash or two of thunder," reported the local paper the next day. "But the air was filled with the roar of the wind and was echoing with the tearing, rending sound made by the wooden grandstand top." This, too, fell down upon the panicked spectators as the v-shaped front section was pushed inward toward the seats. Many avoided injury by dropping between the seats, but over 30 others were less fortunate. Some were hurt as they stood paralyzed with fright, others when they jumped off the back part of the stands in a desperate attempt to escape. Many who sustained serious injuries had to be hospitalized. **Richard P. McWilliams**, 42, and H. C. Everhart were picked up by the wind and hurled several feet into the wreckage as they ran down the grandstand runway. McWilliams was killed instantly and Everhart suffered severe trauma to his face and body. He, fortunately, survived. **William Barker**, 67, who had his skull fractured by the falling roof, died the next day. The storm then crossed the river to Norfolk, where it tore the roof off of a warehouse and dropped it onto a group of seven workmen laying railroad track on a street nearby, killing four of them.[11]

As a heavy rain began to fall, players tore down the screening in front of the first base seats and entered the stands to rescue the injured. Others in the area rushed to help as well. Within a half hour all those suffering severe injuries had been taken to area hospitals. The storm itself dissipated almost as quickly as it arrived. Landis, seated in the front row on the third base side of the stadium, was uninjured. Describing the storm as "a swirling, rushing, tearing black wind," the commissioner said later that he was "grateful that the wind did not crush the left section, for that was packed with women and children and many would have perished." Before leaving Portsmouth later that day, he commended the players and others in the stands for keeping calm and assisting in the rescue efforts.[12]

In a situation eerily similar to what occurred in Portsmouth, sudden "tornadic winds" resulted in three fatalities and massive destruction when they ripped through the city of Augusta, GA, on the night of May 24, 1955. The area had been under a tornado watch since mid-afternoon, but officials at Jennings Stadium, home of the Class A South Atlantic League Augusta Tigers, decided to go ahead with that evening's game against the Montgomery (AL) Rebels anyway. Shortly before 9:00 P.M., with the game in the top of the fifth and the Rebels leading 2 to 0, winds in excess of 80 miles per hour suddenly struck the stadium. While most fans and players scrambled for shelter inside the park itself or made a mad dash to their cars, **David Thomas**, 12, **Sam Madison**, 13, and **Wee Bennett**, 25, all of whom had been watching the game from beneath a tree outside the park, crouched behind the outfield wall surrounding the field. It was an act of sheer desperation, because a 100-foot section of the massive structure, "parts of which blew down with monotonous regularity," had been condemned several weeks earlier. This area was roped off and posted with danger signs, but the three apparently ignored the warnings in their panic.[13]

Inside the stadium, one of the ushers heard "a 'thunderous rumble.'" Rushing outside, he saw "tons of concrete brick and blocks come tumbling down." When he and the groundskeeper went closer to get a better look at the destruction, they heard faint cries for help. Digging frantically through the rubble, they discovered the three victims. Bennett, whose skull was crushed, was found dead. Thomas and Madison were still alive, but both died a short time later in the emergency room of a local hospital. Thomas suffered "severe chest injuries" and Madison "a multiple fracture and possible internal injuries."[14]

Amateur Weather-Related Fatalities

Percy F. W. Barrows, 18, Charles Goetz, 15, and about four other boys were among a group of fans watching a game in Crotona Park in the Bronx, NY, on September 5, 1903, when a severe thunderstorm suddenly struck. While some of the fans scurried for the shelter of a nearby building, the boys ran diagonally across the park toward a large tree. Just as they reached their destination, a bolt of lightning hit the tree, splitting it in two. All the boys were knocked to the ground, but most recovered by the time help arrived. Barrows and Goetz remained unconscious as they were transported to a local hospital. Barrows was pronounced dead on arrival, but Goetz eventually revived and was sent home.[15]

Donald Touart, 21, **Stephen Touart**, 19, **John Green, Charles Thomas,** and a large group of other fans were enjoying the conclusion of a game between company teams in an open field just outside Mobile, AL, on the late afternoon of May 27, 1906, when "a terrific stroke of lightning ... descended from almost a perfectly clear sky." As a light rain began to fall, Arthur Moody, 19, who had been acting as umpire, was just handing the prize money to the winning team's captain when the bolt struck Moody on the left side of his head, ran down his right leg, then out his right foot before spreading among the crowd around him. While those still standing ran off in panic, about 15 or 20 fans and players lay unconscious on the ground. After their initial fright subsided, those players and fans who were not injured returned to assist those who were. Moody, the Touart brothers, Green, and Thomas were killed immediately by the blast, their clothes tattered and torn and their bodies "badly lacerated and blackened almost beyond description." The others, though severely burned, recovered; none of the players was killed.[16]

Albert Skuhra, 30, **Walter Handl**, 18, **Irving Woellert**, 20, **Anton Klauck**, 14, and **William Knudsen**, 16, were killed instantly when lightning struck the grandstand shortly before the start of a July 23, 1906, afternoon game in Manitowoc, WI. A raging thunderstorm drove fans and players to seek shelter in or near the stand. The bolt hit the roof of the stand, then traveled down metal support cables, entering the seating area near the entrance gate. Skuhra and Klauck were in the seats when they were killed, while the other three victims were leaning against the outside structure of the stand in an attempt to keep out of the heavy rain. At least three other fans were severely injured by the strike.[17]

Everett Sloan, 14, and about 250 other fans were awaiting the start of a game between teams from Yorktown and Muncie, IN, on May 15, 1909, when a sudden severe windstorm flipped over the new covered grandstand at the Yorktown ballpark. A light rain began to fall as a dark cloud approached the stand about 3:15 P.M., shortly before game time. Most thought it to be a passing storm when, just as it reached the ballpark, "the cloud swooped down and struck the stand fairly. There was a creaking of timbers, a shrieking of women and the groans of injured men and the cloud passed on." The entire grandstand and the attached player clubhouse were turned upside down by the "twister." Young Sloan, who was standing in back of the stand, was struck on the top of his head by a falling beam from the roof of the structure. He was killed instantly, while approximately 20 other fans were injured. More fortunate were the Yorktown players locked inside their dressing room under the stand. Although they were "rolled around in the room like dice in the box" when the grandstand was blown over, none of them was hurt.[18]

Weston Fry, 19, and **Tom Halverson**, 14, were huddled under an umbrella watching a game between teams Lead and Deadwood, SD, in Lead on July 20, 1909, when lightning from a sudden storm struck the top of the umbrella during the fifth inning. Both young men were killed instantly and about a dozen other fans were knocked unconscious by the strike.[19]

Daniel Druding, 14, described by his coach as "the nicest kid on the team," was supposed to play in an Arlington Heights (IL) Boys Baseball League game on the afternoon of June 16, 1973. When he arrived at the park, however, the game had been canceled because of inclement weather. He decided to stay anyway to watch the final innings of a game in which his brother was playing. Lightning struck as he stood under a tree, the bolt traveling from his head, through his body, and down his left leg, killing him instantly.[20]

Major League Field-Related Fatalities

As mentioned above, a number of stadium fires in the last decade of the nineteenth century, along with the desire to provide safer and more luxurious facilities for a rapidly expanding fan base, led to the construction of more modern baseball stadiums. Oddly enough, the most tragic event in major league history occurred at the first such new stadium to be constructed — the Philadelphia Baseball Park (later known as the Baker Bowl), home to the Phillies until 1938. Small by today's standards (seating capacity never exceeded 20,000), it was built of concrete, brick, steel and wood after a fire had destroyed the original wooden structure in August 1894. It was also the first stadium to employ cantilevered supports for its upper decks rather than vertical posts. "The Hump," as it was sometimes called, was dedicated on May 2, 1895.[21]

On August 8, 1903, a crowd of nearly 11,000 was watching the Phillies play the Boston Beaneaters (Braves). During the fourth inning of the second game of a doubleheader, there was a disturbance on the street outside the left field stands. Many in the stands rushed to the top of the bleachers to see what the trouble was, and, as the crowd grew, the bleacher balcony that overhung Fifteenth Street collapsed, hurtling fans thirty feet to the street below. The "dense mass of humanity ... struck amid blood curdling cries, and lay crushed, broken and mangled, in heaps and swaths, bodies overlapping bodies, many unconscious, but more struggling frantically in pain or fright." **William J. Graham**, 25, **Albert B. Rodgers**, 65, **Joseph Edgar**, 45, **George L. Cunningham, Sr.**, 47, **Matthew P. Reed**, 39, **Nicholas Moser**, 51, **Louis E. McGrath**, 23, **Robert L. Cling**, 30, **Samuel E. Kelly**, 11, **James Howden**, 33, **Edward Williamson**, 63, and **William I. Garwood**, 58, were either killed instantly or died within days of the tragedy; nearly 300 others were injured.[22]

After an extensive investigation it was determined that the wooden beams supporting the overhang were rotted at the point where they attached to the concrete wall of the 8-year-old stadium. At the inquest, the coroner's jury placed the blame on the Philadelphia Baseball Club, Limited, owners of the grounds. The incident resulted in multiple lawsuits and various court rulings. As far as the game that day, the umpire called it because of "panic," the first time a professional baseball game had ever ended for this reason.[23]

Structural problems were partly responsible for this tragedy, which underscores the importance of stadium design and maintenance in public safety. Sometimes touted as "the best ath-

Lining up for seats at Baker Bowl

The Baker Bowl was home to the Philadelphia Phillies from 1895 to 1938. On August 8, 1903, the left field overhanging balcony collapsed onto the street below, killing 12 and injuring hundreds (courtesy National Baseball Hall of Fame Library, Cooperstown, NY).

letic ground in the world," the park was in reality a transitional phase between the wooden facilities of the past and the all-concrete and steel structures that began to be built a decade later. While only the 5,500-seat grandstand was composed of concrete and steel, the remainder of the stadium used wooden flooring and supports, a factor that was to prove fatal.[24]

Testimony at the coroner's inquest revealed the tragic flaws in the design of the stadium. The stands had never been thoroughly inspected since their completion in 1896 and the builder testified that the type of lumber used had a life span of only seven to nine years when exposed to weather. It was determined that the wood had rotted because tin covering had been nailed to the wooden floor support beams. Water leaked in through the nail holes, trapping the water inside. Ironically, the tin that was supposed to keep the wood from rotting ended up causing the decay. Of the 50 fallen support beams, half were completely rotten and 24 others were in advanced stages of decay. The builder argued that the balcony area had been designed as a walkway, not an area for fans to congregate.

Upon completion of the inquest, the jury recommended more stringent inspections of public buildings and "places of amusement." Building inspectors in turn-of-the-century Philadelphia were only allowed access to sites with permission of the owner or after complaints were made. Consequently, after final inspection upon completion of construction, most buildings were never inspected again. Unfortunately, lax building codes and safety inspections were the rule across the nation at the time. Accidents like this one are unlikely to happen today because of advanced building techniques and stricter codes. Routine inspections of the type recommended by the 1903 Philadelphia inquest jury have become standard in today's society.[25]

The Baker Bowl was again the scene of tragedy when three sections of seating in the lower right field pavilion area over the visitors' dugout collapsed during the first half of the seventh inning of a May 14, 1927, game between the Phillies and the St. Louis Cardinals, killing **Fred Haas**, 50, and injuring over 50 other spectators. The wooden stands in this area of the park began to fill with thousands of additional fans seeking shelter from rain that started to fall during the third inning. Shortly after the seventh inning began, there was "a low cracking and creaking" sound, followed by a settling-

Police and others inspect the section of lower right field pavilion stands that collapsed during a May 14, 1927, game at the Baker Bowl. One fan died from a heart attack as a result of the accident (courtesy National Baseball Hall of Fame Library, Cooperstown, NY).

movement in the seating area. The crowd rose as one in a state of panic and proceeded to run "screaming with terror, fighting like demons, trampling each other under foot in their anxiety to escape." Seconds later there was "a thunderous crash" as the seats gave way. Fortunately, the few seconds' aural warning before the full collapse may have saved lives and prevented many more injuries because it gave most of the fans time to either jump over the Cards' dugout onto the field or to dash to the back of the stands under the pavilion. Players seated in the dugout streamed onto the field to see what the commotion was about.[26]

Police and ambulances from eight hospitals rushed to the scene of the calamity. Aid stations were set up on the field as the stadium was cleared of fans. In less than half an hour order had been restored and the injured were receiving on-site treatment or were being transported to one of the responding hospitals. Haas, the only fan to be killed, died not from injuries received, but from a heart attack brought on "undoubtedly by excitement and terror of the crash." When an inquest two weeks later determined that Haas suffered from "chronic heart disease," the Phillies were cleared of any responsibility for his death.[27]

The day after the tragedy, Phillies officials laid the blame not on any structural weakness in that area of the stands, but on overcrowding that resulted from the rain. Stating that the stands had been "thoroughly overhauled at the expenditure of a large sum of money" several months earlier and that the area had undergone "a careful examination" prior to opening day, they also claimed that fan frenzy in the bottom of the sixth when the Phillies scored eight runs contributed to the disaster. At one point in the scoring onslaught, the crowd "leaped to its feet, stamped and shouted and screamed in its joy. This was the straw, apparently, which cracked the already overweighted supports."[28]

Games were played at the Philadelphia Athletics' Shibe Park until a decision was made on what to do about the right field seating area. A preliminary investigation conducted shortly after the collapse placed the blame on advanced rot caused by rain leaking into the interior of the upper joists of the wooden main double girder supporting the center of the pavilion. It was "a latent concealed defect" within the central support structure "which could not have been discovered before the accident unless the entire stand had been ripped apart." There was considerable talk about condemning the entire right field pavilion area until it underwent complete reconstruction. The city coroner, in fact, opined that the "grandstand at the Phillies ball park is the worst constructed I have ever seen." He insisted that the wooden support girders be replaced with concrete and steel supports, stating that if this were not done and another tragedy occurred, he would "endeavor to fix blame on those responsible." While the completed inspection found advanced rot in the main girder and "partial decay" among other support joists in the area, Morris Brooks, head of Philadelphia's Bureau of Building Inspection, adamantly declared the stadium to be "in very good condition in spite of its age." He asserted, "Personally, I do not think that much more than a week's work will be required to restore the stadium to a condition of safety." The Phillies agreed to spend more than $40,000 to completely rebuild the lower stands, including reinforcing every wooden girder and adding better drainage to keep water from collecting on the girders. Although the job involved "more than a week's work," the area was quickly repaired and the stadium was back in use later that summer. It would remain the home of the Phillies for ten more seasons.[29]

Major League Exhibition Field-Related Fatalities

In a once-in-a-lifetime match-up, Walter Johnson and Christy Mathewson were slated to go toe-to-toe in an exhibition game in Tulsa, OK, on October 28, 1913. The scene of the battle was Tulsa's South Main Street Baseball Park, and excitement was at a fever pitch. For days the local press promoted the contest between two of baseball's greatest pitchers. Many businesses shut down for the afternoon, and schools closed early so that everyone would have the opportunity to attend. And turn out they did: nearly 5,000 fans jammed the bleachers surrounding the field in spite of a cold wind that swept the stands. A military band from Fort Sill, OK, played while spectators and officials, including Oklahoma governor Lee Cruce, took their seats. Shortly before game time, just as a military unit from Fort Logan H. Roots near Little Rock, AR, walked beneath the right field stands, the entire section collapsed without warning. "Little noise was made by the collapse," reported the *Tulsa World*, "and it came so suddenly that not even a scream was heard." Later investigation showed that these roofless stands, built four years earlier of "light pieces of lumber," had rotted due to exposure to the weather.[30]

An estimated 500 fans were in the stands when it collapsed; many of them were seriously injured. Surprisingly, only one person was killed, **Pvt. Chester Taylor**, 20, of Company L of the Ninth U.S. Infantry out of Fort Roots. He died two hours after being pulled from the rubble, never regaining consciousness. As victims were rescued from the debris and transported by private auto or by ambulance to area hospitals, officials tried to maintain order among the other fans. There was a moment of panic in the left field bleachers directly across the way, but those in the central grandstand remained in their seats. The band continued to play, which helped to calm the crowd, as did a decision to begin the game early. Seeing players take the field to start warming up diverted the attention of the remaining fans from the tragedy unfolding near them. Once all the injured had been removed from the park, the game itself commenced amid the threat of snow. This much anticipated contest was somewhat anti-climactic after what had occurred earlier. The game remained scoreless until the fourth inning, when Mathewson gave up two runs. George "Hooks" Wiltse, pitching in relief, surrendered four more runs in the fifth. Johnson, relying on his "terrific speed, his fast-breaking curve and his delusive drop ball," pitched a complete game, winning 6 to 0, while allowing eight hits and one walk with eight strikeouts.[31]

Minor League Field-Related Fatalities

During a game on the evening of July 15, 2003, **Christine Ewing**, 22, plunged 25 feet from an artificial climbing wall erected next to Taylor Stadium on the campus of the University of Missouri-Columbia, home field of the independent Frontier League Mid-Missouri Mavericks. The portable structure, located just outside the fence surrounding the stadium, was neither owned nor rented by the team, but had been set up by a locally-owned climbing company to attract fans attending Mavericks games. The victim's mother, who witnessed her daughter's fall, said that "she went backwards and kind of flipped backwards and landed on her head on the asphalt down below." Ewing, who never regained consciousness, died from "severe head trauma" early the next day at an area hospital.[32]

An investigation found that Ewing fell because the safety cable attached to the harness holding her snapped at a point where it was rusted, frayed, and covered with duct tape. When police subsequently discovered that Marcus Frank Floyd, 30, owner of the wall, had ignored a warning from the previous owner a year earlier to replace the cable because of its condition and had failed to act in spite of e-mail notices from the manufacturer to replace all safety cables annually, he was charged with involuntary manslaughter. At his trial in mid–June 2004, the judge declared a mistrial when the jury remained deadlocked 10–2 following deliberations for nine hours. In late October he pled guilty to a charge of misdemeanor assault and was sentenced to 30 days in jail and two years' probation. He was also subject to a separate wrongful death lawsuit, settling that with the victim's family for $700,000 in June 2004.[33]

Amateur Field-Related Fatalities

James "Jack" McCurdy, a carpenter working at the Chippewa Falls, WI, baseball field, died instantly during a May 30, 1894, game against the St. Paul (MN) Diamonds when the newly-erected grandstand collapsed suddenly as he labored underneath it. The stands were being used for the first time when it folded under the weight of 400 fans, many of whom were injured in the accident. The roof over the stands also started to fall, but several quick-thinking spectators prevented further tragedy by bracing it with wooden boards they found nearby.[34]

Eugene Fishel, 11, was killed when the grandstand at Washington Park in Bedford, IN, collapsed without warning during a game between teams from Bloomington and Bedford on the afternoon of August 10, 1924. "Bedlam ensued," reported the local press, "as with a crash, the timbers gave way, catapulting the closely packed crowd to the ground. Shrieks of women and children, as they fell amid the debris of the wooden stand, added to the terror of the crowd, which packed the park to capacity." Nearly 350 fans were in this section of the stands when it fell and many of them were injured. As the roof itself began to fall on the crowd, a number of other spectators ran to prop it up with their hands, allowing those trapped beneath time to scramble out. Parked cars pinned under the collapsed roof on the other end of the stands also helped prevent further death and injury. Young Fishel died within moments after being struck on the head by falling timbers.[35]

Joseph Pizzoli, 50, was sitting on a curb watching a street game in Chicago, IL, on the evening of August 11, 1933, when a car traveling in excess of 60 miles per hour hit another car broadside, pushing it up on the sidewalk. Pizzoli was killed instantly, and Joseph Amado, one of the players, was seriously injured. The two passengers in the struck automobile were also hurt. The driver of the speeding car fled the scene of the accident.[36]

Appendix A:
Uncategorized Fatalities

The following deaths could not be categorized because of a lack of detail in the accounts.

PLAYERS

Date of Death	Name, Age	Place of Death	Injury
5/20/1870	Gardner Brown, 15	Philadelphia, PA	Hit on head by ball (*New York Times*, 5/22/1870)
5/11/1882	Charles Gould, 12	Boston, MA	Fractured skull (*N.Y. Clipper*, 5/20/1882)
4/20/1883	William Collins, 21	Big Rapids, MI	Struck on neck by ball while running bases (*Evening News*, Detroit, MI, 4/21/1893)
9/21/1885	Henry Fleming, 19	Brooklyn, NY	Hit in temple by ball (*Brooklyn Eagle*, 9/22/1885)
9/26/1898	Charles Long, NA	Gouldsboro Station, PA	Hit by pitched ball (*Washington Post*, 9/27/1898)
7/09/1907	Oscar Jackson, NA	Sterling, IL	Struck on neck by ball (*Chicago Daily Tribune*, 7/10/1907)
7/22/1914	Herbert Davis, 10	Bloomington, IN	Hit by ball which ruptured his appendix (*Bloomington Evening World*, 7/23/1914)
5/03/1915	Henry McKee, NA	Mt. Gilead, OH	Hit in temple by ball (*Marion Daily Star*, 5/3/1915)
5/29/1915	Herman Hansen, 21	Washington, DC	Died from blood clot on the brain as a result of injury during a game (*Washington Post*, 5/31/1915)
6/19/1915	Van Houten, NA	NA	Collision with another player caused internal injuries (*New York Times*, 6/21/1915)
7/22/1915	Faye Burdick, 28	Olean, PA	Hit on nose by ball (*Potter County Journal*, 7/28/1915)
3/10/1918	George Dewey Sinks, 19	Norfolk, VA	Struck in chest by ball (*Newark [OH] Daily Advocate*, 3/16/1918)
3/13/1919	Paul Olinger, 17	Washington, DC	Struck on head by ball (*Washington Post*, 3/14/1919)
8/17/1920	Carl Jager, NA	Kalamazoo, MI	Hit on head by thrown ball (*Chicago Daily Tribune*, 8/18/1920)
?/?/1923	Herman Seulau, NA	Chicago, IL	Hit by thrown ball (*Chicago Daily Tribune*, 7/12/1923)
5/02/1927	Clifford Swift, 17	Dubuque, IA	Injured during game (*Chicago Daily Tribune*, 5/3/1927)
9/14/1930	Arthur J. Hamel, 8	Norwich, CT	Struck in chest by thrown ball (*New York Times*, 9/15/1930)
4/19/1932	Clifford Spalding, 17	Bethel, CT	Hit on head by ball (*New York Times*, 4/21/1932)
9/18/1932	Karl F. Mueller, 19	St. Paul, MN	Hit on head by ball (*Bismarck Tribune*, 9/19/1932)
6/09/1934	Walter Huber, 20	Buffalo, NY	Hit on head by ball (*New York Times*, 5/6/1938)
7/20/1939	Dante Cretara, 18	Ossining, NY	Hit in left temple by ball (*New York Times*, 7/23/1939)
8/29/1939	Ettore Pero, 16	New York, NY	Hit on head by ball (*New York Times*, 8/30/1939)
9/07/1942	Walter Plute, 19	Canonsburg, PA	Head injury (*New York Times*, 9/8/1942)

Date of Death	*Name, Age*	*Place of Death*	*Injury*
7/09/1957	Lewis Moore, Jr., 14	North East, MD	Hit by ball (*Washington Post and Times Herald*, 7/11/1957)
7/13/1963	James L. Palmison, 22	Sandusky, OH	Hit behind ear by ball (*Sandusky Register*, 7/19/1963)

FANS

Date of Death	*Name, Age*	*Place of Death*	*Injury*
8/25/1915	Forester Adams, 13	Whitesburg, KY	Hit by thrown ball (*New York Times*, 8/27/1915)
5/24/1916	John J. Callahan, 8	Boston, MA	Struck on head by ball (*Boston Daily Globe*, 5/25/1916)
4/08/1922	Horace Bryant, 8	Lizella, GA	Hit by ball (*Washington Post*, 4/9/1922)

UNKNOWN

Date of Death	*Name, Age*	*Place of Death*	*Injury*
6/29/1903	Newton Vannorn, 17	Coshocton, OH	Struck on head by foul tip (*Atlanta Constitution*, 7/1/1903)
6/01/1908	Norman Wiche, 16	Carthage, OH	Hit by thrown ball (*Washington Post*, 6/3/1908)
7/02/1910	Alonzo Compton, 18	Vineyard, TX	Hit by foul ball (*Chicago Daily Tribune*, 7/4/1910)
6/13/1915	Allen W. Blosser, 22	Uniontown, PA	Struck on head by ball (*Atlanta Constitution*, 6/14/1915)
7/23/1920	Henry Hammett, 21	Atlanta, GA	Sustained broken neck during fight with friend (7/25/1920, *Atlanta Constitution*)
6/01/1925	Fred A. Muller, 5	Eureka, CA	Hit by a batted ball (*Sacramento Bee*, 6/2/1925)
7/13/1928	William Callin, 13	Frostburg, MD	Struck in neck by ball, fracturing vertebra (*New York Times*, 7/14/1928)
7/02/1930	Jesse L. Holderman, 8	Pine Grove, PA	Struck over heart by thrown ball (*New York Times*, 7/4/1930)

Appendix B:
Unconfirmed Fatalities

The following fatalities were gathered from lists of baseball-related deaths that appeared in major newspapers around the country during the late 19th and early 20th centuries. We were able to verify many of the deaths on our preliminary lists and include them in the appropriate chapters. During the verification process, we discovered that some of these supposed baseball related deaths were not baseball-related at all and in some cases the person did not actually die. In addition, we found that the dates given were often not the dates of the incidents or death, but were the dates the incidents were reported in the newspapers.

Following are names and places of those incidents for which we could not locate any further information.

1888

Brooklyn Eagle, 3/3/1889

Date	Name	Place of Death	Injury
7/16/1888	James J. Finnegan	Paterson, NJ	Struck on nose and lips by pitched ball
8/26/1888	John Golden	Cedar Glade, AR	Struck on head by pitched ball
9/01/1888	Henry Zickemeyer	Bloomville, OH	Struck over heart by foul tip
90/8/1888	NA	Lodi, OH	Spectator struck on head by foul ball

1905

Washington Post, 12/10/1905

Date	Name	Place of Death	Injury
7/07/1905	Charles Anderson	Tell City, IN	Struck over heart by pitched ball
7/25/1905	Johnny Hurd	Jefferson City, MO	Struck on head by pitched ball

1906

Los Angeles Times, 10/28/1906

Date	Name	Place of Death	Injury
4/12/1906	William Garrison	Camden, NJ	Ruptured blood vessel while swinging at ball
4/15/1906	James H. Benson	Philadelphia, PA	Stroke of apoplexy while watching game
5/30/1906	George C. Hackett	Philadelphia, PA	Struck by batted ball while watching game
6/16/1906	Thomas P. Baker	Camden, NJ	Hit by bat
7/02/1906	Joseph Schneider	Philadelphia, PA	exhaustion
NA	George T. Snyder	NA	heart attack

Washington Post, 12/16/1906

Name	Hometown	Injury
Thomas Barlow	Philadelphia, PA	Hit by bat

Cumberland Evening News, 8/6/1906

Name	Place of Death	Injury
Carl Stauler	Saginaw, MI	Over-exertion while running bases
Eddie Geers	Tennessee	Hit by a batted ball
John Kosielmak	Detroit, MI	Struck on jaw by batted ball

1907

Washington Post, 10/27/1907

Date	Name	Place of Death	Injury
8/01/1907	Manville Phillips	Erie, PA	Hit over heart by ball

1908

"Death List of 1908" (source unknown), 11/12/1908

Name, Age	Place of Death	Injury
Bernard Bowser, 7	Pittsburgh, PA	Struck on head by ball
Charles Leebove, 6	Pittsburgh, PA	Hit by batted ball
Dennis J. Burns, 11	Philadelphia, PA	Struck on head by ball while walking by a game
Everet Rickards, 10	Philadelphia, PA	Hit by car while retrieving ball
Frank Phillips, 9	Pittsburgh, PA	Struck in mouth by ball
George Dagills, NA	Shenandoah, VA	NA
George McGleason, NA	Cincinnati, OH	NA
Peter J. Jensen, NA	North Hackensack, NJ	Struck in temple by batted ball
William Aubin, NA	Pawtucket, RI	Struck in head by pitched ball

1909

Indianapolis Star, 12/26/1909

Date	Name, Age	Place of Death	Injury
5/16/1909	William Harrison, 17	Gastonville, PA	Struck in head by batted ball
6/10/1909	Coleman Moulton, 22	Montgomery, WV	Heart attack while throwing ball
7/10/1909	John Chenault, NA	French Lick, IN	Struck over heart by pitched ball
7/17/1909	Hewitt Spillman, 26	Glasgow, KY	Overexertion
8/01/1909	Charles Black, NA	Big Stone Springs, KY	Fell while making a catch, breaking his neck
9/27/1909	Alexander Moore, 20	Bristol, TN	Struck in neck by ball

1910

Chicago Daily Tribune, 10/31/1910

Name, Age	Place of Death	Injury
Elmer Rich, 15	Brooklyn, NY	Stuck on head by batted ball while watching game
John Halpin, NA	Brooklyn, NY	Collapsed while throwing ball
Phillip Kiatler, NA	Peoria, IL	Heart attack while watching game
Phillip Forney, NA	El Reno, OK	Struck over left eye by ball while umpiring
William Johnson, NA	Olive, OK	Struck below right ear by pitched ball

1913

Chicago Daily Tribune, 12/15/1913

Date	Name	Place of Death	Injury
5/18/1913	B. Parroto	Chicago, IL	Struck over heart by pitched ball
6/01/1915	C. Brown	Chicago, IL	Struck on head by pitched ball
6/23/1915	F. W. Reed	Harvey, IL	Struck on head by pitched ball
6/23/1915	M. McCoy	Chicago, IL	Struck on head by pitched ball
8/30/1915	L. Roberts	Philadelphia, PA	Struck on head by pitched ball

1914

Chicago Daily Tribune, 12/6/1914

Date	Name	Place of Death	Injury
4/15/1914	B. Shaffer	Fort Madison, IA	Hit by pitched ball
6/17/1914	L. Boyce	Toledo Beach, MI	Hit by pitched ball
6/22/1914	S. Hirshberg	Chicago, IL	Struck on head by bat
6/29/1914	H. Allen	Youngstown, OH	Hit by pitched ball
7/15/1914	W. Bange	Elgin, IL	Hit by foul tip
8/16/1914	J. Feinberg	New York, NY	Collision
8/20/1914	Roy Brink	Laineburg, MN	Overexertion
8/21/1914	C. K. Lunt	Rock, ME	Collision
8/28/1914	C. L. Mackey	Moundsville, WV	Hit by pitched ball

1915

Chicago Daily Tribune, 10/24/1915

Date	Name	Place of Death
5/12/1915	C. Albro	St. Johns, MI
5/26/1915	A. McDougall	Denver, CO
6/11/1915	B. Ammous	Tacoma, WA
6/22/1915	W. A. Mullholand	Saginaw, MI
7/80/1915	H. Lynk	Bryn Mawr, PA
7/18/1915	T. D. Greenwood	Gross Plains, TX
7/21/1915	R. Davidson	Philadelphia, PA
8/06/1915	W. Hunt	Buckhannon, WV
10/09/1915	D. Orpe	Nakoma, ND

1919

Los Angeles Times, 1/3/1920

Date	Name	Place of Death
11/13/1919	Cary R. Miller	New York, NY

Appendix C:
Chronology of All Fatalities

The following deaths are listed chronologically. For details, consult chapters 1 through 15.

1860s

Date of Death	Name, Age	Status	Place of Death	Cause
10/18/1862	Jim Creighton, 21	Player	Brooklyn, NY	Internal injury
07/09/1869	Unnamed boy, 16	Player	Newark, NJ	Hit by train

1870s

Date of Death	Name, Age	Status	Place of Death	Cause
04/30/1874	Harry Bernstein, 10	Player	Philadelphia, PA	Bat blow to head
08/16/1876	Willis Jones, 22	Player	Holly Springs, MS	Attacked with bat
06/11/1877	John Emmet Crowder, 17	Player	Richmond, VA	Ruptured blood vessel
08/12/1877	John Quigley, 19	Player	Wappingers Falls, NY	Collision
08/22/1877	Addison Banker, 24	Player	Great Bend, PA	Shot
05/19/1878	Martin Head, 16	Player	Johnston, RI	Ruptured blood vessel
07/09/1878	James J. Crowley, 14	Player	New York, NY	Bat blow to head
070/9/1878	Willie Lawshe, 22	Player	Atlanta, GA	Attacked with bat
07/12/1879	John Campbell, 12	Player	Providence, RI	Bat blow to stomach

1880s

Date of Death	Name, Age	Status	Place of Death	Cause
09/05/1881	Benjamin Shorrock, 23	Player	Haledon, NJ	Batted ball to chest
08/14/1882	Thomas Toppin, 17	Fan	Chester, PA	Thrown ball to head
09/15/1883	Bob Robert, NA	Player	Dooly, GA	Health-related
05/15/1884	John O. Fortune, 16	Player	Pittsburgh, PA	Attacked with coal
06/22/1884	Nicholas Newmayer, NA	Player	Central City, CO	Lightning
10/01/1884	Roscoe Conkling, 16	Fan	Riverhead, NY	Bat blow to head
05/23/1885	George Lassette, 7	Player	New York, NY	Thrown ball to chest
07/31/1885	King Cherry, NA	Fan	Opelika, AL	Heart-related
08/15/1885	Louis Henke, NA	Player	Atlanta, GA	Collision
08/14/1886	William Morrissey, 22	Umpire	Medford, MA	Batted ball to chest
06/13/1887	Edward Likely, 23	Player	Lincoln, NE	Batted ball to head
07/09/1887	Eddie McDade, 15	Player	Manayunk, PA	Batted ball to neck
08/21/1887	Otto Bronson, 18	Player	Hamilton, NY	Beaning
090/7/1887	John Gale, 40	Fan	Brooklyn, NY	Batted ball to head

Date of Death	Name, Age	Status	Place of Death	Cause
02/22/1888	J. C. Johnson, 21	Fan	Chattanooga, TN	Attacked with bat
05/30/1888	Harry Brown, 19	Player	Salem, MA	Bat blow
06/30/1888	William Grainey, 21	Umpire	Brockton, MA	Batted ball to neck
07/22/1888	Edward Pousch, 18	Player	Columbus, OH	Beaning
08/19/1888	Michael Murray, 24	Player	Rochester, NY	Beaning
08/29/1888	Samuel Stainbrook, NA	Umpire	Kincaid, KS	Batted ball to neck
03/30/1889	Orlando Poe, 12	Player	Detroit, MI	Heart-related
06/11/1889	Arthur E. Miller, 12	Player	Glen Cove, NY	Bat blow
06/15/1889	Davidson Hall, 28	Fan	Sunbright, TN	Stabbed
90/22/1889	Thomas J. Godfrey, 25	Player	Castleton, NY	Beaning
09/29/1889	John Walters, 20	Player	Richmond, IN	Beaning
10/24/1889	Thomas E. Mandery, 17	Player	New York, NY	Beaning

1890s

Date of Death	Name, Age	Status	Place of Death	Cause
05/26/1890	Ben Myers, 19	Player	Montgomery, AL	Pitched ball to neck
03/NA/1891	Joseph Stendenbard, 15	Player	San Antonio, TX	Batted ball to temple
05/08/1891	George Anderson, 12	Player	Chicago, IL	Attacked with bat
09/20/1891	Ralph B. Stanley, 20	Player	Carson City, NV	Beaning
06/18/1893	Max Meindel, 25	Player	Altoona, PA	Beaning
08/20/1893	Peter Hyland, 23	Player	Chicago, IL	Beaning
08/20/1893	David McLaughlin, 24	Fan	Boston, MA	Foul ball to head
05/30/1894	Jack McCurdy, NA	Fan	Chippewa Falls, WI	Stands collapsed
06/12/1894	S. C. Griffith, NA	Player	Tampa, FL	Beaning
10/27/1894	Joseph Kercher, 13	Player	Kutztown, PA	Batted ball to chest
04/16/1895	George Cowan, 22	Player	Oberlin College, OH	Beaning
06/30/1895	William C. Dewees, NA	Player	Philadelphia, PA	Beaning
06/30/1895	Morris Davis, 13	Player	Taylor Bottoms, KY	Beaning
06/30/1895	Harvey George, 21	Player	Decatur, IN	Health-related
08/20/1895	Joe Richardson, NA	Player	Brenham, TX	Attacked with bat
09/02/1895	George Paulson, 14	Fan	New York, NY	Foul ball to head
09/08/1895	Benjamin Myers, 20	Player	Washington, DC	Collision
09/21/1895	John Dean, NA	Player	Boscobel, WI	Batted ball to head
06/01/1897	William J. Williams, 14	Player	Minneapolis, MN	Pitched ball to chest
06/07/1897	Walter H. Gorr, 8	Fan	Middletown, NY	Foul ball to stomach
06/20/1897	Austin Smith, 18	Player	Sandy Hill, NY	Beaning
080/9/1897	Cal Taylor, NA	Player	Eufaula, AL	Attacked with stick
08/14/1897	Joseph Collins, 10	Fan	Boston, MA	Foul ball to head
04/13/1899	Charles Dial, NA	Player	Grass Valley, CA	Beaning
04/24/1899	Thomas Kelley, 16	Player	Madison, WI	Collision
04/29/1899	Sam Powell, 19	Umpire	Lowndesboro, AL	Attacked with bat
05/06/1899	Hugh Cavanagh, 22	Player	Montclair, NJ	Pitched ball to chest
05/30/1899	Edward Conner, NA	Player	Lawrence, MA	Batted ball to chest
08/07/1899	John Stillane, 12	Player	New York, NY	Fall
08/26/1899	Eldrakin Potter, 14	Player	Suffolk, VA	Pitched ball to chest
08/28/1899	Unnamed convict, NA	Player	Valdosta, GA	Thrown ball to head

1900s

Date of Death	Name, Age	Status	Place of Death	Cause
06/24/1900	George Lakin, 19	Player	Baltimore, MD	Beaning
08/04/1900	Ward M. Snyder, 23	Player	Homewood, PA	Batted ball to chest
09/03/1900	Joseph Marsh, 23	Player	Dalton, MA	Batted ball to head

Date of Death	Name, Age	Status	Place of Death	Cause
04/28/1901	F. E. Kirkpatrick, NA	Player	Madera, CA	Collision
06/29/1901	Simon Cohen, 11	Fan	New York, NY	Foul ball to head
08/28/1901	Elmore Silvers, 23	Player	Quincy, FL	Beaning
09/19/1901	Joseph Collins, 13	Fan	Lowell, MA	Foul ball to head
04/11/1902	W. W. Marsh, NA	Player	Rivermont, VA	Fall
05/04/1902	John Schutz, Jr., NA	Manager	Syracuse, NY	Electrocuted
05/11/1902	Walter L. Myles, 18	Player	West Chester, PA	Beaning
05/18/1902	Ernest Seneiel, 12	Fan	Chicago, IL	Foul ball to chest
06/10/1902	Reade Jarman, 24	Player	Charlottesville, VA	Batted ball to neck
07/05/1902	Charles Harrington, NA	Player	Midlothian, TX	Batted ball to stomach
07/08/1902	Hubert Jones, 14	Fan	Belleville, AR	Foul ball to chest
10/25/1902	Stanton Walker, 20	Fan	Morristown, OH	Foul ball/knife
04/11/1903	Aaron Sokolski, NA	Fan	Orange, TX	Pitched ball to head
04/13/1903	Punch Arnold, 15	Player	Newnan, GA	Pitched ball to chest
05/31/1903	Charles Kelly, 25	Fan	Pittsburgh, PA	Shot
06/24/1903	Robert L. Shannon, 23	Player	Washington, DC	Thrown ball to neck
07/25/1903	Calvin Phillippi, 26	Player	Jonestown, PA	Pitched ball to neck
08/08/1903	William J. Graham, 25	Fan	Philadelphia, PA	Balcony collapsed
08/08/1903	Albert B. Rodgers, 65	Fan	Philadelphia, PA	Balcony collapsed
08/08/1903	Joseph Edgar, 45	Fan	Philadelphia, PA	Balcony collapsed
08/08/1903	George Cunningham, 47	Fan	Philadelphia, PA	Balcony collapsed
08/08/1903	Matthew P. Reed, 39	Fan	Philadelphia, PA	Balcony collapsed
08/08/1903	Nicholas Moser, 51	Fan	Philadelphia, PA	Balcony collapsed
08/08/1903	Louis E. McGrath, 23	Fan	Philadelphia, PA	Balcony collapsed
08/08/1903	Robert L. Cling, 30	Fan	Philadelphia, PA	Balcony collapsed
08/08/1903	Samuel E. Kelly, 11	Fan	Philadelphia, PA	Balcony collapsed
08/08/1903	James Howden, 33	Fan	Philadelphia, PA	Balcony collapsed
08/08/1903	Edward Williamson, 63	Fan	Philadelphia, PA	Balcony collapsed
08/08/1903	William I. Garwood, 58	Fan	Philadelphia, PA	Balcony collapsed
08/13/1903	William Higgins, 20	Player	Fontana, KS	Thrown ball to head
08/21/1903	Allan Newman, 25	Player	Pawtucket, RI	Batted ball to head
09/05/1903	Percy F. W. Barrows, 18	Fan	Bronx, NY	Lightning
05/01/1904	Frank Duncan, 20	Player	Baltimore, MD	Batted ball to head
07/09/1904	Frank Herbert, NA	Player	Dayton, OH	Collision
07/11/1904	Hiram Williamson, 22	Player	Cherry Hill, MD	Beaning
07/11/1904	Charles Jeffries, 28	Player	McKeesport, PA	Lightning
07/11/1904	Joseph Barrett, 16	Player	Cumberland, MD	Lightning
07/NA/1904	Gertrude Jaeger, 9	Fan	Elizabethport, NJ	Foul ball to chest
08/07/1904	Verne Lowe, 19	Player	Dresden, OH	Beaning
09/05/1904	Wendell Miller, 12	Fan	Glen Ellyn, IL	Foul ball to head
09/17/1904	Albert Johnson, 32	Player	River Forest, IL	Batted ball to chest
10/01/1904	John Garcia, 28	Player	Jamaica, NY	Health-related
03/10/1905	John Hilton, NA	Player	Huntsville, AL	Heatstroke
040/8/1905	Eugene Harris, 15	Player	Asheville, NC	Batted ball to head
04/24/1905	Alfred Moyer, 10	Fan	Allentown, PA	Bat blow to head
05/01/1905	Jesse Strode, 22	Player	Gillette, AR	Pitched ball to chest
05/17/1905	Olin Francis, 29	Player	Bristol, VA	Heart-related
05/21/1905	James Miles, NA	Fan	Brooklyn, NY	Batted ball to head
05/22/1905	Edward Johnston, 28	Player	Chicago, IL	Heart-related
06/10/1905	Henry Diehl, 20	Player	Wooster, OH	Beaning
06/18/1905	Frank C. Wilcox, 19	Player	Auburn, ME	Pitched ball to head
06/19/1905	Sarah Swanboam, 58	Fan	Brooklyn, NY	Thrown ball to head
06/24/1905	Patrick Cosgrove, 70	Fan	Peru, IL	Collision
07/05/1905	Harry Exley, 12	Fan	Savannah, GA	Bat blow to head
07/09/1905	A. Harten, NA	Player	Altoona, IA	Stroke
07/29/1905	Lloyd C. Grout, 15	Player	Cedar Rapids, IA	Beaning
07/29/1905	Frederick Whittaker, 19	Player	Hamilton Terrace, NJ	Batted ball to chest

Date of Death	Name, Age	Status	Place of Death	Cause
7/30/1905	Estel Payton, 16	Player	Ottumwa, IA	Batted ball to chest
8/03/1905	J. W. Maher, 44	Fan	Pittsburgh, PA	Stroke
8/31/1905	Walter Buchanan, 14	Player	Elida, OH	Pitched ball to stomach
9/04/1905	Joseph McDonald, NA	Player	Mount Holly, NJ	Beaning
4/15/1906	Robert Norton, 12	Fan	Jersey City, NJ	Foul ball to head
5/24/1906	Jesse Robertson, NA	Player	Norfolk, VA	Beaning
5/26/1906	Howard Newton, 17	Player	Kansas City, MO	Pitched ball to chest
5/26/1906	Frank Wesan, 14	Player	Philadelphia, PA	Bat blow to head
5/27/1906	Stach Wisnoski, 20	Player	Houston, TX	Thrown ball
5/27/1906	Arthur Moody, 19	Umpire	Mobile, AL	Lightning
5/27/1906	Donald Touart, 21	Fan	Mobile, AL	Lightning
5/27/1906	Stephen Touart, 19	Fan	Mobile, AL	Lightning
5/27/1906	John Green, NA	Fan	Mobile, AL	Lightning
5/27/1906	Charles Thomas, NA	Fan	Mobile, AL	Lightning
6/12/1906	Reuben Walt, 30	Player	Herndon, PA	Thrown ball to head
6/16/1906	Ed Puckett, NA	Player	Grassy Lick, KY	Attacked with bat
6/17/1906	Morgan Doran, 21	Fan	New York, NY	Pitched ball to head
6/22/1906	Edward P. Dillon, NA	Player	Conway, PA	Beaning
6/26/1906	Herbert M. Whitney, 27	Player	Waterloo, IA	Beaning
7/01/1906	Attillio Marino, 12	Player	Philadelphia, PA	Thrown ball to chest
7/01/1906	Charles McDonald, 17	Player	Philadelphia, PA	Beaning
7/04/1906	John Aulting, NA	Player	Fleetwood, PA	Beaning
7/04/1906	John Leak, NA	Fan	Wadesboro, NC	Attacked with bat/knife
7/23/1906	Albert Skuhra, 30	Fan	Manitowoc, WI	Lightning
7/23/1906	Walter Handl, 18	Fan	Manitowoc, WI	Lightning
7/23/1906	Irving Woellert, 20	Fan	Manitowoc, WI	Lightning
7/23/1906	Anton Klauck, 14	Fan	Manitowoc, WI	Lightning
7/23/1906	William Knudsen, 16	Fan	Manitowoc, WI	Lightning
7/25/1906	W. H. Williams, NA	Player	Soperton, GA	Pitched ball to chest
8/11/1906	Thomas F. Burke, 26	Player	Lynn, MA	Beaning
8/28/1906	Casper Musselman, 19	Player	Catasauqua, PA	Pitched ball to chest
9/16/1906	Kune Schilling, 13	Fan	Milwaukee, WI	Foul ball to neck
9/19/1906	John Hoge, 21	Player	Martins Ferry, OH	Collision
10/9/1906	McKee, NA	Player	Rolla, MO	Collision
4/19/1907	Orrie McWilliams, 15	Player	Deep River, IA	Choking
4/28/1907	Arthur Reed, 19	Player	Washington, DC	Attacked with bat
5/12/1907	Edward Bowe, 13	Fan	Troy, NY	Foul ball to head
5/26/1907	William King, 26	Player	St. Denis, MD	Pitched ball to chest
5/31/1907	William Steth, 20	Player	Little Falls, MN	Beaning
6/08/1907	Harry Randall, 16	Player	Derby, CT	Pitched ball to chest
6/14/1907	Harold Brown, 15	Player	Mount Pleasant, IA	Bat blow to head
6/30/1907	Albert LaPlant, 22	Player	St. Anthony, IA	Lightning
7/04/1907	Rorie Young, 21	Player	Grovetown, GA	Shot
8/05/1907	John McCue, 32	Fan	Harlem, NY	Thrown brick to head
8/17/1907	Daniel V. McKeon, 22	Manager	Newark, NJ	Batted ball to head
8/24/1907	Charles L. Clemons, NA	Player	Brooklyn, NY	Beaning
3/18/1908	S. H. Smith, NA	Player	Auburn, AL	Thrown ball to head
4/01/1908	Manuel N. Lefkowith, 13	Fan	Roxbury, MA	Thrown ball to head
4/20/1908	Ben Rice, NA	Player	Sparks, GA	Heart-related
4/22/1908	Catherine Murray, 58	Fan	New York, NY	Foul ball to chest
5/01/1908	William Haverkamp, 13	Fan	Grand Rapids, MI	Thrown bottle to head
5/24/1908	John R. Perry, 23	Player	St. Louis, MO	Health-related
5/27/1908	Robert W. Pierce, 15	Player	Wickford, RI	Batted ball to chest
5/28/1908	Charles Lempka, 14	Player	Poughkeepsie, NY	Pitched ball to chest
5/31/1908	John Wulkotte, NA	Player	Cincinnati, OH	Batted ball to head
6/17/1908	William D. Schutte, 17	Player	Knoxville, PA	Heart-related
6/22/1908	August Senecae, 18	Player	Bridgeton, RI	Beaning

Date of Death	Name, Age	Status	Place of Death	Cause
6/22/1908	Edward Haas, 27	Player	Brookline, PA	Shot
70/1/1908	George Washington, 34	Player	Winsted, CT	Heart Attack
7/04/1908	Paul Morgan, 21	Player	Springfield, SC	Pitched ball to chest
7/06/1908	Harry Cole, NA	Player	Benton, PA	Beaning
7/17/1908	Andrew Luksia, 7 mos.	Fan	Pittsburgh, PA	Thrown ball to head
7/18/1908	Willie Hudson, 14	Fan	Chicago, IL	Fall
8/24/1908	George Fleischman, 24	Player	Stapleton, NY	Beaning
10/8/1908	Henry T. McBride, NA	Fan	New York, NY	Fall
2/23/1909	George C. Franklin, 26	Player	Imperial, CA	Beaning
3/14/1909	Dominick Cerone, 6	Player	New York, NY	Attacked with brick
4/24/1909	Leonard DeLong, NA	Player	Lamont, IA	Collision
5/15/1909	Leander Holmgreen, 19	Player	Ellsworth, PA	Batted ball to chest
5/15/1909	Lewis Mould, 22	Player	Pittsburgh, PA	Hit by streetcar
5/15/1909	Everett Sloan, 14	Fan	Yorktown, IN	Stands collapsed
5/20/1909	Arthur Burroughs, 9	Player	Central Falls, RI	Bat blow to chest
5/26/1909	Leo Smith, 19	Player	Kokomo, IN	Collision
5/31/1909	Alfred Vollmer, 17	Player	Ecorse, MI	Pitched ball to chest
6/01/1909	John Donaldson, 36	Umpire	Zelienople, PA	Batted ball to head
7/04/1909	Walter Schwartz, 13	Player	Saginaw, MI	Beaning
7/05/1909	William MacNamara, NA	Player	Kingsland, NJ	Collision
7/06/1909	Wilson E. Losch, 12	Player	Reading, PA	Fall
7/18/1909	Will Whitely, NA	Fan	Selma, AL	Attacked with bat
7/20/1909	Weston Fry, 19	Fan	Lead, SD	Lightning
7/20/1909	Tom Halverson, 14	Fan	Lead, SD	Lightning
7/22/1909	Andrew Brown, 9	Player	Pittsburgh, PA	Drowning
7/26/1909	Harry Rubes, NA	Player	Spencer, IA	Pitched ball to chest
7/26/1909	Eugene Swinbank, 17	Player	Chicago, IL	Pitched ball to chest
8/03/1909	Edward Kloss, 12	Fan	Detroit, MI	Collision
8/10/1909	William Altman, NA	Fan	Moorehead, KY	Foul ball to chest
8/15/1909	George King, NA	Fan	Beckwith, CA	Attacked with bat
8/16/1909	Benson Smith, 14	Player	Chicago, IL	Pitched ball to head
8/20/1909	Clarence Thomas, NA	Player	Black Creek, VA	Batted ball to chest
8/26/1909	William Bedford, NA	Player	Atlantic City, NJ	Lightning
8/29/1909	Robert Myers, 65	Fan	Chicago, IL	Heart-related
9/04/1909	John Stauffer, 35	Player	Pittsburgh, PA	Heart-related
9/12/1909	John Coffey, 9	Fan	Manhattan, NY	Foul ball to head
9/15/1909	Charles Pinkney, 20	Player	Dayton, OH	Beaning
9/24/1909	Oliver P. Thompson, 13	Player	Washington, DC	Hit by hearse

1910s

Date of Death	Name, Age	Status	Place of Death	Cause
3/23/1910	Fred D. Redahan, 16	Player	Portland, ME	Heart-related
3/26/1910	Roy Duncan, 18	Player	Kittaning, PA	Batted ball to head
3/28/1910	James C. Allen, 14	Player	Reading, PA	Batted ball to head
4/11/1910	Rudolph Ruhling, 15	Player	New York, NY	Beaning
4/17/1910	Frank Burns, NA	Player	Troy, NY	Beaning
4/17/1910	William Schmidt, 28	Player	Freeburg, IL	Pitched ball to chest
4/24/1910	Louis Rose, 10	Player	Jersey City, NJ	Drowning
4/28/1910	Frank Breitweiser, 18	Player	New York, NY	Batted ball to head
5/13/1910	Jesse Sprouse, 12	Player	Alexandria, VA	Attacked with bat
5/19/1910	Harry Becker, 14	Player	Bronx, NY	Batted ball to stomach
5/29/1910	Frank Kostchryz, 15	Player	Cleveland, OH	Beaning
5/29/1910	Walter J. Garson, 34	Player	Cleveland, OH	Heart-related
6/18/1910	Charles E. Moran, 23	Player	LaPorte, IN	Bat blow to side

Date of Death	Name, Age	Status	Place of Death	Cause
06/25/1910	Leonard Hand, 21	Player	Dayton, KY	Batted/thrown ball to head
07/02/1910	Marcus Goldwater, 48	Fan	Los Angeles, CA	Heart-related
07/04/1910	Leonard Massengale, 27	Player	Augusta, GA	Beaning
07/23/1910	Robert Hudson, NA	Fan	Max Meadows, VA	Shot
07/25/1910	H. D. Edwards, NA	Player	Montclair, NJ	Bat blow to head
07/25/1910	Inez Stephenson, 2	Fan	Indianapolis, IN	Thrown ball to chest
07/27/1910	Albert Stephenson, 15	Player	Camden, NJ	Thrown ball to knee
08/10/1910	Howard Layer, 12	Player	Cornfield Point, MD	Beaning
08/13/1910	Sherman K. Rott, NA	Player	Charleston, SC	Heart-related
08/20/1910	Wayne Hinkle, 19	Player	Rye Beach, OH	Beaning
08/28/1910	Kid Iverson, NA	Player	Brooks, GA	Shot
08/28/1910	Harvey Mayes, NA	Player	Brooks, GA	Shot
09/01/1910	George Quick, NA	Fan	Huntsville, AL	Foul ball to side
09/02/1910	Mary Ludek, 8	Fan	Chicago, IL	Foul ball to stomach
09/04/1910	Edward Ballard, 20	Player	Wisner, WI	Batted ball to chest
09/05/1910	Jim Barrett, NA	Player	Brooks, GA	Shot
09/07/1910	Edward W. Hoge, 12	Player	Washington, DC	Thrown ball to head
10/24/1910	Samuel James, 30	Player	Dana, IN	Batted ball to temple
NA/1911	Son Williams, NA	Umpire	Briar Creek, GA	Shot
04/15/1911	Frank P. Lawrence, 21	Player	Santa Paula, CA	Beaning
05/07/1911	Bertrand Frick, 17	Player	Ravenna, OH	Beaning
05/22/1911	Edmond F. Pierdon, 55	Fan	New York, NY	Heart-related
05/30/1911	Edna Thumm, 15	Fan	Pittsburgh, PA	Foul ball to head
06/25/1911	John H. King, 17	Player	Bridgeport, CT	Beaning
07/06/1911	Chauncey Olliner, 12	Player	Guilford, CT	Beaning
07/17/1911	Edward Gabryszak, 10	Fan	Chicago, IL	Foul ball to stomach
07/28/1911	John Freeman, 14	Player	Washington, DC	Batted ball to head
08/13/1911	Herbert Turner, 13	Player	Hillyard, WA	Beaning
08/15/1911	Harry Greenhood, 12	Player	Philadelphia, PA	Batted ball to neck
08/25/1911	Michael Dougherty, NA	Fan	Chicago, IL	Thrown ball to stomach
09/17/1911	William Schmidt, 21	Player	Chicago, IL	Beaning
05/04/1912	George S. Hiett, 27	Player	Washington, DC	Beaning
06/09/1912	Homer Norris, 10	Player	Wellston, OH	Batted ball to chest
07/09/1912	Albert Bohen, 15	Player	Rockford, IL	Beaning
07/21/1912	George Campbell, 6	Player	Kearny, NJ	Pitched ball to foot
09/07/1912	Bugs Raymond, 30	Fan	Chicago, IL	Kicked/attacked with bat
09/19/1912	Harry Kerr, 20	Player	Orient, IA	Beaning
04/01/1913	J. C. Hays, NA	Fan	Decherd, TN	Pitched ball to head
04/14/1913	Paul Murphy, 9	Player	Walton, MI	Batted ball to chest
05/07/1913	Francis Jenks, 15	Player	Hanover, NH	Collision
05/16/1913	Leo Clair Cummings, 12	Player	Pittsfield, MA	Batted ball to head
05/21/1913	Mrs. John Hosie, NA	Fan	Harrison, NJ	Batted ball to stomach
05/25/1913	James Baneskiewicz, 12	Fan	Baltimore, MD	Foul ball to head
05/26/1913	Vance Faught, 19	Player	Cozad, NE	Beaning
05/31/1913	Fritz Greenwald, 21	Player	Holland, NY	Batted ball to head
060/1/1913	Paris Smith, 18	Player	Anacortes, WA	Beaning
06/02/1913	William Wiggins, 22	Player	Kearney, NJ	Beaning
06/17/1913	J. Whetstone, 24	Player	New Orleans, LA	Collision
06/22/1913	Harvey C. Harned, 21	Scorekeeper	Jersey City, NJ	Thrown ball
06/24/1913	Michael Ruth, 26	Player	Jasonville, IN	Thrown ball to head
06/29/1913	Bob Nell, 47	Umpire	Bullitt Co., KY	Attacked with bat
10/28/1913	Chester Taylor, 20	Fan	Tulsa, OK	Stands collapsed
02/06/1914	Nicholas Fernicola, 26	Player	Newark, NJ	Bat blow to head
02/19/1914	Bessie Lee Rice, 8	Fan	Gulfport, MS	Thrown ball to head
04/11/1914	John Nelson, 18	Player	Brooklyn, NY	Batted ball to head
04/18/1914	Robert O. Mahaffey, 19	Player	Chicago, IL	Heart-related
05/08/1914	Louis Sweetstein, 13	Player	Detroit, MI	Health-related

Date of Death	Name, Age	Status	Place of Death	Cause
05/19/1914	Willis F. Davis, 19	Player	Wichita, KS	Collision
05/25/1914	John Hardy, 17	Player	Philadelphia, PA	Batted ball to head
05/31/1914	Roy Mimms, 30	Player	Fort Worth, TX	Pitched ball to chest
05/31/1914	Gaulando, NA	Player	Ladd, IL	Collision
06/01/1914	Bill Hammer, 21	Player	Tompkinsville, KY	Beaning
06/01/1914	Frank Boucher, 22	Player	Rockville, CT	Beaning
06/07/1914	Charles Wellman, 13	Player	Chicago, IL	Batted ball to head
06/07/1914	Charles Clarke, 18	Player	Harlem, NY	Heart-related
06/08/1914	Thomas Gilpin, NA	Player	Sparks, OK	Batted ball to chest
06/28/1914	Leo Levestue, 25	Player	Fall River, MA	Beaning
06/28/1914	Joseph D. Adam, 14	Fan	Chicago, IL	Batted ball to chest
07/01/1914	Binks Alton, 30	Player	Mineral Point, WI	Batted ball to head
07/04/1914	Joseph Snyder, 21	Player	Medina, OH	Pitched ball to chest
07/17/1914	Mike Bellevic, 13	Player	Litchfield, IL	Pitched ball to knee
09/07/1914	Walter Sanders, NA	Player	Salisbury, MO	Beaning
09/21/1914	James Savio, 22	Player	Fort Wayne, IN	Batted ball to wrist
09/29/1914	Stanislaw Klich, 15	Player	East St. Louis, IL	Attacked with bat
10/13/1914	Eddie Gray, 10	Player	Riverton, ID	Batted ball to chest
02/20/1915	Harry C. Posz, 16	Player	St. Louis, MO	Thrown ball to head
04/15/1915	Paul Zeigler, 16	Player	Grass Lake, MI	Bat blow to head
04/18/1915	Robert Howison, 10	Player	Richmond, VA	Batted ball to head
04/18/1915	John DeRoche, Jr., 16	Fan	Freehold, NJ	Foul ball to head
04/25/1915	William Downing, NA	Player	Needham, MA	Beaning
05/01/1915	Lewis Wasson, 26	Player	Indianapolis, IN	Beaning
05/01/1915	William La Lone, 11	Player	Seattle, WA	Hit by bus
05/09/1915	Thomas Jackson, 20	Player	Monticello, AR	Collision
05/11/1915	Roy Wolff, 27	Fan	Denver, CO	Thrown brick to head
05/13/1915	William E. Crawford, 15	Player	Hanover, PA	Beaning
05/17/1915	Walter Jannusch, 18	Player	Des Plaines, IL	Beaning
05/22/1915	James Chapman, 19	Umpire	Bisbee, AZ	Batted ball to head
05/22/1915	Charles Seymour, 16	Player	Payson, IL	Pitched ball to chest
05/23/1915	Guy W. Ommert, 17	Player	Palmyra, PA	Beaning
05/23/1915	Lloyd Kennedy, 20	Player	Fargo, ND	Bat blow to side
05/24/1915	George Wesley, NA	Player	Price, UT	Beaning
05/26/1915	William Davidson, 13	Player	Thompson, OH	Batted ball to head
05/30/1915	Speck Wyss, 22	Player	Peoria, IL	Collision
06/01/1915	Oscar Genter, 17	Player	Evansville, IN	Pitched ball to head
060/1/1915	Victor E. Craig, 36	Scorekeeper	Wilkes-Barre, PA	Foul ball to head
06/01/1915	Chauncey Martin, 45	Fan	Brooklyn, NY	Heart-related
06/12/1915	William Wine, 25	Player	Queens, NY	Health-related
06/26/1915	Elbert Osborne, NA	Security	Dorchester, VA	Shot
07/05/1915	Lock L. Lann, NA	Fan	Aberdeen, MS	Shot
070/6/1915	A. J. Waller, 23	Player	Dearborn, MO	Beaning
07/10/1915	Roy Plymell, 22	Player	London, OH	Batted ball to head
07/12/1915	Percy E. Williams, NA	Player	San Francisco, CA	Beaning
07/13/1915	Lamar Carn, 24	Player	Memphis, TN	Batted ball to head
07/25/1915	Percy Damon, 26	Player	Hanover, MA	Pitched ball to head
07/28/1915	William E. Coman, 52	Fan	Boston, MA	Heart-related
07/31/1915	Landon Bell, 23	Player	Middletown, CT	Health-related
08/01/1915	Edward Hafferkamp, 34	Player	St. Louis, MO	Beaning
08/11/1915	Roy Dean, NA	Player	Covington, OK	Beaning
08/15/1915	Jack Selby, 43	Fan	Island, KY	Shot
08/19/1915	George Cox, 13	Player	Philadelphia, PA	Beaning
08/22/1915	Edward Scradis, 4	Fan	Pittsburgh, PA	Bat blow to chest
090/1/1915	Banker Duer, NA	Fan	Clinton, IA	Foul ball to head
09/24/1915	Karl Vollmer, 11	Player	Baden, MO	Beaning
09/23/1915	Russell Kistler, 29	Player	Harrisburg, PA	Beaning

Date of Death	Name, Age	Status	Place of Death	Cause
10/10/1915	Thomas Fisher, 5	Fan	Gillespie, IL	Foul ball to heart
04/23/1916	Shirley Phillips, 16	Player	Belington, WV	Pitched ball to chest
05/18/1916	Franklin Hoen, 18	Player	Mount Airy, PA	Pitched ball to head
05/21/1916	George White, 22	Player	Detroit, MI	Pitched ball to chest
05/24/1916	James D. Irwin, 15	Player	Oil City, PA	Pitched ball to chest
06/19/1916	Johnny Dodge, 27	Player	Mobile, AL	Beaning
08/07/1916	Martin Meyer, 24	Player	Jamaica, NY	Beaning
08/08/1916	Robert Wacker, NA	Player	Milwaukee, WI	Beaning
05/30/1917	Robert Wagner, NA	Player	Danielsville, PA	Beaning
05/30/1917	Peter McManus, 18	Player	Stamford, CT	Pitched ball to chest
06/21/1917	Henry Ayres, 16	Player	New York, NY	Shot
07/14/1917	Andrew Dammer, NA	Player	Chicago, IL	Beaning
06/02/1918	E. P. Webb, 46	Fan	Indianapolis, IN	Plane crash
06/23/1918	John Britton, 60	Fan	New York, NY	Foul ball to head
03/19/1919	William Lewis, 14	Player	St. Clairsville, OH	Batted ball to knee
04/23/1919	Clarence Bender, 22	Player	McKees Rocks, PA	Batted ball to chest

1920s

Date of Death	Name, Age	Status	Place of Death	Cause
06/05/1920	William Biersdorff, 21	Player	Chicago, IL	Batted ball to chest
07/24/1920	Carl King, NA	Player	Willacoochee, GA	Lightning
08/17/1920	Ray Chapman, 29	Player	New York, NY	Beaning
03/27/1921	Lawrence G. Sumner, 20	Player	Blacksburg, VA	Bat blow to chest
05/15/1921	Stanley Rivett, 9	Fan	Streator, IL	Foul ball to chest
05/30/1921	Joseph Conway, 35	Fan	Pittsburgh, PA	Shot
05/30/1921	Jesse Barron, 29	Fan	Pittsburgh, PA	Shot
06/06/1921	James Audrey Ensor, 11	Player	Towson, MD	Batted ball to head
06/11/1921	Louis Fetyk, 22	Player	Bronx, NY	Heart-related
06/NA/1921	Patrick Lynch, 40	Fan	Wellersburg, PA	Foul ball to neck
08/09/1921	Lester Frye, NA	Player	Lisbon Falls, ME	Beaning
12/19/1921	Dace Smith, 25	Workman	Memphis, TN	Construction accident
04/16/1922	Mike Davenport, NA	Player	Milledgeville, GA	Collision
04/30/1922	Earl Heuer, 25	Player	Staten Island, NY	Beaning
04/30/1922	Arno Schmeiser, NA	Player	Osman, WI	Beaning
05/06/1922	Michael Finn, 61	Owner	Omaha, NE	Heart-related
05/07/1922	Alfred Kenning, 65	Fan	Detroit, MI	Heart-related
05/07/1922	Julius Van Overmeer, NA	Fan	Detroit, MI	Stroke
05/27/1922	Charles Baldwin, 19	Player	Chase, MD	Pitched ball to chest
07/01/1922	Cy Long, 24	Player	Newton, NC	Lightning
07/17/1922	Charles Bouzek, 33	Umpire	Fenton, MO	Attacked with bat
07/29/1922	John L. Kallapka, 21	Fan	Follansbee, WV	Shot
09/09/1922	Leon Scanlon, 19	Player	Rosemont, PA	Beaning
06/09/1923	Leroy Kellogg, NA	Player	Princeton, NJ	Collision
07/26/1923	Michael Donohue, 26	Player	Coaldale, PA	Beaning
10/07/1923	Grady Ard, 18	Player	Pace, FL	Pitched ball to stomach
04/05/1924	Nicholas Dunn, 14	Player	Brooklyn, NY	Hit by car
04/13/1924	John Veal, 9	Player	Santa Ana, CA	Thrown ball to chest
05/27/1924	H. B. Miltenberger, NA	Fan	St. Louis, MO	Heart-related
05/31/1924	Frank Farriar, NA	Fan	Troy, NY	Foul ball to head
08/10/1924	Eugene Fishel, 11	Fan	Bedford, IN	Stands collapsed
09/02/1924	Gilmore Pickett, 21	Fan	High Point, NC	Lightning
06/01/1925	Clement Skidinski, 13	Player	Chicago, IL	Hit by truck
06/05/1925	Margaret Rudar, 16 mos.	Fan	Pittsburgh, PA	Batted ball to head
06/14/1925	Eugene McGrath, 34	Player	Linoleumville, NY	Pitched ball to chest
06/18/1925	Edward McKenna, 9	Player	Jersey City, NJ	Hit by train

Date of Death	Name, Age	Status	Place of Death	Cause
6/22/1925	Albert Green, 19	Fan	Griffin, GA	Shot
7/4/1925	Ulysses Lee, 63	Fan	Long Island, NY	Heart-related
7/11/1925	John Wells, 54	Fan	Rockaway, NJ	Heart-related
7/18/1925	Thomas Hanley, 32	Player	Jersey City, NJ	Beaning
7/22/1925	George Halabe, 26	Workman	Fort Slocum, NY	Lightning
8/2/1925	Chester Mendizs, 11	Fan	Staten Island, NY	Foul ball to head
8/24/1925	Rudolph Solomon, 20	Player	Cobleskill, NY	Thrown ball to head
8/24/1925	Harlan Fogel, 21	Fan	Stroudsburg, PA	Foul ball to head
9/6/1925	John Dowd, 34	Fan	Elizabeth, NJ	Foul ball to head
3/23/1926	William A. Estergreen, 15	Player	Atlantic City, NJ	Thrown ball to head
7/4/1926	Nick Damore, 12	Fan	Youngstown, OH	Foul ball to head
7/11/1926	Orville Allen, 31	Player	Taylorsville, IL	Beaning
3/23/1927	John G. Carpenter, 10	Player	San Antonio, TX	Fall
5/9/1927	Anthony Esposito, 13	Player	Brooklyn, NY	Pitched ball to chest
5/14/1927	Fred Haas, 50	Fan	Philadelphia, PA	Heart-related
5/16/1927	Richard Matthews, 14	Player	Pittsburgh, PA	Collision
5/25/1927	Richard McWilliams, 42	Fan	Portsmouth, VA	Windstorm-related
5/26/1927	William Barker, 67	Fan	Portsmouth, VA	Windstorm-related
6/12/1927	Peter Denock, 16	Player	Pittsburgh, PA	Pitched ball to stomach
6/24/1927	Stanley A. Nelson, 27	Player	Utica, NY	Pitched ball to chest
6/26/1927	Margaret Miller, 15	Fan	Prospect, PA	Batted ball to head
7/13/1927	Pete Mann, 20	Player	Macon, GA	Blow to chest
7/15/1927	Frank Rigler, 22	Player	East Helena, MT	Beaning
7/20/1927	Walter Warren, 35	Fan	Fort Branch, IN	Attacked with bat
8/9/1927	Philip J. Harris, NA	Player	Delmar, NY	Bat blow to head
9/26/1927	Patrick J. McTavey, 38	Umpire	Long Island, NY	Fistfight
2/12/1928	James Fancker, NA	Workman	Monterey, CA	Construction accident
5/10/1928	Mary Novak, 8	Fan	Union Center, NY	Batted ball to head
6/10/1928	William A. Tierney, 18	Player	Englewood, NJ	Beaning
6/26/1928	Louis M. Rossignol, 44	Fan	Macon, GA	Heart-related
8/12/1928	Raymond Binkowski, 9	Player	Chicago, IL	Hit by car
8/27/1928	James Lageiffe, 10	Player	New York, NY	Hit by car
9/3/1928	William S. Buerger, 51	Fan	Utica, NY	Foul ball to head
9/16/1928	Frank Janik, 24	Player	Buffalo, NY	Beaning
09/16/1928	Paul Vernon McCord, 8	Fan	Mount Kisco, NY	Thrown ball to chest
12/NA/1928	Walter Lawson, 53	Fan	Shreveport, LA	Thrown ball to head
04/28/1929	Dominick Espanela, 14	Fan	Croton, NY	Pitched ball to chest
5/13/1929	Edward Kusiak, 20	Player	Ludlow, MA	Beaning
5/14/1929	Lee Porter, 28	Fan	Akron, OH	Thrown bottle to head
5/19/1929	Joseph Carter, 60	Fan	Bronx, NY	Stampede
5/19/1929	Eleanor Price, 17	Fan	Bronx, NY	Stampede

1930s

Date of Death	Name, Age	Status	Place of Death	Cause
1/8/1930	Alexander Heinemann, 52	Owner	New Orleans, LA	Suicide
5/7/1930	Donald Donovan, 17	Player	Lawrence, MA	Lightning
5/17/1930	Walter F. Busch, 58	Fan	Washington, DC	Heart-related
6/19/1930	Howard J. Collins, 18	Player	West Chester, PA	Batted ball to head
6/19/1930	George Tuohey, 17	Fan	Chester, PA	Foul ball to stomach
6/28/1930	Joseph G. Nieberding, 16	Player	Pittsburgh, PA	Attacked with bat
9/16/1930	Joseph Czorniak, 15	Player	Chicago, IL	Fistfight
3/2/1931	Bruno Cia, 6	Player	Chicago, IL	Hit by car
4/30/1931	Ursula Thompson, 3	Fan	Washington, DC	Bat blow
6/9/1931	Norman Evans, 35	Player	Rock Hill, SC	Beaning

Date of Death	Name, Age	Status	Place of Death	Cause
10/4/1931	John Salo, 38	Security	Passaic, NJ	Pitched ball to head
10/11/1931	A.F. Leeiz, 51	Player	Chicago, IL	Heart-related
11/29/1931	Edward Swanson, 15	Player	Los Angeles, CA	Fall
3/13/1932	Lucien D. Robinson, 74	Fan	Tampa, FL	Heart-related
4/19/1932	Anthony Judiniewicz, 20	Player	Milwaukee, WI	Beaning
4/24/1932	Joseph Stephenson, 9	Fan	San Antonio, TX	Thrown ball to head
4/25/1932	Floyd Miller, 12	Player	Wahpeton, ND	Bat blow to head
5/21/1932	Herman Hoppenjans, 72	Fan	Covington, KY	Heart-related
5/26/1932	Henry Nemetz, 25	Player	Shelby, MS	Lightning
5/30/1932	Raffaele Massucci, 43	Fan	Summit, NJ	Foul ball to head
6/11/1932	Alvert Muzzio, 8	Player	New York, NY	Batted ball to chest
6/16/1932	Frank Logan, II, 26	Player	Philadelphia, PA	Beaning
6/28/1932	Max Zanderer, NA	Fan	Bronx, NY	Heart-related
7/14/1932	Balzer B. Klein, 26	Player	Wilton, ND	Beaning
9/28/1932	Edward S. Thompson, 67	Fan	Bronx, NY	Heart-related
3/19/1933	Michael Levy, 14	Player	Baltimore, MD	Batted ball to head
4/20/1933	William Nicklaus, 16	Player	Butler, NJ	Pitched ball to chest
5/7/1933	James Linde, 11	Player	Cincinnati, OH	Bat blow to head
5/29/1933	Charles Edward Lee, 18	Player	State College, PA	Lightning
6/2/1933	Philip Azarella, Jr., 13	Player	Dunkirk, NY	Beaning
6/4/1933	Kenneth A. Meehan, 28	Player	Orange, MA	Beaning
6/11/1933	Michael J. Burke, 50	Player	San Mateo, CA	Heart-related
6/25/1933	Patsy Cappola, 10	Fan	New York, NY	Batted ball to head
7/3/1933	Jake Batterton, 19	Player	Omaha, NE	Beaning
7/19/1933	Edward Drazek, 14	Fan	Amsterdam, NY	Bat blow to head
7/24/1933	John M. Moore, 56	Fan	Glens Falls, NY	Heart-related
8/11/1933	Joseph Pizzoli, 50	Fan	Chicago, IL	Hit by car
3/27/1934	Donald Weber, 13	Player	Redlands, CA	Bat blow to head
5/3/1934	Howard McBeck, 16	Player	Poughkeepsie, NY	Beaning
5/15/1934	Victor Weinman, 15	Fan	Philadelphia, PA	Bat blow to head
6/27/1934	Jack Smith, 12	Player	Amityville, NY	Thrown ball to stomach
7/9/1934	Theodore Wager, 30	Player	Dansville, NY	Beaning
7/22/1934	Raymond Ater, NA	Player	Pampa, TX	Beaning
7/19/1935	Joseph Welch, 16	Player	Detroit, MI	Lightning
8/10/1935	Roger Calvert, 13	Fan	Annapolis, MD	Foul ball to head
8/13/1935	Cal Wilson, 32	Player	Stantonville, TN	Attacked with bat
10/6/1935	Boyd Loendorf, 26	Player	Richey, MT	Beaning
5/13/1936	Roy Hinkley, 11	Player	Rochester, NY	Hit by train
5/31/1936	Michael Lally, 70	Fan	Greenwich, CT	Heart-related
6/16/1936	Allen H. Kerr, 49	Fan	New Haven, CT	Heart-related
6/28/1936	Harry Kronenberg, 24	Player	Brooklyn, NY	Beaning
9/2/1936	George Tkach, 21	Player	Winnipeg, Canada	Beaning
10/11/1936	John Przeciemski, 22	Player	West New York, NJ	Collision
10/22/1936	Ralph Musick, 18	Player	Roanoke, VA	Bat blow to head
3/28/1937	Russell Pierson, Jr., 14	Player	Orange, NJ	Batted ball to head
4/17/1937	George Knotts, 18	Player	Corning, AR	Beaning
5/30/1937	Marvin Carey, 12	Player	Perry, NY	Collision
8/22/1937	Donald Fromelt, 21	Player	Bristol, SD	Collision
8/29/1937	Stanley M. Rees, 38	Player	Lexington, KY	Heart-related
5/19/1938	Norma Jean Stewart, 4	Fan	Detroit, MI	Batted ball to chest
5/23/1938	Raymond Blackburn, 14	Player	Gloucester, NJ	Batted ball to stomach
7/14/1938	Norman Macdonald, 52	Fan	Brooklyn, NY	Foul ball to head
7/21/1938	Skeeter Ebnet, 23	Player	Winnipeg, Canada	Beaning
7/23/1938	Leo Fitch, 19	Player	Albany, NY	Batted ball to head
8/26/1938	George McCarthy, 19	Player	Oswego, NY	Beaning
8/28/1938	Robert Lewis Perry, 16	Player	Westmoreland, TN	Pitched ball to chest

Date of Death	Name, Age	Status	Place of Death	Cause
9/29/1938	Nicholas Mongero, 21	Player	Yorktown Heights, NY	Beaning
3/5/1939	Robert Siberry, 13	Player	Greenville, OH	Beaning
5/3/1939	Wallace Montgomery, 32	Fan	Hot Springs, AR	Fall
5/4/1939	Robert Rodriguez, 26	Player	Folsom, CA	Collision
5/30/1939	Harry Newman, 27	Player	Detroit, MI	Collision
6/4/1939	Robert Jures, 11 mos.	Fan	New York, NY	Batted ball to head
6/14/1939	Richard Leahy, 17	Player	Jersey City, NJ	Bat blow to head
6/21/1939	Wilbur McFall, NA	Player	Danville, VA	Lightning
6/21/1939	Charlie Bolden, NA	Player	Danville, VA	Lightning
6/24/1939	Horace G. Evans, 66	Fan	Frostburg, MD	Heart-related
7/13/1939	Norman Ingram, 14	Player	Burlington, IA	Batted ball to chest
7/31/1939	Paul McMillan, 3	Fan	Brunswick, GA	Bat blow to head
8/15/1939	John Noga, 16	Player	Chicago, IL	Beaning
8/16/1939	Henry Jimenez, 6	Player	New York, NY	Hit by car

1940s

Date of Death	Name, Age	Status	Place of Death	Cause
8/25/1940	Frank W. Davis, 63	Fan	Washington, DC	Heart-related
4/10/1941	Albert Davidson, Jr., 19	Player	Columbus, OH	Beaning
5/18/1941	Thomas Kantos, 24	Player	Chicago, IL	Pitched ball to chest
5/26/1941	Valentine Hoelzer, Jr., 21	Player	Queens, NY	Beaning
6/24/1941	William Fahy, Jr., 17	Player	Jersey City, NJ	Beaning
7/20/1941	Paddy Kreitz, 55	Player	Portland, OR	Heart-related
6/3/1942	Edith Mae Brooks, 8	Fan	Richmond, VA	Batted ball to chest
8/24/1942	Saul Cola, 10	Player	Bronx, NY	Fall
8/30/1942	Howard Swamp, 14	Player	Menasha, WI	Collision
10/3/1942	Pinky Hargrave, 44	Groundsman	Ft. Wayne, IN	Heart-related
9/30/1943	Clarence Stagemyer, 32	Fan	Washington, DC	Thrown ball to head
5/13/1945	Russell Liller, 9	Player	Keyser, WV	Bat blow to head
7/31/1945	Raymond Phillips, 40	Manager	Butler, WI	Lightning
7/31/1945	William Simerlein, 16	Player	Butler, WI	Lightning
7/31/1945	Peter Hillstrom, 14	Player	Butler, WI	Lightning
8/15/1945	Joseph L. Fielding, 50	Fan	New York, NY	Heart-related
10/8/1945	Emil W. Fehring, 60	Fan	Chicago, IL	Heart-related
5/3/1947	Ray Brubaker, 51	Manager	Waterloo, IA	Heart-related
6/13/1947	Daniel Kuechle, 26	Player	Buffalo, NY	Collision
6/19/1947	Walter Gibbs, Jr., 6	Player	Newark, NJ	Bat blow to head
7/10/1947	Stormy Davis, 20	Player	Sweetwater, TX	Beaning
8/12/1947	Norman Eschbach, 19	Player	Pennsburg, PA	Lightning
8/12/1947	Stanford Buck, 21	Player	Pennsburg, PA	Lightning
3/22/1948	Richard Mulcahy, Jr., 18	Player	Hingham, MA	Beaning
4/24/1948	James R. McLaren, NA	Fan	Brooklyn, NY	Heart-related
5/11/1948	Robert Osgood, 19	Player	Richmond, IN	Heart-related
6/4/1948	John Argo, Jr., 19	Player	Memphis, TN	Beaning
11/23/1948	Kenneth Maxfield, 39	Player	San Bernardino, CA	Beaning
3/15/1949	James Feilen, 11	Player	Chicago, IL	Bat blow to head
5/22/1949	Mikel Davis, 6	Player	Los Angeles, CA	Thrown ball to chest
7/31/1949	Allen L. Joyner, 23	Player	Baker, FL	Lightning
7/31/1949	Harry Moore, 24	Player	Baker, FL	Lightning
8/1/1949	Joe Taylor, 20	Player	Baker, FL	Lightning
8/7/1949	Harold Jensen, 26	Player	Urbana, OH	Lightning

1950s

Date of Death	Name, Age	Status	Place of Death	Cause
3/24/1950	Joseph Stefanelli, 14	Player	Newark, NJ	Batted ball to head
5/20/1950	James L. Roundtree, 24	Fan	Bradley, SC	Shot
5/21/1950	Morris E. Stanley, 35	Player	Florissant, MO	Batted ball to head
6/11/1950	Stanford B. Twente, NA	Fan	Houston, TX	Shot/suicide
7/2/1950	Robert F. Morris, 16	Player	Helena, MT	Lightning
7/3/1950	Lawrence Bulanek, 7	Player	Houston, TX	Batted ball to chest
7/4/1950	Barney Doyle, 56	Fan	New York, NY	Shot
8/30/1950	Thomas Graham, 16	Player	Frankford, PA	Lightning
6/10/1951	Ottis Johnson, 24	Player	Headland, AL	Beaning
6/11/1951	Robert M. Klingler, 10	Player	Emlenton, PA	Thrown ball to head
6/16/1951	Andy Strong, 23	Player	Alexandria, LA	Lightning
6/29/1951	Dick Conway, 19	Player	Ogden, UT	Thrown ball to chest
8/18/1951	Drew Thomas, 12	Player	Haynesville, LA	Pitched ball to chest
3/31/1952	Howard Prince, 13	Fan	Bronx, NY	Thrown ball to head
4/2/1952	Gary Eldon Moore, 16	Player	Comanche, OK	Thrown ball to chest
4/18/1952	Thomas Cummiskey, 54	Editor	Bronx, NY	Heart-related
4/21/1952	Sam Neal, 50	Groundsman	Longview, TX	Electrocuted
5/18/1952	Kenneth Eckman, 12	Player	Oak Lawn, IL	Fall on glass
3/3/1953	Clyde Milan, 65	Coach	Orlando, FL	Heart-related
3/31/1953	Gene Reynolds, 19	Player	Big Spring., TX	Electrocuted
3/31/1953	Robert Brown, 18	Player	Big Spring., TX	Electrocuted
4/5/1953	Herb Gorman, 27	Player	San Diego, CA	Heart-related
5/9/1953	Donald Schipani, 14	Player	Boston, MA	Collision
5/16/1953	John S. Barry, 70	Fan	Milwaukee, WI	Heart-related
5/24/1953	Carmella Olivo, 32	Fan	New York, NY	Stabbed
5/26/1953	William Weeks, 12	Fan	St. Louis, MO	Heart-related
5/27/1953	Joseph Eilbacher, 50	Fan	Chicago, IL	Heart-related
8/1/1953	Donald Walrath, 19	Player	Hopedale, OH	Beaning
7/2/1954	Mac Smith, 23	Player	Hagerstown, MD	Health-related
7/6/1954	Una Tumelty, 18	Fan	Brooklyn, NY	Heart-related
7/26/1954	Walker W. Sanford, 72	Fan	Charlottesville, VA	Heart-related
4/19/1955	Eddie Tharpe, 12	Player	Varnville, SC	Pitched ball to chest
4/20/1955	Edward G. Mason, 59	Fan	Brooklyn, NY	Heart-related
5/14/1955	Chad Pickens, 16	Player	Weirton, OH	Thrown ball to head
5/24/1955	David Thomas, 12	Fan	Augusta, GA	Windstorm-related
5/24/1955	Sam Madison, 13	Fan	Augusta, GA	Windstorm-related
5/24/1955	Wee Bennett, 25	Fan	Augusta, GA	Windstorm-related
6/27/1955	Terry Dickey, 8	Player	Fairfield, IL	Beaning
7/11/1955	Mark Bogenholm, 7	Player	Chicago, IL	Bat blow to chest
5/30/1956	Donald Jolk, 23	Player	Renton, WA	Beaning
7/31/1956	Halvis Martin Fletcher, 13	Player	Baton Rouge, LA	Pitched ball to chest
4/18/1957	Kim McCarren, 7	Player	Silver Spring, MD	Thrown ball to neck
6/6/1957	Pat Blackwell, 10	Player	Valsetz, OR	Batted ball to head
6/29/1957	Gladys Marion Dunn, 58	Fan	Los Angeles, CA	Heart-related
5/5/1958	Elmer Gene Keever, 17	Player	Asheville, NC	Heart-related
5/13/1958	Carl Allman, 15	Player	Wilmer, TX	Batted ball to head
5/18/1958	Wm. Whitla, Jr., 3 mos.	Fan	San Bernardino, CA	Thrown ball to head
6/11/1958	John F. Jones, 39	Player	New York, NY	Heart-related
7/25/1958	Johnny DiMiceli, 7	Player	Smithtown, NY	Thrown ball to neck
9/1/1958	Francis J. Ahern, 58	Fan	San Francisco, CA	Heart-related
9/14/1958	Robert Pitts, 12	Batboy	Centreville, VA	Thrown ball to head
10/6/1958	Vincent F. Haggerty, 50	Fan	Bronx, NY	Heart-related
11/9/1958	Emmit J. Goodbody, 53	Coach	Chula Vista, CA	Heart-related
6/30/1959	Gary F. Klingler, 10	Player	Indianapolis, IN	Lightning

1960s

Date of Death	Name, Age	Status	Place of Death	Cause
3/18/1960	Dixie Howell, 40	Player	Hollywood, FL	Heart-related
5/22/1960	Timothy McDoniel, 16	Player	Newark, AR	Pitched ball to chest
8/29/1960	Dominic LaSala, 68	Fan	Miami, FL	Foul ball to head
5/17/1961	Barry B. Babcock, 9	Player	Temple City, CA	Pitched ball to chest
5/29/1961	George McCormick, 10	Batboy	Park Ridge, IL	Batted ball to head
7/15/1961	Jerry Lynn Dodson, 13	Player	Louisville, KY	Thrown ball to neck
5/5/1962	Henry Verzyl, 19	Player	Queens, NY	Thrown ball to head
7/29/1962	Arnold Barrett, 23	Player	Bronx, NY	Bat blow
4/29/1964	Charles Greenlief, 15	Player	Normantown, WV	Beaning
7/30/1964	Jerry Highfill, 13	Batboy	Wenatchee, WA	Batted ball to head
5/9/1965	Ray Eaton, 32	Player	Hopkinsville, KY	Thrown ball to head
6/16/1965	Carl Knutson, Jr., 13	Player	South San Gabriel, CA	Pitched ball to chest
7/26/1965	Len Handel, 34	Writer	Anaheim, CA	Foul ball to head
3/17/1966	Louis J. Lise, 18	Player	New Rochelle, NY	Batted ball to head
6/23/1966	William B. McDonald, 46	Fan	Island Lake, IL	Heart-related
5/20/1967	Charles Dowd, Jr., 18	Player	Perth Amboy, NJ	Thrown ball to head
7/5/1967	Stuart Schechtman, 15	Player	Queens, NY	Thrown ball to head
7/28/1967	Lucille Larimer, 60	Fan	Chicago, IL	Heart-related
5/7/1968	James E. Kimball, 10	Player	Portland, OR	Batted ball to chest
6/16/1969	Bill Ferguson, 15	Player	Vinita, OK	Collision
8/5/1969	George J. Shramek, 24	Fan	Baltimore, MD	Fall/suicide

1970s

Date of Death	Name, Age	Status	Place of Death	Cause
4/10/1970	Rufus Mack, 33	Fan	St. Louis, MO	Shot
5/3/1970	Cal Drummond, 52	Umpire	Des Moines, IA	Batted ball to head
5/18/1970	Kurt Salha, 9	Player	Los Banos, CA	Pitched ball to chest
5/20/1970	Alan Fish, 14	Fan	Los Angeles, CA	Foul ball to head
6/25/1970	David Piritano, 12	Player	Chicago, IL	Pitched ball to chest
6/16/1971	John Adams, 11	Player	Escondido, CA	Thrown ball to chest
7/22/1971	Gary Pettitt, 22	Fan	Pittsburgh, PA	Fall
7/22/1971	C. Maynard Nichols, 62	Fan	Bronx, NY	Heart-related
8/25/1971	Glenn Shober, 37	Fan	Philadelphia, PA	Fall
4/18/1972	Joseph Farrell, 17	Fan	Pittsburgh, PA	Fall
7/16/1972	Leo Boswell, 12	Player	Chicago, IL	Hit by car
5/13/1973	John Wade, 19	Player	Lake Havasu City, AZ	Lightning
6/16/1973	Daniel Druding, 14	Fan	Arlington Heights, IL	Lightning
6/22/1973	Clifford Knight, 8	Fan	Fort Wayne, IN	Thrown ball to chest
5/24/1974	Pard Pearce, 78	Umpire	Newport, RI	Heart-related
8/22/1974	Alfredo Edmead, 18	Player	Rocky Mount, NC	Collision
6/16/1975	Paul Adamansky, 8	Player	New York, NY	Lightning
8/22/1975	Steve Hutchison, 20	Player	Kansas City, KS	Beaning
4/11/1976	John Corbett, 73	Fan	Philadelphia, PA	Heart-related
11/30/1976	William Zimmerman, 17	Player	Rancho Palos Verdes, CA	Batted ball to knee
7/11/1977	Dennis P. Dunne, 34	Fan	Chicago, IL	Heart-related
6/21/1978	Robert Roggatz, 10	Player	Lincolnwood, IL	Thrown ball to chest
6/23/1978	Dennis Wucki, 13	Player	Chicago, IL	Batted ball to head
9/4/1978	Joseph Wagner, 58	Fan	Baltimore, MD	Heart-related
9/4/1978	Minzio Bazarozza, 75	Fan	Baltimore, MD	Heart-related
5/17/1979	Dennis Clement, 15	Player	Allenstown, NH	Collision

1980s

Date of Death	Name, Age	Status	Place of Death	Cause
6/1/1980	Kenneth A. Hahn, 18	Player	Constantine, IN	Lightning
6/18/1980	Gerald Piotter, Jr., 9	Player	Indianapolis, IN	Pitched ball to chest
8/25/1980	Edward Huntoon, 23	Fan	Miami, FL	Shot
8/25/1980	Charles Matanis, 24	Fan	Miami, FL	Shot
7/13/1980	Bruce Winick, 28	Fan	New York, NY	Fall/suicide
12/9/1981	Jose Martin Solis, 15	Player	Dallas, TX	Batted ball to chest
3/5/1982	Scott Halbrook, 19	Player	Corvallis, OR	Collision
6/6/1984	Anthony Perry, 30	Fan	San Francisco, CA	Fall
8/7/1984	Adriano Martinez, 18	Player	Long Island, NY	Lightning
5/1/1985	Mark Leddy, 21	Fan	New York, NY	Fall
5/16/1986	Edward Joyce, 53	Fan	Chicago, IL	Fall
3/11/1988	Daniel McCarthy, 42	Fan	Bradenton, FL	Hit by car
3/21/1988	Edd Roush, 94	Fan	Bradenton, FL	Heart-related
8/1/1988	Elmer Rader, 64	Fan	Norristown, PA	Foul ball to head
4/27/1989	Mike Wurzer, 20	Fan	Kansas City, MO	Fall

1990s

Date of Death	Name, Age	Status	Place of Death	Cause
3/18/1990	William Ryan Wojick, 10	Player	Citrus Park, FL	Pitched ball to chest
5/14/1990	Ronaldo Romero, 19	Player	Fayetteville, NC	Heart-related
5/30/1990	Bruce Edgerley, 16	Player	Beaufort, SC	Batted ball to chest
8/6/1992	Matthew G. Laven, 28	Intern	Little Rock, AR	Suicide
5/8/1993	Brian Korbin, 9	Player	Charlottesville, VA	Heart-related
5/17/1993	Joseph Matteucci, 17	Fan	Castro Valley, CA	Attacked with bat
8/14/1993	Clifford Toolerton, 75	Fan	Pittsburgh, PA	Fall
6/28/1994	Michael Marano, 12	Player	Bensonhurst, NY	Pitched ball to chest
4/16/1995	Jason Smyly, 6	Player	Saraland, AL	Batted ball to chest
4/1/1996	John McSherry, 51	Umpire	Cincinnati, OH	Heart-related
4/5/1996	Danny Ledezma, 22	Fan	Avenal, CA	Attacked with bat
5/14/1996	Bernie Wanko, 63	Fan	South Bend, IN	Heart-related
3/17/1997	Vincent Ceceri, 56	Coach	North Scituate, RI	Heart-related
5/5/1997	Kriston Palomo, 16	Player	Torrance, CA	Collision
6/24/1997	Julius Riofrir, 17	Player	Glendale, CA	Batted ball to head
2/26/1998	David Cadena, 17	Player	Laredo, TX	Pitched ball to chest
6/4/1998	Jacob Watt, 6	Player	Lexington, IL	Batted ball to chest
7/18/1998	Nicholas A. Graham, 19	Player	Providence, RI	Heart-related
4/25/1999	Francisco Munoz, 37	Fan	Bronx, NY	Fall
5/25/1999	Corey Smith, 13	Player	North Columbus, OH	Pitched ball to chest
6/26/1999	Andrew Cook, 5	Player	Omaha, NE	Thrown ball to chest
7/14/1999	William DeGrave, 39	Workman	Milwaukee, WI	Construction accident
7/14/1999	Jerome Starr, 52	Workman	Milwaukee, WI	Construction accident
7/14/1999	Jeffrey Wischer, 40	Workman	Milwaukee, WI	Construction accident
8/8/1999	Ben Jackson, 22	Player	Thomasville, GA	Lightning
8/12/1999	Brandy Mitchell, 9	Player	Michigan City, IN	Batted ball to head

2000s

Date of Death	Name, Age	Status	Place of Death	Cause
3/27/2000	Shawn Barnes, 15	Player	Madison, IN	Thrown ball to chest
5/16/2000	Diana Smith, 32	Fan	Ozark, AL	Shot
5/16/2000	Edward McQuinn, II, 35	Fan	Ozark, AL	Shot

Date of Death	Name, Age	Status	Place of Death	Cause
5/17/2000	Ricky Smith, 35	Fan	Ozark, AL	Shot/suicide
4/21/2000	Ryan Garrison, 12	Player	Racine, WI	Heart-related
5/24/2000	Devin Beck, 11	Player	Ammon, ID	Aneurysm
6/11/2000	Ryan Blanco, 7	Player	Centereach, NY	Batted ball to chest
5/21/2001	Unnamed boy, 3	Player	Rochester, NY	Attacked with bat and brick
6/27/2001	Brendan Grant, 18	Player	Belmont, MA	Collision
5/5/2002	Caleb Slaton, 11	Player	Russellville, KY	Thrown ball to chest
5/17/2002	Nader Parman, II, 7	Player	East Cobb, GA	Batted ball to chest
6/5/2002	Daniel Rice, 47	Coach	Buffalo Grove, IL	Lightning
6/29/2002	Jason Malone, 11	Player	Berea, OH	Heart-related
8/23/2002	Victoria Lampe, 28	Fan	Orlando, FL	Health-related
2/17/2003	Steve Bechler, 23	Player	Ft. Lauderdale, FL	Heatstroke/Ephedra
3/24/2003	Scott Rosenberger, 17	Player	Elkville, IL	Heart-related
5/9/2003	John Ashmore, 13	Player	Fayette County, GA	Pitched ball to chest
7/15/2003	Christine Ewing, 22	Fan	Columbia, MO	Fall
7/26/2003	Brandon Patch, 18	Player	Great Falls, MT	Batted ball to head
9/17/2003	Todd E. Adams, 35	Fan	San Francisco, CA	Fall
9/19/2003	Marc Antenorcruz, 25	Fan	Los Angeles, CA	Shot
9/21/2003	Justin Saccone, 15	Player	Melbourne, KY	Pitched ball to chest
9/23/2003	Rick Conyers, 49	Coach	Norcross, GA	Heart-related
10/8/2003	Lyle Greunke, 63	Umpire	Omaha, NE	Heart-related
6/8/2004	Rudie Bachman, 15	Player	Stanford, IL	Heart-related
7/9/2004	Harry Udvare, 58	Umpire	Muskego, WI	Heart-related
7/27/2004	Ryan Nielsen, 17	Player	West Jordan, UT	Batted ball to neck
7/30/2004	James A. Kolata, 48	Fan	Milwaukee, WI	Fall
1/19/2005	Matthew Miulli, 17	Player	Tampa, FL	Heart-related
4/12/2005	Jeremy Rourke, 15	Fan	Palmdale, CA	Attacked with bat
4/14/2005	Scott Marangi, 47	Umpire	Villa Park, IL	Heart-related
8/3/2005	Unnamed grandfather, NA	Fan	Cincinnati, OH	Heart-related
9/27/2005	Robbie Levine, 9	Player	Merrick, NY	Heart-related
7/12/2006	Glenn Kelly, 66	Fan	Fort Atkinson, WI	Fall
7/29/2006	Denise Quickenton, 29	Fan	Boston, MA	Health-related
9/18/2006	Samuel L. Noe, 61	Fan	Dandridge, TN	Shot
9/18/2006	Jerry D. Shands, 63	Fan	Dandridge, TN	Shot
9/18/2006	Ellen D. Shands, 62	Fan	Dandridge, TN	Shot
2/24/2007	Chris Gavora, 17	Player	Grapevine, TX	Batted ball to head
3/17/2007	Des Hamilton, 53	Coach	Jacksonville, FL	Heart-related
7/23/2007	Mike Coolbaugh, 35	Coach	Little Rock, AR	Batted ball to neck
11/1/2007	Cayden Huels, 4	Fan	Wesley Chapel, FL	Pitched ball to chest

Chapter Notes

Preface

1. "Foul Play: Fan Fatalities in Twentieth-Century Organized Baseball," reprinted from *Nine: A Journal of Baseball History and Culture* 12, no. 1 (Fall 2003), by permission of the University of Nebraska Press, © 2003 by the University of Nebraska Press; "'I Guess I Forgot to Duck': On-Field Player Fatalities in the Minor Leagues," reprinted from *Nine: A Journal of Baseball History and Culture* 11, no. 2 (Spring 2003), by permission of the University of Nebraska Press, © 2003 by the University of Nebraska Press.

2. For further background on how news reporting changed over time, see Hazel Dicken-Garcia, *Journalistic Standards in Nineteenth-Century America* (Madison, WI: University of Wisconsin Press, 1989), and Andie Tucher, "In Search of Jenkins: Taste, Style, and Credibility in Gilded-Age Journalism," *Journalism History* 27 (Summer 2001): 50–55.

3. "Baseball Enthusiast Is Killed," *Chicago Daily Tribune*, July 10, 1897, 2; "Fatally Injured," *Columbus (OH) Dispatch*, July 10, 1897, 2; "Cut His Arm Off," *Daily Times (Portsmouth, OH)*, July 10, 1897, 8.

Introduction

1. "Baseball Is 'Deadliest Sport' According to New York Doctor," *Chicago Daily Tribune*, August 22, 1920, A4; "Most Dangerous Recreation Is Found to Be Baseball," *New York Times*, July 8, 1930, 10; "Baseball Tops Deaths in New York Survey," *Los Angeles Times*, August 17, 1951, C3; Lou Pavlovich, Jr., "Baseball Deaths Outstrip Football, 2–1," *Collegiate Baseball*, January 6, 1984, 1.

2. Robert E. Coughlin, "Fatalities in Athletic Games and Deaths of Athletes," *New York Medical Journal* 105 (June 23, 1917): 1204–05; "Baseball Is 'Deadliest Sport,'" A4.

3. Thomas A. Gonzales, "Fatal Injuries in Competitive Sports," *Journal of the American Medical Association* 146, no. 16 (August 18, 1951):1506–11.

4. Gonzales, "Fatal Injuries," 1508, 1510. This finding is in line with what our study shows: head injuries were the most common cause of player fatalities prior to the widespread use of the batting helmet.

5. Pavlovich, "Baseball Deaths," 1. Interestingly, when deaths for all ages of participants during this same 8-year period are compared, football led with 260 fatalities followed by baseball with 183.

6. United States Consumer Product Safety Commission, "Reducing Youth Baseball Injuries with Protective Equipment," *Consumer Product Safety Review* 1, no. 1 (1996): 1–4.

7. Coughlin, "Fatalities in Athletic Games," 1204–05.

8. Gonzales, "Fatal Injuries," 1506.

9. Frederick O. Mueller and Jerry L. Diehl, *Annual Survey of Football Injury Research, 1931–2005* (Chapel Hill, NC: National Center for Catastrophic Sport Injury Research, 2006), http://www.unc.edu/depts/nccsi/SurveyofFootballInjuries.htm (accessed May 12, 2006). "Indirect" causes are defined as "Those fatalities which are caused by systemic failure as a result of exertion while participating in football activity or by a complication which was secondary to a non-fatal injury."

10. National Center for Catastrophic Sport Injury Research, *Twenty-Second Annual Report, Fall 1982–Spring 2004* (Chapel Hill, NC: National Center for Catastrophic Sport Injury Research, 2005), http://www.unc.edu/depts/nccsi/AllSport.htm (accessed May 12, 2006). As in the report above, "indirect" causes are defined as "Those injuries which are caused by systemic failure as a result of exertion while participating in a sport activity or by a complication which was secondary to a non-fatal injury."

Chapter 1

1. Shirley Povich, "This Morning with Shirley Povich," *Washington Post*, June 21, 1940, 21.

2. Peter Morris, *A Game of Inches: The Stories Behind the Innovations that Shaped Baseball: The Game on the Field* (Chicago: Ivan R. Dee, 2006), 101–107, 181–185.

3. Morris, 183; "Baseball Gossip," *National Police Gazette*, September 29, 1888, 3. While one must be cautious in applying motive or causality when looking at raw statistics, there clearly were more hit batsmen in the late nineteenth and early twentieth centuries according to hit-by-pitch statistics provided by *Retrosheet.Org*. The average number per team in the major leagues ranged from a low of 40 in 1916 to a high of 72 in 1898 and 1899. By 1916 these figures began to decline significantly, fluctuating between the low 20s to the upper 30s per team yearly from the mid–1910s to the early 1990s. Interestingly, the average is again increasing, ranging between 50 to 60 hit batters per team yearly since the mid–1990s.

4. Harry A. Williams, "'Bean' Ball Should Be Placed on Blacklist," *Los Angeles Times*, June 8, 1913, VII7; Edward Burns, "What About This Bean Ball Craze, Mr. President?," *Chicago Daily Tribune*, May 26, 1937, 25.

5. Povich, "This Morning," 21. Povich is referring to the beaning death of Cleveland's Ray Chapman in 1920. See account that follows.

6. Arthur Daley, "Lethal Weapon," *New York Times*, May 26, 1955, 43; Dan Daniel, "Giles Enforcing 'Hush' Rule on Umps," *Sporting News*, April 4, 1956, 2.

7. "Ted Williams Faces Showdown on Helmet," *Los Angeles Times*, March 12, 1958, C1; John Drebinger, "Red Sox Triumph as Yanks Suffer Fifth Defeat in Six Exhibition Starts," *New York Times*, March 14, 1958, 32; "Williams to Wear Helmet," *Los Angeles Times*, March 15, 1958, A2. One further argu-

ment against helmets was made by National League umpire Jocko Conlan, who claimed that "those helmets are an inviting target for pitchers to throw at." While agreeing that helmets did provide protection, he did not "think so many pitchers would be aiming at the hitters' noggins if they were just wearing their baseball caps without any protective covering." Conlan's fear is not borne out by hit-by-pitch statistics. The average per team in the National League decreased from nearly 30 in 1955 — the year before the headgear was required in the league — to 25 in 1956. While it increased to nearly 30 again in 1957, it remained in this range for the next several years. Of course, how many of these hit batsmen were victims of *deliberate* beanings is not known. See Frank Finch, "Ump Puts Bean Ball Blame on Helmets," *Los Angeles Times*, May 25, 1958, E4.

8. Morris, 442–443; Kate Ledger, "Safety Did Not Come First," *Sports Illustrated*, July 14, 1997.

9. "Batters Wear Polo Helmets as Safeguard," *Washington Post*, May 31, 1937, 14; "Dean and Di Maggio Injuries Spur Talk of Diamond Safety," *Newsweek*, May 8, 1939, 26.

10. James F. Dawson, "National League Seeks Modification of Rule to Obstruct Optioning of Players," *New York Times*, February 5, 1941, 24; "M'Phail Orders Use of Helmets in Dodgers' Chain," *Chicago Daily Tribune*, March 9, 1941, E2; Roscoe McGowen, "Plastic Protectors Inside Caps Will Be Worn by Dodger Batters," *New York Times*, March 9, 1941, S1.

11. "A MacPhail Proposal," *New York Times*, November 25, 1941, 34.

12. "Plastic Cap That Saved Adcock Is Brainchild of Pirates' Rickey," *New York Times*, August 3, 1954, 22; Jack Brodsky, "Keep Your Head On," *New York Times Magazine*, July 31, 1955, 46; "No Baseball Rule Requires Players Use Protective Caps," *Washington Post and Times Herald*, August 3, 1954, 21.

13. "Make Safety Caps Mandatory," *The Sporting News*, August 12, 1953, 12; Daley, "Lethal Weapon," 43.

14. "Yanks Ask 'Protection,'" *New York Times*, March 31, 1956, 9; "Players Must Don Helmets, Says Harridge," *Chicago Daily Tribune*, March 12, 1958, B3; "Across the Years with the Rule Book," *Sporting News*, June 5, 1976, 28; "New Rule Adopted on Saving Games," *Sporting News*, January 26, 1974, 39.

15. "Little League Has Safer Helmet," *Chicago Daily Tribune*, March 27, 1958, D5; Milton Bracker, "Little League Works to Cut Injuries," *New York Times*, August 31, 1959, 27. Today safety experts are recommending that youth baseball adopt face masks for batters as well. See Joel S. Pasternack, Kenneth R. Veenema, and Charles M. Callahan, "Baseball Injuries: A Little League Survey," *Pediatrics* 98, no. 3 (September 1996): 445–447.

16. "Chapman Hit, Fracture of Skull Feared," *Cleveland (OH) Plain Dealer*, August 17, 1920, 1, 17; William Slocum, "Chapman's Body Arrives Home Today," *Cleveland Plain Dealer*, August 18, 1920, 1, 10; "Thought It Wild Pitch," *Cleveland Plain Dealer*, August 18, 1920, 14.

17. Slocum, "Chapman's Body," 10; "Chapman Hit," 1; Carl Mays, "My Attitude Toward the Unfortunate Chapman Affair," *Baseball Magazine*, November 1920, 576–577.

18. "Ban Johnson, Asked to Bar Carl Mays, from Baseball, Puts Off Decision," *Cleveland Plain Dealer*, August 18, 1920, 14; "Umpires Query Mays' Argument," *Cleveland Plain Dealer*, August 19, 1920, 16; Henry P. Edwards, "Ban Johnson Will Take No Action Against Carl Mays for His Pitching," *Cleveland Plain Dealer*, August 21, 1920, 12; "Ban Is Once More Wrong," *New York Times*, August 22, 1920, 17. Members of the Indians' squad, with the support of the St. Louis Browns and Washington Senators players, attempted to organize a boycott of Mays, but this action, too, failed when Johnson moved to squelch it. For a comprehensive account of the Chapman affair, see Mike Sowell, *The Pitch That Killed* (New York: Macmillan, 1989).

19. "Whitney Is Dead," *Burlington (IA) Hawk-Eye*, June 27, 1906, 2.

20. "Whitney Is Dead," 2; "Body Is Sent Home," *Burlington (IA) Hawk-Eye*, June 28, 1906, 2.

21. "Swift Inshoot May Be Fatal," *Boston Daily Globe*, August 10, 1906, 5. In some news accounts, Edward Yeager is sometimes referred to as Joseph Yeager. This misinformation has led to the erroneous conclusion that the misidentified "Joseph" Yeager was major league player Joe Yeager. In 1906, "Little Joe," as he was sometimes known, was a utility infielder with the New York Highlanders, with whom he batted .301. To add to the confusion, Joe Yeager had been a pitcher in his early career.

22. "Inshoot Was Fatal," *Boston Daily Globe*, August 12, 1906, 15; "Funeral of Thos. F. Burke," *Boston Daily Globe*, August 15, 1906, 8.

23. "Yeager Arrested," *Boston Daily Globe*, August 19, 1906, 7; "Yeager Discharged," *Boston Daily Globe*, August 21, 1906, 3; "Accident Not Crime," *Sporting News*, August 25, 1906, 1. It is not uncommon for an arrest to be made in an investigation into an accidental death. In most cases it is a mere formality to determine cause and circumstances.

24. "Second Baseman Charles Pinkney Fatally Injured by Pitched Ball; Aged Father Witnesses Accident," *Dayton (OH) Daily News*, September 15, 1909, 10; "Hit by Hageman; May Not Recover," *Grand Rapids (MI) Herald*, September 15, 1909, 10.

25. "Second Baseman Charles Pinkney Fatally Injured," 10; "Pinkney Dies as Result of Injury," *Grand Rapids (MI) Herald*, September 16, 1909, 10. The game ended with Grand Rapids winning 5 to 4. Oddly, this would make Hageman the losing pitcher in the first game and the winning one in the second.

26. "Pinkney Dies," 10. While Hageman's "grief knew no bounds" after Pinkney's death, he did go on to a brief major league career. He pitched for the Red Sox in 1911 and 1912, appearing in four games and going 0–2. And in 1914 he split the year between the Cardinals (2–4) and the Cubs (1–1), appearing in 28 games.

27. "Great Umpire Calls Third Strike on Charley Pinkney," *Dayton (OH) Daily News*, September 15, 1909, 1; W. L. Connors, "A Tribute to Charley Pinkney," *Dayton (OH) Daily News*, September 18, 1909, 12.

28. "John Dodge Killed by a Pitched Ball," *Sporting News*, June 22, 1916, 1; "Player Dodge Dead; Hit by Pitched Ball," *Washington Post*, June 20, 1916, 8; "Raise Fund of $1500 for Sister of Johnny Dodge," *Boston Daily Globe*, August 12, 1916, 5.

29. "Tom Rogers Hurls No-Hit, No-Run, No-Man-to-First," *Atlanta Constitution*, July 12, 1916, 10.

30. David L. Fultz, "An Object Lesson," *Baseball Magazine*, September 1916, 83–84. One of the signatories to the condolence letter was Jake Daubert, slick fielding first baseman for both the Brooklyn Dodgers (1910–1918) and the Cincinnati Reds (1919–1924). The sad death of this outstanding player will be covered in a later chapter.

31. "Player Hit on Head by Pitched Ball Near Death," *Chicago Daily Tribune*, July 3, 1933, 14; "Player Struck on Head by Ball Dies of Injury," *Chicago Daily Tribune*, July 4, 1933, 19; "Batterton Burial Services to Be Held in Los Angeles," *Los Angeles Times*, July 4, 1933, A10.

32. "Maroons Beat Superior 8 to 1 in Fine Game," *Winnipeg (Manitoba) Free Press*, August 28, 1936, 16; "Inquest Jury Lays No Blame for Death of Baseball Player," *Winnipeg (Manitoba) Free Press*, September 5, 1936, 1.

33. "Hope Now Held for the Life of Injured Superior Ball Player," *Win-*

nipeg (Manitoba) Free Press, August 31, 1936, 14; "Condition of George Tkach Is Unfavorable," *Winnipeg (Manitoba) Free Press*, September 1, 1936, 12; "Baseball Player Dies," *Winnipeg (Manitoba) Free Press*, September 3, 1936, 1.

34. Scott Young, "Ebnet Beaned," *Winnipeg (Canada) Free Press*, July 18, 1938, 12; "Linus (Skeeter) Ebnet," *Sporting News*, 12. According to Tom Hawthorn, Young, who recently passed away, is the father of rock musician Neil Young. See Tom Hawthorn, "Skeets Killed by Pitch," in *Dominionball: Baseball Above the 49th*, ed. Jane Finnan Dorward (Cleveland, OH: Society for American Baseball Research, 2005), 25–29.

35. Young, "Ebnet Beaned," 12.

36. "Ebnet Dies," *Winnipeg (Manitoba) Free Press*, July 22, 1938, 1.

37. "Longhorn Star First Fatality in O.B. in '47," *Sporting News*, July 23, 1947, 14; Joseph M. Overfield, "Tragedies and Shortened Careers," in *Total Baseball V*, ed. John Thorn (New York: Viking Penguin, 1997), 164; "Player Hit by Baseball Dies," *New York Times*, July 11, 1947, 19. Davis' father was C.A. "Stormy" Davis, who had played in the low minors for over 15 years.

38. "Clifton Hurls Two-Hitter; Browns, Headland Here Today," *Dothan (AL) Eagle*, June 3, 1951, 18; "Ottis Johnson Suffers Fractured Skull; Benched Indefinitely," *Dothan (AL) Eagle*, June 3, 1951, 18; Ken Brooks, *The Last Rebel Yell* (Lynn Haven, FL: Seneca Park Publishers, 1986), 48.

39. "Johnson's Condition Remains 'Unchanged,'" *Dothan (AL) Eagle*, June 6, 1951, 8; "Browns to Serve as Pallbearers; at Funeral of Ottis Johnson Today," *Dothan (AL) Eagle*, June 11, 1951, 8.

40. "Withdrawal Threatened If Jack Clifton Pitches," *Dothan (AL) Eagle*, June 13, 1951, 12; Brooks, *Last Rebel Yell*, 44.

41. "Mrs. Johnson Says Ottis Would Want Jack Clifton to Play," *Dothan (AL) Eagle*, June 13, 1951, 12; Brooks, *Last Rebel Yell*, 44.

42. Brooks, *Last Rebel Yell*, 44; "Browns Forfeit to Headland," *Dothan (AL) Eagle*, June 13, 1951, 6; Furman Bisher, "Injury from Pitch Fatal to Dothan Player," *Sporting News*, June 20, 1951, 18; "Clifton Hurls No-Hitter, Wildness Costs Two Runs," *Sporting News*, June 20, 1951, 18.

43. Edgar G. Brands, "Border Loop Stays in Ring with 4 Clubs," *Sporting News*, July 4, 1951, 16; Edgar G. Brands, "Two League Heads Resign, One Returns," *Sporting News*, July 11, 1951, 41; "Smith Delays Withdrawal One Week in Return for All Rights to His Club," *Dothan (AL) Eagle*, June

26, 1951, 7; "Halstead Resigns; New Four Club League Considered," *Dothan (AL) Eagle*, June 29, 1951, 6.

44. Brands, "Two League Heads," 41, 46; Brooks, *Last Rebel Yell*, 44, 46; Lloyd Johnson and Miles Wolff, eds., *The Encyclopedia of Minor League Baseball*, 2nd ed. (Durham, NC: Baseball America, 1997), 404.

45. "Clifton Announces Retirement," *Sporting News*, February 27, 1952, 33; Edsel Johnson, Jr., to David Jones, August 4, 2000, National Baseball Hall of Fame.

46. "Baseball Hit His Head," *New York Sun*, August 24, 1908, 5; "Player Hit by Baseball Dies," *New York Sun*, August 25, 1908, 9; "Ball Catcher, Hit on Head, Dies," *New York Times*, August 25, 1908, 14.

47. "Otto Bronson," *Madison (NY) Observer*, August 24, 1887, 3.

48. "A Boy Killed by a Baseball," *Washington Post*, July 23, 1888, 1.

49. "Killed by a Pitched Ball," *New York Times*, August 20, 1888, 1.

50. "Killed in a Baseball Game," *New York Times*, September 23, 1889, 8.

51. "Local," *Cambridge City (IN) Tribune*, October 3, 1889, 2.

52. "Death Caused by a Baseball," *New York Times*, October 26, 1889, 2.

53. "Baseball," *Los Angeles Times*, September 21, 1891, 1.

54. "Killed by a Ball," *Washington Post*, June 19, 1893, 4; "Max Meindel," *Tyrone (PA) Herald*, June 22, 1893, 5.

55. "Pitcher Kills the Man at Bat," *Chicago Daily Tribune*, August 21, 1893, 1.

56. "Killed by a Pitched Ball," *Washington Post*, June 13, 1894, 6.

57. "A Fatal Blow," *Cleveland Plain Dealer*, April 17, 1895, 6.

58. "Pitcher Drops Dead in the Box," *Chicago Daily Tribune*, July 1, 1895, 1.

59. "Pitcher Drops Dead in the Box," 1.

60. "Ball Player Killed Sunday," *Atlanta Constitution*, June 21, 1897, 2.

61. "Baseball Player Dead," *Los Angeles Times*, April 14, 1899, 4.

62. "Boy Killed by a Baseball," *New York Times*, June 25, 1900, 7.

63. "Silvers Killed in Game of Ball," *Atlanta Constitution*, August 29, 1901, 2.

64. "Killed by a Baseball," *New York Times*, May 12, 1902, 5.

65. "Ball Player Dies," *Washington Post*, July 12, 1904, 8.

66. "Killed by a Pitched Ball," *Washington Post*, August 8, 1904, 8.

67. "Killed by Pitched Ball," *Massillon (OH) Independent*, June 15, 1905, 7; "Local Happenings," *Massillon (OH) Independent*, June 15, 1905, 5.

68. "Hit by a Ball; Lloyd Grout

Dies," *Cedar Rapids (IA) Republican* July 30, 1905, 12.

69. "M'Donald Dies from Baseball Injury," *Trenton (NJ) Times*, September 5, 1905, 3.

70. "Killed by Pitched Ball," *Washington Post*, May 26, 1906, 5.

71. "Inshoot on Temple Kills," *Chicago Daily Tribune*, June 23, 1906, 2.

72. "Police Will Stop Sunday Ball Games," *Philadelphia Inquirer*, July 3, 1906, 9.

73. "Killed by Pitched Ball," *Philadelphia Inquirer*, July 5, 1906, 6.

74. "Sporting," *Racine (WI) Daily Journal*, June 1, 1907, 17.

75. "Killed by Baseball," *Boston Daily Globe*, August 26, 1907, 5.

76. "Pitched Ball Kills Boy," *Chicago Daily Tribune*, June 23, 1908, 3.

77. "Ball Player Hit by Ball," *Morning Press (Bloomsburg, PA)*, July 6, 1908, 1; "Death Claims Ball Player," *Morning Press (Bloomsburg, PA)*, July 7, 1908, 1.

78. "Ball Player Killed," *Imperial Valley (CA) Press*, February 27, 1909, 1.

79. "Hit by Pitched Ball, Boy Dies," *Detroit News*, July 5, 1909, 3.

80. "Blow from Baseball Kills a Boy," *New York Times*, April 12, 1910, 4.

81. "Pitched Balls Kill Two Young Players," *New York Times*, April 18, 1910, 3.

82. "Baseball Fatal to Two; One Hurt," *Cleveland Plain Dealer*, May 30, 1910, 1–2.

83. "Skull Fractured," *Augusta (GA) Chronicle*, June 29, 1910, 12; "Mr. Massesgale [sic] Dead from Baseball Injury," *Augusta (GA) Chronicle*, July 4, 1910, 8; "Short Sketch of L. R. Massengale," *Augusta (GA) Chronicle*, July 5, 1910, 9.

84. "Funeral of Baseball Victim," *Washington Post*, August 13, 1910, 14.

85. "Baseball Kills a Student," *Chicago Daily Tribune*, August 21, 1910, 5.

86. "Killed by a Pitched Ball," *Los Angeles Times*, April 18, 1911, I15.

87. "Killed by a Pitched Ball," *Washington Post*, May 8, 1911, 2.

88. "Killed by Pitched Ball," *Washington Post*, June 27, 1911, 2.

89. "Boy Killed by Baseball," *Atlanta Constitution*, July 8, 1911, 2.

90. "Killed by Pitched Ball," *Los Angeles Times*, August 14, 1911, I3.

91. "William Schmidt," *Chicago Daily News*, September 18, 1911, 4.

92. "Baseball Kills a Player," *Washington Post*, May 5, 1912, 1.

93. "Baseball Hurt Proves Fatal," *Rockford (IL) Daily Register*, July 9, 1912, 1.

94. "Ball Game Causes Death," *Register and Leader (Des Moines, IA)*, September 20, 1912, 2.

95. "Broke M'Carty's Neck," *Daily Northwestern (Oshkosh, WI)*, May 26, 1913, 9.

96. "Baseball Blows Fatal," *Washington Post*, June 3, 1913, 8.

97. "Boy Hurt in Baseball Game Dies in Hospital," *Reno (NV) Evening Gazette*, June 2, 1913, 6.

98. "Two Baseball Deaths," *Atlanta Constitution*, June 2, 1914, 9.

99. "3 Hit by Baseballs Die," *New York Times*, June 2, 1914, 1.

100. "Killed by Baseball," *Boston Daily Globe*, June 29, 1914, 9.

101. "Killed by Pitched Ball," *Atlanta Constitution*, September 8, 1914, 10.

102. "Killed by Pitched Ball," *Washington Post*, April 26, 1915, 2.

103. "Baseball Player Hurt," *Indianapolis Star*, May 2, 1915, 1; "Death and Funeral Notices," *Indianapolis Star*, May 3, 1915, 12.

104. "Killed by Pitched Ball," *Atlanta Constitution*, May 15, 1915, 3.

105. "Pitched Ball Kills Boy," *Chicago Daily Tribune*, May 18, 1915, 11.

106. "Killed by Pitched Ball," *Washington Post*, May 24, 1915, 3.

107. "Wesley Who Was with Helena in 1914 Is Killed," *Helena (MT) Independent*, May 28, 1915, 8.

108. "Killed by Pitched Ball," *Chicago Daily Tribune*, July 7, 1915, 11.

109. "Baseball Player Dies as Result of Injury," *San Francisco Chronicle*, July 13, 1915, 4.

110. "Killed by Pitched Ball," *Atlanta Constitution*, August 2, 1915, 5.

111. "Personal Mention," *Enid (OK) Daily Eagle*, August 11, 1915, 3; "Roy Dean," *Enid (OK) Daily Eagle*, August 15, 1915, 1.

112. "Boy Held for Baseball Accident," *Philadelphia Inquirer*, August 20, 1915, 3.

113. "Boy Dies After Being Struck on Head by Baseball," *St. Louis Post-Dispatch*, September 24, 1915, 1.

114. "Player's Death Is Cause of Postponed Game at Marysville," *The Patriot (Harrisburg, PA)*, September 25, 1915, 11; "Pitched Ball Kills Player," *New Oxford (PA) Item*, September 30, 1915, 1.

115. "Dies After Baseball Game," *Olean (NY) Evening Herald*, August 8, 1916, 1; "Baseball Injury Fatal," *Washington Post*, August 8, 1916, 6.

116. "Ball Player Killed," *Kokomo (IN) Daily Tribune*, August 9, 1916, 1.

117. "Semipro Player Killed, Hit in Temple by Pitcher," *Boston Daily Globe*, May 31, 1917, 5.

118. "Amateur Baseball Player Killed by Pitched Ball," *Chicago Daily Tribune*, July 15, 1917, 1.

119. "L. Frye of Freeport Team Killed by Pitched Ball," *Chicago Daily Tribune*, August 10, 1921, 19.

120. "Killed by Pitched Ball," *New York Times*, May 1, 1922, 8.

121. "Pitched Ball Victim Well Known Teacher," *Sheboygan (WI) Press-Telegram*, May 2, 1922, 2; "Manitowoc, Wis., Teacher, Hit by Bean Ball, Dies," *Chicago Daily Tribune*, May 4, 1922, 17.

122. "Killed by Pitched Ball," *New York Times*, September 11, 1922, 17.

123. "Baseball Injury Fatal," *New York Times*, July 27, 1923, 10.

124. "Killed by a Pitched Ball," *New York Times*, July 19, 1925, E1.

125. "Semi-Pro Ball Player, Hit in Head by Pitcher, Dies," *Chicago Daily Tribune*, July 12, 1926, 17.

126. "Frank Rigler Dies of Injuries Received in Game at East Helena," *Helena (MT) Independent*, July 16, 1927, 1; "Frank Rigler Memorial Game to Be Played Wednesday at East Helena," *Helena (MT) Independent*, July 21, 1927, 7; "Smelterites Win Frank Rigler Memorial Contest by 9 to 0 Score," *Helena (MT) Independent*, July 28, 1927, 7.

127. "Struck by Baseball, Dies," *New York Times*, June 11, 1928, 21.

128. "Baseball Player Killed When Hit by Pitched Ball," *Buffalo (NY) Evening News*, September 17, 1928, 14.

129. "Late News Briefs," *Lowell (MA) Sun*, May 13, 1929, 13; "Player Struck by Baseball Dies," *New York Times*, May 14, 1929, 8.

130. "Lando Man Badly Injured by Ball," *Evening Herald (Rock Hill, SC)*, June 8, 1931, 6; "Norman Evans Dies from Injury Caused by Ball Saturday," *Evening Herald (Rock Hill, SC)*, June 10, 1931, 1.

131. "Hit by a Pitched Ball, Season's First Victim Dies," *Milwaukee Journal*, April 19, 1932, 3.

132. "Dies from Blow of Baseball," *New York Times*, June 17, 1932, 3; "Haverford Athlete Hit by Ball, Dies," *Chester (PA) Times*, June 17, 1932, 1.

133. "Local Baseball Player Killed by Pitched Ball," *Bismarck (ND) Tribune*, July 14, 1932, 1; "Jury Finds Klein Death Accidental," *Bismarck (ND) Tribune*, July 15, 1932, 5.

134. "Baseball Injuries Fatal," *Washington Post*, June 3, 1933, 15.

135. "Baseball Player Killed When Hit by Pitched Ball," *Chicago Daily Tribune*, June 5, 1933, 22.

136. "Wild Ball Kills Youth," *New York Times*, May 4, 1934, 6.

137. "Man Hit by Baseball Dies," *New York Times*, July 10, 1934, 19.

138. "Pampa Shortstop Fatally Injured," *San Antonio (TX) Express*, July 23, 1934, 9.

139. "Wild Pitch Kills Montana Ballplayer," *Helena (MT) Daily Independent*, October 7, 1935, 6.

140. "Brooklyn Man Dies of Baseball Injury," *New York Times*, June 29, 1936, 16.

141. "Baseball Game Fatal to Youth," *Fayetteville (AR) Daily Democrat*, April 19, 1937, 1.

142. "Hit by Pitched Ball, Dies," *New York Times*, August 27, 1938, 28.

143. "Baseball Pitch Fatal to Youth," *New York Times*, September 30, 1938, 12.

144. "Baseball Kills Boy," *Washington Post*, March 6, 1939, 4.

145. "Youth, 16, Killed by Pitched Ball in Park Game," *Chicago Daily Tribune*, August 16, 1939, 24.

146. "Dies from Baseball Injury," *New York Times*, April 12, 1941, 24.

147. "Youth Hit by Ball Dies," *New York Times*, May 27, 1941, 25.

148. "Boy, Struck by Baseball, Dies," *New York Times*, June 25, 1941, 23.

149. "Hingham High Star, Hit on Head by Ball, Dies," *Boston Daily Globe*, March 23, 1948, 1.

150. "John S. Argo Jr.," *Commercial Appeal (Memphis, TN)*, June 5, 1948, 18.

151. Bill Nowlin, "Baseball and Death in Iowa," *The National Pastime: A Review of Baseball History* 24 (2004): 107–109.

152. "Baseball Player, Hit by Pitched Ball, Dies," *Los Angeles Times*, November 24, 1948, C2; "Baseball Player Dies After Being Hit on Head by Pitched Ball," *Modesto (CA) Bee*, November 23, 1948, 4.

153. "Donald Walrath, Struck by Ball, Dies of Injuries," *Steubenville (OH) Herald Star*, August 1, 1953, 1.

154. "8-Year-Old Boy Dies of Injury in Sandlot Game," *Washington Post and Times Herald*, June 29, 1955, 29.

155. "Father of Three Killed when Struck by Pitch," *Chicago Daily Tribune*, May 31, 1956, D2; "Sandlotter Dies After Beaning," *Walla Walla (WA) Union-Bulletin*, May 31, 1956, 9.

156. "Pitched Ball Kills Freshman," *The Daily Review (Hayward, CA)*, April 30, 1964, 24.

157. "Batter Dies After Being Hit by Pitch," *Chicago Tribune*, August 23, 1975, C6.

Chapter 2

1. KidSource Online, "CPSC Releases Study of Protective Equipment for Baseball, June 4, 1996," KidSource Online, http://www.kidsource.com/CPSC/baseball.6.10.html (accessed October 10, 2005). The commission analyzed 88 game-related fatalities that occurred between 1973 and 1995. They found that 68 deaths re-

sulted from ball impact, 13 from bat impact. Of the 68 ball-related deaths, 38 were from chest blows, 21 from beanings. The CPSC recommends softer balls and chest protectors for batters as methods for reducing *commotio cordis* fatalities.

2. "Tom Farrell's Pitched Ball Kills P. Mann," *Asheville (NC) Citizen*, July 14, 1927, 1–2. Farrell never made it to the major leagues.

3. "Pitched Ball Kills R. Mann, Macon Infielder," *Macon (GA) Telegraph*, July 14, 1927, 1; "Macon Third Baseman Killed When Hit by Pitched Ball," *Atlanta Constitution*, July 14, 1927, 1; "Macon Pitcher Guards Body of Dead Player," *Washington Post*, July 15, 1927, 15. Mann's older brother, Johnny, who had played for Asheville earlier and Macon the year before, was playing third base for the Wichita Falls (TX) Spudders of the Class A Texas League at the time of fatality. The following season he would appear in six games for the Chicago White Sox.

4. "Pitched Ball Kills R. Mann," 1. Larry Gardner, manager of the Asheville Tourists, must have been especially unnerved by Mann's death. In 1920, he was a teammate of Ray Chapman, and witnessed Carl Mays' fatal beaning of the Cleveland shortstop.

5. "Macon Pitcher Guards Body," 15; "Pitcher Exonerated for Killing Player," *Los Angeles Times*, July 15, 1927, 11.

6. "Killed by a Pitched Ball," *Chicago Daily Tribune*, June 2, 1897, 4.

7. "Death on the Diamond," *Washington Post*, May 7, 1899, 2.

8. "Killed by Baseball," *Washington Post*, August 27, 1899, 10.

9. "Heart Stopped by Swift Ball," *Atlanta Constitution*, April 14, 1903, 9.

10. "Killed in a Baseball Game," *New York Times*, July 26, 1903, 9.

11. "Killed by a Pitched Ball," *Chicago Daily Tribune*, May 2, 1905, 1.

12. "Nearby Happenings," *Van Wert (OH) Daily Bulletin*, September 2, 1905, 5; "A Blow in the Stomach Kills a Boy," *Democratic Standard (Coshocton, OH)*, September 8, 1905, 7.

13. "Boy Killed in Game of Ball with Friends," *Lincoln (NE) Evening News*, May 28, 1906, 14.

14. "Player Killed by Pitched Ball," *Allentown (PA) Democrat*, August 29, 1906, 2.

15. "Killed by Pitched Ball," *Washington Post*, May 27, 1907, 1.

16. "Killed by Pitched Ball," *New York Times*, June 9, 1907, 2.

17. "Pitched Ball Kills Player," *Washington Post*, May 29, 1908, 4.

18. "Killed by Pitched Ball," *Washington Post*, July 6, 1908, 6.

19. "Boy Killed by Pitched Ball," *Chicago Daily Tribune*, June 1, 1909, 2.

20. "Killed by a Pitched Ball," *Chicago Daily Tribune*, July 28, 1909, 11.

21. "Eugene Swinbank, 17 Years Old, Fatally Hit Near Heart," *Chicago Daily Tribune*, September 27, 1909, 3; "Ball Kills the Player," *Quincy (IL) Daily Herald*, September 27, 1909, 1.

22. "Ball Player Killed," *Los Angeles Times*, April 19, 1910, 16.

23. "Thrown Ball Kills Boy," *New York Times*, July 22, 1912, 7.

24. "Fort Worth, Texas," *New York Times*, June 2, 1914, 1.

25. "Pitched Ball Kills Player," *Chicago Daily Tribune*, July 5, 1914, B1.

26. "Death Result of Being Hit by Base Ball," *Litchfield (IL) News-Herald*, July 17, 1914, 4; "Funeral Saturday Morning," *Litchfield (IL) News-Herald*, July 18, 1914, 2.

27. "Three Victims Added to Toll of Baseball," *Chicago Daily Tribune*, May 24, 1915, 10.

28. "Wild Pitch Kills Player," *Evansville (IN) Courier*, June 2, 1915, 1.

29. "Baseball Kills Boy Player," *Washington Post*, April 24, 1916, 7.

30. "Pitched Ball Kills Young Married Man," *Detroit News*, May 22, 1916, 14.

31. "Boy Killed by Pitched Ball," *Washington Post*, May 25, 1916, 9.

32. "Captain of Prep Nine Killed by Pitched Ball," *Chicago Daily Tribune*, May 31, 1917, 13.

33. "Baltimore Sandlotter Killed in Ball Game," *Washington Post*, May 30, 1922, 10.

34. "Ball Player Dies of Injury," *Washington Post*, October 8, 1923, 5.

35. "Killed by Pitched Ball as 2,000 Look On; Veteran Struck Over Heart in Sunday Game," *New York Times*, June 15, 1925, 3; "Clears Pithcer [sic] of Batter's Death," *New York Times*, June 16, 1925, 26.

36. "Player Killed by Pitched Ball," *New York Times*, June 25, 1927, 13.

37. "High School Ball Player Is Killed by Pitched Ball," *Chicago Daily Tribune*, April 21, 1933, 25.

38. "Youth Killed by Pitched Ball," *New York Times*, August 29, 1938, 4.

39. "Batter Killed by Pitched Ball in Park Game," *Chicago Daily Tribune*, May 19, 1941, 22.

40. "Haynesville Youth Killed by Baseball," *Shreveport (LA) Times*, August 19, 1951, 1.

41. "Varnville Seventh Grader Killed When Hit by Ball," *The State (Columbia, SC)*, April 20, 1955, 8A; "Pitched Ball Kills Student at Varnville," *News and Courier (Charleston, SC)*, April 20, 1955, 11A. Some news accounts report that he was struck on the chest by a batted ball. See "Batted Ball Kills Boy," *The News (Newport, RI)*, April 20, 1955, 10.

42. "Boy, 13, Killed by Pitch When Struck on Chest," *Chicago Daily Tribune*, August 1, 1956, B2.

43. "State Elks Golf Tourney Opens Saturday at Hinton," *Charleston (WV) Gazette*, May 24, 1960, 12; "Baseball Player, 16, Dies," *New York Times*, May 24, 1960, 46.

44. "Little Leaguer Struck in Chest, Killed by Ball," *Los Angeles Times*, May 19, 1961, B1; "500 Attend Funeral of Little League Victim," *Los Angeles Times*, May 21, 1961, FA.

45. "Star Player, 13, Dies when Struck by Pitch," *Los Angeles Times*, June 17, 1965, 3; Jerry Cohen, "Family Grieves over Star Player's Death," *Los Angeles Times*, June 18, 1965, SG8; "Pony Leaguers Weep at Funeral of Teammate," *Los Angeles Times*, June 20, 1965, E4.

46. "Los Banos Little Leaguer Is Hit by Baseball, Dies," *Fresno (CA) Bee*, May 19, 1970, 1.

47. "Boy, 12, Killed During Game of Baseball," *Chicago Tribune*, June 26, 1970, E2.

48. "Pitched Ball Kills Little Leaguer," *South Bend (IN) Tribune*, June 19, 1980, 1.

49. Kathleen Ovack, "Little Leaguer Killed by Pitch," *St. Petersburg (FL) Times*, March 19, 1990, 1B; Kathleen Ovack and Bill Duryea, "Family, Ballplayers Struggle with Little Leaguer's Death," *St. Petersburg (FL) Times*, March 20, 1990, 1B.

50. "Boy Killed in Baseball Mishap," *New York Times*, June 29, 1994, B3.

51. "Quick Hits," *San Antonio (TX) Express-News*, February 28, 1998, 2C; "Funeral Arrangements Made for Laredo Students, Coach," *San Antonio (TX) Express-News*, March 1, 1998, 4C.

52. "Boy, 13, Dies After Baseball Hits Chest," *Columbus Dispatch*, May 26, 1999, 4B; Doug Alden, "In a Fraction of a Heartbeat, Freak Accident Kills Young Ballplayers," *Associated Press State and Local Wire*, July 4, 1999.

53. Chris Reinolds and Brenden Sager, "Baseball to Chest Claims Boy's Life," *Atlanta Journal-Constitution*, May 11, 2003, 1C; Bill Montgomery and Brenden Sager, "Baseball to Chest Claims Boy's Life," *Cox News Service*, May 10, 2003.

54. "Teen Dies After Being Hit by Pitch in Youth Baseball Game," *Associated Press State and Local Wire*, September 22, 2003; "Boy Hit by Pitch Died of Rare Heart Occurrence, Coroner Says," *Associated Press State and Local Wire*, September 23, 2003.

55. "A Catcher Killed by a Ball," *New York Times*, June 1, 1890, 2.

56. "Died from Injury," *Daily Kennebec Journal (Augusta, ME)*, June 19, 1905, 1.

57. "Hit by Pitched Ball; Dies,"

Chicago Daily Tribune, July 26, 1906, 4.

58. "Pitched Ball Kills a Boy," *Chicago Daily Tribune*, August 17, 1909, 4.

59. "Skull Fractured by Ball," *Boston Daily Globe*, July 26, 1915, 13.

60. "Baseball Injury Fatal to Youth," *Washington Post*, May 20, 1916, 9.

61. "Baseball Kills a Boy as He Misses Curve," *New York Times*, May 10, 1927, 29; "Cleared of Boy's Death," *New York Times*, May 11, 1927, 28.

62. "Struck by Baseball, Player, 16, Is Killed," *Washington Post*, June 13, 1927, 1.

Chapter 3

1. Robert Kemp Adair, *The Physics of Baseball*, 2nd ed. (New York: Harper Perennial, 1994), 33, 56.

2. "Rookie Killed When Baseball Hits His Chest," *Ogden (UT) Standard Examiner*, June 30, 1951, 1; Les Goates, "Twin Falls Player Dies After Being Hit by Thrown Ball," *Sporting News*, July 11, 1951, 40; "Player Killed as Thrown Ball Hits Above Heart," *Chicago Daily Tribune*, June 30, 1951, B2.

3. "Baseball Listed Cause of Death," *Ogden (UT) Standard Examiner*, July 1, 1951, 1; "Physician Rules Thrown Baseball Killed Athlete," *Chicago Daily Tribune*, July 1, 1951, A3.

4. "Killed by a Base Ball," *Valdosta (GA) Times*, August 29,1899, 3.

5. "Killed by a Baseball," *New York Times*, May 24, 1885, 7.

6. "Killed on Ball Field," *Washington Post*, June 25, 1903, 2.

7. "Threw the Ball That Killed Him," *New York Times*, May 28, 1906, 9.

8. "Catcher Killed by Muffed Ball," *Philadelphia Inquirer*, July 2, 1906, 2; "Inquest for Base Ball Victims," *Philadelphia Inquirer*, July 4, 1906, 2.

9. "Was Killed Playing Ball," *Atlanta Constitution*, March 20, 1908, 11.

10. "Fatally Hurt at Baseball," *Philadelphia (PA) Inquirer*, July 28, 1910, 4.

11. "Boy Killed by Brother," *Washington Post*, September 8, 1910, 2.

12. "Baseball Game Proves Fatal to S. A. Boy," *Santa Ana (CA) Daily Register*, April 14, 1924, 3.

13. "Pitcher Solomon Dies," *Oneonta (NY) Star*, August 25, 1925, 8.

14. "Boy at Play Killed by Baseball," *New York Times*, March 24, 1926, 26.

15. "Boy Hit by Baseball Dies," *New York Times*, June 28, 1934, 12.

16. "Boy, 6, Killed as Baseball Strikes Chest," *Los Angeles Times*, May 23, 1949, 16.

17. "10 Year Old Boy Killed When Hit by Baseball," *Chicago Daily Tribune*, June 12, 1951, B4; "Youngster Killed by Thrown Baseball," *Times Record (Troy, NY)*, June 12, 1951, 25.

18. "Baseball Strikes, Kills State Youth," *Tulsa (OK) Daily World*, April 3, 1952, 1.

19. "Chad Pickens, Injured Weir Player, Dies," *Steubenville (OH) Herald Star*, May 14, 1955, 1.

20. "Boy, 7, Hit by Ball, Is 2d Baseball Fatality," *Washington Post and Times Herald*, April 19, 1957, A1.

21. "Baseball Kills Boy, 7," *New York Times*, July 27, 1958, 48.

22. "Sailor Killed by Baseball," *New York Times*, May 6, 1962, 83.

23. "Baseball Kills Youth," *Daily Review (Hayward, CA)*, June 18, 1971, 24.

24. Tanya Eiserer, "Boy Dies in Freak Accident," *Omaha World Herald*, June 28, 1999, 9.

25. "Boy's Organs Donated After Death from Rare Heart Syndrome," *Associated Press State and Local Wire*, May 8, 2002.

26. "Killed While Running Bases," *Kansas City (MO) Star*, August 14, 1903, 1.

27. "Killed by Baseball," *Washington Post*, June 13, 1906, 3.

28. "Blow from Ball Fatal," *Washington Post*, June 26, 1913, 9.

29. "Boy Is Killed by Thrown Ball in One-a-Cat Game," *St. Louis Post-Dispatch*, February 21, 1915, pt. 3, 1.

30. Bill Nowlin, "Baseball and Death in Iowa," *The National Pastime: A Review of Baseball History* 24 (2004): 107–109; "Victim of Ball Game Tragedy," *Cedar Rapids (IA) Gazette*, May 4, 1949, 14.

31. "Baseball Strikes Boy, Kills Him," *Courier Journal (Louisville, KY)*, July 16, 1961, 17.

32. "Ray Eaton, 32, Dies in Baseball Accident," *Kentucky New Era (Hopkinsville, KY)*, May 10, 1965, 1–2.

33. "Baseball Injury Fatal to Boy," *New York Times*, May 21, 1967, S12.

34. "Queens Ballplayer, 15, Killed by a Thrown Ball," *New York Times*, July 7, 1967, 19.

35. "Death Takes Big Day from Little Leaguer," *Chicago Tribune*, June 23, 1978, 3.

36. "High School Player Dies After Being Struck by a Thrown Ball," *Associated Press State and Local Wire*, March 28, 2000.

Chapter 4

1. David Plaut, ed., *Speaking of Baseball: Quotes and Notes on the National Pastime* (Philadelphia: Running Press, 1993), 75.

2. Richard M. Greenwald, Lori H. Penna, and Joseph J. Crisco, "Differences in Batted Ball Speed with Wood and Aluminum Baseball Bats: A Batting Cage Study," *Journal of Applied Biomechanics* 17 (2001): 241–252.

3. Rochelle L. Nicholls and others, "Bat Kinematics in Baseball: Implications for Ball Exit Velocity and Player Safety," *Journal of Applied Biomechanics* 19 (2003), 283–94; "The Bat's Too Good," *New Scientist* 179, no. 2410 (August 30, 2003): 39.

4. Morris, 431–442. Oddly, the *Official Rules of Major League Baseball* still do not mandate the use of a mask, chest protector, or shin guards. The only requirements are in Rule 1.12, which regulates the dimensions of the catcher's mitt, and Rule 1.16 (d), which states that "all catchers shall wear a catcher's protective helmet, while fielding their position" (*Official Rules of Major League Baseball* (Chicago: Triumph Books, 2006), 12–15).

5. "Killed at the Bat," *New York Times*, September 6, 1881, 2.

6. "Ball Player Killed," *Dallas Morning News*, July 6, 1902, 8.

7. "Killed by a Batted Ball," *Washington Post*, April 9, 1905, 8.

8. "Ball from the Bat Kills Boy Pitcher," *New York Times*, May 20, 1910, 1.

9. "Pitcher Dies from Injuries," *Indianapolis Star*, June 26, 1910, 17.

10. "Baseball Kills Boy," *Washington Post*, July 29, 1911, 1.

11. "Batted Ball Kills Boy," *Washington Post*, June 7, 1921, 3.

12. "Boy, 8, Killed by Baseball," *New York Times*, June 12, 1932, 3.

13. "Man Killed When Hit by Baseball Batted by Nephew in Family Game," *St. Louis Post-Dispatch*, May 22, 1950, 7A.

14. "Houston Boy Killed While Playing Ball," *Galveston (TX) News*, July 5, 1950, 18.

15. "Baseball Injury," *City News Service, Inc.*, June 23, 1997; "Baseball Death,: *City News Service, Inc.*, June 24, 1997.

16. John Nicholas, "9-Year-Old Girl Dies Playing Ball with Friends," *South Bend (IN) Tribune*, August 14, 1999, A1.

17. Bob Anez, "Battle Over Baseball Bats Reaches Legislature," *Associated Press State and Local* Wire, February 17, 2005; Todd Wilkinson, "In Little League Batter's Box, It's Safety Vs. Homers," *Christian Science Monitor*, April 22, 2005, 1.

18. Mike Cronin, "Tears and Laughter for a Fallen Friend," *Salt Lake (UT) Tribune*, August 31, 2004, C1.

19. Marissa Alanis, "Teammates of Grapevine Player Wait and Pray," *Dallas Morning News*, February 24, 2007; Marissa Alanis and Brandon George, "Grapevine Teen's Organs Donated," *Dallas Morning News*, February 27, 2007; Marissa Alanis, "District Makes Helmets Required in Batting Cages," *Dallas Morning News*, February 28, 2007.

20. "Killed on the Ball Field," *New York Times*, July 11, 1887, 1.

21. "Killed by a Foul Tip," *Chicago Daily Tribune*, September 22, 1895, 7.

22. "Catcher Conner Killed by a Foul Ball," *Washington Post*, May 31, 1899, 9.

23. "Foul Tip Killed Catcher Snyder," *Pittsburgh Post*, August 5, 1900, 2; "Young Catcher Killed in a Game," *Pittsburgh Press*, August 5, 1900, 1.

24. "Returns Pitched Ball and Falls Dead," *Chicago Daily Tribune*, August 1, 1905, 1.

25. "Killed in Baseball Game," *Boston Daily Globe*, May 28, 1908, 4.

26. "Foul Tip Fatal," *Washington Post*, June 1, 1908, 8.

27. "Foul Tip Kills Catcher," *Washington Post*, September 6, 1910, 11.

28. "Boy Killed by Batted Ball," *Public Ledger (Philadelphia)*, August 16, 1911, 2; "Boy, Struck by Ball, Is Instantly Killed," *Philadelphia Inquirer*, August 16, 1911, 1. Some national papers misspell the victim's name, calling him Greenwood, and mistakenly report that he was watching the game near the catcher. See "Foul Tip Kills Youngster," *Chicago Daily Tribune*, August 16, 1911, 13.

29. "Foul Tip Kills Ball Player," *Chicago Daily Tribune*, June 10, 1912, 11.

30. "Golf Ball Kills Boy of 12," *Washington Post*, May 17, 1913, 1.

31. "Foul Tip Kills a Catcher," *New York Times*, June 1, 1913, 9.

32. "Pittsburgh's First Diamond Death Due to Foul Tip," *Chicago Daily Tribune*, April 24, 1919, 19; "Man Killed, Boy Hurt by Base Balls," *Tyrone (PA) Daily Herald*, April 25, 1919, 1.

33. "Boy Killed in Baseball Game," *New York Times*, May 24, 1938, 11.

34. "Foul Tip Kills Brother," *New York Times*, July 15, 1939, 3.

35. "Burial Monday for Boy Killed in Baseball Game," *Chicago Tribune*, June 26, 1978, 15; "Second Baseball Death in Chicago," *Post-Standard (Syracuse, NY)*, June 26, 1978, 1.

36. "Blow by a Baseball Caused Boy's Death," *Indiana (PA) Evening Gazette*, December 11, 1981, 17.

37. "Killed by a Batted Ball," *Los Angeles Times*, March 29, 1891, 9.

38. "Killed by a Baseball," *New York Times*, October 28, 1894, 17.

39. "Killed by Batted Ball, *Washington Post*, June 11, 1902, 1.

40. "Man Struck by Baseball Dies as Crowd Watches," *Chicago Daily Tribune*, September 18, 1904, 1.

41. "Killed by a Batted Ball," *New York Times*, July 30, 1905, 1.

42. "Ball Player," *Steubenville (PA) Herald Star*, May 17, 1909, 1; "Player Killed by Batted Ball," *Pittsburgh Press*, May 16, 1909, 2.

43. "Ball Kills Boy," *Atlanta Constitution*, April 16, 1913, 8.

44. "Dies After Baseball Game," *New York Times*, April 13, 1914, 1.

45. "Baseball Victim Dies," *Philadelphia Inquirer*, May 26, 1914, 6.

46. "Batted Baseball Kills a Boy," *Chicago Daily Tribune*, June 8, 1914, 2.

47. "Batted Ball Kills Mineral Point Man," *Wisconsin State Journal (Madison, WI)*, July 2, 1914, 6.

48. "Hit on Arm by Ball; Dies from Effects," *Fort Wayne (IN) Daily News*, September 21, 1914, 2.

49. "Hit by Ball — Dies," *Republican-News (Hamilton, OH)*, May 26, 1915, 7.

50. "Young London Ball Player Is Killed," *Columbus Evening Dispatch*, July 12, 1915, 9.

51. "Ohio Boy First Victim of 1919 Baseball Injury," *Chicago Daily Tribune*, March 20, 1919, 13.

52. "Batted Ball Kills Schoolboy," *New York Times*, March 20, 1933, 32.

53. "Batted Ball Kills Boy," *New York Times*, March 26, 1950, 51.

54. "Batted Ball Kills Little Leaguer," *Los Angeles Times*, June 8, 1957, A6.

55. "Player Killed by Line Drive at Ball Game," *Dallas Morning News*, May 14, 1958, 1.

56. "Youth Killed by Baseball," *New York Times*, March 18, 1966, 80.

57. "Little Leaguer, 10, Hit by Pop Fly, Dies," *Los Angeles Times*, May 9, 1968, E11; "Youngster Dies in Baseball Game," *Walla Walla (WA) Union-Bulletin*, May 8, 1968, 21.

58. Tony Bartelme, "Beaufort Youth Killed by Ball," *News and Courier (Charleston, SC)*, June 1, 1990, 1–2.

59. "News Briefs," *Birmingham News*, April 20, 1995, 4B.

60. Jessica Dayton, "Child's Death Ruled Accidental," *Copley News Service*, July 23, 1998.

61. Tracy Connor, "Baseball Kills L.I. Boy, 7, in Backyard," *New York Post*, June 12, 2000, 16; "Boy, 7, Killed in Backyard Baseball Game," *Associated Press State and Local Wire*, June 12, 2000.

62. Clint Williams, "Boy, 7, a Rare Statistic in Death," *Atlanta Journal-Constitution*, May 21, 2002, 1B.

63. "Killed by Batted Ball," *Washington Post*, May 2, 1904, 3.

64. "Killed on the Bases," *Boston Daily Globe*, March 28, 1910, 6.

65. "Boy Killed by Batted Ball," *Washington Post*, April 29, 1910, 3.

66. "Chadds Ford Youth, Struck by Ball, Dies," *Chester (PA) Times*, June 19, 1930, 1.

67. "A Death on the Field," *St. Louis Globe-Democrat*, December 18, 1887, 25.

68. "Joseph Marsh Killed," *North Adams (MA) Evening Transcript*, September 4, 1900, 6.

69. "Obituary," *Bristol (RI) Phoenix*, August 25, 1903, 3.

70. "Killed in Ball Game," *Times-Dispatch (Richmond, VA)*, August 22, 1909, 8D.

71. "Boy, 17, Hit by Baseball, Dies of Coronary," *Los Angeles Times*, December 1, 1976, 3.

72. "Killed Playing Baseball," *Boston Daily Globe*, March 29, 1910, 4; "James C. Allen," *Berks and Schuylkill Journal (Reading, PA)*, April 2, 1910, 2.

73. "Killed by Batted Ball," *Atlanta Constitution*, October 25, 1910, 4.

74. "Foul Ball Is Fatal to Baseball Player," *Atlanta Constitution*, June 9, 1914, 6.

75. "Killed by Batted Ball," *Idaho (Idaho Falls) Register*, October 16, 1914, 1.

76. "Boy, Hurt in Baseball Game, Dies at Hospital," *Richmond Times-Dispatch*, April 19, 1915, 10.

77. "Skull Broken by Ball," *Commercial Appeal (Memphis, TN)*, July 11, 1915, 10; "Obituaries," *Commercial Appeal (Memphis, TN)*, July 14, 1915, 7.

78. "Foul Kills Baseball Player in Grant Park," *Chicago Daily Tribune*, June 6, 1920, A6.

79. "Blow on Head by Batted Ball Fatal to Boy of 14," *Chicago Daily Tribune*, March 29, 1937, 19.

80. "Blow Is Fatal to Ballplayer," *Knickerbocker News (Albany, NY)*, July 23, 1938, 8A.

81. "Fatal Game of Base-Ball," *New York Times*, May 3, 1874, 10.

82. "Accidentally Killed by His Comrade," *New York Times*, July 10, 1878, 5.

83. "Batted to Death," *Boston Daily Globe*, July 13, 1879, 1.

84. "Killed by a Baseball Bat," *New York Times*, May 31, 1888, 2.

85. "Fatally Hurt at Baseball," *New York Times*, June 12, 1889, 8.

86. "Slide for Home Plate Fatal," *Chicago Daily Tribune*, May 27, 1906, 2.

87. "Blow by Bat Proves Fatal," *Ottumwa (IA) Courier*, June 17, 1907, 6.

88. "Boy Killed by Baseball Bat," *Chicago Daily Tribune*, May 21, 1909, 4.

89. "Baseball Catcher Is Killed," *Chicago Daily Tribune*, June 19, 1910, 4.

90. "Another Baseball Victim," *Los Angeles Times*, July 27, 1910, 16.

91. "Student Dies from a Blow," *New York Times*, February 7, 1914, 20.

92. "Student's Death Accidental," *Grass Lake (MI) News*, April 22, 1915, 1.

93. "Three Victims Added to Toll of Baseball," *Chicago Daily Tribune*, May 24, 1915, 10.

94. "Bat Slips; Kills Student," *Washington Post*, March 29, 1921, 3.

95. "Slip of Baseball Bat Kills Player," *New York Times*, August 10, 1927, 8.

96. "Blow with Bat Causes Death," *Los Angeles Times*, April 26, 1932, 4.

97. "Boy Bleeds to Death from Injury in Playing Baseball," *Chicago Daily Tribune*, May 8, 1933, 1.

98. "Death Held Accident," *Los Angeles Times*, March 28, 1934, 4.

99. "Youth Struck with Bat During Ball Game Dies," *Washington Post*, October 25, 1936, M12.

100. "Struck by Bat, Player Dies," *New York Times*, June 15, 1939, 16.

101. "Bat Slips from Player, Kills W. Va. Youth," *Washington Post*, May 15, 1945, 3.

102. "Ball Player, 6, Killed," *New York Times*, June 20, 1947, 3.

103. "Inquest to Be Held Today in Death of Boy Struck by Bat," *Chicago Daily Tribune*, March 16, 1949, 26.

104. "Hit on Chest by Ball Bat, Boy of 7 Dies," *Chicago Daily Tribune*, July 12, 1955, 3.

105. "Man Killed in Baseball Game," *New York Times*, July 30, 1962, 6.

Chapter 5

1. George Vass, "Mayhem on the Grass," *Baseball Digest*, July 1966, 35.

2. Barry P. Boden, Robin Tacchetti, and Fred O. Mueller, "Catastrophic Injuries in High School and College Baseball Players," *American Journal of Sports Medicine* 32, no. 5 (July-August 2004): 1191–92. The authors divided catastrophic injuries into three categories: fatal, nonfatal ("permanent neurologic functional disability"), and serious ("no significant permanent functional disability"). They also suggest that catastrophic collision injuries could be reduced by better training in calling for fly balls, stricter enforcement of the rules prohibiting "malicious and intentional contact," and either the outright prohibition of head-first sliding or better training in

sliding around a fielder. See pages 1190 and 1194.

3. One of the Old-Timers, "Players Do Not Thrill Fans as in Olden Days: Henke an Example," *Atlanta Constitution*, December 19, 1915, A3. Henke's first name is sometimes reported as "Lewis" or "Lew." Marshall D. Wright, *The Southern Association in Baseball, 1885–1961* (Jefferson, NC: McFarland, 2002), 6. Charles Levis, who played for both Chattanooga and Macon that season, also had six home runs.

4. "The National Game," *Atlanta Constitution*, August 15, 1885, 5.

5. "Poor Henke," *Atlanta Constitution*, August 16, 1885, 9. It is possible that Marr, if he was wearing a glove, was unfamiliar with it. While first basemen began using fingerless gloves without padding around 1875, unpadded fingerless gloves for other fielders were introduced slowly from 1877 to 1882. (It was not until the late 1880s that padded gloves with fingers became popular.) Since outfielders were one of the last to start using gloves, it is conceivable that Marr, an outfielder (and sometimes catcher), may not have used a glove while playing his usual left-field position. Although the news account did not comment on it one way or another, it did report that "the ball coming with extraordinary swiftness bounced out of his *hands*" (authors' emphasis). Marr went on to a four-year major league career as a utility infielder and outfielder, playing briefly with the Cincinnati Red Stockings in 1886, and then with the Columbus Solons and the Cincinnati Reds from 1889 to 1891. For a brief history of the glove, see Stephen Wong, *Smithsonian Baseball: Inside the World's Finest Collections* (New York: Smithsonian Books, 2005), 38–42.

6. "Poor Henke," 9.

7. "For the Benefit of Henke's Family," *Atlanta Constitution*, August 18, 1885, 5. The season ended with Atlanta in first place, Augusta second, and Nashville third.

8. "'Red' Herbert Knocked Out," *Dayton (OH) Daily News*, July 8, 1904, 2nd edition, sec. 2, 2.

9. "Came from the Rear and Won," *Dayton (OH) Daily News*, July 9, 1904, 2nd edition, sec. 2, 2; "'Red' Herbert Was Popular," *Dayton (OH) Daily News*, July 11, 1904, 1st edition, 4.

10. The newspaper reported that the doctors believed Herbert would have eventually died from the typhus fever even if the collision had not occurred. "'Red' Herbert Was Popular," 4; "Benefit Game Talked Of," *Dayton (OH) Daily News*, July 12, 1904, 2nd

edition, 8; "Herbert's Widow," *Dayton (OH) Daily News*, July 14, 1904, 2nd edition, 8.

11. "Firecracker League," *Fort Wayne (IN) Daily News*, May 21, 1909, 15; "Third Sacker Is Badly Hurt," *Kokomo (IN) Daily Tribune*, May 24, 1909, 8. Ironically, Smith probably should have been scratched for that game. He had badly twisted his ankle fielding a ground ball during the previous day's game, and the team physician had recommended that he rest it for several days.

12. "Third Sacker," 8. Although Bluffton tied the game at two apiece that inning and went ahead by a run the next, Kokomo eventually won the game 4 to 3 with a run in their half of the ninth.

13. "Death of Leo Smith," *Kokomo (IN) Daily Tribune*, May 26, 1909, 1; "Funeral of Leo Smith," *Kokomo (IN) Daily Tribune*, May 27, 1909, 7; "Game Not Allowed," *Kokomo (IN) Daily Tribune*, May 28, 1909, 8.

14. "A Sad Loss," *Sports Illustrated*, September 2, 1974, 11.

15. Bob Teitlebaum, "Salem Swings with Its .400 Dominican Duo," *The Sporting News*, June 8, 1974, 41; "Salem Outfielder Dies After On-Field Collision," *Sporting News*, September 7, 1974, 43.

16. Bob Teitlebaum, "Voice on Phone — 'Alfredo's Dead,'" *Sporting News*, September 7, 1974, 43.

17. "Collision Kills Young Star," *Charlotte (NC) Observer*, August 24, 1974, 1B, 4B.

18. "Voice On Phone," 43.

19. "The Dark Side of Ball Playing," *Poughkeepsie (NY) Daily Eagle*, July 9, 1877, 3; "Sad News — Death of Quigley the Ball Player," *Poughkeepsie (NY) Daily Eagle*, August 13, 1877, 3; "Inquest," *Poughkeepsie (NY) Daily Eagle*, August 14, 1877, 3; "Dan Brouthers Dies at 74; Baseball Slugger of '80's," *Poughkeepsie (NY) Eagle News*, August 3, 1932, 1–2; Joseph M. Overfield, "Dennis Joseph Brouthers," in *Baseball's First Stars: The Second Volume*, edited by Frederick Ivor-Campbell (Cleveland, OH: Society for American Baseball Research, 1996), 11–12.

20. "Killed at a Ball Game," *Washington Post*, September 10, 1895, 3.

21. "Fatal Ball Game," *Wisconsin State Journal (Madison)*, April 24, 1899, 1.

22. "Baseball Fatality," *Los Angeles Times*, April 30, 1901, 4.

23. "Young Hoge Has Lockjaw Attack," *Wheeling (WV) Intelligencer*, September 17, 1906, 1; "John Hoge Dead," *Wheeling (WV) Intelligencer*, September 20, 1906, 1.

24. "2 Run for Baseball; 1 Killed,"

Chicago Daily Tribune, October 11, 1906, 1; "Foot Ball Player Killed," *Moberly (MO) Weekly Democrat*, October 12, 1906, 1.

25. "Mt. Ayr," *Cedar Rapids (IA) Republican*, April 28, 1909, 3.

26. "Dies of Ball Game Injury," *New York Times*, July 7, 1909, 4.

27. "Boy's Death Due to Baseball Injuries," *Boston Daily Globe*, May 9, 1913, 9.

28. "Ball Player Dies of Broken Neck," *Daily Picayune (New Orleans)*, June 18, 1913, 3.

29. "Deaths and Funerals," *Wichita (KS) Eagle*, May 20, 1914, 9.

30. "Killed Playing Ball," *Streator (IL) Daily Free Press*, June 5, 1914, 2.

31. "Thomas Jackson," *Monticellonian (Monticello, AR)*, May 13, 1915, 5.

32. "Semi-Pro Player Dies After Game," *Peoria (IL) Daily Journal*, August 30, 1915, 14; "Dead Ball Player to Be Buried Wednesday," *Peoria (IL) Daily Journal*, August 31, 1915, 4.

33. "G. M. C. Athlete's Injuries Fatal," *Atlanta Constitution*, April 17, 1922, 9.

34. "Fatal Slide to Second," *New York Times*, June 11, 1923, 2; Obituary, *Daily Princetonian (Princeton, NJ)*, June 14, 1923, 2.

35. "High School Boy Killed," *Yorkville (York, SC) Enquirer*, May 13, 1924, 4; "Frank Caldwell," *Yorkville (York, SC) Enquirer*, May 16, 1924, 5.

36. "Ball Game Injury Causes Boy's Death," *Pittsburgh Press*, May 16, 1927, 8.

37. "Killed Playing Baseball," *New York Times*, October 12, 1936, 17.

38. "4 Dead, 5 Injured in Area Accidents on Eve of Holiday," *Rochester (NY) Democrat and Chronicle*, May 31, 1937, 15.

39. "Fatal Accident," *Webster (SD) Journal*, August 26, 1937, 1.

40. "Felon Is Killed in Folsom Ball Game," *Sacramento (CA) Bee*, May 5, 1939, 14.

41. "Injuries Fatal to Ball Player," *Detroit News*, May 31, 1939, 24.

42. "Young Menasha Ball Player Is Fatally Injured," *Appleton (WI) Post-Crescent*, August 31, 1942, 4; "Takes Life After Being Questioned at Police Office," *Appleton (WI) Post- Crescent*, August 28, 1942, 12.

43. "'Freak' Injury Fatal to Ballplayer, 26," *Buffalo (NY) Evening News*, June 13, 1947, 1.

44. "Baseball Injury Fatal to Boy, 15," *Los Angeles Times*, June 18, 1969, B1.

45. "Boy, 15, Hurt in School Baseball Collision, Dies," *Los Angeles Times*, May 19, 1979, C7.

46. "OSU Slugger Slips in Coma After Collision," *Corvallis (OR) Gazette-Times*, March 3, 1982, 15, 17; "Baseball Player, 19, Dies," *Corvallis (OR) Gazette-Times*, March 5, 1982, 1, 12; "Halbrook Death Termed a 'Freak,'" *Corvallis (OR) Gazette-Times*, March 6, 1982, 7.

47. Eric Sondheimer, "Baseball Player Declared Brain Dead," *Daily News (Los Angeles)*, May 5, 1997.

48. Brian MacQuarrie, "Teen Player Dies After Collision with a Teammate," *Boston Globe*, June 29, 2001, A1; Caroline Louise Cole, "Fund-Raiser to Honor Fallen Ballplayer, *Boston Globe*, June 13, 2002, 8.

Chapter 6

1. "Says Athletes Ruin Men," *Chicago Daily Tribune*, June 13, 1905, 1.

2. James C. Whorton, "'Athlete's Heart': The Medical Debate Over Athleticism, 1970–1920," *Journal of Sport History* 9, no. 1 (Spring 1982): 36.

3. Paul D. Thompson, "Historical Concepts of the Athlete's Heart," *Medicine and Science in Sports and Exercise* 36, no. 3 (March 2004): 365; Whorton, 37.

4. *The Gale Encyclopedia of Medicine*, s.v. "Athletic Heart Syndrome," by John T. Lohr (accessed December 27, 2006).

5. Domenico Corrado, Cristina Basso, and Gaetano Thiene, "Essay: Sudden Death in Young Athletes," *Lancet* 366 (December 17, 2005): S47–S48.

6. Corrado, S47.

7. John Thorn, "Jim Creighton," *The Baseball Biography Project*, http://bioproj.sabr.org/ (accessed March 8, 2006).

8. Unidentified news clipping dated 1911, Jim Creighton Player File, National Baseball Hall of Fame, Cooperstown, NY. According to Tom Shieber at the National Baseball Hall of Fame, Creighton did not hit any home runs during that game.

9. "The National Game," *New York Times*, August 30, 1881, 4. The *New York Times* was engaging more in wishful thinking than in fact. The paper's position seems to have been based almost entirely on its distaste for the game of baseball as evidenced in the concluding statement: "Our experience with the national game of baseball has been sufficiently thorough to convince us that it was in the beginning a sport unworthy of men, and that it is now, in its fully developed state, unworthy of gentlemen. Cricket will probably become as popular here in the course of a few years as it is in England, and we shall be contented to play a game worth playing, even if it is English in its origin, without trying to establish a national game of our own."

10. Thorn; "The Premature Death of Baseball's First Superstar (1862)," in *Early Innings: A Documentary History of Baseball, 1825–1908*, comp. and ed. Dean Sullivan (Lincoln, NE: University of Nebraska Press, 1995), 47–48.

11. Thorn. The authors are indebted to Tom Shieber, senior curator at the National Baseball Hall of Fame, for sharing his research and insight on Creighton's death.

12. Dave Sheinin, "O's Prospect Bechler Dies of Heatstroke; Pitcher, 23, Collapsed in Sunday's Workout," *Washington Post*, February 18, 2003, D1.

13. Sheinin, D1.

14. The lawyer for the manufacturer of the particular brand Bechler was taking, Xenadrine RFA-1, disputed the role ephedra might have played, stating, "The fact that the medical examiner found traces of ephedra in Mr. Bechler's system does not mean that Mr. Bechler died from ephedra. He died from heatstroke." Murray Chass, "Pitcher's Autopsy Lists Ephedra as One Factor," *New York Times*, March 14, 2003, D5; Kevin Kelly, "Orioles Rookie Dies After Workout," *St. Petersburg (FL) Times*, February 18, 2003, 1C.

15. "Heart Attack Causes Death of Marion Baseball Player," *Palladium-Item and Sun Telegram (Richmond, IN)*, May 12, 1948, 1; "Obituary," *The Sporting News*, May 19, 1948, 34.

16. "Heart Attack," 1; "Obituary," 34.

17. Phil Collier, "Death Summons Pad Herb Gorman," *San Diego Union*, April 6, 1953, A14; Jack Murphy, "Wet-Eyed Infielder Offered Assistance," *San Diego Union*, April 6, 1953, A14; "Gorman, Padre Outfielder, Dies During Game," *San Diego Union*, April 6, 1953, A1; "Heart Attack During Game Fatal to Padres' Gorman," *The Sporting News*, April 15, 1953, 34. Gorman showed great promise early on when, as a 19-year-old first baseman on his 1945 San Francisco–based Coast Guard baseball team, he was "believed to be the youngest manager of any service team." See "Youngest Service Pilot Leads Coast Guard Team," *The Sporting News*, May 31, 1945, 11.

18. Gorman's wife said later that although her husband had not been ill, he did tell her he was feeling tired the morning of the game. Collier, A14; "Gorman, Padre Outfielder, Dies," A1.

19. Murphy, A14; "Gorman, Padre Outfielder, Dies," A1; "Heart Attack During Game," 34.

20. Collier, A14.

21. "Heart Attack During Game," 34.

22. "Player Collapses, Dies at Stadium," *Morning Herald (Hagerstown, MD)*, July 3, 1954, 1; "Hagerstown Player Dies on Field After Rapping Hit," *The Sporting News*, July 14, 1954, 52.

23. Smith, who was the first athlete at his Chickamauga, GA, high school to captain the football, basketball, and baseball teams in the same year, had served in the Marines until August 1953. "Player Collapses," 1; "Hagerstown Player Dies," 52.

24. Frank Colley, "Mac Smith's Death Takes All Glory out of Winning Game," *Morning Herald (Hagerstown, MD)*, July 3, 1954, 16.

25. John C. Hoffman, "Howell Shines After 19 Years in Minors," *The Sporting News*, September 14, 1955, 3; "Howell, Ex-Chisox Hurler, Succumbs to Heart Attack," *The Sporting News*, March 30, 1960, 24.

26. "Howell, Ex-Chisox Hurler," 24; Millard Howell, Certificate of Death, Florida State Board of Health, Bureau of Vital Statistics, March 19, 1960.

27. "Obituaries," *The Sporting News*, May 28, 1990, 39; Chip Wilson and John Glennon, "Rangers Pitcher Collapses," *Gaston (NC) Observer*, May 15, 1990, 1; John Glennon and Chip Wilson, "Rangers Pitcher Romero Dies After Collapse Monday," *Charlotte (NC) Observer*, May 16, 1990, 1C–2C.

28. Glennon and Wilson, "Rangers Pitcher Romero Dies," 1C–2C.

29. Glennon and Wilson, "Rangers Pitcher Romero Dies," 1C–2C.

30. Chip Wilson and John Glennon, "Pitcher's Death Due to Natural Causes," *Gaston (NC) Observer*, June 1, 1990, 9.

31. "Caught the Ball and Died," *New York Times*, October 2, 1904, 1.

32. "Negro Pitcher Drops Dead," *Trenton (NJ) Evening Times*, July 2, 1908, 13; "Pitcher Drops Dead," *Sporting Life*, July 11, 1908, 5.

33. "Ball Player Dies at Game's End," *Chester (PA) Times*, July 26, 1949, 13; Alan J. Pollock, *Barnstorming to Heaven: Syd Pollock and His Great Black Teams* (Tuscaloosa, AL: University of Alabama Press, 2006), 157–159.

34. "Georgia Gossip," *Atlanta Constitution*, September 21, 1883, 2.

35. "Local Brevities," *Detroit Free Press*, March 31, 1889, 18; "Base Ball Killed Him," *Brooklyn Eagle*, April 1, 1889, 4.

36. "Pitcher Drops Dead in the Box," *Chicago Daily Tribune*, July 1, 1895, 1; "'Two More Nails in My Coffin,'" *Fort Wayne (IN) Gazette*, July 2, 1895, 1.

37. "Virginia Obituary," *Washington Post*, May 18, 1905, 4.

38. "Chicago Ball Player Dies in Game," *New York Times*, May 23, 1905, 2.

39. "Fell Dead Playing Ball," *Atlanta Constitution*, April 22, 1908, 9.

40. "Boy Scared to Death by Practical Joker Who Jumped from Bushes," *Pittsburgh (PA) Post*, June 18, 1908, 3.

41. "Pitched Ball That Won and Then Fell Dead," *Pittsburgh Press*, September 5, 1909, 1; "Striking Out Last Man, Pitcher Falls Dead as Crowd Cheers," *Pittsburgh Sunday Post*, September 5, 1909, 1. When Stauffer's death was reported in the out-of-town papers two days later, many fabricated details were added. According to the *New York Times*, for example, Stauffer was called in to relieve the starting pitcher in the bottom of the ninth inning with the bases full, no one out, and his team leading by just one run. "He dashed into the box," continued the story, "and began to pitch without warming up. A fly to the outfield meant a tied score, and a hit or fumble perhaps the game. Stauffer made the first batter strike out on three pitched balls. It took five pitches to retire the second man. There was wild confusion as he faced the heaviest batter of the Victors [the opposing team]. He made this man swing at three fast ones, and the game was over." With the final out, "the crowd rushed on the field to carry Stauffer off, but as he stepped from the box he clasped his hand over his heart and fell dead." The *Boston Daily Globe* added that "the crowd was still cheering Stauffer when he died." See "Won Ball Game and Died," *New York Times*, September 6, 1909, 1; "Pitches Himself to Death," *Boston Daily Globe*, September 6, 1909, 3.

42. "Dropped Dead After Game," *Boston Daily Globe*, March 24, 1910, 6.

43. "Baseball Fatal to Two; One Hurt," *Cleveland Plain Dealer*, May 30, 1910, 1–2.

44. "Drops Dead Beside Home Plate," *News and Courier (Charleston, SC)*, August 14, 1910, 24.

45. "Pitcher Drops Dead in Box," *Waterloo (IA) Times-Tribune*, April 19, 1914, 8; "Death Due to Heart Disease," *Chicago Daily Tribune*, April 21, 1914, 15.

46. "Dies Playing Baseball," *New York Times*, June 8, 1914, 1.

47. "Soldier Dies in Ball Game," *New York Times*, June 13, 1915, 5.

48. "Dies Running Bases," *New York Times*, June 12, 1921, 9.

49. "Ball Player Stricken, Dies," *Chicago Daily Tribune*, October 12, 1931, 3.

50. "Mike Burke Stricken on Ball Field," *San Mateo (CA) Times*, June 12, 1933, 1; Tay Pay Magilligan, "Great Leader Passes from Game," *San Mateo (CA) Times*, June 12, 1933, 7.

51. "Stanley M. Rees Dies Suddenly," *Lexington (KY) Herald*, August 30, 1937, 1.

52. "'Paddy' Kreitz 'Called Out': Dies in Baseball Game," *The Oregonian (Portland, OR)*, July 21, 1941, sec. 3, 1.

53. "High School Athlete Dies on Ball Field," *Asheville (NC) Citizen*, May 6, 1958, 1.

54. "John F. Jones," *New York Times*, June 13, 1958, 23.

55. "Baseball Player, 9, Dies of Heart Attack," *Washington Times*, May 9, 1993, A12.

56. "Rites Set for 'Nick' Grahma [sic], 19, Who Collapsed While Playing Baseball," *Providence (RI) Journal-Bulletin*, July 22, 1998, 6C.

57. Jennie Tunkieicz, "Boy Who Collapsed Had Enlarged Heart, Report Says," *Milwaukee Journal Sentinel*, May 11, 2000, 3B.

58. Susan Jaffe, "Farewell to Star Player," *Cleveland Plain Dealer*, July 1, 2002, B1.

59. "Coroner: Heart Disease Apparently Killed Teen at Baseball Practice," *Associated Press State and Local Wire*, March 26, 2003.

60. M. K. Guetersloh, "Teen Collapses, Dies Shortly After Ballgame," *The Pantagraph (Bloomington, IL)*, June 10, 2004, A1.

61. Saundra Amrhein, "Alonso Baseball Player Dies After Tryout," *St. Petersburg (FL) Times*, January 20, 2005, 3B; Bill Varian, "For Athlete, Baseball Was Life," *St. Petersburg (FL) Times*, January 22, 2005, 1B.

62. Richard Weir, "Lil' League's Big Tragedy, Boy, 9, Dies at Practice," *Daily News (New York, NY)*, September 29, 2005, 2.

63. "Death of a Base-Ball Player on the Home-Run," *Daily Dispatch (Richmond, VA)*, June 12, 1877, 1.

64. "A Warning to Base-Ball Players," *New York Times*, May 27, 1878, 2; "The Day," *Newport (RI) Daily News*, May 20, 1878, 2.

65. "Ball Player Dies After Getting Overheated," *Birmingham (AL) News*, March 11, 1905, 1.

66. "Drops Dead While Playing Baseball," *Register and Leader (Des Moines, IA)*, July 11, 1905, 10.

67. "Boy Ball Player Strangles," *Register and Leader (Des Moines, IA)*, April 21, 1907, 1. As with the Stauffer case above, McWilliams' death was one that was wildly exaggerated by the national press. According to one contemporary account, McWilliams was catching during a game and choked on the candy while attempting to tag a runner scoring from third: "McWilliams caught the ball, but immediately fell to the ground in a violent fit of strangulation. Help was summoned, but the boy was dead before physicians

could reach his side. The body was removed to the McWilliams home, and a gum-drop was found to be lodged securely in the windpipe." This account was repeated in at least one recent baseball book. See "Choked to Death Playing Ball," *Vicksburg (TN) Evening Post*, April 25, 1907, 1; Joel Zoss and John Bowman, *Diamonds in the Rough: The Untold Story of Baseball* (Chicago: Contemporary Books, 1996), 354–355.

68. "Lightning Kills Joseph J. Howard," *St. Louis Globe-Democrat*, May 25, 1908, 1, 10; "Burial Permits," *St. Louis Globe-Democrat*, May 26, 1908, 10; "Ball Player Dies on Field," *St. Louis Post-Dispatch*, May 25, 1908, 9. This case was also one for which the national press fabricated details. Both the *Washington Post* and the *Chicago Daily Tribune* reported that Perry died while throwing out a runner attempting to steal home. Perry, "anxious to make up for an error...," proclaimed the *Post*, "today put forth so great an effort in a long throw from deep left field to the home plate that he burst a blood vessel and fell dead." The *Tribune*, not to be outdone, added, "The throw was perfect and as the catcher put out the runner Perry fell forward on his face dead." See "Gives Life for a Put-Out," *Washington Post*, May 25, 1908, 9, and "Millionaire Golfer Is Killed by Lightning," *Chicago Daily Tribune*, May 25, 1908, 1.

69. "Too Much Base Ball Causes Boy's Death," *Detroit News*, May 8, 1914, 1.

70. "Middletown Pitcher Drops Dead," *New York Times*, August 1, 1915, S3; "Dies After a Home Run," *New York Times*, August 1, 1915, 15.

71. Corey Taule, "Doctor: Aneurysm, Not Baseball, Led to Boy's Death," *Idaho Falls (ID) Post Register*, May 27, 2000, A1.

Chapter 7

1. "'Shoeless' Tasby Sheds Steel Spikes as Lightning Flashed," *The Sporting News*, July 29, 1959, 10.

2. E. Brian Curran and Ronald L. Holle, "Lightning Fatalities, Injuries, and Damage Reports in the United States from 1959–1994," *NOAA Technical Memorandum NWS SR-193*, October 1997, http://www.nssl.noaa.gov /papers/techmemos/NWS-SR-193/ techmemo-sr193.html (accessed January 23, 2007); Ronald L. Holle, "Number of Lightning Deaths by State from 1995 to 2004," National Weather Service Lightning Safety, June 18, 2005, http://www.lightningsafety. noaa.gov/stats/ 95-04_Deaths_by_

state.pdf (accessed January 23, 2007); Michael Cherington and Carol Vervalin, "Lightning Injuries — Who Is at Greatest Risk?," *Physician and Sportsmedicine* 18, no. 8 (August 1990): 58–61. While most lightning deaths today occur among individuals engaged in sports or recreational activities, this was not always the case. Farmers and others working outdoors comprised the largest category of victims prior to the middle of the last century. See Michael Cherington, "Lightning Injuries in Sports: Situations to Avoid," *Sports Medicine* 31, no. 4 (2001): 301–308.

3. Cherington and Vervalin, 61; Cherington, "Lightning Injuries," 306.

4. "Snakes Break Up the Game," *New York Times*, April 25, 1889, 5; "Snake Bite New Hazard on Tarheel Diamond," *Washington Post*, October 16, 1928, 13.

5. "Baby Black Snake Decides a Pennant," *New York Times*, July 31, 1949, S1.

6. Ryan Finley, "Beesball Game Shortened to Five Innings," *Arizona Daily Star (Tucson, AZ)*, March 25, 2005, A1, A13; Bob Baum, "Swarm Cancels Baseball Game," *Ventura (CA) County Star*, March 25, 2005, 2.

7. "Lightning Kills Crowley Outfielder During Game," *The Sporting News*, June 27, 1951, 18; "Outfielder for Crowley Killed by Bolt," *Alexandria (LA) Daily Town Talk*, June 18, 1951, 1.

8. "Outfielder for Crowley," 1.

9. Some in the crowd speculated that the lightning was attracted to the metal button on the top of Strong's cap. "Outfielder for Crowley," 1, 20; "Lightning Kills Crowley," 18.

10. Mack Owens, "Sports-Specting," *Alexandria (LA) Daily Town Talk*, June 19, 1951, 12; "Lightning Kills Crowley," 18. The impact of the incident led to the cancellation of the following night's game between the same two teams when players refused to take the field after lightning was seen in the area. See "Outfielder for Crowley," 20.

11. "Lightning Kills Player on a Baseball Diamond," *Chicago Daily Tribune*, August 27, 1909, 2; "Ball Player Hit by Electric Bolt, *Atlanta Constitution*, August 27, 1909, 4; Lightning Kills Player," *Washington Post*, August 27, 1909, 8.

12. "Two Ball Players Killed by Lightning," *Richmond Times-Dispatch*, June 22, 1939, 1.

13. "Killed by Lightning," *New York Times*, June 24, 1884, 2.

14. "Destructive Storm Deals Heavy Blow," *Pittsburgh Post*, July 12, 1904, 1, 8; "Bolt Kills Ball Player," *Pittsburgh Press*, July 12, 1904, 5. The local Pittsburgh newspapers differed in

some details of the incident. The *Post* reports that he was the team's left fielder who was due to report shortly to "the New York club of the American [L]eague." The *Press* stated that Jeffries was a pitcher who was scheduled to join the Toronto (Canada) Maple Leafs of the Class A Eastern League a few days later. In either event, he appears to have been a player with considerable talent.

15. "Players Killed by Lightning," *Washington Post*, July 12, 1904, 8.

16. "Base Ball Team Struck by Bolt," *Waterloo (IA) Daily Courier*, July 2, 1907, 6.

17. "Lightning During Game Kills Baseball Player at Willachoochee [sic], Ga.," *Albany (GA) Herald*, July 25, 1920, 1.

18. "Cy Long Killed by Lightning," *Charlotte (NC) Observer*, July 2, 1922, 1; "Lightning Killed Young Cyril Long," *Charlotte (NC) News*, July 2, 1922, 9.

19. "Seventh Day of Heat Sets Record of 87; 5 Die, 8 Overcome," *New York Times*, May 8, 1930, 1; "Lightning Hits Bleacher; 1 Dead," *Logansport (IN) Press*, May 8, 1930, 1.

20. "Lightning Kills Ball Player During Game," *Commercial Appeal (Memphis, TN)*, May 27, 1932, 13.

21. "Lightning Kills Ball Player, Stuns Others at Penn State," *New York Times*, May 30, 1933, 20.

22. "City to Blister Over Week-End," *Detroit News*, July 20, 1935, 1–2.

23. "Bolt Stuns Butler, Leaves Three Dead," *Milwaukee Journal*, August 1, 1945, 1, 3.

24. "Lightning Kills Two Pennsburg Ballplayers," *Morning Call (Allentown, PA)*, August 13, 1947, 1, 5.

25. "Lightning Kills 2 Ballplayers, Panics Crowd," *Washington Post*, August 1, 1949, 1; "Third Ball Player Dies After Lightning Hits During Game," *Chicago Daily Tribune*, August 2, 1949, A6.

26. "Others to Ground," *Steubenville (OH) Herald Star*, August 8, 1949, 1.

27. "Lightning Kills Anaconda Ballplayer Here," *Independent Record (Helena, MT)*, July 3, 1950, 1.

28. "Lightning Kills Boy, 16, at Play in Frankford," *Philadelphia Inquirer Public Ledger*, August 31, 1950, 1, 12.

29. "Death from Sky Strikes Fast at Little Leaguer," *Indianapolis Star*, July 1, 1959, 1.

30. "Lightning Bolt Strikes, Kills Pitcher," *Washington Post*, May 14, 1973, D5; Tom Paegel, "Moist Air from Gulf Brings Rain, Thunder, Lightning," *Los Angeles Times*, May 15, 1973, A3, A20.

31. Robert D. McFadden, "Boy, 8, Is Killed and 5 Girls Are Injured by

Lightning Under Tree in Central Park," *New York Times*, June 17, 1975, 22.

32. "Lightning Kills Baseball Player," *South Bend (IN) Tribune*, June 2, 1980, 1.

33. Tom Demoretcky and Dennis Hevesi, "Ballplayer Killed by Lightning," *Newsday (Long Island, NY)*, August 8, 1984, 3; "Game Near End When Bolt Hit," *Newsday (Long Island, NY)*, August 9, 1984, 3; "League Cancels Season After Fatality," *Newsday (Long Island, NY)*, August 10, 1984, 25. Maria Pichardo, Martinez's mother, sued the North Patchogue Medford Youth Athletic Association and the Eastern Suffolk Baseball Umpires Association "to recover damages for wrongful death and conscious pain and suffering." Pichardo's suit charged the two associations with negligence because they did not call the game when the weather turned threatening. In 1991 the New York Supreme Court's Appellate Division ruled against Pichardo, stating that "by electing to continue to play baseball in weather conditions which were readily apparent (at some point in the game, thunder was heard and some lightning was seen in the distance), the plaintiff's decedent [Martinez] assumed the risks inherent in continued play." Furthermore, this "assumption of the risk" was "voluntary" since "the plaintiff has failed to present any evidence that the decedent was ordered to continue to play or that there existed an economic compulsion or other circumstance which impelled the decedent to continue to play." See *Maria Pichardo, etc., respondent, v. North Patchogue Medford Youth Athletic Assoc., Inc., et al, appellants, et al, defendants*, 172 A.D. 2d 814 (N.Y. Supr. Ct. App. Div., 2d Dept. 1991), http://0-www.lexisnexis.com.library.winthrop.edu:80/universe.

34. "Valdosta State Pitcher Struck, Killed by Lightning During Game," *Associated Press State and Local Wire*, August 10, 1999.

35. "New-Jersey," *New York Times*, July 10, 1869, 8.

36. "Killed While Playing Baseball," *New York Times*, August 8, 1899, 10.

37. "Killed While Playing Baseball," *Washington Post*, April 12, 1902, 8.

38. "Killed by Street Car While Playing Baseball," *Pittsburgh Press*, May 16, 1909, 2.

39. "Skull Fractured Playing Ball," *Philadelphia Inquirer*, July 7, 1909, 2.

40. "Boy Drowned in River While Chasing Ball," *Pittsburgh Press*, July 23, 1909, 10; "Leaps After Baseball Into Allegheny River, Leftfielder Drowns," *Pittsburgh Post*, July 23, 1909, 1.

41. "Funeral Hack Kills," *Washington Post*, September 25, 1909, 2.

42. "4 Drown, 4 Saved in Sunday Boating," *New York Times*, April 25, 1910, 2; "Singular Fatality," *Sporting Life*, May 7, 1910, 3.

43. "Lad, Playing Ball, Killed by Jitney," *Seattle Times*, May 2, 1915, 5.

44. "Two Boys Killed by Autos," *New York Times*, April 6, 1924, 3.

45. "Autos Crush Out 5 Lives; Death Toll in May 77." *Chicago Daily Tribune*, June 2, 1925, 6.

46. "Accident Witnesses Hide in Sanctuary," *Los Angeles Times*, June 19, 1925, 5.

47. "Boy, 10, Breaks Neck at Play," *San Antonio (TX) Express*, March 24, 1927, 1.

48. "Six Die in Day as Result of Auto Accidents," *Chicago Daily Tribune*, August 13, 1928, 5.

49. "Automobile Kills Boy Playing Ball," *New York Times*, August 28, 1928, 9.

50. "Boy, 6, Killed by Auto as He Plays in Street," *Chicago Daily Tribune*, March 3, 1931, 8.

51. "Boy's Baseball Injuries Fatal," *Los Angeles Times*, November 30, 1931, 16.

52. "Engine Kills Boy Playing in Ball Game," *Democrat and Chronicle (Rochester, NY)*, May 14, 1936, 1.

53. "Boy, 6, Killed by Automobile," *New York Times*, August 17, 1939, 22.

54. "Killed in Baseball Game," *New York Times*, August 25, 1942, 18.

55. "Oaklawn Pupil Fatally Hurt While Playing Ball," *Chicago Daily Tribune*, May 19, 1952, C4.

56. "Two Howard College Youths Die in Electrical Accident," *Midland (TX) Reporter-Telegram*, April 1, 1953, 5.

57. "E. Boston Boy Killed; Crashed Into Wall in Sandlot Ball Game," *Boston Globe*, May 10, 1953, 18.

58. "Girl Killed by Auto on South Side," *Chicago Tribune*, July 18, 1972, A6.

Chapter 8

1. Brenda Jo Bredemeir and David L. Shields, "Values and Violence in Sports Today," *Psychology Today* 17 (October 1985): 23, 25–26.

2. Bredemeir and Shields, 29.

3. David B. Huang, Don R. Cherek, and Scott D. Lane, "Laboratory Measurement of Aggression in High School Age Athletes: Provocation in a Nonsporting Context," *Psychological Reports*, 85 (1999): 1261; Chris S. Strobel, David L. Cook, and Carolyn M. Hoffman, "A Preliminary Investigation of Expected Aggression in the Sport of Baseball," *Applied Research in Coaching and Athletics Annual* (1995): 16, 22–23.

4. Alan S. Reifman, Richard P. Larrick, and Steven Fein, "Temper and Temperature on the Diamond: The Heat-Aggression Relationship in Major League Baseball," *Personality and Social Psychology Bulletin*, 17, no. 5 (1991): 580, 585. In another study of HBP incidents, the researcher found that during the 1950s and 1960s when baseball was beginning to integrate, African American batters were hit at a much greater rate than white batters. Fortunately, this appears no longer to be the case. See Thomas A. Timmerman, "Violence and Race in Professional Baseball: Getting Better or Getting Worse?," *Aggressive Behavior* 28 (2002): 109–116.

5. Daniel L. Wann, "Essay: Aggression in Sport," *Lancet* 366 (December 2005): S31.

6. "Knocked Senseless with a Base Bat," *Brenham (TX) Daily Register*, August 20, 1895, 3; "Charged with Murder," *Brenham (TX) Daily Register*, August 21, 1895, 3.

7. "Negroes in Baseball Riot," *Washington Post*, August 29, 1910, 8; "Brooks," *Fayetteville (GA) News*, September 9, 1910, 5.

8. "Murder: Willis Jones (White) Murdered by Marsh Walker (Colored) at Holly Springs, Mississippi," *Memphis Daily Appeal*, August 18, 1876, 1.

9. "Shot by His Brother," *Evening Gazette (Port Jervis, NY)*, August 21, 1877, 1; "A Base Ball Tragedy — Brother Against Brother," *Boston Daily Globe*, August 21, 1877, 5; "Murdered by His Brother," *New York Times*, August 23, 1877, 2.

10. "The Baseball Tragedy," *Daily Constitution (Atlanta)*, July 10, 1878, 4; "Carl Mitchell's Case," *Daily Constitution (Atlanta)*, December 18, 1878, 1; "Not Guilty!,'" *Daily Constitution (Atlanta)*, December 19, 1878, 1.

11. "One Boy Kills Another," *Pittsburgh Dispatch*, May 16, 1884, 2.

12. "There Seems to Be Little Doubt," *Chicago Evening Journal*, May 15, 1891, 3; "A Coroner's Jury," *Chicago Evening Journal*, May 16, 1891, 11; "E. L. Jones," *Chicago Evening Journal*, May 23, 1891, 7; "It Was Not 'Reddy,'" *Chicago Evening Journal*, May 25, 1891, 7.

13. "He Killed a Baseball Player," *Atlanta Constitution*, August 10, 1897, 1; "Taylor's Slayer Arrested," *Atlanta Constitution*, August 29, 1897, A15.

14. "Killed with a Ball Bat," *Mt. Sterling (KY) Advocate*, June 20, 1906, 6; "Karrick Acquitted," *Mt. Sterling (KY) Advocate*, June 27, 1906, 2.

15. "Blow Causes Boy's Death,"

Washington Post, April 29, 1907, 3; "Three Inquests Are Held," *Washington Post*, April 30, 1907, 16; "Crime Not Capital One," *Washington Post*, October 16, 1907, 11; "Murder Verdict Disputed," *Washington Post*, October 18, 1907, 2; "Ross Sentenced for Manslaughter," *Washington Post*, December 14, 1907, 4; "17 Convicts for Atlanta," *Atlanta Constitution*, January 23, 1908, 5.

16. "Shot Through the Head by His Companion," *Augusta (GA) Chronicle*, July 5, 1907, 4.

17. "Edward Haas Accidentally Killed by W. F. Mason," *Pittsburgh Post*, June 23, 1908, 1, 4; "The Unloaded Gun," *Pittsburgh Post*, June 24, 1908, 4; "Man Who Slew Friend Prostrated," *Pittsburgh Press*, June 23, 1908, 1.

18. "Boy Killed with a Brick," *New York Times*, March 15, 1909, 1.

19. "Jury Exonerates Boy," *Washington Post*, May 14, 1910, 16; "Jesse Sprouse Is Buried," *Washington Post*, May 15, 1910, 3.

20. "Klich," *Daily Journal (East St. Louis, IL)*, September 29, 1914, 3; "Wielder of Fatal Base-Ball Bat Is Sought by Police," *Daily Journal (East St. Louis, IL)*, October 1, 1914, 1; "Open Verdict in Death of East Side Boy," *Daily Advocate (Belleville, IL)*, October 1, 1914, 4.

21. "Accused Boy Says Police Beat Him," *Washington Post*, December 21, 1917, 9; "Moynihan Boy Convicted," *New York Times*, December 22, 1917, 5; "Moynihan Sentenced," *New York Times*, December 29, 1917, 6. A self-identified female military recruiter tried to get a suspended sentence if she could get Moynihan in the navy. The judge rejected the offer, stating "I do not think this reference to having Moynihan enlist in the navy has been made with authority from naval officers. I have repeatedly refused such requests before, for I believe service in the army or navy of the United States should be regarded as a badge of honor and not a refuge to escape the consequences of crime."

22. "Blow Kills Boy; Park Guard Held," *Pittsburgh Press*, June 28, 1930, 1, 5; "Slayer of Boy Asks 'Leave,'" *Pittsburgh Press*, June 30, 1930, 19; "Police to Prevent Park Ball Games," *Pittsburgh Press*, July 2, 1930, 21; "5 Women on Jury for Murder Trial," *Pittsburgh Press*, October 27, 1930, 1; "Murder Trial Defense Opens," *Pittsburgh Press*, October 28, 1930, 21; "Murder Jury Gets Bat Slaying Case," *Pittsburgh Press*, October 29, 1930, 1; "Slayer of Boy Fights Verdict," *Pittsburgh Press*, October 30, 1930, 10; "City Employees Raise Fund for Paroled Bat Slayer," *Pittsburgh Press*, February 27, 1931, 1, 4.

23. "Boy, 15, Killed in Quarrel at School Baseball Game," *Chicago Daily Tribune*, September 17, 1930, 3.

24. "Tragic Death of W. Cal Wilson, *McNairy County Independent (Selmer, TN)*, August 16, 1935, 1; "Jury Deadlocked in Walls Case; Unable to Agree," *McNairy County Independent (Selmer, TN)*, July 3, 1936, 1; "Two Murder Sentences in Court Last Week," *McNairy County Independent (Selmer, TN)*, October 2, 1936, 1; "Adjourned Term of Circuit Court," *McNairy County Independent (Selmer, TN)*, October 16, 1936, 1. This murder resulted in a second death. Brothers Gerry and Troy Scott of Selmer, TN, got into an argument "about the striking of Wilson, who was to blame, and things of that kind...." When Gerry threatened his brother with a shotgun, their father, Lon, attempted to separate his two sons. In the struggle that followed, the gun went off. The blast struck the elder Scott over the heart, killing him instantly. Gerry was arrested for the murder of his father. See "Second Death in Baseball Fight — Feeling High," *Lexington (TN) Progress*, August 16, 1935, 2; "Son Kills Father During Quarrel," *McNairy County Independent (Selmer, TN)*, August 16, 1935, 1.

25. "John Kekis, "Police Say Six-Year-Old Beat to Death Toddler Brother," *Associated Press State and Local Wire*, May 31, 2001; Ben Dobbin, "Mother of 3-Year-Old Who Was Beaten to Death Is Shot in the Leg," *Associated Press State and Local Wire*, September 5, 2001; "No Charges for Boy, 6, Who Killed Brother, 3," *Times Union (Albany, NY)*, June 1, 2001, B2.

Chapter 9

1. Arthur F. Long, "Great Pitching Stunts," *Baseball Magazine*, January 1911, 63; Russ Newland, "Old Timers Set to Pay Honor to Connie Mack," *Reno (NV) Evening Gazette*, March 19, 1941, 13; David Nemec, *The Great Encyclopedia of 19th Century Major League Baseball* (New York: Donald I. Fine Books, 1997), 193.

2. "A Famous Ballplayer Dead," *Binghamton (NY) Republican*, May 22, 1891, 1; "Whitney Gone, Too," *Sporting Life*, May 30, 1891, 1; "Grasshopper Jim' Once Mate of Mack," *Anaconda (MT) Standard*, January 11, 1914, 31.

3. If Whitney was injured in a game as detailed by Maul, it would have to have been in 1888, the only year in which Whitney played in Washington while Maul and Kuehne

both played for Pittsburgh. The authors could find no independent account of such an accident. Furthermore, Whitney never mentioned a game-related injury when speaking about his illness. In fact, he believed his consumption was hereditary, which is also medically inaccurate. See "Did a Batted Ball Kill Whitney?," *Chicago Daily Tribune*, April 20, 1897, 8; "Whitney Gone," 1; Harold Dellinger, "James Evans Whitney (Grasshopper Jim)," in *Nineteenth Century Stars*, ed. Mark Rucker and Robert L. Tiemann (Kansas City, MO: Society for American Baseball Research, 1989),138; Harold Dillenger, e-mail message to Bob Gorman, May 1, 2006.

4. There is disagreement as to Collins' correct name. Some sources also report it as George Hubbert Collins or as Hulbert W. Collins. The authors have selected the name currently approved by the Biographical Committee of the Society for American Baseball Research. See the *SABR-L Digest* for April 10, 2007, April 11, 2007, and April 12, 2007.

5. "Badly Injured," *Brooklyn (NY) Daily Eagle*, July 21, 1891, 2; "Burns and Collins Doing Well This Morning," *Brooklyn (NY) Daily Eagle*, July 21, 1891, 2.

6. "Burns and Collins Doing Well," 2; "Burns and Collins Are Doing Well," *Brooklyn (NY) Daily Eagle*, July 22, 1891, 2; Dean A. Sullivan, "Hubert B. Collins," in *Baseball's First Stars* (Cleveland: Society for American Baseball Research, 1996): 33. When Collins returned to the lineup, he played left field for the remainder of the season.

7. "Death of a Brooklyn Ball Player," *Brooklyn (NY) Daily Eagle*, May 23, 1892, 6; "A Famous Player Gone," *Sporting Life*, May 28, 1892, 2; "Seven Thousand Spectators at the Benefit Game," *Brooklyn (NY) Daily Eagle*, May 30, 1892, 4.

8. "Death of Hub Collins," *Chicago Daily Tribune*, May 24, 1892, 7; "Sporting Notes," *Cedar Rapids (IA) Evening Gazette*, June 11, 1892, 13; "Ball Field Accidents," *Washington Post*, March 15, 1908, S3; "Death Lurks in Speedy Sports," *Cedar Rapids (IA) Evening Gazette*, May 27, 1910, 4. Interestingly, the 1908 story incorrectly states that Collins collided with Darby O'Brien while the 1910 account reports that Collins collided with Harry Stover in Boston.

9. Sullivan, 33; "Death of a Brooklyn Ball Player," 6.

10. A contemporary sports columnist believed that Collins' illness was aggravated by "dangerous weather" early in the season. "While Collins gave up his life by reason of exposure

to wet and cold upon the ball field," he asserted, "many more players have at the same time laid the seeds of disease in their systems which will bear serious fruit in the near future." He argued that the season should not begin until May when the weather had turned milder. See C. P. Caylor, "Bismark of Baseball," *Cedar Rapids (IA) Evening Gazette*, June 11, 1892, 13.

11. "The Sporting World," *Sunday Herald (Syracuse, NY)*, December 5, 1886, 5; "Death of James I. Say," *The Sun (Baltimore, MD)*, June 25, 1894, 6; City of Baltimore, Health Department, "Certificate of Death — James Say," June 23, 1894, Baltimore, MD. The authors could find no independent contemporary account of a sliding accident involving Say.

12. "National Leaguers," *Cedar Rapids (IA) Evening Gazette*, January 2, 1897, 4; "Won the First Game," *Washington Post*, April 17, 1896, 8; "Jimmy Rogers a Scrapper," *Washington Post*, August 10, 1897, 8; "O'Brien Is Now a Senator," *Washington Post*, July 4, 1896, 8. The *Post* bemoaned the loss of Rogers. "As an emergency infielder," wrote the paper, "he was certainly valuable to the Senators; without him the club will be lacking in a reliable substitute player."

13. "For the Baseball Fans," *Washington Post*, October 27, 1896, 8; "Billy Lush Married," *Washington Post*, October 29, 1896, 8; "M'Gunnigle to Be Deposed," *Washington Post*, January 6, 1897, 8; "Shake-Up in the Colonels," *Washington Post*, June 17, 1897, 8; "In Major League Circles," *Galveston (TX) Daily News*, June 27, 1897, 21. Although Rogers may have described himself as "a shy and retiring chap" and been called "genial" by others, that was not always the case. After an August 9, 1897, minor league doubleheader in which Rogers' team took both games, he got into a fistfight with a fan named Jackson who had been heckling him. "Rogers struck Jackson two terrific blows," according to one account of the brawl, "and he [Jackson] went down in a heap with a badly cut face and it is feared a broken leg. An angry crowd gathered and Rogers was hurried away to avoid further trouble." See "Two Terrific Blows," *Boston Daily Globe*, August 10, 1897, 3.

14. "Cast Offs in Demand," *Washington Post*, June 18, 1897, 8; "Springfield Interested," *Boston Daily Globe*, January 31, 1898, 4; "Jimmy Rogers at Springfield," *Washington Post*, July 8, 1897, 8; "Baseball Notes," *Washington Post*, August 25, 1898, 8; "The World of Sport," *Washington Post*, January 22, 1899, 23; "Baseball Notes," *Washington Post*, May 28, 1899, 20. Rogers' teammates at

Springfield included future Hall-of-Famer Dan Brouthers and Danny Green, discussed later in this chapter.

15. "To Be Settled Out of Court," *Washington Post*, July 24, 1896, 8; "Ball Player Rogers Dead," *Washington Post*, January 22, 1900, 8; State of Connecticut, "Certificate of Death — James F. Rogers," January 21, 1900, Bridgeport, CT; *Mosby's Medical, Nursing, and Allied Health Dictionary*, 5 ed., s.v. "meningoencephalitis," http://0- gale net.galegroup.com.library.winthrop.ed u/.

16. "Baseball Notes," *Washington Post*, June 3, 1902, 9; "Baseball Notes," *Washington Post*, October 14, 1902, 8; "Gardner to Manage Toronto," *Boston Daily Globe*, February 7, 1903, 5; "To Strengthen Torontos," *Manitoba (Winnipeg) Free Press*, August 8, 1903, 6.

17. "Famous Local Pitcher, James Gardner, Dead," *Pittsburgh Dispatch*, April 25, 1905, 9; "Jimmie Gardner Has Answered Last Call," *Pittsburgh Press*, April 24, 1905, 1; "Diamond Loses Favorite," *Pittsburgh Post*, April 25, 1905, 8.

18. "News Nuggets," *Sporting Life*, June 24, 1905, 10.

19. "Fatalities in Sport," *Washington Post*, December 10, 1905, S2; "Two Ball Players Die," *Atlanta Constitution*, September 20, 1905, 2; "Bill Taylor's Sad End," *Altoona (PA) Mirror*, September 16, 1905, 12.

20. Joe Dittmar, "'Doc' Powers' Shocking End," *The National Pastime: A Review of Baseball History* 13 (1993): 62–65. Newspapers at the time often listed Powers' first name as Maurice. See "Powers at Point of Death," *Washington Post*, April 26, 1909, 4, and "'Doc' Powers Very Low," *The New York Times*, April 26, 1909, 8, as examples.

21. Dittmar, 63; Robert Brayden, "Intussusception," *Clinical Reference Systems*, November 2006, http://0-galenet.galegroup.com.library.winthro p.edu/.

22. Dittmar, 63–64.

23. Joe Dittmar, e-mail message to Bob Gorman, December 15, 2005; "Belt Buckle," *Cincinnati Enquirer*, May 9, 1909.

24. Dittmar, e-mail; Brayden; Andriy Zhelekh, "Adult Intussusception," *Journal of Diagnostic Medical Sonography* 23 (March-April 2007): 97–100. According to Brayden, "the exact cause of intussusception is not known. It sometimes happens when a child has a cold or other viral illness associated with swollen glands in the abdomen. There are glands located in the wall of the intestine and swelling of these glands can cause the bowel to telescope." Zhelekh found that about five percent of intussusception cases occurs

among adults and that it usually has some underlying internal cause. In one recent case, for example, the underlying cause in an adult female patient was determined to be "a benign polyp in the small bowel."

25. Mike Shatzkin, ed., *The Ballplayers* (New York: Arbor House, 1990), 409; Billy Evans, "The Growl of the Wolves," *Liberty*, July 2, 1927, 55.

26. Shatzkin, 409; "Umpire Arrested for Assault on Player He Had Ordered from Grounds," *Lima (OH) Times-Democrat*, July 8, 1903, 4; "No Game," *Lincoln (NE) Daily Evening News*, April 12, 1906, 1; Lloyd Johnson and Miles Wolff, eds., *The Encyclopedia of Minor League Baseball*, 2 ed. (Durham, NC: Baseball America, 1997), 149, 153.

27. "Danny Green Ill," *Reno (NV) Evening Gazette*, July 31, 1912, 3; "The World of Sport," *Lincoln (NE) Daily News*, November 22, 1913, 8.

28. "Danny Green Insane," *Racine (WI) Journal-News*, January 19, 1914, 9; "Camden, N.J., Jan. 19," *Daily Northwestern (Oshkosh, WI)*, January 19, 1914, 8; "Famous Ball Player Dead," *Bucks County (PA) Gazette*, November 13, 1914, 3; "Noted Ball Player Dead," *Washington Post*, November 10, 1914, 8; "Danny Green Dead," *Atlanta Constitution*, November 11, 1914, 11. Oddly, in some accounts Green's "only child" is said to be a boy named Edward instead of a girl as reported in the 1913 stories. And, according to at least one contemporary news clipping that the authors found in Green's player file located in the National Baseball Hall of Fame library, his head injury was reportedly due to a bat, not a pitched ball. Furthermore, several large national newspapers including *The Washington Post* and *The Atlanta Constitution* stated his injury occurred while he played for Minneapolis (MN) Millers of the same league as the Milwaukee Brewers, the team for which Green actually played.

29. State of New Jersey, Bureau of Vital Statistics, "Certificate and Record of Death — Daniel Green," November 8, 1914, Blackwood, NJ; Frank Russo, e-mail message to SABR-L Digest, February 27, 2007; Frank Russo, e-mail message to SABR-L Digest, January 31, 2005.

30. "Boston Gets Pitcher Pape Cheap," *Middletown (NY) Times-Press*, August 9, 1909, 7; "Red Sox Release Pitcher Pape," *Chicago Daily Tribune*, May 18, 1910, 12; "Larry Pape Pitches 14 Innings of Five Hits and Brockton Wins 1 to 0," *Boston Daily Globe*, August 18, 1910, 6; "Arellanes and Pape to Pitch for Red Sox," *Boston Daily Globe*, January 5, 1911, 7; "Red Sox Team Av-

erage .262," *Boston Daily Globe*, October 4, 1909, 5.

31. "Red Sox Open Here April 8," *Boston Daily Globe*, January 15, 1913, 7; "Pape Case Shows Injustice of Present Baseball Rule," *Washington Post*, January 21, 1913, 8; "Pape Quits Baseball," *Washington Post*, May 24, 1913, 8; "Larry Pape Is Now a Beaver," *Los Angeles Times*, November 24, 1913, III3; "Larry Pape Is Sent to Buffalo," August 31, 1914, III2.

32. Richard Guy, "Larry Pape, a Former Pitcher, Dies Suddenly in Swissvale; Gossip of the Athletes," *Pittsburgh Gazette Times*, July 23, 1918, 10; "Larry Pape Dies of Injury," *The Sporting News*, August 1, 1918, 1; Commonwealth of Pennsylvania, Department of Health, "Certificate of Death," July 21, 1918, Swissvale, PA. The authors suspect the cause released to the public was intentionally erroneous for reasons of privacy and to save his surviving family any potential embarrassment as to the real cause. In addition, the authors could not find any contemporary account of any injury he sustained during his playing career. A 1974 article, however, reported that Pape had been injured by a line drive to the stomach while pitching to Eddie Collins of the Philadelphia Athletics in a 1912 game and that this injury ended his season, but the author does not contend it was in any way responsible for his death in 1918. Instead, he asserts Pape died from "cancer of the stomach," something much closer to the truth. See Tom Rieger, "Pape's Ill-Fated Career," *Enterprise*, August 1, 1974, 3.

33. "Tigers Finish in Fifth Place," *Lincoln (NE) Daily Star*, September 28, 1914, 7; "The Spotlight on Sports," *Lincoln (NE) Daily News*, February 16, 1915, 9; "Triple Play Demonstrated," *Los Angeles Times*, July 4, 1915, VII1; "'Doc' Crandall of the Angels Has Fine P.C.L. Record," *Oakland (CA) Tribune*, May 7, 1925, 23; "Lynn Scoggins Retires," *Los Angeles Times*, September 21, 1917, 15; "Body of Scoggins Taken to Texas," *The State (Columbia, SC)*, August 18, 1923, 3.

34. "Body of Scoggins," 3; "Lynn S. Scoggins Dies at Hospital," *The State (Columbia, SC)*, August 17, 1923, 10; State of South Carolina, Bureau of Vital Statistics, "Certificate of Death — Lynn J. Scoggins," August 16, 1923, Columbia, SC; Lee Allen, "Cooperstown Corner," *The Sporting News*, April 13, 1968, 6.

35. Jim Sandoval, "Jake Daubert," *The Baseball Biography Project*, Society for American Baseball Research, http://bioproj.sabr.org (accessed June 1, 2005); William C. Kashatus, *Diamonds in the Coalfields* (Jefferson, NC: McFarland, 2002), 94–97.

36. Sandoval, "Jake Daubert"; "Reds Divide with Cards," *New York Times*, May 29, 1924, 12; "Daubert, Reds' 1st Sacker, Sent Home for Rest," *Chicago Daily Tribune*, June 5, 1924, 25; "Snappy Sports," *Lima (OH) News*, June 10, 1924, 12; "Reds Finally Complete Deal for Charley Dressen," *Zanesville (OH) Signal*, June 11, 1924, 14; "Dodgers Defeat Reds; Errors Aid Victors," *Washington Post*, June 18, 1924, S1; "The Telosport," *Zanesville (OH) Signal*, June 26, 1924, 14. By some counts, Daubert's beaning was at least the eighth of his career.

37. "Daubert May Manage Portland Coast League Team Next Season," *Zanesville (OH) Times-Signal*, September 7, 1924, 9; "Reds Beat Cards, 10–1," *New York Times*, September 28, 1924, S3; "Jake Daubert Under the Knife," *Zanesville (OH) Times Recorder*, October 2, 1924, 10; "Jake Daubert Resting O.K. after Operation," *Chicago Daily Tribune*, October 3, 1924, 25; "Daubert Is 'Doing Well,'" *Washington Post*, October 4, 1924, S2; "Jake Daubert, Reds' Veteran Star, Near Death in Cincinnati," *Chicago Daily Tribune*, October 8, 1924, 17; "Daubert Is Sinking, Little Hope Remains," *New York Times*, October 9, 1924, 19; "Jake Daubert Dies from Appendicitis," *New York Times*, October 10, 1924, 15.

38. Sandoval, "Jake Daubert"; State of Ohio, "Certificate of Death — Jacob E. Daubert," October 9, 1924, Cincinnati, OH; J. W. Heintzman to Cincinnati Base Ball Club Co., November 29, 1924, National Baseball Hall of Fame, Cooperstown, NY; "Death Again Visits the Cincinnati Reds," *The Sporting News*, October 16, 1924, 4; "Reds and Giants Split Twin Bill; Cubs Are Back in Fourth Place," *Portsmouth (OH) Daily Times*, September 17, 1924, 12; "Exhume Body of Jake Daubert," *Chicago Daily Tribune*, September 17, 1925, 21; "Daubert's Widow Sues," *New York Times*, August 11, 1929, 23; "Daubert's Widow Files Suit for Compensation," *Chicago Daily Tribune*, August 11, 1929, A7; Jim Sandoval, e-mail message to Bob Gorman, November 30, 2005.

39. "Roy Crabb's Funeral to Be on Wednesday," *Democrat-News (Lewistown, MT)*, April 1, 1940; Jerry E. Clark, *Anson to Zumer: Iowa Boys in the Major Leagues* (Omaha, NE: Making History, 1992), 53–54; State of Montana, "Standard Certificate of Death," March 30, 1940, Lewistown, MT.

40. "Death of John McDonough," *Fort Wayne (IN) Journal*, July 23, 1884, 2; "May Disband," *Fort Wayne (IN) Journal*, June 24, 1884, 1.

41. "May Disband," 1; "Notes," *Fort Wayne (IN) Journal*, June 26,

1884, 1; "Beaten Again," *Fort Wayne (IN) Journal*, July 1, 1884, 1; "Notes," *Fort Wayne (IN) Journal*, July 8, 1884, 1; "Friends of John McDonough," *Fort Wayne (IN) Journal*, July 22, 1884, 1; "Death of John McDonough," 1.

42. "Mac Is Dead," *Fort Wayne (IN) Sentinel*, July 22, 1884, 3; "McDonough Dying," *Daily Gazette (Fort Wayne, IN)*, July 21, 1884 6; "McDonough Gone," *Daily Gazette (Fort Wayne, IN)*, July 23, 1884, 6; "Death of John McDonough," 1.

43. "Left Again," *Fort Wayne (IN) Journal*, May 30, 1884, 3; "Forging Ahead," *Fort Wayne (IN) Journal*, June 18, 1884, 1; State of Michigan, County of Macomb, "Record of Deaths," vol. A, 233.

44. "Galveston Shut Out," *Galveston (TX) Daily News*, July 29, 1895, 2; "George Dean," *Galveston (TX) Daily News*, August 13, 1895, 2; "George Dean," *Galveston (TX) Daily News*, August 18, 1895, 4; "George Dean Dead," *Galveston (TX) Daily News*, August 19, 1895, 2; "The Game of Life Ended," *Daily Light (San Antonio, TX)*, August 19, 1895, 4; "Autopsy Held," *Galveston (TX) Daily News*, August 20, 1895, 8. "Typhoid malarial fever" is a Civil War medical term used "to describe the many cases of camp fever that combined elements from typhoid fever, malarial remittent fever, and scurvy to varying degrees." See Paul Smith, *Archaic Medical Terms: A Resource for Genealogists and Historians*, http://www.paul_smith.doctors.org.uk/ArchaicMedicalTerms.htm (accessed May 17, 2007).

45. Jeffrey Powers-Beck, *The American Indian Integration of Baseball* (Lincoln, NE: University of Nebraska Press, 2004), 183–184; William C. Kashatus, *Money Pitcher: Chief Bender and the Tragedy of Indian Assimilation* (University Park, PA: Pennsylvania State University Press, 2006), 27, 95; "Bender Ran Amuck on Steamer," *News and Courier (Charleston, SC)*, July 21, 1908, 12; "'Chief' J. C. Bender," *The State (Columbia, SC)*, July 21, 1908, 6; "Bender Fined and Benched," *News and Courier (Charleston, SC)*, July 24, 1908, 8.

46. "League Closes Today for the 1911 Season," *Edmonton (Alberta) Daily Bulletin*, September 2, 1911, 6; "Baseball Player Dropped Dead" *Edmonton (Alberta) Daily Bulletin*, September 25, 1911, 10; "Eskimo Fielder Drops Dead as He Enters Room," *Edmonton (Alberta) Journal*, September 25, 1911, 1.

47. "Bender Dies of Heart Failure," *News and Courier (Charleston, SC)*, September 27, 1911, 8; "John Bender Dies in Baseball Game," *Evening Sentinel (Carlisle, PA)*, September 30, 1911, 4; "Caught on the Fly," *Sporting Life*,

October 7, 1911, 6; Kashatus, 95; Powers-Beck, 184, 217.

48. "Latest News by Telegraph Briefly Told," *Sporting Life*, August 24, 1912, 5; "Death Roll," *Steubenville (OH) Weekly Herald*, August 16, 1912, 2; "Medical Certificate of Death — William Craig," Steubenville, OH, August 15, 1912.

49. "Death by the Bat," *Atlanta Constitution*, May 30, 1874, 3; "A Murder Was Committed," *Forest and Stream*, June 4, 1874, 263; "Melancholy Affray," *North-East Georgian (Athens, GA)*, June 3, 1874, 3.

50. John Hix, "Strange As It Seems," *Washington Post*, January 14, 1933, 15; "Baseball Centennial Oddities," *Burlington (NC) Daily Times-News*, March 9, 1939, 12; "Sporting Odds," *Collier's*, August 16, 1947, 75; H. Allen Smith and Ira L. Smith, "The Old Ballgame," *Saturday Evening Post*, July/August 2000, 74. On page 62 of this latter publication, the editor assures readers that "these incidents actually took place and were covered in the newspapers of the day."

51. "The Corpse Scored," *Baseball Magazine*, January 1914, 57–58; Rich Marazzi, "Baseball Rules Corner," *Baseball Digest*, January/February 2006, 88.

52. "Lefty" Ranweiler, "Sports of the Century," in *The Centennial History of Kandiyohi County* (Willmar, MN: Kandiyohi County Historical Society, 1970), 323. The authors also searched the *Proquest Historical Newspapers* database and the *NewspaperArchive.com* database for each of the names given for the individuals involved, but could find no contemporary accounts of the incidents. The only "Thielman" who appears in baseball news during that time is Henry Thielman, pitcher for Brooklyn Dodgers in 1903. He died in 1942.

53. "Badger Umps Saw Man Score After Dying on Third," *La Crosse (WI) Tribune*, August 19, 1907, 2; "Player Died on Third Base, but Scored Run," *Star Publications (Chicago)*, September 19, 1907, 6; "Queer Tale of Baseball Field," *Galveston (TX) Daily News*, October 24, 1907, 4. Anderson must have been quite a character. Earlier in 1907, he was beaten up at the boarding house where he lived by a fellow boarder, Joseph Haberman, because Haberman became convinced Anderson was trying to steal the affections of the landlady. Apparently Haberman was attracted to the landlady and became incensed when he learned that Anderson was bringing her small gifts from his baseball travels. Anderson agreed to drop assault charges after his assailant agreed to pay $35 for damage done to Anderson's clothing and $4.92

in court costs. See "Ump Anderson Given a Beating," *La Crosse (WI) Tribune*, July 31, 1907, 2.

54. "The Corpse Scored," 57.

55. "Moccasin Bites Outfielder," *Washington Post*, April 26, 1907, 8; "Caught Ball, Lost Leg," *New York Times*, April 26, 1907, 1; "Snake Bites Ball Player," *Washington Post*, July 24, 1909, 1; "Wins Game, Snake Bite Kills," *New York Times*, July 24, 1909, 1; "Fielder, Chasing Fly, Is Bitten by Snake," *Syracuse (NY) Herald*, July 24, 1909, 8; "Ball Player Killed by Snake," *Fort Wayne (IN) Sentinel*, July 24, 1909, 10; Joel Zoss and John Bowman, *Diamonds in the Rough: The Untold History of Baseball* (Chicago: Contemporary Books, 1996), 355; Johnson and Wolff, 167.

56. *Oxford Illustrated Companion to Medicine*, 2001, s.v. "snake bite," http://0-web.ebscohost.com.library.winthrop.edu/.

57. "Injured in Ball Game, Boy Dies," *Ithaca (NY) Daily Journal*, April 4, 1910, 5; *Dorland's Illustrated Medical Dictionary*, 2003, s.v. "meningitis," http://www.credoreference.com/entry/4181356.

58. "Died from Base Ball Injury," *Sporting Life*, June 11, 1910, 1; Daniel J. Sexton and Eric L. Westerman, "Tetanus," *UpToDate*, 15 (August 2007), http://www.utdol.com/utd/content/topic.do?topicKey=oth_bact/40603.

59. "Baseball Kills Policeman," *New York Times*, June 23, 1910, 1; *The Royal Society of Medicine Health Encyclopedia*, 2000, s.v. "erysipelas," http://www.credoreference.com/entry/2227586; Loretta Davis, "Erysipelas," *Emedicine from WebMD*, http://www.emedicine.com/derm/topic129.htm (accessed November 25, 2007).

60. "Bone Sliver in Heart Causes Boy's Death," *Atlanta Constitution*, November 30, 1912, 4; "Hayes," *Philadelphia Inquirer*, November 29, 1912, 15.

61. "Child Hit by Ball Dies at Yelm from Injuries," *Tacoma (WA) Tribune*, May 8, 1915, 2; "Obituary," *Tacoma (WA) Tribune*, May 9, 1915, 17; *McGraw-Hill Concise Encyclopedia of Science and Technology*, 2004, s.v. "Tuberculosis," http://www.credoreference.com/entry/5974083.

62. "Hit by Ball, He Dies of Illness," *South Bend (IN) Tribune*, June 24, 1935, 10; *Chamber's 21st Century Dictionary*, 2001, s.v. "streptococcus," http://www.credoreference.com/entry/1230864.

Chapter 10

1. Larry Gerlach, "Death on the Diamond: The Cal Drummond Story," *National Pastime: A Review of Baseball History* 24 (2004): 14–16; "Cal Drummond, Ex-Major League Umpire, Dies at 52," *Greenville (SC) News*, May 4, 1970, 9.

2. Gerlach, 15.

3. Gerlach, 15; "Cal Drummond," 9; "Veteran Umpire Cal Drummond Died Sunday," *Ames (IA) Daily Tribune*, May 4, 1970, 11; "Autopsy Shows Brain Damage Caused the Death of Umpire," *Muscatine (IA) Journal*, May 4, 1970, 8; "Rios Hurt Again," *The Sporting News*, May 23, 1970, 44.

4. "Youth Killed During Chiefs Batting Practice," *Wenatchee (WA) Daily World*, July 31, 1964, 1; "13-Year-Old Wenatchee Boy Killed in Batting Practice," *The Sporting News*, August 15, 1964, 38. Breeden would appear briefly with the Cincinnati Reds in 1969 and the Chicago Cubs in 1971.

5. Doug Crise, "Death of Mike Coolbaugh," *Arkansas (Little Rock) Democrat-Gazette*, July 24, 2007; S. L. Price, "A Death in the Baseball Family," *Sports Illustrated*, September 24, 2007, 56–57, 60.

6. Price, 60; Todd Traub, "Danger on the Diamond," *Arkansas (Little Rock) Democrat- Gazette*, July 29, 2007.

7. "Umpire's Death Is Caused by Foul Tip," *Cleveland Plain Dealer*, November 24, 1911, 11; State of Ohio, Bureau of Vital Statistics, "Certificate of Death — Edward Cermak," Cleveland, OH, November 24, 1911.

8. "Umpire Morrissey Killed," *Boston Globe*, August 15, 1886, 1; "Killed by a Foul Ball," *New York Times*, August 15, 1886, 2.

9. "Killed by a Pitched Ball," *New York Times*, July 1, 1888, 2; "Killed by a Base Ball," *Boston Daily Globe*, July 7, 1888, 3; "All Right to Have an Umpire Killed," *Sunday Herald (Syracuse, NY)*, July 22, 1888, 1.

10. "An Umpire Killed," *Daily Northwestern (Oshkosh, WI)*, August 30, 1888, 1; "Epitome of the Week," *Freeborn County Standard (Albert Lea, MN)*, September 5, 1888, 11; "A Fatal 'Foul,'" *National Police Gazette*, September 22, 1888, 2.

11. "Killed by Baseball," *Washington Post*, August 18, 1907, 3; "Batted Ball Kills Captain of a Team," *Fitchburg (MA) Daily Sentinel*, August 28, 1907, 5.

12. "Death from Foul Ball Batted by His Brother," *Pittsburgh Post*, June 2, 1909, 2.

13. "Killed by a Thrown Ball," *New York Times*, June 23, 1913, 16; "Killed

by Thrown Ball," *Gettysburg (PA) Times,* June 23, 1913, 3; "Killed by Foul Tip," *Boston Daily Globe,* June 23, 1913, 6.

14. "Hit with Baseball Saturday; Dies in Night Following," *Bisbee (AZ) Daily Review,* May 25, 1915, 5.

15. "Skull Fractured by Base Ball," *Wilkes-Barre (PA) Record,* June 2, 1915, 5.

16. "Killed by a Baseball," *New York Times,* October 5, 1931, 3; "Honor Baseball Victim," *New York Times,* October 6, 1931, 10; "1,000 See Bunion Derby Reach End in New York," *Washington Post,* May 27, 1928, M17.

17. "Fairfax Boy Is Killed by Baseball, *Washington Post and Times Herald,* September 15, 1958, A1; "Recent Deaths," *Fairfax (VA) Herald,* September 19, 1958, 1.

18. "George, a Game Boy, Plays Ball — To the End," *Chicago Daily Tribune,* May 30, 1961, 3; "Cub Scouts in Tribute to Ball Player," *Chicago Daily Tribune,* June 1, 1961, C5.

19. "Sports Editor Len Handel Fatally Hurt by Foul Ball," *Sporting News,* August 7, 1965, 38; "Sports Editor Was Hit by Foul Ball," *Chicago Tribune,* July 27, 1965; B3; "Editor Dies After Being Hit by Ball," *Fresno (CA) Bee,* July 27, 1965, 26; Al Carr, "Sports Ala Carr," *Los Angeles Times,* August 1, 1965, OC18; "Widow of Sports Writer Files Suit," *Los Angeles Times,* April 23, 1966, OC14; "Editor Death Suit Lost by Widow," *Independent (Long Beach, CA),* April 2, 1970, 27.

20. "Dies in Yankees' Dugout," *New York Times* April 19, 1952, 15; "Heart Attack Fatal to Movietone Editor," *Charleston (WV) Gazette,* April 19, 1952, 8; "Joe's Jersey in Fame's Hall," *Lima (OH) News,* April 19, 1952, 5.

21. Shirley Povich, "65-Year-Old Hit by Heart Attack After Fungo Drill," *Washington Post,* March 4, 1953, 16; "Clyde Milan Dead; Baseball Coach, 65," *New York Times,* March 4, 1953, 27; Ira L. Smith, *Baseball's Famous Outfielders* (New York: A. S. Barnes, 1954), 88–93.

22. Joe Kay, "Umpire John McSherry Collapses During Game," *Associated Press Sports News,* April 1, 1996; Murray Chass, "Umpire Dies After Collapsing on Field," *New York Times,* April 2, 1996, B7; Ken Allan, "Death on the Diamond," *Referee,* April 2006, 76–77.

23. Kay; Chass, B7, B9; Allan, 76–77. "Sudden cardiac death" is most often caused either by "ventricular fibrillation," a condition in which "the lower chamber of the heart quivers instead of pumping in an organized rhythm," or "ventricular tachycardia,"

in which the heart beats rapidly, "usually over 100 beats per minute." For a victim to avoid brain death, CPR "must begin within four to six minutes and advanced life support measures must begin within eight minutes." See Dorothy Stonely, "Sudden Cardiac Death," *Gale Encyclopedia of Medicine,* 3rd ed., http://0-find.galegroup.com. library.winthrop.edu/.

24. "Finn, Part Owner Omaha Club, Sees Homer Hit; Dies," *Sunday World Herald (Omaha, NE),* May 7, 1922, 1,12; "Funeral Services Held Yesterday for Mike Finn," *Morning World Herald (Omaha, NE),* May 8, 1922, 1; "Heart Disease Fatal to Baseball Veteran," *The Sporting News,* May 11, 1922, 2.

25. "Phillies' Pilot Dies Suddenly," *Terre Haute (IN) Tribune,* May 4, 1947, 1; "Ray Brubaker Rites Set for Wednesday," *Terre Haute (IN) Tribune,* May 5, 1947, 5; "Ray Brubaker, 51, Stricken on Bench," *The Sporting News,* May 14, 1947, 16.

26. "'Pinky' Hargrave, Baseball Star, Dies of Heart Attack," *News-Sentinel (Ft. Wayne, IN),* October 3, 1942, 1–2. Hargrave's older brother, Eugene "Bubbles" Hargrave, was also a major league catcher, spending 12 seasons from 1913 to 1930 with the Chicago Cubs, Cincinnati Reds, and New York Yankees. Bubbles helped convert his younger sibling from an infielder to a catcher early in Pinky's career.

27. "Sandlot Coach Dies at Game," *San Diego Union,* November 10, 1958, B3.

28. "Umpire Walter Pearce Dies at Cardines Game," *Newport (RI) Daily News,* May 25, 1974, 2, 10.

29. Brian D. Mockenhaupt, "Ponaganset Mourns Loss of Coach," *Providence (RI) Journal-Bulletin,* March 19, 1997, 1C.

30. Beth Warren, "Youth Coach Dies," *Atlanta Journal-Constitution,* September 25, 2003, 1JJ.

31. John Fey, "Funeral Services Are Set Today for Longtime Umpire Greunke," *Omaha World-Herald,* October 11, 2003, 5C.

32. Scott Williams, "Umpire Dies on Diamond He Loved," *Milwaukee Journal Sentinel,* July 13, 2004, 1B.

33. "High School Ump Dies on Field in Villa Park," *Chicago Daily Herald,* April 15, 2005, 3; Kevin Schmit, "Behind the Mask Was a Man, and His Death Touched Many," *Chicago Daily Herald,* May 6, 2005, 1.

34. Chase Goodbread, "Longtime Area Baseball Coach Hamilton Collapses, Dies," *Florida (Jacksonville) Times-Union,* March 18, 2007, C8.

35. "Union: Workers Feared Strong, Gusting Winds," *Tampa (FL) Tribune,* July 16, 1999, 5; "Accident

Puzzle Coming Together," *Wisconsin State Journal (Madison, WI),* July 16, 1999, 1A; "3 Ironworkers' Families Sue, Saying Lift Was Unsafe," *Milwaukee Journal Sentinel,* August 13, 1999, 1; "Wisconsin Supreme Court's Decision Remains After Big Blue Settlement," *Wisconsin Law Journal,* January 18, 2006.

36. "One Killed, Five Hurt in Cave-In," *Commercial Appeal (Memphis, TN),* December 20, 1921, 1; "Negroes Recovering," *Commercial Appeal (Memphis, TN),* December 21, 1921, 15.

37. "Workman Killed by Electric Shock," *Los Angeles Times,* February 13, 1928, 18; "Prexy Honors Lefty O'Doul at Dedication," *Los Angeles Times,* February 23, 1928, B3.

38. "Electricity Kills Park Attendant," *Syracuse (NY) Herald-Journal,* April 23, 1952, 29; "Caretaker Is Electrocuted Lowering Flag at Longview," *The Sporting News,* April 30, 1952, 33.

39. "Wire Screen Placed to Protect Life Deals Out Death at Athletic Field," *Post-Standard (Syracuse, NY),* May 5, 1902, 6; "Will Locate the Blame," *Post-Standard (Syracuse, NY),* May 6, 1902, 7; "Sets Blame for Death of Schutz," *Post-Standard (Syracuse, NY),* May 14, 1902, 7; "Sues Three Companies," *Evening Herald (Syracuse, NY),* December 30, 1902, 9.

40. "Lightning Strikes Down Five," *Mobile (AL) Register,* May 28, 1906, 1.

41. "Lightning Kills 4; Six Others Stunned," *New York Times,* July 23, 1925, 1, 3.

42. "Bolt Stuns Butler, Leaves Three Dead," *Milwaukee Journal,* August 1, 1945, 1,3.

43. Steve Zalusky, "Coach Dies Two Days After Struck by Lightning," *Chicago Daily Herald,* June 6, 2002, 1.

Chapter 11

1. David Q. Voigt, "America's Manufactured Villain — the Baseball Umpire," *Journal of Popular Culture* 4, no.1 (Summer 1970), 1–21.

2. Bill James, *The Bill James Historical Baseball Abstract* (New York: Villard Books, 1988), 38; John A. Heydler, as quoted in Harold Seymour, *Baseball: The Early Years* (New York: Oxford University Press, 1960), 290; Francis C. Richter, "The Cost of Rowdy Ball," in *Grandstand Baseball Annual 2000* (Downey, CA: J. M. Wayman, 2000), 95–98. Richter's essay was originally published in the 1919 *Reach Guide* as a response to Christy Mathewson and his call for a return to "real old-fashioned feud in base ball."

3. Brick Owens, "Dodging the Brickbats with the Umpire," *Washington Post*, April 8, 1928, MS5; "Strenuous Life of an Umpire," *Washington Post*, June 30, 1907, M3.

4. James, 57; Ban Johnson, as quoted in Jonathan Fraser Light, *The Cultural Encyclopedia of Baseball*, 2 ed. (Jefferson, NC: McFarland, 2005), 25; "Pitcher M'Ginnity Also Expelled," *Janesville (WI) Daily Gazette*, August 29, 1901, 2; "Sporting," *Racine (WI) Daily Journal*, August 24, 1901, 8.

5. Billy Evans, "Twenty Years a Big League Umpire," *Liberty*, June 27, 1925, 32–36; "Hedges May Be Fined," *Washington Post*, September 17, 1907, 9; James, 136.

6. D. W. Rainey, "Assaults on Umpires: a Statewide Survey," *Journal of Sport Behavior* 17, no. 3 (September 1994). The survey also found that "alcohol consumption is frequently involved in assaults by softball players."

7. "Fatal End of a Ball Game," *Birmingham News*, May 1, 1899, 7; ""Umpire Killed in a Fight," *Chicago Daily Tribune*, May 2, 1899, 1; "Baseball Umpire Killed," *New York Times*, May 2, 1899, 8; "Killed the Umpire," *The Star (Sandusky, OH)*, May 5, 1899, 4.

8. "Crime to Kill an Umpire," *Boston Daily Globe*, November 21, 1911, 16; "Umpires Get Aid of Appeals Court," *Atlanta Constitution*, November 21, 1911, 3; *Young v. The State*, 10 GA App. 116.

9. For more information on this case, see Bob Gorman, "Kill the Umpire, or the Case of the Fatal Lick," *Elysian Fields Quarterly: The Baseball Review* 21, no. 2 (Spring 2004), 45–49.

10. "Spectator Kills Umpire of County Baseball Game," *St. Louis Post-Dispatch*, July 17, 1922, 1; "Verdict Holds Boy for the Death of Baseball Umpire," *St. Louis Post-Dispatch*, July 18, 1922, 1–2; "Youth Declares He Doesn't Remember Killing Umpire," *St. Louis Post-Dispatch*, May 3, 1923, 3; "Jury Still Out in Trial of Youth Who Killed Umpire," *St. Louis Post-Dispatch*, May 4, 1923, 3; "Slayer of Umpire Gets Four Years in Reformatory," *St. Louis Post-Dispatch*, May 5, 1923, 3.

11. Details on this case came for a collection of newspaper clippings kept by Mary McTavey, widow of the deceased, in a Diamond Composition Book, now housed at the National Baseball Hall of Fame in Cooperstown, NY. Nearly $2,000 was raised for McTavey's family through a series of fund-raising baseball and basketball games and by individual contributions.

12. "Heinemann Kills Himself in Baseball Park He Loved," *Times-Picayune (New Orleans)*, January 9, 1930, 1, 10.

13. "Heinemann Kills Himself," 1, 10.

14. "Heinemann Kills Himself," 1, 10; "Throng Mourns at Last Rites for Heinemann," *Times-Picayune (New Orleans)*, January 10, 1930, 2.

15. "Illinois Man Shoots G'Town Man, Kills Self," *Commercial Appeal (Memphis, TN)*, August 7, 1992, B3; "Ray Winder Intern Expected to Recover," *Arkansas (Little Rock) Democrat Gazette*, August 8, 1992; "Center Still Offering Aid to Veterans," *Arkansas (Little Rock) Democrat Gazette*, August 23, 1992.

16. "Policeman Slain at Dorchester," *Big Stone Gap (VA) Post*, June 30, 1915, 1.

17. Mac Davis, *Lore and Legends of Baseball* (New York: Lantern Press, 1953), 216. The Davis account was probably based on contemporary national newspaper reports, which stated that "Jennings' skull is fractured and he cannot recover." See "Broke Skull of the Umpire," *Atlanta Constitution*, August 22, 1901, 1.

18. "Used Base Ball Bat," *Terre Haute (IN) Express*, August 22, 1901, 4; "Ex-Vigo Convict Assaults Umpire," *Evening Gazette (Terre Haute, IN)*, August 21, 1901, 1; "Marcellus Forbes Killed Himself," *Evening Gazette (Terre Haute, IN)*, July 6, 1903, 1; Sullivan County Historical Society, *Sullivan County, Indiana, Cemetery Records*, vol. 3 (Sullivan, IN: Sullivan County Historical Society, 1983), 148.

19. "A Deplorable Catastrophe," *Darlington (SC) News*, September 5, 1889, 1; "A Base Ball Tragedy," *News and Courier (Charleston, SC)*, September 1, 1889, 1. Some news accounts give Dargan's first name as Leon.

20. "Deplorable Catastrophe," 1; "Hear the Other Side," *News and Press (Darlington, SC)*, September 4, 1889, 1; "A Base Ball Tragedy," 1.

21. "Good News from Wadesboro," *News and Courier (Charleston, SC)*, September 2, 1889, 1; "The Darlington Tragedy," *News and Courier (Charleston, SC)*, September 5, 1889, 1; "He Killed the Baseball Umpire," *Chicago Daily Tribune*, September 5, 1889, 1; Anson County (NC) Historical Society, e-mail message to Bob Gorman, January 3, 2006.

22. This story came to light because of the persistence of the Charleston *News and Courier*. The paper had been in contact with residents of Darlington who insisted that Marshall was very much alive. The paper claimed to have cautioned King to "be careful of your facts," but he did not listen to the paper's warnings. See "The Darlington Tragedy," *News and Courier (Charleston, SC)*, September 6, 1889, 1.

Chapter 12

1. "Dangerous Spectator Sports, Shoe Shines, the Two-Day Weekend and DIY Opium," *Esquire*, January 2006.

2. Frank Fitzpatrick, "After Hockey Death, Baseball Gets a Safety Reminder," *Knight-Ridder/Tribune News Service*, April 9, 2002; Sam Walker, "Batter Up! Batten Down," *Wall Street Journal*, August 3, 2001, W1, W4.

3. J. Gordon Hylton, "A Foul Ball in the Courtroom: The Baseball Spectator Injury as a Case of First Impression," *Tulsa Law Review*, 38, no. 3 (Spring 2003); David Nemec, *The Great Encyclopedia of 19th-Century Major League Baseball* (New York: Donald I. Fine Books, 1997), 217; David Nemec, *The Official Rules of Baseball: An Anecdotal Look at the Rules of Baseball and How They Came to Be* (Guilford, CT: Lyons Press, 1999), 151–154.

4. Hylton; Nemec, *Great Encyclopedia*, 125; *Spalding's Official Base Ball Guide for 1878* (Chicago: A. G. Spalding and Brother, 1878), 3; "Recreation Park," *Detroit (MI) Post and Tribune*, April 28, 1879, 4; Troy Soos, *Before the Curse: The Glory Days of New England Baseball, 1858–1918*, rev. ed. (Jefferson, NC: McFarland, 2006), 47–48; "Base Ball," *New York Clipper*, February 19, 1870, 363. A 1911 editorial in *Baseball Magazine*, noting that "almost every grandstand is partially protected by a wire netting designed to prevent the passage of foul balls into the crowd of spectators," asked "if it would not be advisable to have the entire grandstand protected in this manner. It would certainly go a long way toward minimizing accidents among the spectators." Of particular concern were female and elderly fans, whom the magazine felt were "particularly defenceless [sic] against this chance danger." See "Baseball Dangers," *Baseball Magazine*, December 1911, 106.

5. When nets were first introduced in the late 1800s, some parks removed them because of fan protests. For example, several days after owners installed screens in 1884 at the Wright Street Grounds, home of the Western League Milwaukee Brewers, they were taken down because of fan complaints. See "The World of Sport," *Milwaukee (WI) Daily Journal*, July 3, 1884, 1.

6. Hylton; Andrew T. Pittman, "Foul Balls and Assumption of Risk," *Journal of Physical Education, Recreation, and Dance* 78, no. 1 (January 2007): 8; James C. Kozlowski, "Law Review: Spectator Injury Outside the Stands," *Parks and Recreation* 41, no. 1 (January 2006): 32.

7. Hylton; Pittman, 9; Kozlowki, 32–35; Charles Toutant, "Play Ball! (Carefully)," *New Jersey Law Journal*, September 19, 2005; *Maisonave v. Newark Bears*, 881 A.2d 700 (2005), http://0-web.lexis-nexis.com.library. winthrop.edu/; *Reider v. State*, 897 So.2d 893 (2005), http://0-web.lexis-nexis.com.library.winthrop.edu/.

8. Dorothy Townsend, "Boy, 14, Dies After Being Hit on Head by Dodger Foul Ball," *Los Angeles Times*, May 21, 1970, 1; *Fish v. Los Angeles Dodgers Baseball Club*, 56 Cal. App. 3d 620 (1976), http://0-web.lexis-nexis.com.library.winthrop.edu/.

9. *Fish v. Dodgers*.

10. "A Boy Got His First Baseball ... It Killed Him," *Chicago Tribune*, May 22, 1970, C1; *Fish v. Dodgers*.

11. *Fish v. Dodgers*.

12. *Fish v. Dodgers*.

13. *Fish v. Dodgers*; "Dodgers Absolved in Death of Boy Hit by Baseball," *Los Angeles Times*, September 27, 1973, OC1. The jury verdict was appealed on technical grounds, mainly concerning the judge's failure to give proper instructions to the jury. On March 26, 1976, the California Court of Appeal reversed the decision of the jury on these grounds and allowed Fish's parents to continue their suit. On April 23, a petition by the Dodgers for a rehearing was denied and on May 26 a hearing by the California Supreme Court was also denied. A search of *Lexis-Nexis* and other relevant sources failed to provide further information as to the final disposition of this suit.

14. Early newspaper reports spell the victim's last name as "Lascala." Tommy Fitzgerald, "Raydon's 3-Hitter Beats Marlins, 5–0," *Miami (FL) News*, August 28, 1960, 2C; Steve Trumbull, "Marlin Fan's Death First in Baseball?," *Miami (FL) Herald*, August 31, 1960, 1C.

15. Trumbull, 1C; Erwin Potts, "Baseball Fan Hit by Foul Undergoes Brain Surgery," *Miami (FL) Herald*, August 29, 1960, 1C; "Man Hit by Ball Dies of Injuries," *Miami (FL) Herald*, August 30, 1960, 1C; "Ball Game Spectator Hit on Head," *Miami (FL) News*, August 30, 1960, 2A.

16. "Elizabeth Man Killed by Batted Ball," *Washington Post*, September 7, 1925, 1.

17. "Killed by a Batted Ball," *New York Times*, September 8, 1887, 2.

18. "Killed by a Baseball," *Boston Daily Globe*, August 21, 1893, 1.

19. "Boy Killed by a Baseball," *New York Times*, September 4, 1895, 2; "Amateur Ball Players Under Arrest," *Boston Daily Globe*, September 5, 1895, 8; "City and Vicinity," *New York Times*, September 7, 1895, 8.

20. "Walter H. Gorr," *The Argus (Middletown, NY)*, June 7, 1897, 8.

21. "Was Struck on Head," *Boston Daily Globe*, August 15, 1897, 3.

22. "Killed by a Foul Ball," *New York Times*, June 30, 1901, 8.

23. "Struck by Baseball," *Lowell (MA) Daily Mail*, September 20, 1901, 1.

24. "Batted Ball Kills a Boy," *Chicago Daily Tribune*, May 20, 1902, 1.

25. "Boy Killed by Foul Ball," *Atlanta Constitution*, July 9, 1902, 11.

26. Accounts of this fatality have varied, both at the time of Walker's death and in more recent stories. The authors base their information on the story appearing in *The Belmont Chronicle* published in St. Clairsville, OH, the community with a newspaper closest to Morristown. Other accounts state that he either was the scorer or that he was passing the knife on to the umpire. See "Peculiar Accident," *Belmont Chronicle (St. Clairsville, OH)*, October 30, 1902, 1; "Peculiar and Fatal Accident," *Daily Examiner (Bellefontaine, OH)*, October 27, 1902, 1; "A Unique Accident," *Sporting Life*, November 8, 1902, 1; John Bowman and Joel Zoss, *Diamonds in the Rough: The Untold History of Baseball* (New York: Collier Macmillan, 1989), 356.

27. "Baseball Kills Girl," *Afro-American Ledger (Baltimore, MD)*, July 30, 1904, 2.

28. "Boy Is Killed by a Baseball," *Chicago Daily Tribune*, September 6, 1904, 8.

29. "Killed by a Baseball," *New York Times*, May 22, 1905, 1. An Associated Press report appearing at the time stated that Miles was a catcher who suffered a fractured skull when a pitched ball struck him between the eyes. He reportedly was not wearing a mask at the time. See "Killed by Pitched Ball," *Los Angeles Times*, May 23, 1905, II3.

30. "Baseball Kills a Boy," *New York Times*, April 16, 1906, 1.

31. "Ball Kills a Boy," *Milwaukee Journal*, September 17, 1906, 3.

32. "Boy Struck by Baseball Died," *New York Times*, May 13, 1907, 4.

33. "Baseball Kills Woman," *Washington Post*, April 23, 1908, 1. Another newspaper reported that it was a "tossed ball" instead. See "Woman Killed by Baseball," *Atlanta Constitution*, April 24, 1908, 7.

34. "Killed by Foul Tip," *Marion (OH) Weekly Star*, August 14, 1909, 3.

35. "Foul Ball Kills a Boy," *New York Times*, September 13, 1909, 1.

36. "Killed by Foul Ball," *Atlanta Constitution*, September 2, 1910, 8.

37. "Batted Baseball Kills Girl,"

Chicago Daily Tribune, September 3, 1910, 3.

38. "Hit by Baseball; Dies," *Pittsburgh Post*, May 31, 1911, 1; "Blow from Batted Ball Kills Young Girl," *Pittsburgh Press*, May 31, 1911, 8. The account of this incident appearing in the *New York Times* is greatly exaggerated. See "Girl Killed by Foul Ball," *New York Times*, May 31, 1911, 20.

39. "Boy Fan Killed by Baseball," *Chicago Daily Tribune*, July 18, 1911, 3.

40. "Baseball Kills Woman," *New York Times*, May 22, 1913, 1; "Batted Ball Kills Woman," *Washington Post*, May 22, 1913, 2.

41. "Players in Fatal Game Are Dismissed," *Evening Sun (Baltimore, MD)*, May 26, 1913, 12; "Players in Fatal Ball Game Freed," *Baltimore (MD) American*, May 27, 1913, 14; "Tragic Sequel to Boy's Death," *Baltimore (MD) American*, May 28, 1913, 16; "Double Funeral Today," *Baltimore (MD) American*, May 29, 1913, 14.

42. "Boy Killed by Batted Ball," *Chicago Daily Tribune*, June 29, 1914, 18.

43. "Killed by Batted Ball," *Washington Post*, April 19, 1915, 2.

44. "Charlotte Game Called Off," *Daily Times (Davenport, IA)*, September 3, 1915, 16.

45. "Line Drive Kills Child," *Chicago Daily Tribune*, October 11, 1915, 14.

46. "Batted Ball Kills Spectator," *New York Times*, June 24, 1918, 17.

47. "Nine-Year-Old Lad Killed by Foul Ball," *Atlanta Constitution*, May 18, 1921, 12.

48. "Killed by Batted Ball," *Washington Post*, June 23, 1921, 3.

49. "Foul Tip Kills Baseball Spectator," *New York Times*, June 1, 1924, E5.

50. "Baseball Kills Baby Being Carried by Mother on Northside," *Pittsburgh Post*, June 6, 1925, 1; "Sixteen-Months-Old Babe Killed by Batted Ball," *Charleroi (PA) Mail*, June 6, 1925, 1.

51. "Boy Killed by Foul Ball," *New York Times*, August 3, 1925, 17.

52. "Baseballs Kill Two; Pitcher and 'Fan,'" *Washington Post*, August 25, 1925, 1.

53. "Boy Is Killed by Batted Ball," *Youngstown (OH) Vindicator*, July 6, 1926, 1.

54. "Baseball Strikes Girl, Resulting in Death at Hospital," *Johnstown (PA) Tribune*, June 27, 1927, 13.

55. "Union Center Child Killed by Batted Ball While She Skips Rope in School Yard," *Binghamton (NY) Press*, May 11, 1928, 10.

56. "Man Hit by Ball from Son's Bat Dies of Injury," *Utica (NY) Daily Press*, September 4, 1928, 3.

57. "Struck by Baseball, Boy Dies

in Hospital," *Chester (PA) Times*, June 20, 1930, 1.

58. "Killed by a Batted Ball," *New York Times*, May 31, 1932, 9.

59. "Batted Ball Kills Boy, 10," *New York Times*, June 26, 1933, 4.

60. "Struck by Baseball, District Youth Dies," *Washington Post*, August 11, 1935, 3.

61. "Killed at Play," *Detroit News*, May 20, 1938, 37.

62. "Blow by Baseball Fatal," *New York Times*, July 16, 1938, 2.

63. "Baby Killed by Batted Ball," *New York Times*, June 5, 1939, 16.

64. "Eight-Year-Old Child Killed at Playground as Ball, Hit 225 Feet, Strikes Her Over Heart," *Richmond (VA) Times-Dispatch*, June 4, 1942, 1, 5; "Edward Lucas Faces Charge in Girl's Death," *Richmond (VA) Times-Dispatch*, June 5, 1942, 7; "Child's Death Is Declared Accidental," *Richmond (VA) Times-Dispatch*, June 6, 1942, 4. Lucas claimed that while he personally had never played with a hard ball on that field before, at least one of his teammates (the only witness at the hearing) said he himself had played baseball there previously.

65. Margaret Gibbons, "Borough, Baseball League Settled with Estate of Man Killed by Foul Ball," *The Legal Intelligencer*, October 29, 1997, 8.

66. Shirley Povich, "This Morning with Shirley Povich," *Washington Post*, February 20, 1946, 12.

67. Povich, "This Morning," 12.

68. "Wild Throw Fatal to Fan," *New York Times*, October 1, 1943, 22; "Death of Fan Was Accident," *Washington Post*, October 1, 1943, B1. The Senators won that game 6 to 2, then took the second 7 to 4, to clinch second place in the American League, their best finish in seven years.

69. Society for American Baseball Research, *Minor League Baseball Stars*, vol. 3 (Cleveland, OH: SABR, 1992), 128; Richard Scheinin, *Field of Screams: The Dark Underside of America's National Pastime* (New York: W. W. Norton, 1994), 194–195.

70. "Sports Hit Hard," *Galveston (TX) Daily News*, May 31, 1928, 9; "Blame Baseball Blow for Death of Colored Fan," *The Bee (Danville, VA)* December 22, 1928, 4; "Negro Fan Dies from Blow," *The Sporting News*, January 3, 1929, 2; "Fan Dies When Hit by Ball, and Shires Is Sued," *News-Palladium (Benton-Harbor, MI)*, March 28, 1929, 13.

71. "Negro Fan Dies," 2; "Sox Pilot Faces Damage Claim," *Evening Tribune (Albert Lea, MN)*, March 28, 1929, 14; "Jury Exonerates Shires of Blame for Fan's Death," *Chicago Daily Tribune*, March 29, 1929, 31; "Art Shires Sued for $25, 411 in Death of

Negro Baseball Fan," *The Sporting News*, April 4, 1929, 7.

72. "Art Shires Sued," 7; "Jury Exonerates Shires," 31; "Suit Against Shires in Killing Reopened." *San Antonio (TX) Light*, May 21, 1929, 8; "Federal Court Reinstates Case Against Shires," *Chicago Daily Tribune*, May 21, 1929, 27.

73. "Suit Against Shires Taken Off Docket," *Los Angeles Times*, January 12, 1930, E9; "Shires to Pay Widow of Man Killed $500," *San Antonio (TX) Light*, January 12, 1930, pt. 6, 1; "Caught on the Fly," *The Sporting News*, January 16, 1930, 8. One reason Shires may not have been in court himself was that on January 10, 1930, he was in Boston facing Boston Braves catcher Al Spohrer in the ring. It would be Shires' last professional bout before Commissioner Landis forced him to choose between quitting or be banned from baseball. He was awarded a TKO over Spohrer in the fourth round of this bogus match. See "Art Shires Closes Ring Career with Win Over Brave Catcher," *Dallas Morning News*, January 11, 1930, 13.

74. "A Boy's Sad Death," *Chester (PA) Times*, August 15, 1882, 3; "The Toppin Inquest," *Chester (PA) Times*, August 16, 1882, 3.

75. "Killed by a Baseball," *New York Times*, April 12, 1903, 1.

76. "Baseball Kills Woman," *New York Times*, June 21, 1905, 1.

77. "Killed by a Pitched Ball," *New York Times*, June 18, 1906, 1.

78. "Killed by Baseball," *Boston Daily Globe*, April 3, 1908, 16.

79. "Hit by Ball and Dies," *Washington Post*, July 19, 1908, 16. Another newspaper does not give the name of the victim, but reports that the father was named Andrew Luksia. See "Babe Killed by Baseball," *Chicago Daily Tribune*, July 18, 1908, 4.

80. "Baby Is Struck by Baseball," *Indianapolis Star*, July 25, 1910, 1; "Baby Hit by Ball Dies," *Indianapolis Star*, July 26, 1910, 14; "Gets Release from Jail by Pleading of Friends," *Indianapolis Star*, July 27, 1910, 3; "Reports on Baby's Death," *Indianapolis Star*, July 29, 1910, 10; "Man Whose Wild Throw Killed Baby Dismissed," *Indianapolis Star*, July 30, 1910, 14.

81. "Man Killed by a Baseball," *Chicago Daily Tribune*, August 27, 1911, 6; "Deaths," *Daily News (Chicago, IL)*, August 28, 1911, 15.

82. "Chief of Police at Decherd Killed," *Nashville (TN) Banner*, April 2, 1913, 4.

83. "Little Girl Is Killed by Thrown Baseball," *Atlanta Constitution*, February 20, 1914, 2; "Blow of Baseball Kills Child," *Daily Picayune (New Orleans, LA)*, February 20, 1914, 5. The

Picayune story reports the child's age as 5.

84. "Boy Killed by Baseball," *New York Times*, September 17, 1928, 15.

85. "Baseball Kills Lad Viewing Game from Behind Catcher," *New York Times*, April 29, 1929, 20.

86. "Boy Killed When Struck Behind Ear by Thrown Ball at San Pedro Park," *San Antonio (TX) Express*, April 25, 1932, 1; "Ball Game Death Called Accident," *San Antonio (TX) Express*, April 26, 1932, 18.

87. "Baseball Kills Boy, 13," *New York Times*, April 1, 1952, 31.

88. Harry Weisberger, "Wild Baseball Strikes, Kills 3-Month-Old Baby," *Daily Sun (San Bernardino, CA)*, May 19, 1958, B1.

89. Local newspaper accounts differ as to whether this accident occurred at a baseball or a softball game. See "Boy Killed When Hit by Baseball," *Journal-Gazette (Ft. Wayne, IN)*, June 23, 1973, 1; "Wild Throw Kills Youth at Ball Game," *Fort Wayne (IN) News-Sentinel*, June 23, 1973, 6A.

90. "Florida Boy, 4, Dies After Baseball Hits His Chest, Stops His Heart," *Associated Press*, November 3, 2007; Thomas Lake and Helen Anne Travis, "Boy, 4, Killed by Ball in Park," *St. Petersburg (FL) Times*, November 3, 2007, 1A.

91. "General News Notes," *Syracuse (NY) Standard*, October 3, 1884, 2; "Killed by a Baseball Bat," *Washington Post*, October 2, 1884, 1.

92. "Killed with a Bat," *Pittsburgh Times*, April 25, 1905, 1.

93. "Died from Blow of a Baseball Bat," *Savannah (GA) Morning News*, July 6, 1905, 12. The *Atlanta Constitution* reported that the batter had slung the bat in anger after striking out, but the local paper made no mention of this being the case. See "Killed with a Baseball Bat," *Atlanta Constitution*, July 6, 1905, 9.

94. "Four-Year-Old Boy Hurt Fatally at Ball Game," *Pittsburgh Post*, August 23, 1915, 2; "Freed on Own Recognizance," *Pittsburgh Post*, August 24, 1915, 4.

95. "Youth Held After Child Dies at Baseball Game," *Washington Post*, May 1, 1931, 4.

96. "Amsterdam Boy Struck by Bat Succumbs," *Schenectady (NY) Gazette*, July 20, 1933, 5.

97. "Broken Bat Causes Boy's Death," *New York Times*, May 16, 1934, 14.

98. "Bat Kills Boy, 3, at Game," *New York Times*, August 1, 1939, 42.

99. "May Cost Life," *Bureau County (IL) Record*, June 27, 1906, 10; "Succumbs to Injury," *Ottawa (IL) Journal*, July 4, 1906, 3.

100. "Injured at Ball Game, Boy

Dies," *Detroit News*, August 4, 1909, 14.

Chapter 13

1. Louis Effrat, "Yankees Beat Browns in Tenth," *New York Times*, April 29, 1953, 22; "Gang Fight Shocking Setback — For Kids," *The Sporting News*, May 13, 1953, 12.

2. As Francois Thebaud, French sports journalist and founder of one of Europe's leading soccer magazines, once wrote about the game he loved, "No other sport has ever been plagued into mourning by catastrophes on such a scale." See Francois Thebaud, "A Red Card for the Round Ball," *UNESCO Courier*, December 1992; Steve Rushin, "A Stain on the Game: The Mass Deaths of Fans Is Soccer's Recurring Tragedy, but It's Barely Noticed Here," *Sports Illustrated*, May 21, 2001; "Soccer Riots Plague Africa," *Amusement Business*, May 28, 2001, 10. Even soccer deaths pale in comparison with the number killed at Roman chariot races. Over 30,000 died in one year alone (532 B.C.E.) during these contests. See Jack C. Horn, "Fan Violence: Fighting," *Psychology Today*, October 1985, 30.

3. One survey of newspaper coverage of fan violence (involving 5 or more persons) at all levels (high school, college, professional, and other) identified 170 incidents over a 12-year period (1960–1972), or slightly more than 14 per year. Incidents included "running on the playing field or court and disrupting an event, fighting with fans or players, throwing missiles, and vandalism." The incidents by sport are 43 in football, 36 in baseball, 35 in basketball, 17 in boxing, 15 in hockey, and 24 in other sports combined. See Jerry M. Lewis, "Fan Violence: An American Social Problem," *Research in Social Problems and Public Policy* 2 (1982): 182; Julian Roberts and Cynthia Benjamin, "Spectator Violence in Sports: A North American Perspective," *European Journal on Criminal Policy and Research* 8 (June 2000): 163–181.

4. Francis C. Richter, "The Cost of Rowdy Ball," in *Grandstand Baseball Annual 2000* (Downey, CA: J. M. Wayman, 2000), 95–98; Fred Stein, *A History of the Baseball Fan* (Jefferson, NC: McFarland, 2005), 28–30.

5. Stein, 31, 35–36, 182–186; Bill James, *The Bill James Historical Baseball Abstract* (New York: Villard Books, 1988), 136; Jonathan Fraser Light, *The Cultural Encyclopedia of Baseball*, 2nd ed. (Jefferson, NC: McFarland, 2005), 227.

6. Kirk L. Wakefield and Daniel L. Wann, "An Examination of Dysfunctional Sport Fans: Method of Classification and Relationships with Problem Behaviors," *Journal of Leisure Research* 38, no. 2 (2006): 168–186; Stephen Starksports, "Sports Fans Mad, Bad, and Dangerous to Know: American Spectators Losing Good Reputation," *Atlanta Journal and Constitution*, July 14, 1991, 1D; Ian Love, "Baseball Moves to Curb Unruly Fan Behavior," *Los Angeles Times*, March 16, 1986, 12. For a thorough analysis of sports crowd behavior, see Daniel L. Wann, Merrill J. Melnick, Gordon W. Russell, and Dale G. Pease, *Sport Fans: The Psychology and Social Impact of Spectators* (New York: Routledge, 2001).

7. Wann et al., *Sports Fans*, 129–130; John McManus, "Alcohol: A Touchy Subject," *The Sporting News*, May 1, 1989, 49.

8. Wakefield and Wann, 171, 177, 179; Stuart P. Taylor, Charles B. Gammon, and Deborah R. Capasso, "Aggression as a Function of the Interaction of Alcohol and Threat," *Journal of Personality and Social Psychology* 34, no. 5 (1976): 938–941.

9. Charles Leerhsen and John McCormick, "When Push Comes to Shove," *Newsweek*, May 16, 1988, 73; Jay Coakley, *Sport in Society: Issues and Controversies*, 7th ed. (New York: McGraw-Hill, 2001), 197.

10. Craig Wolff, "Unruliness an Ugly Pastime for Some Baseball Fans," *New York Times*, June 16, 1985; Scott D. Lane, Don R. Cherek, and Cynthia J. Pietras, "Alcohol Effects on Human Risk Taking," *Psychopharmacology* 172, no. 1 (2004): 74.

11. Laurence Steinberg, "Risk Taking in Adolescence: New Perspectives from Brain and Behavioral Science," *Current Directions in Psychological Science* 16, no. 2 (2007): 56.

12. Leerhsen and McCormick, 73; Jack McCallum and Richard O'Brien, "Hard Rain," *Sports Illustrated*, November 4, 1996.

13. William Oscar Johnson, "Sports and Suds: The Beer Business and the Sports World Have Brewed Up a Potent Partnership," *Sports Illustrated*, August 8, 1988, 68–82; Leerhsen and McCormick, 72–73; Wakefield and Wann, 181.

14. Wolff; Jonathan Williams, "Safety Fence Eyed at Stadium: Authority to Meet in Wake of Fatality," *Pittsburgh (PA) Post-Gazette*, April 20, 1972, 1; Fr. John Hissrich, e-mail message to Bob Gorman, June 5, 2002.

15. Harold Seymour, *Baseball: The Early Years* (New York: Oxford University Press, 1989), 289; Love, 12.

16. "Death Closes Roof Stands," *Chicago Daily Tribune*, July 19, 1908, 6. Chicago was not the only venue with stands located on top of surrounding buildings. Several major league parks at the time, including those in Washington, DC, Boston, MA, and Philadelphia, PA, had similar stands near them as well. See "May See Games from Roofs," *Washington Post*, September 10, 1908, 14; "Seeing the Ball Games in Boston Without Paying a Cent," *Boston Daily Globe*, September 19, 1909, SM 4; "Mackmen Blank the Tigers," *Chicago Daily Tribune*, September 19, 1909, C1.

17. "Death Closes," 6; "Hit by Ball and Dies," *Washington Post*, July 19, 1908, 16; "Grand Stands on Roofs Are Called Nuisance by Court," *Chicago Daily Tribune*, January 19, 1910, 13.

18. "The Cubs Win the Pennant," *New York Times*, October 9, 1908, 1–3; "Paid with Life to See Game," *New York Times*, October 9, 1908, 3; "Chicago Goes Wild Over Cub's Victory," *New York Times*, October 9, 1908, 3.

19. "Man Who Fell to Death at Stadium Identified," *Evening Sun (Baltimore)*, August 6, 1969, D3; Doug Brown, "Oriole Potpourri," *Evening Sun (Baltimore)*, August 6, 1969, C1.

20. "East McKeesport Boy Takes Fatal Shortcut at Game," *Pittsburgh Post-Gazette*, April 19, 1972, 1; Jonathan Williams, "Safety Fence Eyed at Stadium," *Pittsburgh Post-Gazette*, April 20, 1972, 1; Jonathan Williams, "Stadium Death Inquest Slated," *Pittsburgh Post-Gazette*, April 22, 1972, 1; Fr. John Hissrich, e-mail message to Bob Gorman, June 5, 2002.

21. Lloyd Vye, the manager of the Vet, stated that "people don't understand how far out of the way you have to go to get to that area" and that with "construction going on, it wasn't a mystery to me that the plate was missing." As to why there was no one preventing fans from using the walkway, Vye explained that "the security guards who keep fans out of the scoreboard area usually leave when the game ends and the crowd has dispersed." There was disagreement as to how well lighted the area was. When a number of other fans claimed that the lights were out in the vicinity of the scoreboard, Vye replied, "the electrician assured me the maintenance lights were never turned out." In February 1972, Shober's widow filed a $3.1 million lawsuit against the city of Philadelphia, the Phillies team, and the architectural firms that helped design the stadium. See James S. Lintz, "Phillies Fan's Fatal Plunge Tied to Plate Left Off Pit," *Philadelphia Inquirer*, August 26, 1971, 1; "Family Sues for Death in Ball Park,"

Delaware County (PA) Daily Times, February 19, 1972, 2.

22. "Baseball Fan Falls to His Death," *Associated Press,* July 13, 1980; "A Queens Man Commits Suicide in Leap Off Shea Stadium Ramp," *New York Times,* July 14, 1980, B6; "Domestic News," *Associated Press,* July 14, 1980.

23. "Fan Dies in Plunge at Candlestick," *San Francisco Chronicle,* June 7, 1984, 1, 22.

24. "Shea Spectator Dies After Fall," *New York Times,* May 2, 1985, B15; "Mets' Fan Falls to Death," *The Post (Frederick, MD),* May 3, 1985, B4.

25. "Upper-Deck Fall Kills Fan at Sox Game," *Chicago Tribune,* May 17, 1986, sec. 2, 5.

26. Sharon Bond, "Car Hits Fan Chasing Foul Ball in Bradenton," *St. Petersburg (FL) Times,* March 11, 1988, 1B; Kathy Subko, "Man Hit While Chasing Ball Dies," *St. Petersburg (FL) Times,* March 12, 1988, 5B.

27. "Fan Dies After Fall at Stadium," *Kansas City (MO) Times,* April 28, 1989, E1; Steve Kaut, "Tragedy at Royals Stadium," *Kansas City (MO) Star,* April 28, 1989, 3A; "Fall Fatal to Fan at Royals Stadium," *Pacific Stars and Stripes,* April 30, 1989, 34.

28. "Stadium Fall Kills Man," *Pittsburgh Post-Gazette,* August 16, 1993, B4.

29. Brian Lewis, Larry Celona, Angela Mosconi, and Bill Sanderson, "Fan Dies in Stadium Plunge," *New York Post,* April 26, 1999, 7; Angela Mosconi, "Dean Man's Family Spurns Yanks' Help, *New York Post,* May 1, 1999, 14.

30. "Fan Dies at Pacific Bell Park in Bid to Retrieve Sunglasses," *San Francisco Chronicle,* September 18, 2003, A15; Alan Gathright, "Alcohol Cited in 1st Death at Pacific Bell Park," *San Francisco Chronicle,* September 19, 2003, A22.

31. "Man Dies After Falling Off Escalator at Miller Park," *Associated Press State and Local Wire,* July 31, 2004; "Baseball Fan Dies in Miller Park Fall," *Capital Times (Madison, WI),* July 31, 2004, 3A.

32. Bob Purvis, "Family Wants Answers from Police After Man's Death," *Milwaukee Journal Sentinel,* July 21, 2006, B1; Bob Purvis, "Family of Man Who Died After Being Shoved by Officers Files Notice of Claim," *Milwaukee Journal Sentinel,* November 7, 2006.

33. "Dies in Fall from Fence at Spa Ball Park," *Sentinel-Record (Hot Springs, AR),* May 4, 1939, 1; "Final Rites for Montgomery Today," *Sentinel-Record (Hot Springs, AR),* May 5, 1939, 2.

34. "Airplane to Drop Some Balls

Where Soldiers Perform," *Indianapolis Star,* May 29, 1918, 10; "Aviation Team to Play Taylor's A.B.C.s Today," *Indianapolis Star,* June 1, 1918, 10; William Ash, "A.B.C.s and Soldiers to Scrap Again," *Indianapolis Star,* June 2, 1918, 3.

35. "Airplane to Drop," 10. The plane, which had been in a crash earlier that spring, was sent to the Speedway camp for repairs and was being used at the Speedway to help train student fliers. See "Gearhart Held to Have Chance," *Indianapolis Star,* June 4, 1918, 8.

36. "Ball Game Postponed When an Airplane Falls in Park Killing U. S. Aero Captain," *Indianapolis Star,* June 3, 1918, 9; "Flier Killed, Another Hurt in Crash at Baseball Park," *Indianapolis Star,* June 3, 1918, 1, 3.

37. "Flier Killed," 1, 3; "Gearhart Held," 8; "Maj. Gearhart Improving," *Indianapolis Star,* June 8, 1918, 5.

38. "Flier Killed," 1, 3; "Gearhart Held," 8.

39. Interestingly, this event occurred at the height of Prohibition (1920–1933) when beer was not sold at ballparks. None of the news accounts even hinted at alcohol-consumption being involved, so unless some of the miscreant fans had smuggled liquor into the stadium, this particular riot could not be blamed on "Demon Rum." Gordon Cobbledick, "Pop Bottles Fly as Macks Trim Indians, 4–2," *Cleveland Plain Dealer,* May 12, 1929, 1C, 4C; "Umpire Hit by Bottle Is Worse," *Cleveland Plain Dealer,* May 13, 1929, 1; "Umpire Assaulted as Athletics Win," *New York Times,* May 12, 1929, 5S; "Ball Game Riot Is Fatal to Akronite," *Akron (OH) Beacon Journal,* May 15, 1929, 1.

40. Cobbledick, 1C; "Umpire Assaulted," 5S.

41. "Ball Game Riot," 1; Sam Otis, "Wake Up, Cleveland!," *Cleveland Plain Dealer,* May 13, 1929, 19.

42. "Blow on Head Brings Death," *Evening Press (Grand Rapids, MI)* May 2, 1908, 1, 6; "Parks Not Guilty," *Evening Press (Grand Rapids, MI),* December 19, 1908, 7.

43. "Blow on Head," 1, 6.

44. "Parks Not Guilty," 7.

45. "Race Riot Rages in Harlem Streets," *New York Times,* August 5, 1907, 1; "Two Badly Hurt in Race Riot," *The Sun (New York, NY),* August 5, 1907, 1. These two papers disagreed as to the racial composition of the two teams. The *New York Times* described both teams as all-white, while *The Sun* said one was white, the other black. In all likelihood *The Sun* was correct.

46. "Race Riot Rages," 1; "Two Badly Hurt," 1; "More Attacks on Ne-

groes," *New York Times,* August 6, 1907. 2; "Five Thousand in Race Riot," *Boston Daily Globe,* August 5, 1907, 9.

47. "Race Riot Rages," 1; "Two Badly Hurt," 1; "Victim of Race Riot Dies," *New York Times,* August 6, 1907, 2.

48. Don Jensen, "Bugs Raymond," *The Baseball Biography Project,* Society for American Baseball Research, http://bioproj.sabr.org/ (accessed July 26, 2005); Jack Kavanagh, "Bugs Raymond," *Baseball Research Journal,* 26 (1997): 125–127.

49. "'Bugs' Raymond Dies Suddenly," *Chicago Daily Tribune,* September 8, 1912, C1.

50. "Coroner to Investigate," *Los Angeles Times,* September 9, 1912, 11; "'Bugs' Raymond Died of Violence," *Chicago Daily Tribune,* September 10, 1912, 3; "'Bugs' Raymond Was Slain," *New York Times,* September 10, 1912, 7.

51. "Two Men Struck on Head and One Is Likely to Die," *Rocky Mountain News (Denver),* May 10, 1915, 3; "Man Struck by Brick at Ball Game Is Dead," *Rocky Mountain News (Denver),* May 13, 1915, 8; Frank Newhouse, "Liners from the Amateurs' Bats," *Denver Post,* May 16, 1915, 2.

52. An autopsy later that day found the brain uninjured, but death was caused when the ruptured artery filled the brain cavity with blood, "thus pressing the brain back from the skull nearly an inch." See, "Another Tragedy," *Daily Times (Chattanooga, TN),* February 23, 1888, 5.

53. "Gave Himself Up," *Daily Times (Chattanooga, TN),* February 24, 1888, 6; "M'Gill in Court," *Daily Times (Chattanooga, TN),* February 25, 1888, 6.

54. "Criticized Her Acting," *Los Angeles Times,* September 23, 1899, 2; "Julia Morrison Before Bar of Justice," *Daily Times (Chattanooga, TN),* January 5, 1900, 5; "Julia Morrison on the Stand," *Daily Times (Chattanooga, TN),* January 6, 1900, 5–6; "Temporary Insanity Miss Morrison's Plea," *Daily Times (Chattanooga, TN),* January 7, 1900, 4; "The Trial of Julia Morrison," *Daily Times (Chattanooga, TN),* January 8, 1900, 5; "Was Julia Morrison Insane," *Daily Times (Chattanooga, TN),* January 9, 1900, 4–5; "Morrison Case Goes to the Jury Today," *Daily Times (Chattanooga, TN),* January 10, 1900, 4–5.

55. "Trial of Julia Morrison," 5; "Once Indicted," *Boston Daily Globe,* January 8, 1900, 2; "Miss Morrison 'Not Guilty,'" *Daily Times (Chattanooga, TN),* January 11, 1900, 4. Julia Morrison crops up in another scandal the following year. Apparently she had been taking lessons in hypnotism from one Professor J. R. V. Silver in New

York. After competing the sixth lesson at her home, they went out to dinner. Suddenly the professor's enraged wife and young son appear, unbeknownst to him, behind his back. Mrs. Silver, angry at finding her husband with the lovely actress, proceeded to lash him with "a heavy dog whip." The philandering academic was able to make his way through the crowded restaurant and flee by passing cab. For her part, Morrison claimed not to know that Silver was married. "I think his wife treated him right," she explained later. "He had no right to ask me to dine with him." See, "Disturbed at Their Meal," *Atlanta Constitution*, July 1, 1901, 3.

56. "Negro Butchered at Pleasant Hill," *Charlotte (NC) News*, July 5, 1906, 1; "A Brutal Killing," *Charlotte (NC) Daily Observer*, July 6, 1906, 7.

57. "Made a Base Hit," *Monroe (LA) News-Star*, July 20, 1909, 5; "Ball Player Kills Negro with a Bat," *Atlanta Constitution*, July 19, 1909, 7.

58. "Man Killed at Beckwith Sunday in a Dispute Arising Out of a Ball Game," *Plumas (Quincy, CA) National Bulletin*, August 16, 1909, 1; "Jones Held for Trial on Murder Charge," *Plumas (Quincy, CA) National Bulletin*, August 19, 1909, 1; "Trial of J. C. Jones for the Murder of Geo. King Being Heard by Jury," *Plumas (Quincy, CA) National Bulletin*, September 23, 1909, 1.

59. "Trial of J. C. Jones," 1; "Guilty of Murder in Second Degree Verdict of Jury at Trial of Jones," *Plumas (Quincy, CA) National Bulletin*, September 27, 1909, 1;

60. "Guilty of Murder," 1; "J. C. Jones Sentenced to Term of 14 Years in Prison," *Plumas (Quincy, CA) National Bulletin*, October 7, 1909, 3. Several jurors afterwards remarked on the role that alcohol played in the events, finding that "this unfortunate murder had its origin in booze, that both sides to the controversy had imbibed to such an extent that, while not drunk, they were in such condition as to magnify and resent any slight offense and precipitate just such an unfortunate row as resulted in the death of one man and the ruin of the life of another." See "Guilty of Murder," 1.

61. "Jones Murder Case Reversed by Court," *Plumas (Quincy, CA) National Bulletin*, July 17, 1911, 1; "Second Trial of J. C. Jones for the Murder of Geo. King Results in Prompt Acquittal," *Plumas (Quincy, CA) National Bulletin*, October 23, 1911, 1.

62. "Spectators Riot at Ft. Branch Go; One Fan Injured," *Evansville (IN) Courier*, July 18, 1927, 7; "Suspect in Fatal Ft. Branch Fight Is Missing Now," *Evansville (IN) Courier*, July 23,

1927, 3; "Widow Testifies in Bat Murder," *Evansville (IN) Courier*, October 19, 1927, 1, 3.

63. "Suspect in Fatal Ft. Branch Fight," 3; "Probe of Fatal Melee at Ball Game Is Opened," *Evansville (IN) Courier*, July 21, 1927, 1,3; "Ft. Branch Miner Wielded Deadly Bat, Man Swears," *Evansville (IN) Courier*, July 31, 1927, 1, 6.

64. "Fred Stone Held in Bat Killing," *Evansville (IN) Courier*, July 26, 1927, 1, 2; "Drop Murder Charge in Ball Bat Slaying," *Evansville (IN) Courier*, July 30, 1927, 5; "Alleged Bat Slayer Faces Trial Oct. 18," *Evansville (IN) Courier*, September 23, 1927, 5.

65. "Widow Testifies," 1, 3; "Stone, on Stand, Admits Slugging Warren with Bat," *Evansville (IN) Courier*, October 20, 1927, 1, 3; "Bat Killing Case to Jury Today," *Evansville (IN) Courier*, October 21, 1927, 1; "Ft. Branch Man Found Guilty of Assault, Battery," *Evansville (IN) Courier*, October 22, 1927, 1.

66. "Town Asks, 'Why?' After a Little-League Killing," *New York Times*. May 23, 1993, 18; "Youth to Stand Trial in Slaying at Ball Game," *San Francisco Chronicle*, November 10, 1993, A17; Peter Fimrite, "Mother Turns Grief for Slain Son into Anti-Violence Campaign," *San Francisco Chronicle*, May 29, 1995, A17.

67. The umpire, who rushed to aid the stricken player, later told authorities who had thrown the rock. This action led to death threats against the umpire and an attempt to burn down his home early on the morning of May 18. When authorities decided not to prosecute the pitcher who had injured Messina, the calls and threats against the umpire ceased. See ""Baseball Brawl Brings Death; Ump Threatened," *St. Petersburg (FL) Times*, May 20, 1993, 1A; "Arraignment Postponed in Deadly Brawl," *San Francisco Chronicle*, May 20, 1993, A24.

68. Catherine Bowman, "Not-Guilty Plea in Little League Bat Homicide," *San Francisco Chronicle*, August 12, 1993, A17; "Youth to Stand Trial,"A17; "Teenager Sentenced in Baseball-Bat Killing," *San Francisco Chronicle*, April 23, 1994, A20.

69. Anastasia Hendrix, "Inmate Is Killed in Brawl," *Fresno (CA) Bee*, April 7, 1996, B1.

70. Charles F. Bostwick and Karen Maeshiro, "Moment of Rage," *Daily News (Los Angeles)*, April 14, 2005, N1; Charles F. Bostwick, "Murder Conviction Disputed," *Daily News (Los Angeles)*, October 27, 2006; AV1.

71. "13-Year-Old Gets 12 Years for Baseball Bat Killing," *Ventura County (CA) Star*, July 29, 2005, 5; Caitlin

Liu, "Boy, 13, Gets 12 Years for Murder," *Los Angeles Times*, July 29, 2005, B1.

72. Bostwick; Karen Maeshiro, "Ball-Bat Slaying Charge Reduced," *Daily News (Los Angeles)*, January 23, 2007, AV1; Karen Maeshiro, "State Appeals Reduction of Charge in Bat Slaying," *Daily News (Los Angeles)*, February 7, 2007, AV3; "Briefly," *Daily News (Los Angeles)*, February 23, 2007, AV3.

73. While the area newspaper did not give a reason for the assault, the *National Police Gazette* reported that Hall was angered over a decision by Staples awarding a player a base-on-balls. The *Gazette* made no mention of Hall throwing rocks at Staples, but said that Staples stabbed Hall after Hall called him a liar. See "The Umpire Makes His Escape," *Knoxville (TN) Journal*, June 16, 1889, 1; "On Trial for Murder," *Knoxville (TN) Daily Journal*, June 20, 1889, 8; "Sporting Notes," *National Police Gazette*, July 6, 1889, 11.

74. "Woman Slain at a Baseball Game in Central Park, Killer Is Mobbed," *New York Times*, May 25, 1953, 1, 17; "Fans Bat Down Woman's Killer at Ball Game," *Chicago Daily Tribune*, May 25, 1953, 10; "Indicted in Central Park Slaying," *New York Times*, July 11, 1953, 28; "53 Lynchless, Race Report to Drop Index," *Washington Post*, December 31, 1953, 5.

75. "Mystery Shot Kills Polo Grounds Fan in 50,000 Crowd," *The Sporting News*, July 12, 1950, 54; "Mystery Bullet Kills Baseball Fan in Midst of Crowd at Polo Grounds," *New York Times*, July 5, 1950, 1, 22.

76. "Mystery Bullet," 22. When word reached some of the Dodger players on the field that there had been a shooting, "they were talking more about the shooting than the ball game," according to second baseman Jackie Robinson. The Giants bench reportedly was unaware that anything was amiss.

77. "Youth Questioned in Death at Game," *New York Times*, July 6, 1950, 34.

78. "Search Extended in Mystery Death," *New York Times*, July 7, 1950, 42; "Boy, 14, Admits Firing .45 Pistol at Time of Polo Grounds Killing," *New York Times*, July 8, 1950, 1; "Youth Remanded in Polo Gun Case," *Post-Standard (Syracuse, NY)*, July 27, 1950, 3; "Boy Is Sent to Warwick," *Kingston (NY) Daily Freeman*, August 3, 1950, 15; Joseph McNamara, "And It's One, Two, Three Strikes You're Dead at the Old Ballgame" (undated clipping of a two-page column entitled "The Justice Story" found in the National Baseball Hall of Fame's clipping files, probably

from the magazine section of *New York Daily News*).

79. "Baseball Fan Slain in Opener," *Sunday News and Courier (Jefferson City, MO)*, April 12, 1970, 14; Bill McClellan, "As Busch Goes Down, Mystery Lingers in 1970 Murder There," *St. Louis Post-Dispatch*, November 9, 2005, B1; Bill McClellan, "Conclusion About Killing at Stadium: It's Too Late," *St. Louis Post-Dispatch*, November 20, 2005, C1.

80. McClellan, "As Busch Goes Down," B1; McClellan, "Conclusion about Killing," C1.

81. Henry Schulman, "Police Nab 2 in Fan Shooting," *San Francisco Chronicle*, September 21, 2003, A25; "Two Men Charged with Fatal Shooting in Dodger Stadium Parking Lot," *City News Service*, September 23, 2003; Tim Traeger, "Reward Offered for Suspect in Dodger Stadium Shooting," *Pasadena (CA) Star-News*, September 23, 2003; Bill Hetherman, "Witness: Argument Led to Shooting at Stadium," *Pasadena (CA) Star-News*, August 12, 2004; "Two Ordered to Stand Trial for Fatal Shooting in Dodger Stadium Parking Lot," *City News Service*, February 4, 2004; "Man Sentenced to 50-to-Life in Deadly Stadium Shooting," *City News Service*, October 26, 2004. There was speculation early on that the conflict might have arisen because of the intense rivalry between Dodgers and Giants fans, but this turned out not to be the case. The victim was not wearing Giants apparel and no one testified that the altercation started because of team loyalties.

82. Hetherman, "Witness"; "Man Sentenced to 50-to-Life"; Louis Galvan, "L. A. Suspect Sought in Fresno," *Fresno (CA) Bee*, September 26, 2003, B1,; "Man Charged with Murder of Giants Fan at Dodger Stadium Pleads Innocent," *Associated Press State and Local Wire*, October 16, 2003; Tim Traeger, "2nd Man Held in Stadium Shooting," *San Gabriel Valley (CA) Tribune*, December 2, 2003; "One Man Pleads No Contest to Voluntary Manslaughter in Stadium Shooting," *City News Service*, August 9, 2004; Bill Hetherman, "Jury Convicts Man in Shooting at Dodger Game," *Pasadena (CA) Star-News*, August 16, 2004.

83. Some accounts report Twente's first name as "Stamford." In addition, at least three different ages were given for the victim, 30, 48, and 50. See "Television Audience Is Horrified," *Daily Mail (Anderson, SC)*, June 12, 1950, l; "Suicide at Ball Game Goes on Houston TV: Victim Has Boy in SC," *Index-Journal (Greenwood, SC)*, June 12, 1950, 1; "Television Flashes Scenes in Suicide at Buff Stadium," *Houston*

Post, June 12, 1950, 1–2; "Man, 48, Fatally Shoots Self; TV Shows Body," *Houston Chronicle*, June 12, 1950, 1–2.

84. "Television Audience," 1; "Suicide at Ball Game," 1; "Television Flashes," 1–2; "Man, 48, Fatally Shoots Self," 1, 4.

85. Joan Fleischman, "Ball Park Gunman Kills Two," *Miami (FL) Herald*, August 26, 1980, 1A, 14A; Dan Williams, "Double-Killing Suspect's Parents Terrified by 'Sick Enraged' Son," *Miami (FL) Herald*, August 27, 1980, 1C, 3C.

86. Fleischman, 1A, 14A; Williams, 1C, 3C.

87. "Young Negro Is Shot to Death Late Monday by Solomon George," *Griffin (GA) Semi-Weekly News*, June 25, 1925, 6; "Hearing Planned for Griffin Man Held for Murder," *Atlanta Constitution*, July 26, 1925, A3.

88. "Shooting Ends Baseball Game at Bradley," *Index-Journal (Greenwood, SC)*, May 22, 1950, 5; "Fan Is Killed at Negro Game," *The State (Columbia, SC)*, May 23, 1950, 5B; "Hold Coach for Gun Death of Baseball Fan," *Chicago Defender*, June 3, 1950, 12; "Baseball Fan Killed," *Daily Mail (Anderson, SC)*, May 22, 1950, 1.

89. "One Dead and Six Wounded in Fierce Riot," *Pittsburgh Post*, June 1, 1903, 1–2; "Rioters to Be Brought to Justice," *Pittsburgh Press*, June 1, 1903, 5; "Murderer of Kelly Known," *Pittsburgh Press*, June 2, 1903, 20; "Warrants Out for Rioters," *Pittsburgh Press*, June 3, 1903, 1; "Sailor Rees May Be Freed," *Pittsburgh Press*, June 5, 1903, 1; "Foster in Jail on Riot Charge," *Pittsburgh Press*, June 6, 1903, 2; "Investigation Nearly Ended," *Pittsburgh Press*, June 8, 1903, 1.

90. "Fatal Shooting at Max Meadows," *Roanoke (VA) Times*, July 23, 1910, 1; "Splendid School at Max Meadows," *Roanoke (VA) Times*, July 27, 1910, 8.

91. "Lock L. Lann," *Aberdeen (MS) Examiner*, July 9, 1915, 5.

92. "Killing of Man Delayed Ball Game an Hour," *Owensboro (KY) Inquirer*, August 16, 1915, 1.

93. "Negro Slain After He Kills One, Shoots Four," *Pittsburgh Post*, May 31, 1921, 1, 5.

94. "Negro Slain," 1, 5; "Officer Is Praised for Brave Action," *Pittsburgh Post*, June 1, 1921, 1.

95. "Murder at a Ball Game," *New York Times*, July 30, 1922, 18; "State Briefs," *Charleston (WV) Daily Mail*, August 4, 1922, 11.

96. "Woman Had Filed Complaint Against Ex-Husband," *Associated Press State and Local Wire*, May 18, 2000.

97. Duncan Mansfield, "Tenn. Father Wounded Trying to Grab Gun," *Associated Press Online*, September 21,

2006; Jim Balloch, "Police: Custody Feud Turned Violent," *KnoxNews*, September 20, 2006, http://www.knoxnews.com/kns/local_news/article/0,1406,KNS_347_5006597,00.html.

Chapter 14

1. Lori S. Buns and Patti A. Ellison, "First Aid and Emergency Care at a Major-League Baseball Stadium," *Journal of Emergency Nursing* 18 (August 1992): 332–333.

2. Buns and Ellison, 331–333.

3. O. John Ma, Ronald G. Pirrallo, and Jonathan M. Rubin, "Survey of Medical Services at Major League Baseball Stadiums," *Prehospital and Disaster Medicine* 10 (October-December 1995): 268–271.

4. Daniel R. Witte and others, "Cardiovascular Mortality in Dutch Men During 1996 European Football Championship: Longitudinal Population Study," *British Medical Journal* 321 (December 2000): 1552–1554.

5. "Dies at Baseball Game as Pirates Pass Giants," *Chicago Daily Tribune*, August 4, 1905, 4.

6. "Died at Baseball Game," *New York Times*, May 23, 1911, 4.

7. "Drops Dead at Ball Game," *New York Times*, June 2, 1915, 22.

8. "Man Drops Dead at Fenway Park Game," *Boston Daily Globe*, July 29, 1915, 13; "Fan Drops Dead," *Racine (WI) Journal-News*, July 29, 1915, 9.

9. "Thrills Kill 2 at Ball Games," *Detroit Free Press*, May 8, 1922, 1; "Falk's Homer Wins for White Sox, 9–7," *New York Times*, May 8, 1922, 23.

10. "Reds and Cards Divide," *New York Times*, May 28, 1924, 20.

11. "Norfolk Man Dies at Baseball Game," *Washington Post*, May 18, 1930, M1.

12. "Rev. Dr. Robinson Dies at Ball Game," *New York Times*, March 14, 1932, 17.

13. "Herman J. Hoppenjans," *New York Times*, May 22, 1932, N4.

14. "'Sticky' Heat of 84 Kills 2 and Fells 3," *New York Times*, June 29, 1932, 23.

15. "Edward S. Thompson," *New York Times*, September 29, 1932, 21.

16. "Fan Falls Dead as Indians Rally in Nats' Game," *Washington Post*, August 26, 1940, 1; "Indians Beaten, 5–4; White Sox Nip Yanks, 1–0, Lose, 3–1," *Wisconsin (Madison) State Journal*, August 26, 1940, 12.

17. "Dies at Baseball Game," *New York Times*, August 16, 1945, 10.

18. "Dr. Fehring, 60, Stricken While at Series Game," *Manitowoc*

(WI) Herald-Times, October 9, 1945, 2.

19. "J. R. M'Laren's Funeral," *New York Times*, April 27, 1948, 25.

20. "Heart Attack Fatal to Judge J. S. Barry," *Wisconsin (Madison) State Journal*, May 17, 1953, 1; "Milwaukee Judge Dies Watching Ball Game," *Washington, Post*, May 17, 1953, M16.

21. "Alton Boy Dies After Attending Baseball Game," *St. Louis Post-Dispatch*, May 27, 1953, 22A.

22. "Dies After Heart Attack at White Sox Game," *Chicago Daily Tribune*, May 28, 1953, C6.

23. "Hill Section Girl, 18, Drops Dead as Snider Doubles," *Brooklyn (NY) Eagle*, July 7, 1954, 1.

24. "Edward G. Mason," *New York Times*, April 22, 1955, 25.

25. "Cahill Seen Successor to Chief Ahern," *San Mateo (CA) Times*, September 2, 1958, 1,2; "Say Hey Kid Doesn't Say Much, but Bat Talks Big," *San Mateo (CA) Times*, September 2, 1958, 7.

26. "Vincent F. Haggerty," *New York Times*, October 7, 1958, 35.

27. "Indiana Woman Dies Watching Sox Game," *Chicago Tribune*, July 29, 1967, A8.

28. "C. Maynard Nichols Dies at 62; Puzzle Expert Was Times Aide," *New York Times*, July 24, 1971, 28.

29. Phil Musick, "Doc's Toughest Adversary; Death Is No Stranger," *Los Angeles Times*, April 13, 1976, D1; "Medich Tries to Revive Victim in Philadelphia," *The Sporting News*, April 24, 1976, 29; Jim Henneman, "Medich Saves Stricken Bird Fan," *The Sporting News*, August 5, 1978, 13; "Doctor on Call," *Sports Illustrated*, October 2, 1978, 9.

30. "County Aide Dunne Dies at Sox Park," *Chicago Tribune*, July 12, 1977, 11; William Juneau, "Aide's Widow Hired by Assessor," *Chicago Tribune*, October 7, 1978, S3.

31. "2 Fall Ill at Game, Die," *The Sun (Baltimore, MD)*, September 5, 1978, C16; "Deaths Called Natural," *The Sun (Baltimore, MD)*, September 6, 1978, C3.

32. Tad Reeve, "Baseball Veteran Edd Roush Dies at 94 of a Heart Attack," *Bradenton (FL) Herald*, March 22, 1988, A1, A11; Howard Hall, "'Mr. Baseball' Died Where He Wanted to Be," *Bradenton (FL) Herald*, March 22, 1988, B1; Tad Reeve, "Edd Roush Loved the Game Like It Was His, Only His," *Bradenton (FL) Herald*, March 22, 1988, D1, D3.

33. "Notes from Thursday's Games," *Associated Press*, August 4, 2005; "Players Rally Around Child After Grandfather Collapses," *Associated Press State and Local Wire*, August 5, 2005.

34. Paul Grondahl, "Tragedy at Game Shocks, Saddens; Pregnant Woman from Schenectady Stricken at Fenway, but Baby Survives," *Times Union (Albany, NY)*, August 2, 2006, A1; Jennifer Amy Myers, "$5 Cup of Water Leads Billerica Woman to Seek Fairer Practices," *Lowell (MA) Sun*, April 17, 2007.

35. "Woman Watching Ball Game Dies of Heart Attack," *Los Angeles Times*, June 30, 1957, B1.

36. Matt Kopsea, "Illness of Fan Ends Play at Cove," *South Bend (IN) Tribune*, May 13, 1996, A1; "Fan Stricken at Coveleski Game Dies," *South Bend (IN) Tribune*, May 15, 1996, B5.

37. "Woman Dies in Orlando Rays Minor-League Promotion," *Associated Press State and Local Wire*, August 25, 2002.

38. "A Baseball Spectator Falls Dead," *Atlanta Constitution*, August 1, 1885, 5.

39. "Home Run the Death of Fan," *Washington Post*, August 30, 1909, 4.

40. "Dies Suddenly at Ball Game," *Los Angeles Times*, July 3, 1910, V15.

41. "Thrills Kill 2 at Ball Games," *Detroit Free Press*, May 8, 1922, 1.

42. "Dies at a Ball Game," *New York Times*, July 5, 1925, 2.

43. "Mayor Dies at Ball Game," *New York Times*, July 12, 1925, E7.

44. "Louis Rossignol Passes at Macon of Heart Attack," *Atlanta Constitution*, June 28, 1928, 4.

45. "John H. Moore," *New York Times*, July 26, 1933, 17.

46. "Dies at Baseball Game," *New York Times*, June 1, 1936, 19.

47. "Allen H. Kerr," *New York Times*, June 17, 1936, 23.

48. "Frostburg Mayor Dies at Ball Game," *Washington Post*, June 25, 1939, 6. The obituary in the *New York Times* mistakenly gives his name as "Arch M. Evans." See "Arch M. Evans," *New York Times*, June 26, 1939, 19.

49. "W. W. Sanford," *Washington Post and Times Herald*, July 29, 1954, 18.

50. "Island Lake's Mayor Dies at Baseball Game," *Chicago Tribune*, June 24, 1966, A10.

Chapter 15

1. Josh Leventhal, *Take Me Out to the Ballpark: An Illustrated Tour of Baseball Parks Past and Present* (New York: Black Dog and Leventhal, 2000), 10–11; Michael Gershman, *Diamonds: The Evolution of the Ballpark* (Boston: Houghton Mifflin Co., 1993), 30, 53–59; Bill James, *The Bill James Historical Baseball Abstract* (New York: Villard Books, 1988), 36; Michael Benson, *Ballparks of North America: A Comprehensive Historical Reference to Baseball Grounds, Yards and Stadiums, 1845 to Present* (Jefferson, NC: McFarland, 1989), xxvi–xxvii.

2. Linda Deckard, "Officials Say Safety Precautions at U.S. Stadiums Prevent Tragedies Such as British Soccer Deaths," *Amusement Business*, April 29, 1989.

3. Deckard; Charles Leerhsen and John McCormick, "When Push Comes to Shove," *Newsweek*, May 16, 1988; Benson, xxvii.

4. "Two Killed, 62 Hurt in Yankee Stadium as Rain Stampedes Baseball Crowd; Victims Are Crushed at Bleacher Exit," *New York Times*, May 20, 1929, 1–2; "Clears Ball Club in Stadium Deaths," *New York Times*, May 21, 1929, 33. Two days later, Babe Ruth spent an hour visiting the children and adults still hospitalized as a result of the stampede. He signed baseballs and had his picture taken with several of the victims. See "Babe Ruth Brings Cheer to Hospital," *New York Times*, May 22, 1929, 8.

5. "Two Killed" 2; "Clears Ball Club" 33.

6. "Clears Ball Club" 33; "Sue Over Stadium Panic," *New York Times*, November 7, 1929, 56; "Ask $960,000 Damages of Yankee Baseball Club," *New York Times*, February 11, 1932, 23; "Verdict Is Set Aside in Stadium Suits," *New York Times*, February 17, 1932, 17; "Ruling in Yankee Suit," *New York Times*, July 3, 1932, 3; "34 Claims Settled in Stadium Stampede," *New York Times*, December 16, 1932, 2. Interestingly, the following spring the Yankees announced that the wooden bleachers in "Ruthville" and in centerfield would be replaced with concrete stands at the cost of $150,000. Whether this renovation had anything to do with the rainstorm stampede and the resulting lawsuits is not indicated. See "Yankees Plan New Stand," *New York Times*, March 4, 1933, 16.

7. Howell L. Piner, *Sherman's Black Friday, May 15th, 1896: A History of the Great Sherman Tornado* (Sherman, TX: G. L. Tucker, Jr., 1971, 1896), http://www.rootsweb.com/~txgrayso/black3.html (accessed September 14, 2005); "Death in the Winds," *Chicago Daily Tribune*, May 16, 1896, 1; "The Bronchos Are Safe," *San Antonio Daily Light*, May 16, 1896, 8; "A Deadly Cyclone," *Titusville (PA) Morning Herald*, May 16, 1896, 1. The Texas-Southern League lasted just two years (1895–1896), with the Sherman team folding less than a month after the tornado struck. See "No Game at Sherman," *Galveston (TX) Daily News*, June 12,

1896, 8; "Sherman Disbanded," *Galveston (TX) Daily News*, June 12, 1896, 8.

8. "Lightning Bolt Kills Fireman," *Charlotte (NC) Observer*, September 3, 1924, 1; "Bolt Kills Fireman, Who Fled from Rain," *Washington Post* September 3, 1924, 2.

9. "Landis Visits Portsmouth Today; Beckmen Defeat Bronchos," *Virginian-Pilot and the Norfolk Landmark*, May 25, 1927, 8.

10. "Black Cloud Gives Warning to Crowd in Baseball Park," *Virginian-Pilot and the Norfolk Landmark*, May 26, 1927, 1, 9; "Five Persons Killed, Two Score More Hurt in Storm," *Virginian-Pilot and the Norfolk Landmark*, May 26, 1927, 1–2.

11. "Black Cloud," 1, 9; "Five Persons Killed," 1–2; "Storm Death Toll Increased to Six; Injured Improve," *Virginian-Pilot and the Norfolk Landmark*, May 27, 1927, 1; Six Dead as Result of 2 Roofs Falling During 72-Mile Gale," *Norfolk (VA) Ledger-Dispatch*, May 26, 1927, 1–2.

12. "Judge Landis Is Witness of Tragedy When Gale Hits Portsmouth Baseball Park," *Norfolk (VA) Ledger-Dispatch*, May 26, 1927, 2; "Storm Worst He's Ever Experienced Says Judge Landis," *Virginian-Pilot and the Norfolk Landmark*, May 26, 1927, 1, 9.

13. Bill Lumpkin, "Three Killed as Storm Hits Augusta Ballpark," *Augusta (GA) Chronicle*, May 25, 1955, 1, 3; Johnny Hendrix, "Tiger-Montgomery Game Is Knocked Out by Storm," *Augusta (GA) Chronicle*, May 25, 1955, 8; Bill Lumpkin, ""City Begins Job of Mopping Up After Bout with Tornadic Wind Which Claimed Lives of Three," *Augusta (GA) Chronicle*, May 26, 1955, 10A.

14. Lumpkin, "Three Killed," 1, 3; Hendrix, 8; Lumpkin, "City Begins," 10.

15. "Lightning Kills a Boy," *New York Times*, September 6, 1903, 2.

16. "Lightning Strikes Down Five," *Mobile (AL) Register*, May 28, 1906, 1.

17. "Lightning Kills Five," *Racine (WI) Journal*, July 24, 1906, 1; "Funf Leben endet ein Schlag ["Five Lives Ended in One Instance"], *Manitowoc (WI) Post*, July 29, 1904, 4.

18. "Cyclone Kills Boy and Injures Many Others," *Muncie (IN) Evening Press*, May 17, 1909, 8; "'Twister' Overturned Grandstand; Boy Killed, Fifteen Persons Are Hurt," *Muncie (IN) Sunday Star*, May 16, 1909, 1, 12.

19. "Lightning Hits Bleachers," *Dakota Huronite (Huron, SD)*, July 29, 1909, 2.

20. "Son's Death 'God's Will,' Mother Says," *Chicago Tribune*, June 17, 1973, 2; "Death Notices," *Chicago Tribune*, June 18, 1973, C10.

21. Phillip J. Lowry, *Green Cathedrals* (Reading, MA: Addison-Wesley Publishing, 1992), 207–9; Leventhal, 35.

22. "Four Dead, Some Dying, Many Hurt at Baseball Park," *Public Ledger (Philadelphia)*, August 9, 1903, 1–2; "Five More Dead in Ball Park Tragedy," *Public Ledger (Philadelphia)*, August 10, 1903, 1–2; "Mayor Takes Up the Ball Park Disaster," *Public Ledger (Philadelphia)*, August 11, 1903, 1–2; "Erection of Fatal Balcony Is Described," *Philadelphia Inquirer*, August 19, 1903, 1, 14. Confusion in identifying victims led to discrepancies in various news accounts as to ages.

23. According to one source, the U.S. Supreme Court eventually ruled that neither the owners of the team nor the owners of the grounds were responsible for the injuries and deaths. See Rich Westcott, *Philadelphia's Old Ballparks* (Philadelphia: Temple University Press, 1996), 77–78.

24. Leventhal, 10–11; Benson, 297–98.

25. "Erection of Fatal Balcony," 1, 14; "Censure for the Lessors of Base Ball Park," *Philadelphia Inquirer*, August 20, 1903, 1, 5; "Says Rotten Wood Was in Ball Park," *Public Ledger (Philadelphia)*, August 19, 1903, 2; "Jury Puts Blame on Ball Ground Owners," *Public Ledger (Philadelphia)* August 20, 1903, 2.

26. "1 Dies, 50 Injured in Stand Collapse at Phillies' Park," *Philadelphia Inquirer*, May 15, 1927, 1, 6.

27. "1 Dies," 1, 6; "Phillies Cleared in Death of Man," *Philadelphia Inquirer*, May 28, 1927, 20.

28. "1 Dies," 6; "City May Condemn Entire Pavilion at Phils' Ball Field," *Philadelphia Inquirer*, May 16, 1927, 1,14.

29. "Elliott Demands Complete Safety at Phillies Park," *Philadelphia Inquirer*, May 17, 1927, 1, 7; "Ball Stand Rumors Denied by Brooks," *Philadelphia Inquirer*, May 21, 1927, 3; "$40,000 to Rebuild Stands of Phillies," *Philadelphia Inquirer*, May 24, 1927, 2; Perry Lewis, "Phillies Plan to Get Back Into Own Plant for Last Game of Home Stand," *Philadelphia Inquirer*, May 26, 1927, 22; "Phillies Cleared," 2; Benson, 299–300.

30. "One Killed — 52 Injured," *Tulsa (OK) World*, October 29, 1913, 1; Jack Kavanagh, *Walter Johnson: A Life* (South Bend, IN: Diamond Communications, 1995), 88–89.

31. "One Killed," 1; Kavanagh, 89–90; "One Killed and 50 Injured at World's Tour Ball Game," *Washington Post*, October 29, 1913, 8; "Walter Johnson Reigned Supreme," *Tulsa (OK) World*, October 29, 1913, 1, 12.

32. "Woman Dies After Falling Off Climbing Wall Set Up for Fans at Minor League Baseball Game," *Associated Press State and Local Wire*, July 16, 2003; Kelly Wiese, "Inspections of Climbing Walls, Other Rides Stepped Up Under Legislation," *Associated Press State and Local Wire*, May 22, 2004.

33. Wiese; "Affidavit Shows Rust, Duct Tape Found Where Cable Broke in Fatal Fall," *Associated Press State and Local Wire*, July 19, 2003; Scott Charton, "Owner of Climbing Wall Charged in Woman's Death," *Associated Press State and Local Wire*, August 13, 2003; "Judge Declares Mistrial in Case Involving Climbing Wall Death," *Associated Press State and Local Wire*, June 18, 2004; "Missouri Today," *Associated Press State and Local Wire*, June 26, 2004; "Climbing Wall Owner Pleads to Misdemeanor in Fatal Fall," *Associated Press State and Local Wire*, October 22, 2004.

34. "A Collapse," *Minneapolis Tribune*, May 31, 1894, 1; "Grand Stand Collapsed," *Pioneer Press (St. Paul)*, May 31, 1894, 1.

35. "Collapse of Baseball Stand Traps 350 Persons," *Indianapolis Star*, August 11, 1924, 1; "Bloomington Woman Hurt at Ball Park," *Evening World (Bloomington, IN)*, August 11, 1924, 4.

36. "Auto Plunges Over Curb; Kills 1 at Ball Game," *Chicago Daily Tribune*, August 12, 1933, 16.

Bibliography

Listed below are the books, journals, magazines, newspapers, and other documents used in this study. For the sake of brevity, specific newspaper issues used are noted in the endnotes only.

Books

Adair, Robert Kemp. *The Physics of Baseball*. 2nd ed. New York: Harper Perennial, 1994.

Benson, Michael. *Ballparks of North America: A Comprehensive Historical Reference to Baseball Grounds, Yards and Stadiums, 1845 to Present*. Jefferson, NC: McFarland, 1989.

Brooks, Ken. *The Last Rebel Yell*. Lynn Haven, FL: Seneca Park Publishers, 1986.

The Centennial History of Kandiyohi County. Willmar, MN: Kandiyohi County Historical Society, 1970.

Clark, Jerry E. *Anson to Zumer: Iowa Boys in the Major Leagues*. Omaha, NE: Making History, 1992.

Coakley, Jay. *Sport in Society: Issues and Controversies*. 7th ed. New York: McGraw-Hill, 2001.

Davis, Mac. *Lore and Legends of Baseball*. New York: Lantern Press, 1953.

Dicken-Garcia, Hazel. *Journalistic Standards in Nineteenth-Century America*. Madison, WI: University of Wisconsin Press, 1989.

Dorland's Illustrated Medical Dictionary. St. Louis: Elsevier, 2002. http://www.credoreference.com/entry/4181356.

Dorward, Jane Finnan, ed. *Dominionball: Baseball Above the 49th*. Cleveland, OH: Society for American Baseball Research, 2005.

Gale Encyclopedia of Medicine. 3rd ed. Detroit: Thompson Gale, 2006.

Gershman, Michael. *Diamonds: The Evolution of the Ballpark*. Boston: Houghton Mifflin, 1993.

Grandstand Baseball Annual 2000. Downey, CA: J. M. Wayman, 2000.

Ivor-Campbell, Frederick, ed. *Baseball's First Stars: The Second Volume*. Cleveland, OH: Society for American Baseball Research, 1996.

James, Bill. *The Bill James Historical Baseball Abstract*. New York: Villard Books, 1988.

Johnson, Lloyd, and Miles Wolff, eds. *The Encyclope-dia of Minor League Baseball*. 2nd ed. Durham, NC: Baseball America, 1997.

Kashatus, William C. *Diamonds in the Coalfields*. Jefferson, NC: McFarland, 2002.

_____. *Money Pitcher: Chief Bender and the Tragedy of Indian Assimilation*. University Park: Pennsylvania State University Press, 2006.

Kavanagh, Jack. *Walter Johnson: A Life*. South Bend, IN: Diamond Communications, 1995.

Leventhal, Josh. *Take Me Out to the Ballpark: An Illustrated Tour of Baseball Parks Past and Present*. New York: Black Dog and Leventhal, 2000.

Light, Jonathan Fraser. *The Cultural Encyclopedia of Baseball*. 2nd ed. Jefferson, NC: McFarland, 2005.

Lowry, Phillip J. *Green Cathedrals*. Reading, MA: Addison-Wesley, 1992.

McGraw-Hill Concise Encyclopedia of Science and Technology. New York: McGraw-Hill, 2004. http://www.credoreference.com/entry/5974083.

Morris, Peter. *A Game of Inches: The Stories Behind the Innovations That Shaped Baseball: The Game Behind the Scenes*. Chicago: Ivan R. Dee, 2006.

_____. *A Game of Inches: The Stories Behind the Innovations That Shaped Baseball: The Game on the Field*. Chicago: Ivan R. Dee, 2006.

Mosby's Medical, Nursing, and Allied Health Dictionary. 5th ed. St. Louis: Mosby, 2002.

Mueller, Frederick O., and Jerry L. Diehl. *Annual Survey of Football Injury Research, 1931–2005*. Chapel Hill, NC: National Center for Catastrophic Sport Injury Research, 2006.

National Center for Catastrophic Sport Injury Research. *Twenty-Second Annual Report, Fall 1982–Spring 2004*. Chapel Hill, NC: National Center for Catastrophic Sport Injury Research, 2005.

Nemec, David. *The Great Encyclopedia of 19th Century Major League Baseball*. New York: Donald I. Fine, 1997.

_____. *The Official Rules of Baseball: An Anecdotal*

Look at the Rules of Baseball and How They Came to Be. Guilford, CT: Lyons Press, 1999.

Official Rules of Major League Baseball. Chicago: Triumph Books, 2006.

Piner, Howell L. *Sherman's Black Friday, May 15th, 1896: A History of the Great Sherman Tornado.* Sherman, TX: G. L. Tucker, Jr., 1971, 1896. http://www.rootsweb.com/~txgrayso/black3.html. Accessed September 14, 2005.

Plaut, David, ed. *Speaking of Baseball: Quotes and Notes on the National Pastime.* Philadelphia: Running Press, 1993.

Pollock, Alan J. *Barnstorming to Heaven: Syd Pollock and His Great Black Teams.* Tuscaloosa: University of Alabama Press, 2006.

Powers-Beck, Jeffrey. *The American Indian Integration of Baseball.* Lincoln: University of Nebraska Press, 2004.

Royal Society of Medicine Health Encyclopedia. London: Bloomsbury, 2000. http://www.credoreference.com/entry/2227586.

Rucker, Mark, and Robert L. Tiemann, eds. *Nineteenth Century Stars.* Kansas City, MO: Society for American Baseball Research, 1989.

Scheinin, Richard. *Field of Screams: The Dark Underside of America's National Pastime.* New York: W. W. Norton, 1994.

Seymour, Harold. *Baseball: The Early Years.* New York: Oxford University Press, 1989.

Shatzkin, Mike, ed. *The Ballplayers.* New York: Arbor House, 1990.

Smith, Ira L. *Baseball's Famous Outfielders.* New York: A. S. Barnes, 1954.

Society for American Baseball Research. *Minor League Baseball Stars.* Vol. 3. Cleveland, OH: Society for American Baseball Research, 1992.

Soos, Troy. *Before the Curse: The Glory Days of New England Baseball, 1858–1918.* Rev. ed. Jefferson, NC: McFarland, 2006.

Sowell, Mike. *The Pitch That Killed.* New York: Macmillan, 1989.

Spalding's Official Base Ball Guide for 1878. Chicago: A. G. Spalding and Brother, 1878.

Stein, Fred. *A History of the Baseball Fan.* Jefferson, NC: McFarland, 2005.

Sullivan, Dean, ed. *Early Innings: A Documentary History of Baseball, 1825–1908.* Lincoln: University of Nebraska Press, 1995.

Sullivan County Historical Society. *Sullivan County, Indiana, Cemetery Records.* Vol. 3. Sullivan, IN: Sullivan County Historical Society, 1983.

Thorn, John, ed. *Total Baseball V.* New York: Viking Penguin, 1997.

Wann, Daniel L., Merrill J. Melnick, Gordon W. Russell, and Dale G. Pease. *Sport Fans: The Psychology and Social Impact of Spectators.* New York: Routledge, 2001.

Westcott, Rich. *Philadelphia's Old Ballparks.* Philadelphia: Temple University Press, 1996.

Wong, Stephen. *Smithsonian Baseball: Inside the World's Finest Collections.* New York: Smithsonian Books, 2005.

Wright, Marshall D. *The Southern Association in Baseball, 1885–1961.* Jefferson, NC: McFarland, 2002.

Zoss, Joel, and John Bowman. *Diamonds in the Rough: The Untold Story of Baseball.* Chicago: Contemporary Books, 1996.

Journals

"The Bat's Too Good." *New Scientist* 179 (August 30, 2003): 39.

Boden, Barry P., Robin Tacchetti, and Fred O. Mueller. "Catastrophic Injuries in High School and College Baseball Players." *American Journal of Sports Medicine* 32 (July–August 2004): 1189–1196.

Brayden, Robert. "Intussusception." *Clinical Reference Systems* (November 2006).

Buns, Lori S., and Patti A. Ellison. "First Aid and Emergency Care at a Major-League Baseball Stadium." *Journal of Emergency Nursing* 18 (August 1992): 329–334.

Cherington, Michael. "Lightning Injuries in Sports: Situations to Avoid." *Sports Medicine* 31 (2001): 301–308.

_____, and Carol Vervalin. "Lightning Injuries—Who Is at Greatest Risk?" *Physician and Sportsmedicine* 18 (August 1990): 58–61.

Coughlin, Robert E. "Fatalities in Athletic Games and Deaths of Athletes." *New York Medical Journal* 105 (June 23, 1917): 1204–1205.

Corrado, Domenico, Cristina Brasso, and Gaetano Thiene. "Essay: Sudden Death in Young Athletes." *Lancet* 366 (December 17, 2005): S47–S48.

Dittmar, Joe. "'Doc' Powers' Shocking End." *National Pastime: A Review of Baseball History* 13 (1993): 62–65.

Gerlach, Larry. "Death on the Diamond: The Cal Drummond Story." *National Pastime: A Review of Baseball History* 24 (2004): 14–16.

Gonzalez, Thomas A. "Fatal Injuries in Competitive Sports." *Journal of the American Medical Association* 146 (August 18, 1951): 1506–1511.

Gorman, Bob. "'I Guess I Forgot to Duck': On-Field Fatalities in the Minor Leagues." *Nine: A Journal of Baseball History and Culture* 11 (Spring 2003): 85–96.

_____. "Kill the Umpire, or the Case of the Fatal Lick." *Elysian Fields Quarterly: The Baseball Review* 21 (Spring 2004): 45–49.

_____, and David Weeks. "Foul Play: Fan Fatalities in Twentieth-Century Organized Baseball." *Nine: A Journal of Baseball History and Culture* 12 (Fall 2003): 115–132.

Greenwald, Richard M., Lori H. Penna, and Joseph J. Crisco. "Differences in Batted Ball Speed with Wood and Aluminum Baseball Bats: A Batting Cage Study." *Journal of Applied Biomechanics* 17 (2001): 241–252.

Huang, David B., Don R. Cherek, and Scott D. Lane. "Laboratory Measurement of Aggression in High School Athletes: Provocation in a Nonsporting Context." *Psychological Reports* 85 (1999): 1251–1262.

Hylton, J. Gordon. "A Foul Ball in the Courtroom: The Baseball Spectator Injury as a Case of First Impression." *Tulsa Law Review* 38 (Spring 2003).

Kavanagh, Jack. "Bugs Raymond." *Baseball Research Journal* 26 (1997): 125–127.

Kozlowski, James C. "Law Review: Spectator Injury Outside the Stands." *Parks and Recreation* 41 (January 2006): 32–35.

Lane, Scott D., Don R. Cherek, and Cynthia J. Pietras. "Alcohol Effects on Human Risk Taking." *Psychopharmacology* 172 (2004): 68–77.

Lewis, Jerry M. "Fan Violence: An American Social Problem." *Research in Social Problems and Public Policy* 2 (1982): 175–206.

Ma, O. John, Ronald G. Pirrallo, and Jonathan M. Rubin. "Survey of Medical Services at Major League Baseball Stadiums." *Prehospital and Disaster Medicine* 10 (October–December 1995): 268–272.

Nicholls, Rochelle L., and others. "Bat Kinematics in Baseball: Implications for Ball Exit Velocity and Player Safety." *Journal of Applied Biomechanics* 19 (2003): 283–294.

Nowlin, Bill. "Baseball and Death in Iowa." *The National Pastime: A Review of Baseball History* 24 (2004): 107–109.

Pasternack, Joel S., Kenneth R. Veenema, and Charles M. Callahan. "Baseball Injuries: A Little League Survey." *Pediatrics* 98 (September 1996): 445–448.

Pittman, Andrew T. "Foul Balls and Assumption of Risk." *Journal of Physical Education, Recreation, and Dance* 78 (January 2007): 8–9.

Rainey, D. W. "Assaults on Umpires: A Statewide Survey." *Journal of Sport Behavior* 17 (September 1994).

Reifman, Alan S., Richard P. Larrick, and Steven Fein. "Temper and Temperature on the Diamond: The Heat-Aggression Relationship in Major League Baseball." *Personality and Social Psychology Bulletin* 17 (October 1991): 580–585.

Roberts, Julian, and Cynthia Benjamin. "Spectator Violence in Sports: A North American Perspective." *European Journal on Criminal Policy and Research* 8 (June 2000): 163–181.

Sexton, Daniel J., and Eric L. Westerman. "Tetanus." *UpToDate* 15 (August 2007). http://www.utdol.com/utd/content/topic.do?topicKey+oth_bact/40603.

Steinberg, Laurence. "Risk Taking in Adolescence: New Perspectives from Brain and Behavioral Science." *Current Directions in Psychological Science* 16 (2007): 55–59.

Strobel, Chris S., David L. Cook, and Carolyn M. Hoffman. "A Preliminary Investigation of Expected Aggression in the Sport of Baseball." *Applied Research in Coaching and Athletics Annual* (1995): 16–31.

Taylor, Stuart P., Charles B. Gammon, and Deborah R. Capasso. "Aggression as a Function of the Interaction of Alcohol and Threat." *Journal of Personality and Social Psychology* 34 (1976): 938–941.

Thompson, Paul D. "Historical Concepts of the Athlete's Heart." *Medicine and Science in Sports and Exercise* 36 (March 2004): 363–370.

Timmerman, Thomas A. "Violence and Race in Professional Baseball: Getting Better or Getting Worse?" *Aggressive Behavior* 28 (2002): 109–116.

Toutant, Charles. "Play Ball! (Carefully)." *New Jersey Law Journal,* September 19, 2005.

Tucher, Andie. "In Search of Jenkins: Taste, Style, and Credibility in Gilded-Age Journalism." *Journalism History* 27 (Summer 2001): 50–55.

United States Consumer Product Safety Commission. "Reducing Youth Baseball Injuries with Protective Equipment." *Consumer Product Safety Review* 1 (1996): 1–4.

Voigt, David Q. "America's Manufactured Villain — the Baseball Umpire." *Journal of Popular Culture* 4 (Summer 1970): 1–21.

Wakefield, Kirk L., and Daniel L. Wann. "An Examination of Dysfunctional Sport Fans: Method of Classification and Relationships with Problem Behaviors." *Journal of Leisure Research* 38 (2006): 168–186.

Wann, Daniel L. "Aggression in Sport." *Lancet* 366 (December 2005): S31–S32.

Whorton, James C. "'Athlete's Heart': The Medical Debate Over Athleticism, 1870–1920." *Journal of Sport History* 9 (Spring 1982): 30–52.

"Wisconsin Supreme Court's Decision Remains After Big Blue Settlement." *Wisconsin Law Journal,* January 18, 2006.

Witte, Daniel R., and others. "Cardiovascular Mortality in Dutch Men During 1996 European Football Championship: Longitudinal Population Study." *British Medical Journal* 321 (December 2000): 1552–1554.

Zhelekh, Andriy. "Adult Intussusception." *Journal of Diagnostic Medical Sonography* 23 (March–April 2007): 97–100.

Magazines

Allan, Ken. "Death on the Diamond." *Referee,* April 2006, 76–77.

"Baseball Dangers." *Baseball Magazine,* December 1911, 106.

Bredemeir, Brenda Jo, and David L. Shields. "Values and Violence in Sports Today." *Psychology Today,* October 1985, 23–25, 28–32.

"The Corpse Scored." *Baseball Magazine,* January 1914, 57–58.

"Dangerous Spectator Sports, Shoe Shines, the Two-Day Weekend and DIY Opium." *Esquire,* January 2006.

"Dean and Di Maggio Injuries Spur Talk of Diamond Safety." *Newsweek*, May 8, 1939, 26.

Deckard, Linda. "Officials Say Safety Precautions at U.S. Stadiums Prevent Tragedies Such as British Soccer Deaths." *Amusement Business*, April 29, 1989.

"Doctor on Call." *Sports Illustrated*, October 2, 1978, 9.

Evans, Billy. "The Growl of the Wolves." *Liberty*, July 2, 1927, 53–56.

_____. "Twenty Years a Big League Umpire." *Liberty*, June 27, 1925, 32–36.

Fultz, David L. "An Object Lesson." *Baseball Magazine*, September 1916, 83–84.

Gibbons, Margaret. "Borough, Baseball League Settled with Estate of Man Killed by Foul Ball." *The Legal Intelligencer*, October 29, 1997, 8.

Horn, Jack C. "Fan Violence: Fighting." *Psychology Today*, October 1985, 30–31.

Johnson, William Oscar. "Sports and Suds: The Beer Business and the Sports World Have Brewed Up a Potent Partnership." *Sports Illustrated*, August 8, 1988, 68–82.

Leerhsen, Charles, and John McCormick. "When Push Comes to Shove." *Newsweek*, May 16, 1988, 72–73.

Ledger, Kate. "Safety Did Not Come First." *Sports Illustrated*, July 14, 1997.

Long, Arthur F. "Great Pitching Stunts." *Baseball Magazine*, January 1911, 63–65.

Marazzi, Rich. "Baseball Rules Corner." *Baseball Digest*, January/February 2006, 86–88.

Mays, Carl. "My Attitude Toward the Unfortunate Chapman Affair." *Baseball Magazine*, November 1920, 575–577, 607.

McCallum, Jack, and Richard O'Brien. "Hard Rain." *Sports Illustrated*, November 4, 1996.

"A Murder Was Committed." *Forest and Stream*, June 4, 1874, 263.

Pavlovich, Lou, Jr. "Baseball Deaths Outstrip Football, 2–1." *Collegiate Baseball*, January 6, 1984, 1.

Price, S. L. "A Death in the Baseball Family." *Sports Illustrated*, September 24, 2007, 55–62.

Rieger, Tom. "Pape's Ill-Fated Career." *Enterprise*, August 1, 1974, 3.

Rushin, Steve. "A Stain on the Game: The Mass Deaths of Fans Is Soccer's Recurring Tragedy, but It's Barely Noticed Here." *Sports Illustrated*, May 21, 2001.

"A Sad Loss." *Sports Illustrated*, September 2, 1974, 11.

Smith, H. Allen, and Ira L. Smith. "The Old Ballgame." *Saturday Evening Post*, July/August 2000, 62–63, 74.

"Soccer Riots Plague Africa." *Amusement Business*, May 28, 2001, 10.

"Sporting Odds." *Collier's*, August 16, 1947, 75.

Thebaud, Francois. "A Red Card for the Round Ball." *UNESCO Courier*, December 1992.

Vass, George. "Mayhem on the Grass." *Baseball Digest*, July 1966, 35–42.

Newspapers

CANADIAN

Edmonton Daily Bulletin
Edmonton Journal
Manitoba Free Press
Winnipeg Free Press

NATIONAL

Associated Press Online
Associated Press State and Local Wire
Christian Science Monitor
City News Service
Cox News Service
Knight-Ridder/Tribune News Service
National Police Gazette
Pacific Stars and Strips
Sporting Life
Sporting News
Wall St. Journal

STATE AND D.C.

Alabama

Birmingham News
Dothan Eagle
Mobile Register

Arizona

Arizona Daily Star (Tucson)
Bisbee Daily Review

Arkansas

Arkansas Democrat-Gazette (Little Rock)
Fayetteville Daily Democrat
Monticellonian (Monticello)
Sentinel-Record (Hot Springs)

California

Daily News (Los Angeles)
Daily Review (Hayward)
Daily Sun (San Bernardino)
Fresno Bee
Imperial Valley Press
Independent (Long Beach)
Los Angeles Times
Modesto Bee
Oakland Tribune
Pasadena Star-News
Plumas National Bulletin (Quincy)
Sacramento Bee
San Diego Union
San Francisco Chronicle
San Gabriel Valley Tribune
San Mateo Times
Santa Ana Daily Register
Ventura County Star

Colorado

Denver Post
Rocky Mountain News (Denver)

District of Columbia

Washington Post
Washington Post and Times Herald
Washington Times

Florida

Bradenton Herald
Florida Times-Union (Jacksonville)
Miami Herald
Miami News
St. Petersburg Times
Tampa Tribune

Georgia

Albany Herald
Atlanta Constitution
Atlanta Journal-Constitution
Augusta Chronicle
Daily Constitution (Atlanta)
Griffin Semi-Weekly News
Macon Telegraph
North-East Georgian (Athens)
Savannah Morning News
Valdosta Times

Idaho

Idaho Falls Post Register
Idaho Register (Idaho Falls)

Illinois

Bureau County Record
Chicago Daily Herald
Chicago Daily Tribune
Chicago Evening Journal
Chicago Defender
Chicago Tribune
Daily Advocate (Belleville)
Daily Journal (East St. Louis)
Daily News (Chicago)
Litchfield News-Herald
Ottawa Journal
Peoria Daily Journal
Quincy Daily Herald
Rockford Daily Register
Streator Daily Free Press

Indiana

Cambridge City Tribune
Daily Gazette (Fort Wayne)
Evansville Courier
Evening Gazette (Terre Haute)
Evening World (Bloomington)
Fort Wayne Daily News
Fort Wayne Gazette
Fort Wayne Journal
Fort Wayne News Sentinel
Fort Wayne Sentinel
Indianapolis Star
Journal-Gazette (Fort Wayne)
Kokomo Daily Tribune
Logansport Press
Muncie Evening Press
Muncie Sunday Star

News-Sentinel (Fort Wayne)
The Pantagraph (Bloomington)
South Bend Tribune
Terre Haute Express
Terre Haute Tribune

Iowa

Ames Daily Tribune
Burlington Hawk-Eye
Cedar Rapids Evening Gazette
Cedar Rapids Republican
Daily Times (Davenport)
Muscatine Journal
Ottumwa Courier
Register and Leader (Des Moines)
Waterloo Daily Courier
Waterloo Times-Tribune

Kansas

Wichita Eagle

Kentucky

Courier-Journal (Louisville)
Kentucky New Era (Hopkinsville)
Lexington Herald
Mt. Sterling Advocate
Owensboro Inquirer

Louisiana

Alexandria Daily Town Talk
Daily Picayune (New Orleans)
Monroe News-Star
Shreveport Times
Times-Picayune (New Orleans)

Maine

Daily Kennebec Journal (Augusta)

Maryland

Afro-American Ledger (Baltimore)
Baltimore American
Evening Sun (Baltimore)
Morning Herald (Hagerstown)
The Post (Frederick)
The Sun (Baltimore)

Massachusetts

Boston Daily Globe
Boston Globe
Fitchburg Daily Sentinel
Lowell Daily Mail
Lowell Sun
North Adams Evening Transcript

Michigan

Detroit Free Press
Detroit News
Detroit Post and Tribune
Evening Press (Grand Rapids)
Grand Rapids Herald
Grass Lake News
News-Palladium (Benton-Harbor)

Minnesota

Evening Tribune (Albert Lea)
Freeborn County Standard

Minneapolis Tribune
Pioneer Press (St. Paul)

Mississippi
Aberdeen Examiner

Missouri
Kansas City Star
Kansas City Times
Moberly Weekly Democrat
News and Courier (Jefferson City)
St. Louis Globe-Democrat
St. Louis Post-Dispatch

Montana
Anaconda Standard
Democrat-News (Lewistown)
Helena Independent
Independent Record (Helena)

Nebraska
Lincoln Daily News
Lincoln Daily Star
Lincoln Evening News
Morning World Herald (Omaha)
Omaha World Herald

Nevada
Reno Evening Gazette

New Jersey
Daily Princetonian (Princeton)
Trenton Times

New York
The Argus (Middletown)
Binghamton Press
Binghamton Republican
Brooklyn Daily Eagle
Brooklyn Eagle
Buffalo Evening News
Daily News (New York)
Democrat and Chronicle (Rochester)
Evening Gazette (Port Jarvis)
Evening Herald (Syracuse)
Ithaca Daily Journal
Kingston Daily Freeman
Knickerbocker News (Albany)
Madison Observer
Middletown Times-Press
New York Clipper
New York Post
New York Sun
New York Times
Newsday (Long Island)
Olean Evening Herald
Oneonta Star
Post-Standard (Syracuse)
Poughkeepsie Daily Eagle
Poughkeepsie Eagle News
Post-Standard (Syracuse)
Rochester Democrat and Chronicle
Schenectady Gazette
Sunday Herald (Syracuse)

Syracuse Herald
Syracuse Herald-Journal
Syracuse Standard
Times Record (Troy)
Times Union (Albany)
Utica Daily Press

North Carolina
Asheville Citizen
Burlington Daily Times-News
Charlotte Daily Observer
Charlotte News
Charlotte Observer
Gaston Observer

North Dakota
Bismarck Tribune

Ohio
Akron Beacon Journal
Belmont Chronicle (St. Clairsville)
Cincinnati Enquirer
Cleveland Plain Dealer
Columbus Dispatch
Columbus Evening Dispatch
Daily Examiner (Bellefontaine)
Daily Times (Portsmouth)
Dayton Daily News
Democratic Standard (Coshocton)
Lima News
Lima Times Democrat
Marion Weekly Star
Massillon Independent
Portsmouth Daily Times
Republican-News (Hamilton)
The Star (Sandusky)
Star Publications (Chicago)
Steubenville Herald Star
Van Wert Daily Bulletin
Youngstown Vindicator
Zanesville Signal

Oklahoma
Enid Daily Eagle
Tulsa Daily World
Tulsa World

Oregon
Corvallis Gazette-Times
The Oregonian (Portland)

Pennsylvania
Allentown Democrat
Altoona Mirror
Berks and Schuylkill Journal (Reading)
Bucks County Gazette
Charleroi Mail
Chester Times
Delaware County Daily Times
Evening Sentinel (Carlisle)
Gettysburg Times
Indiana Evening-Gazette
Johnstown Tribune

Morning Call (Allenstown)
Morning Press (Bloomsburg)
New Oxford Item
The Patriot (Harrisburg)
Philadelphia Inquirer
Philadelphia Inquirer Public Ledger
Pittsburgh Dispatch
Pittsburgh Gazette Times
Pittsburgh Post
Pittsburgh Press
Public Ledger (Philadelphia)
Titusville Morning Herald
Tyrone Daily Herald
Tyrone Herald
Wilkes-Barre Record

Rhode Island
Bristol Phenix
Newport Daily News
The News (Newport)
Providence Journal-Bulletin

South Carolina
Daily Mail (Anderson)
Darlington News
Evening Herald (Rock Hill)
Greenville News
Index-Journal (Greenwood)
News and Courier (Charleston)
News and Press (Darlington)
The State (Columbia)
Yorkville Enquirer (York)

South Dakota
Dakota Huronite (Huron)
Webster Journal

Tennessee
Commercial Appeal (Memphis)
Daily Times (Chattanooga)
KnoxNews
Knoxville Journal
Lexington Progress
McNairy County Independent
Memphis Daily Appeal
Nashville Banner
Vicksburg Evening Post

Texas
Brenham Daily Register
Daily Light (San Antonio)
Dallas Morning News
Galveston Daily News
Galveston News
Houston Chronicle
Houston Post
Midland Reporter-Telegram
San Antonio Express
San Antonio Daily Light
San Antonio Light

Utah
Ogden Standard Examiner
Salt Lake Tribune

Virginia
The Bee (Danville)
Big Stone Gap Post
Daily Dispatch (Richmond)
Fairfax Herald
Norfolk Ledger-Dispatch
Palladium-Item and Sun Telegram (Richmond)
Roanoke Times
Times-Dispatch (Richmond)
Virginian-Pilot and the Norfolk Landmark

Washington
Seattle Times
Tacoma Tribune
Walla Walla Union-Bulletin
Wenatchee Daily World

West Virginia
Charleston Daily Mail
Charleston Gazette
Wheeling Intelligencer

Wisconsin
Appleton Post-Crescent
Capital Times (Madison)
Daily Northwestern (Oshkosh)
Janesville Daily Gazette
La Crosse Tribune
Manitowoc Herald-Times
Manitowoc Post
Milwaukee Daily Journal
Milwaukee Journal
Milwaukee Journal Sentinel
Racine Daily Journal
Racine Journal-News
Sheboygan Press-Telegram
Wisconsin State Journal (Madison)

Miscellaneous Documents

Anson County Historical Society. E-mail message to Robert M. Gorman, January 3, 2006.

Cermak, Edward. Certificate of Death. State of Ohio, Bureau of Vital Statistics, November 24, 1911.

Crabb, Roy. Standard Certificate of Death. State of Montana, March 30, 1940.

Craig, William. Medical Certificate of Death. State of Ohio, August 15, 1912.

Creighton, Jim. Player File. National Baseball Hall of Fame, Cooperstown, NY.

Curran, E. Brian, and Ronald L. Holle. "Lightning Fatalities, Injuries, and Damage Reports in the United States from 1959–1994." *NOAA Technical Memorandum NWS SR-193*, October 1997. http://www.nssl.noaa.gov/papers/techmemos/NWS-SR-193/. Accessed January 23, 2007.

Daubert, Jacob E. Certificate of Death. State of Ohio, October 9, 1924.

Daubert, Jake. Player File. National Baseball Hall of Fame, Cooperstown, NY.

Davis, Loretta. "Erysipelas." *Emedicine from WebMD.* http://www.emedicine.com/derm/topic129.htm. Accessed November 25, 2007.

Dellinger, Harold. E-mail message to Robert M. Gorman, May 1, 2006.

Dittmar, Joe. E-mail message to Robert M. Gorman, December 15, 2005.

Fish v. Los Angeles Dodgers Baseball Club. 56 Cal. App. 3d 620 (1976).

Green, Daniel. Certificate and Record of Death. State of New Jersey, Bureau of Vital Statistics, November 8, 1914.

Hissrich, Fr. John. E-mail message to Robert M. Gorman, June 5, 2002.

Holle, Ronald L. "Number of Lightning Deaths by State from 1995 to 2004." National Weather Service Lightning Safety, June 18, 2005. http://www.lightningsafety.noaa.gov/stats/95–04_Deaths_by_state.pdf. Accessed January 23, 2007.

Howell, Millard. Certificate of Death. Florida State Board of Health, Bureau of Vital Statistics, March 19, 1960.

Jensen, Don. "Bugs Raymond." *The Baseball Biography Project.* Society for American Baseball Research. http://bioproj.sabr.org/. Accessed July 26, 2005.

Johnson, Edsel, Jr. Letter to David Jones, August 4, 2000. National Baseball Hall of Fame, Cooperstown, NY.

KidSource Online. "CPSC Releases Study of Protective Equipment for Baseball, June 4, 1996." KidSource Online. http://www.kidsource.com/CPSC/baseball.6.10.html. Accessed October 10, 2005.

Maisonave v. Newark Bears. 881 A.2d 700 (2005).

Maria Pichardo, etc., respondent, v. North Patchogue

Medford Youth Athletic Assoc., Inc., et al, appellants, et al, defendants, 172 A.D. 2d 814 (N.Y. Supr. Ct. App. Div., 2d Dept. 1991).

McTavey, Mary. "Diamond Composition Book." National Baseball Hall of Fame, Cooperstown, NY.

Pape, Laurence Albert. Certificate of Death. Commonwealth of Pennsylvania, Department of Health, July 21, 1918.

Records of Death. State of Michigan, County of Macomb, Vol. A, 233.

Reider v. State. 897 So.2d 893 (2005).

Rogers, James F. Certificate of Death. State of Connecticut, January 21, 1900.

Russo, Frank. E-mail message to *SABR-L Digest,* January 31, 2005, February 27, 2007.

SABR-L Digest, April 10, 2007, April 11, 2007, and April 12, 2007.

Sandoval, Jim. E-mail message to Robert M. Gorman, November 30, 2005.

_____. "Jake Daubert." *The Baseball Biography Project,* Society for American Baseball Research. http://bioproj.sabr.org/. Accessed June 1, 2005.

Say, James. Certificate of Death. City of Baltimore, Health Department, June 23, 1894.

Scoggins, Lynn J. Certificate of Death. State of South Carolina, Bureau of Vital Statistics, August 16, 1923.

Smith, Paul. *Archaic Medical Terms: A Resource for Genealogists and Historians.* http://www.paul_smith.doctors.org.uk/ArchaicMedicalTerms.htm. Accessed May 17, 1997.

Thorn, John. "Jim Creighton." *The Baseball Biography Project,* Society for American Baseball Research. http://bioproj.sabr.org/. Accessed March 8, 2006.

Index